# Light
## of the
# Kingdom

## Biblical Topics
## in the
## Bahá'í Writings

*By JoAnn Borovicka*

T0340848

*Bahá'í*
PUBLISHING

Wilmette, Illinois

Bahá'í Publishing
401 Greenleaf Avenue, Wilmette, Illinois 60091

19  18  17  16          4   3   2   1

**Library of Congress Cataloging-in-Publication Data**

Names: Borovicka, JoAnn, author.
Title: Light of the Kingdom : Biblical Topics in the Baha'i Writings /
By
   JoAnn Borovicka.
Description: Wilmette, Illinois : Baha'i Publishing, 2016. | Includes
   bibliographical references and index.
Identifiers: LCCN 2015051080 | ISBN 9781618511010 (pbk. : alk.
paper)
Subjects:  LCSH: Bible—Bahai interpretations.
Classification: LCC BP378.6 .B67 2016 | DDC 297.9/382—dc23 LC
record available at http://lccn.loc.gov/2015051080

Cover design by Misha Maynerick Blaise
Book design by Patrick Falso

Imagery on front cover comes from the British Library Catalogue of
Illuminated Manuscripts. https://www.bl.uk/catalogues/illuminated-
manuscripts/ILLUMIN.ASP?Size=mid&IllID=52634

# Light
## of the
# Kingdom

*Immerse yourselves in the ocean of My words,*
*that ye may unravel its secrets,*
*and discover all the pearls of wisdom*
*that lie hid in its depths.*

—Bahá'u'lláh, The Kitáb-i-Aqdas, ¶182

*For Mike*

# TABLE OF CONTENTS

**The New Testament**

## Contents

# FOREWORD

I initially approached JoAnn Borovicka's beautiful *Light of the Kingdom* as a seeker with a well-defined goal: as a Christian I wished to learn more about the Bahá'í Faith. I found what I hoped for. I also came away from the book having experienced far more than I expected. Her exploration of biblical topics in the Bahá'í Writings is a comprehensive, extensively researched, and truly enjoyable scholarly work. It is also a profoundly moving volume of devotional literature.

JoAnn writes with wonderful clarity. She is consistently spare and thoughtful. Whether introducing a major biblical theme, a specific passage from Scripture, or an interpretation from the Bahá'í Writings, she deals swiftly with the subject. She obviously cares about what she shares and, at the same time, does not want to get in the way of it.

JoAnn's organization of the book is excellent. Her "Introduction" and "The Nature of the Bible in the Bahá'í Faith" lay a succinct, solid foundation for the methodology and content that follow. In her extensive treatment of the Hebrew and Christian Scriptures, she carefully honors the book-by-book nature of the Bible and at the same time accents themes that receive expression throughout biblical material. As I read, I periodically found myself turning to the two helpful appendices on the Bahá'í Faith and its Central Figures and Institutions. I also, for the sheer fun of it, regularly flipped to the Table of Contents. In addition to giving an instructive overview of the varied literary elements in the Bible, it offers an extensive list of topics that inevitably invite reader exploration. In short, the organization of this book renders it a fine reference resource as well as a book for personal study. This alone entitles it to a long and useful life.

It is precisely at this point, though, that my experience of this book exceeded expectations. The words "reference resource" and "study book" ultimately fall short: *Light of the Kingdom* is also something more. And the "something more" comes through in its nature as true devotional literature. Specifically, it is devotional literature for this age that cries out for differing faiths to dialogue together and to unite in offering the world the richest visions they have been given to share.

As I read, I was repeatedly nurtured and stretched by the texts JoAnn drew together for this volume. At first this happened with the biblical quotations. Familiar to me, they piqued memories I carried within. Swiftly, though, quotations from Writings in the Bahá'í Faith mingled with the Scripture I already knew. These, too, nurtured and stretched me. Such soul-appropriateness does not just happen. The authentic fitting together of words from varied faith traditions demands time and spirit. I had the sense that the author prayed much of the book before she wrote it. Respect permeated her introductions to the passages she offered.

I found myself drawn into open dialogue with what appeared on the pages before me. I learned much about values the Bahá'í Faith has cherished from its nineteenth century beginnings: its positive teachings on science and rational thought, on the rights of women, on the importance of modern biblical scholarship, on responding to the needs of the poor. Interwoven with passages from the Bible and the Bahá'í Writings, I found Bahá'í teachings on matters ranging from angels to the Trinity, to Bread and Blood, to Manifestations, to Jesus, to eternal life. I found places of great concord with my own understanding. I also found differences, fresh perspectives, and an invitation to keep exploring realities that none of us will ever fully grasp. Ultimately, the biblical texts, Bahá'í responses, and JoAnn's spare and quiet words brought me into a far richer place than I sought when I started reading.

*Light of the Kingdom* has its outstanding precedents in religious literature. I'll mention only one here. For the author's role and the effect of the book it appears particularly fitting. The twentieth-century rabbi Martin Buber spent years gathering old Jewish stories for his enduring classic *Tales of the Hassidim*. When finished, he wrote a splendid introduction, then scurried out of the way. He wanted to let the great tradition he had studied so long speak for itself and take his readers where they needed to go.

JoAnn Borovicka has interwoven Bahá'í and Bible Scripture in a beautiful collection, and it is on these spiritual resources she has set her focus. It is to them she directs the gaze of her readers. And whether these readers are Bahá'í, Christian, of another faith tradition, or from no tradition at all, I know that they will encounter the same gifts on these pages that I have.

To hold this book in one's hands is to hold a work of immense scholarship and insight. To read it, to linger here and there in its pages, is to be drawn into the realm of prayer and to the Prayer who seeks to hold us all.

STEVE DOUGHTY
*Author*
*Presbyterian Minister*

# AUTHOR'S NOTE

As a little girl with a child's love for Jesus, I had many questions: Who were the wise men? Where is heaven? Where is my soul and does it really turn black when I sin? What else did Jesus and His Apostles have to eat at the Last Supper? One day, privately, I wrote down several questions as best I could in my child's hand, put the letter in an envelope, and addressed it to the Virgin Mary. (I had been counseled that Jesus was very busy, as was His Father, so if I really wanted my prayers to be heard I should address them to Mary who would then approach Jesus on my behalf. Then my prayers would surely be heard because "a son always listens to his mother.")

I carefully placed the envelope on the blanket at the foot of my bed, confident that morning would bring a response. When I awoke, a quick search through the rumpled covers revealed the envelope, flap still down, seal unbroken. I opened the envelope anyway, just in case, but found nothing beyond my original letter. Disheartened, I threw it away. As I grew older, the number of questions filling my mind grew ever larger and increasingly complex.

When I first heard of the Bahá'í Faith as a young adult, I followed my seeker instincts and investigated the Writings of Bahá'u'lláh. Within just a few pages I felt as if I had been linked to a firehose of knowledge capable of washing away old disappointments, resolving internal quandaries, and reviving my delight in exploring spiritual topics.

One of the unexpected outcomes of studying the Bahá'í Writings is that through them I have developed a greater appreciation and love for the Bible, both the Hebrew and Christian Scriptures. Many Bahá'í teachings are delivered in the form of biblical commentary, and I have found that it is at this point—the point of intersection of different religions—that some of my most exciting discoveries have occurred and my most mystical yearnings have been satisfied.

This book—*Light of the Kingdom*—is a celebration of my journey of inquiry into biblical topics in the Bahá'í Writings, where every question led me to a larger understanding followed by, inevitably, more heartfelt questions. Innumerable friends graciously accompanied me on this journey, and I see their faces on every page. Their generous sharing of knowledge, resources, excitement, opinions, challenges, advice, encouragement and—yes—questions, guided, informed, and fueled the writing of this book. It is impossible to name all of the people who have participated in the various forms that this project has taken over the past fifteen years, but, nevertheless, I wish to extend special thanks to: Jeanne Aguirre, Joseph Borovicka, Michael Borovicka, Bonita Bost, Caroline Dicer, Steve Doughty, Judy Goodwin, Catherine Hosack, Greg Hosack, Virginia Kintz, Greg Kintz, Mary Arlene Kuchakpour, Melissa Mack, Gary Matthews, Michelle McClendon, Carey Murphy, Julie Schaff, Martha Schweitz, Vicki Strother, Mark Swofford, Bahhaj Taherzadeh, Louise Tajuddin, Aziz Tajuddin, Alvin Tompkins, Shahin Vafai, Clarence Whitmire, Frances Worthington, John Worthington, David Young, and Dennis Young.

JoAnn Borovicka
*Greenville, South Carolina*
*September 13, 2015*

# INTRODUCTION

The purpose of this book—*Light of the Kingdom*—is to provide an introductory compilation of Bahá'í teachings on a wide range of topics in the Christian Bible, hereinafter termed "the Bible." To this end, it starts with an overview of the Bahá'í perspective about the Bible in general and then explores Bahá'í guidance on a variety of subjects, starting with the first book of the Old Testament and continuing all the way to the last book of the New Testament. The reader will find that using biblical topics as a framework for studying Bahá'í theology results in not only deeper understandings of the Bahá'í Writings, but insights into Jewish and Christian Scriptures as well.

In the Bahá'í Faith, the world's religions are embraced as serialized chapters in the never-ending Book of God. In this divine Book, the release of each new sacred chapter complements and illuminates previous chapters. Thus the Bahá'í Revelation (a new chapter) offers guidance on many of the sublime spiritual mysteries contained in the previous chapters of Judaism and Christianity. It should be noted that the Bahá'í Writings represent revelatory interpretation; that is, they give contemporary significance to ancient Scripture by revealing inner meanings of the texts for this age. As pointed out by Gerald L. Bruns, Professor Emeritus at the University of Notre Dame, reading the Bible is not all about historical context; indeed, "the whole orientation of Scripture is toward its future, not toward its past" (Bruns, p. 629). The reader will find that studying biblical topics in the Bahá'í Writings offers insights into the Scripture of the past while establishing scriptural relevance in the present and future.

The Bahá'í teachings consist of all of the Writings that carry the authority of Bahá'u'lláh, the Founder of the Bahá'í Faith. In addition to the Writings of Bahá'u'lláh, these include works of: the Báb, the Herald of the Faith; 'Abdu'l-Bahá, the Center of the Covenant; Shoghi

Effendi, the Guardian of the Faith; and the Universal House of Justice, the supreme governing body of the Bahá'í world. The Bahá'í teachings are also expressed in notes taken by others of the speeches and talks given by 'Abdu'l-Bahá, but they do not carry the same authority as the Writings because someone else's notes are not necessarily perfect renderings of His words. For more information on the Central Figures and Institutions of the Bahá'í Faith and the unique line of authority that connects them, see Appendices A and B.

In order for the reader to easily distinguish Scripture and authoritative Bahá'í guidance from scholarly commentary, all of the Writings of the Central Figures of the Bahá'í Faith, as well as those of Shoghi Effendi and the Universal House of Justice and the recorded utterances of 'Abdu'l-Bahá, are presented as indented quotations. Unless otherwise noted, the biblical quotations cited in this book are from the New Revised Standard Version (NRSV) of the Bible.

Although this book uses a question-response format, it is not to be taken as a code of replies or litany of Bahá'í beliefs. This book is like a drop in the ocean. It presents samples of Bahá'í theology as it relates to topics that appear in the Bible—theology that stretches understanding even as it provokes additional questions. Readers who long for more complete Bahá'í commentaries can find all of the referenced sources freely available online at Bahai-Library.com.

# THE NATURE OF THE BIBLE
# IN THE BAHÁ'Í WRITINGS

The Bahá'í Writings embrace the Bible as a cherished collection of religious Scripture. In an inscription in the "Old Bible" of the City Temple in London, 'Abdu'l-Bahá states:

> This book is the Holy Book of God, of celestial Inspiration. It is the Bible of Salvation, the Noble Gospel. It is the mystery of the Kingdom and its light. It is the Divine Bounty, the sign of the guidance of God. (*'Abdu'l-Bahá in London*, p. 18)

As a sign of divine guidance, the Bible can be quoted at all Bahá'í occasions that call for readings from Scripture (see letter written on behalf of Shoghi Effendi, *Developing Distinctive Bahá'í Communities*, section 9.22).

### DO BAHÁ'ÍS BELIEVE THAT THE WORDS OF THE BIBLE
### ARE THE EXACT WORDS OF THE PROPHETS?

While many passages and some entire books are traditionally attributed to ancient Prophets, Bahá'ís recognize that, because of historical circumstances, these texts may not represent the Prophets' exact words. Nevertheless, the spiritual substance of the Bible is believed to have been protected by Providence:

> The Bahá'ís believe that God's Revelation is under His care and protection and that the essence, or essential elements, of what His Manifestations intended to convey has been recorded and preserved in Their Holy Books. However, as the sayings of the ancient Prophets were written down some time later, we cannot categori-

cally state, as we do in the case of the Writings of Bahá'u'lláh, that
the words and phrases attributed to Them are Their exact words.
(From a letter of the Universal House of Justice, dated August 9,
1984, to an individual believer, cited in "Resurrection of Christ"
Memorandum from the Research Department of the Universal
House of Justice, September 14, 1987)

### WHO DO BAHÁ'ÍS BELIEVE WROTE THE BIBLE?

While bound under one cover, the Bible is actually a collection of Holy
Books—a library that includes Jewish and Christian Scriptures, each of
which has its own history of composition. The Bahá'í Writings do not
offer commentary on the authorship of these books, and there is little
internal consensus in either the Jewish or Christian communities on the
historical circumstances surrounding their composition. However, certain
long-standing hypotheses have become central in the field of biblical scholarship, and these would be of note to Bahá'ís, including that: (1) many
of the biblical texts represent traditions that were originally transmitted
orally from generation to generation before being written down; (2) some
texts represent more than one tradition and/or came into existence through
the work of more than one author; and (3) some books are composite
texts that have been woven together by redactors (biblical editors) with
particular motivations (Barton and Muddiman, pp. 1–3; Finkelstein & Silberman, pp. 10–13; Friedman, 1997, 2003; Schniedewind, 2004). These
hypotheses are consistent with Bahá'í guidance on the nature of the Bible.

### DO BAHÁ'ÍS BELIEVE THAT THE STORIES
### IN THE BIBLE ARE TRUE?

For Bahá'ís, the Bible is read as true in substance:

The Bahá'ís believe what is in the Bible to be true in substance. This
does not mean that every word recorded in that Book is to be taken
literally and treated as the authentic saying of a Prophet. (From a
letter of the Universal House of Justice, dated August 9, 1984, to an
individual believer, cited in "Resurrection of Christ" Memorandum
from the Research Department, September 14, 1987)

Bahá'ís believe that all of the biblical texts contain spiritual meanings requiring authoritative interpretation:

> The texts of the Holy Books are all symbolical, needing authoritative interpretation. ('Abdu'l-Bahá *The Promulgation of Universal Peace,* p. 307)

## WHERE DO BAHÁ'ÍS LOOK FOR
## AUTHORITATIVE INTERPRETATION OF THE BIBLE?

First, Bahá'ís depend on the Writings of the Central Figures of the Faith for authoritative interpretation:

> Bahá'ís look first to the Bahá'í Writings for authoritative guidance on what can be taken as literal truth, what needs to be understood symbolically and how to interpret the spiritual meanings in the symbolic passages. (From a letter of the Universal House of Justice, dated January 17, 1978, to an individual believer, cited in "Resurrection of Christ" Memorandum from the Research Department, September 14, 1987)

Secondary sources of Bahá'í guidance on biblical interpretation are the Writings of the Institutions of the Faith and the recorded utterances of the Central Figures (see Appendix B).

## WHAT ROLE DOES HISTORICAL ANALYSIS (HISTORICAL CRITICISM) HAVE IN A BAHÁ'Í UNDERSTANDING OF THE BIBLE?

In light of the Bahá'í principle of the harmony of science and religion, Bahá'ís would appreciate information gleaned by applying methods of historical analysis to the biblical texts, inasmuch as it adds to the knowledge base of biblical studies. The purpose of applying the techniques of historical analysis to a biblical text is to investigate the origin, date of composition, authorship, relationship to other ancient literature, and the author's intended meanings in light of the historical context of the work. Historical analysis techniques study the biblical texts in light of the historical record outside of the Bible, as evidenced in fields such as archaeology, ancient literature, astronomy, and geology.[1] Guidance from 'Abdu'l-Bahá indicates that the extra-biblical record of history is an important tool for determining whether an event mentioned in the Bible could be understood as historical fact. Responding to an inquiry about the historicity of a certain event in the New Testament, He states:

> But as these events have not been recorded in any history, it is evident that they are not to be understood literally but according to their inner meaning. ('Abdu'l-Bahá, *Some Answered Questions,* no. 10.5)

Shoghi Effendi affirms the value of the work of historians in his response to an inquiry about the dates of Prophets in the Adamic Cycle:

> There are no dates in our teachings regarding the actual dates of the Prophets of the Adamic Cycle, so we cannot give any. Tentatively we can accept what historians may consider accurate. (From a letter written on behalf of Shoghi Effendi, dated November 25, 1950, to an individual, in *Compilation of Compilations,* vol. I, no. 64)

"Tentative" is a key word in the above guidance. The issues regarding the study of ancient history and literature are complex, interpretations of data vary, and theories change according to new findings. For the purpose of this book, the 2013 edition of the *Oxford Bible Commentary* has been chosen as a collection of highly respected current biblical scholarship and is the source of the dating and authorship information provided in the "Overview" sections.

## WHAT ABOUT VERSES IN THE BIBLE THAT SEEM CONTRADICTORY?

Apparent contradictions between biblical verses arise either from varying accounts from different authors or because the verses are to be understood symbolically:

---

1. For a study on the value of higher biblical analysis for Bahá'ís, see Stockman's "The Bahá'í Faith and Higher Biblical Criticism."

. . . many passages in Sacred Scripture are intended to be taken metaphorically, not literally, and some of the paradoxes and apparent contradictions which appear are intended to indicate this. (The Universal House of Justice, cited in "Resurrection of Christ" Memorandum from the Research Department, September 14, 1987)

### WHAT IS THE VALUE OF THE SYMBOLIC LANGUAGE OF SCRIPTURE?

Symbolism conveys spiritual realities that are larger than common language:

Divine things are too deep to be expressed by common words. The heavenly teachings are expressed in parable in order to be understood and preserved for ages to come. ('Abdu'l-Bahá, *'Abdu'l-Bahá in London,* p. 79)

Study of, and reflection on, the symbolic stories of Scripture attracts the hearts to the Kingdom of God:

I, therefore, pray in your behalf that you may be given the power of understanding these inner real meanings of the Holy Scriptures and may become informed of the mysteries deposited in the words of the Bible so that you may attain eternal life and that your hearts may be attracted to the Kingdom of God. ('Abdu'l-Bahá, *The Promulgation of Universal Peace,* p. 648)

In addition, the symbolic language of Scripture stretches with growth; its meaning is inexhaustible:

Know assuredly that just as thou firmly believest that the Word of God, exalted be His glory, endureth forever, thou must, likewise, believe with undoubting faith that its meaning can never be exhausted. (Bahá'u'lláh, *Gleanings from the Writings of Bahá'u'lláh,* no. 89.1)

### IS THERE A PARTICULAR VERSION OF THE BIBLE THAT IS RECOMMENDED FOR BAHÁ'ÍS?

There is no official recommendation of a specific version of the Bible for use by Bahá'ís. At the time of the first translations of the Bahá'í Writings into English, the King James Version was *the* principle Bible for the English-speaking world, and it is the King James Version that is most cited in the Bahá'í Writings and the transcribed talks of 'Abdu'l-Bahá. However, there are hundreds of translations of the Bible today, with a few of the most popular being the Amplified Bible (AB) published in 1958, the New International Version (NIV) published in 1978, and the New Revised Standard Version (NRSV) published in 1989. Modern translations, some updated regularly, benefit from the latest discoveries about biblical languages gleaned from the Dead Sea Scrolls and other finds. Although you might have a favorite version of the Bible, many people find that reading different translations enhances their experience of the texts. Unless otherwise noted, the New Revised Standard Version of the Bible is cited in this book.

# THE OLD TESTAMENT

Christians and others have traditionally used the term "Old Testament" to refer to the Scriptures of Judaism that the Church claimed as part of its Jewish heritage and eventually came to see as a portion of its own Bible. In most Christian Protestant Bibles the Old Testament books, excluding the Apocrypha, are presented in this sequence:

| The Books of Moses | The Books of History | The Books of Poetical Writings | The Books of Prophecy |
|---|---|---|---|
| Genesis | Joshua | Job | Isaiah |
| Exodus | Judges | Psalms | Jeremiah |
| Leviticus | Ruth | Proverbs | Lamentations |
| Numbers | 1 Samuel | Ecclesiastes | Ezekiel |
| Deuteronomy | 2 Samuel | The Song of | Daniel |
| | 1 Kings | Solomon | Hosea |
| | 2 Kings | | Joel |
| | 1 Chronicles | | Amos |
| | 2 Chronicles | | Obadiah |
| | Ezra | | Jonah |
| | Nehemiah | | Micah |
| | Esther | | Nahum |
| | | | Habakkuk |
| | | | Zephaniah |
| | | | Haggai |
| | | | Zechariah |
| | | | Malachi |

The Old Testament begins with a universal outlook telling of the creation of the heavens and the earth. Soon the focus narrows and centers on the descendents of Abraham (circa 1800 BC), God's "chosen" people (Deuteronomy 7:6), tracing their growth from a single family to twelve Hebrew tribes, the Israelites, who arise from oppression under the guidance of Moses (circa 1300 BC) and settle in the Promised Land of Canaan. It follows the Israelites through their establishment of a great nation under David and Solomon and their subsequent decline. All of the individual and communal glories and tragedies are told in light of the people's relationship with God. Poetical writings, laws, and prophecies are fitted into the narrative.

# THE BOOKS OF MOSES—OVERVIEW

The first five books of the Old Testament—Genesis, Exodus, Leviticus, Numbers, and Deuteronomy—are called the "Books of Moses" because tradition attributes authorship to Moses. They are also referred to as the Torah (Hebrew for "instruction" or "teaching") and the Pentateuch (Greek for "five scrolls"). The Bahá'í Writings do not offer information on the exact origin or authorship of these books. Biblical scholarship indicates numerous sources and a gradual process of composition (Barton and Muddiman, pp. 1–5). A mainstream theory, the Documentary (or Wellhausen) Hypothesis, states that four independent source documents dating from 900 through 500 BC were woven together by a series of redactors between 700 and 400 BC, thus producing the five Books of Moses that we have today.[2] While this model is challenged by some scholars, it is a dominant theory and a focus of discourse in modern biblical scholarship.

**Genesis** presents two stories of creation, a series of nation origin-stories establishing Abraham's progeny as the chosen people, and a multitude of moral and theological lessons. Scholars note that several features of the text suggest that Genesis was probably written in the sixth century BC. It is widely recognized that "many of the stories in Genesis 1–2 have a family likeness to origin-stories current in the Near-Eastern milieu to which ancient Israel belonged" (Whybray, p. 40).

---

2. For more information on the Documentary Hypothesis and how these four sources are distinguished in textual analysis, see *The Bible Dictionary, Volume Six "The Torah"*; Friedman's *Who Wrote the Bible?* and *The Bible with Sources Revealed;* and Schniedewind's *How the Bible Became a Book*.

**Exodus** tells of the Israelite[3] tribes and their bondage in Egypt, liberation under the guidance of Moses, and movement toward the Promised Land. It is widely accepted by scholars that Exodus had a long history of composition with the initial writing completed in the sixth or seventh century BC and the final composition dating to the late sixth or fifth century BC (see Houston, p. 68).

**Leviticus**, meaning "relating to the Levites" (the priests of Israel), contains laws concerning criminal punishment, sacrificial offerings, the consecration of priests, food restrictions, and other matters. It is widely thought by scholars that Leviticus was composed by priests in a long process with numerous editings. Many of the laws are similar to older Near-Eastern codes of law.[4] The book's final composition is generally dated to the seventh or sixth century BC (see Grabbe, p. 92).

**Numbers**, named for the two census accounts it contains, tells of the Israelites' wandering under the guidance of Moses, explores the application of divine guidance in this sometimes rebellious community, establishes the Israelites on the Plains of Moab, and cites additional laws that emerge through a need to respond to specific situations. It is largely considered by scholars to be a composite of sources from various historical periods with the final redaction completed by 400 BC (see Fretheim, p. 110).

**Deuteronomy**, meaning the "law repeated," presents a version of the Ten Commandments, develops the concept of a Covenant between God and the Israelites, focuses on the conquests necessary to possess the Promised Land, and establishes the Temple in Jerusalem as the exclusive site of worship. Presented as Moses' farewell speech before His death, the

---

3. The Hebrew tribes are called "Israelites" and "children of Israel" many years before the formation of the first nation of Israel because they are all presented as the progeny of Jacob, who was given the name "Israel" (Genesis 32:28). Therefore, in a biblical sense, "Israel" existed before and after land ownership and throughout different stages of political organization (see Dietrich, p. 232).

4. Ancient codes of law that parallel portions of the law in the Torah include the Code of Shuylgi (2094–2047 BC), the Sumerian Code (1800 BC), the Code of Hammurabi (1792–1750 BC), the Hittite Code (1650–1200 BC), and the Middle Assyrian Code (1114–1076 BC) (see Matthews and Benjamin, pp. 102, 113, 115, 120).

book concludes the story of the Exodus. It is largely thought by scholars that the beginnings of the literary development of Deuteronomy began in the time of King Josiah around 622 BC in the nation of Judah "almost certainly in the city of Jerusalem" (Friedman, 1997, p. 116).

# TOPICS FROM THE BOOKS OF MOSES

## GOD

The Book of Genesis starts:

> In the beginning when God created the heavens and the earth, the earth was a formless void and darkness covered the face of the deep, while a wind from God swept over the face of the waters. (Genesis 1:1–2)

There continues throughout the Bible the imagery of an All-Powerful, All-Knowing God Who interacts with His creation, often in human ways.

### WHAT IS THE NATURE OF GOD?

The nature of God is a mystery:

> Exalted, immeasurably exalted, art Thou above the strivings of mortal man to unravel Thy mystery, to describe Thy glory, or even to hint at the nature of Thine Essence. (Bahá'u'lláh, *Gleanings from the Writings of Bahá'u'lláh*, no. 1.3)

Although Scripture and artwork often present God as having a human form and human attributes, these represent human imagination, not the essence of God:

. . . let none construe these utterances to be anthropomorphism, nor see in them the descent of the worlds of God into the grades of the creatures. . . . For God is, in His Essence, holy above ascent and descent, entrance and exit; He hath through all eternity been free of the attributes of human creatures, and ever will remain so. (Bahá'u'lláh, The Seven Valleys, p. 22)

## WHY IS KNOWLEDGE OF THE ESSENCE OF GOD INACCESSIBLE?

The human mind cannot know the essence of God because in order to understand something one must surround it and see it from all angles. Humanity, being part of creation, cannot encompass that which encompasses it:

Furthermore, how can a reality that is originated encompass that Reality which has existed from all eternity? For comprehension is the result of encompassing—the latter must take place in order that the former may occur—and the divine Essence is all-encompassing and can never be encompassed. ('Abdu'l-Bahá, *Some Answered Questions*, no. 59.3–5)

Additionally, it is an observable fact that a lower plane of existence can never fully understand a higher plane:

Moreover, differences of degree in the world of creation are a barrier to knowledge. For example, as this mineral belongs to the mineral kingdom, however far it may rise, it can never comprehend the power of growth. The plants and trees, however far they may progress, cannot imagine the power of sight or of the other senses. The animal cannot imagine the human degree, that is, the spiritual powers. Thus, differences of degree are a barrier to knowledge: The inferior degree cannot comprehend the superior. How then can a reality which is originated comprehend that Reality which has existed from all eternity? ('Abdu'l-Bahá, *Some Answered Questions*, no. 59.6)

The created can never fully understand the Creator.

**WHAT CAN HUMAN BEINGS KNOW ABOUT GOD?**

Human beings can know the signs or attributes of God:

The invisible realm of the Divinity is sanctified and exalted above the comprehension of all beings, and all that can be imagined is mere human understanding. The power of human understanding does not encompass the reality of the divine Essence: All that man can hope to achieve is to comprehend the attributes of the Divinity, the light of which is manifest and resplendent in the world and within the souls of men. ('Abdu'l-Bahá, *Some Answered Questions,* no. 59.7)

When human beings manifest and recognize spiritual virtues, they know something of the attributes of God, because Divinity is the manifestation of spiritual virtues:

Divinity is the effulgence of the Sun of Reality, the manifestation of spiritual virtues and ideal powers." ('Abdu'l-Bahá, *The Promulgation of Universal Peace,* p. 463)

Yet, even the knowledge of the attributes of God is proportionate to human capacity:

Knowing God, therefore, means the comprehension and knowledge of His attributes and not of His Reality. And even this knowledge of His attributes extends only so far as human power and capacity permit, and remains wholly inadequate. ('Abdu'l-Bahá, *Some Answered Questions,* no. 59.7)

**HOW CAN THE CAPACITY TO KNOW THE ATTRIBUTES OF GOD BE INCREASED?**

Knowledge of the attributes of God comes through knowledge of the Divine Manifestation:

The source of all learning is the knowledge of God, exalted be His Glory, and this cannot be attained save through the knowledge of His Divine Manifestation. (Bahá'u'lláh, "Words of Wisdom" *Tablets of Bahá'u'lláh,* p. 156)

The Divine Manifestation, or Messenger of God, is the embodiment of the attributes of God:

> Nay rather, the attribute of sovereignty and all other names and attributes of God have been and will ever be vouchsafed unto all the Manifestations of God, before and after Him, inasmuch as these Manifestations, as it hath already been explained, are the Embodiments of the attributes of God, the Invisible, and the Revealers of the divine mysteries. (Bahá'u'lláh, The Kitáb-i-Íqán, ¶113)

The nature of the Manifestation of God will be explored in the section entitled "The Messenger."

## CREATION

Genesis continues with a sublime story of creation:

> Then God said, "Let there be light"; and there was light. And God saw that the light was good; and God separated the light from the darkness. God called the light Day, and the darkness he called Night. And there was evening and there was morning, the first day. (Genesis 1:3–5)

There follows the creation of the heavens on the second day; the earth and sea on the third; the sun, moon and stars on the fourth; creatures of the sea and air on the fifth; and land creatures as well as the first human beings on the sixth. The act of creation is presented as the intentional and peaceful act of one God, and the world of creation is described as being essentially good (see Whybray, pp. 40–43).

### WHAT IS THE SIGNIFICANCE OF THE GENESIS 1 CREATION STORY?

The Genesis 1 creation story is rich in symbolism that conveys spiritual, not literal, meanings:

> We Bahá'ís do not believe in Genesis literally. We know this world

was not created in seven days, or six, or eight, but evolved gradually over a period of millions of years, as science, has proved. (From a letter written on behalf of Shoghi Effendi, dated October 28, 1949, to an individual believer, in *Lights of Guidance*, no. 1658)

Although biblical genealogies studied with a literal eye indicate that this divine six-day act of creation happened about six to ten thousand years ago (Skehan, p. 18), science shows that the world of creation is much older. According to the Bahá'í principle of the harmony of science and religion, a Bahá'í understanding of the age of our world and its process of evolution would harmonize with the most current understandings of science.

### WHAT IS THE BAHÁ'Í PRINCIPLE OF THE HARMONY OF SCIENCE AND RELIGION?

The principle of the harmony of science and religion states that science and religion are two venues of truth and they must agree, for truth is one:

Bahá'u'lláh teaches that religion must be in conformity with science and reason. If belief and teaching are opposed to the analysis of reason and principles of science, they are not worthy of acceptance. This principle has not been revealed in any of the former Books of divine teaching. ('Abdu'l-Bahá, *The Promulgation of Universal Peace*, p. 611)

Science and religion are like two wings of a bird:

We may think of science as one wing and religion as the other; a bird needs two wings for flight, one alone would be useless. Any religion that contradicts science or that is opposed to it is only ignorance—for ignorance is the opposite of knowledge. ('Abdu'l-Bahá, *Paris Talks*, no. 40.16)

### WHAT DOES CURRENT SCIENCE SAY ABOUT THE AGE OF OUR WORLD?

Latest scientific findings indicate that the age of our universe is about 13.7 billion years; the Earth is about 4.57 billion years; and the oldest fossils found on Earth are about 3.8 billion years. Current science also indicates that the first appearance of the human species is no older than 200,000 years (see Skehan; Miller; Nova). While geological and biological traces read by scientific methods provide information on the age of the earth and certain species, cultural traces of the most ancient civilizations have largely been erased:

> Thus, as you are aware, we have no record of twenty thousand years ago, even though we established before through rational arguments that life on this earth is very ancient—not one or two hundred thousand, or even one or two million years old: It is ancient indeed, and the records and traces of ancient times have been entirely oblitated. ('Abdu'l-Bahá, *Some Answered Questions,* no. 41.3)

### DID THE WORLD OF CREATION HAVE A BEGINNING?

In the big picture, creation has no beginning and will have no end:

> As to thy question concerning the origin of creation, know assuredly that God's creation hath existed from eternity, and will continue to exist forever. Its beginning hath had no beginning, and its end knoweth no end. (Bahá'u'lláh, *Gleanings from the Writings of Bahá'u'lláh,* no. 78.1)

### IS THE WORLD OF EXISTENCE PREEXISTENT WITH GOD?

Preexistence is relative. The condition of *essential* preexistence is a station of God alone:

> The world of existence is contingent, inasmuch as it is preceded by a cause, while essential preexistence hath ever been, and shall remain, confined to God, magnified be His glory. This statement is being made lest one be inclined to conclude from the earlier assertion, namely that creation hath no beginning and no end, that it is preexistent. True and essential preexistence is exclusively reserved to God, while the preexistence of the world is secondary and relative. (Bahá'u'lláh, *The Tabernacle of Unity,* no. 2.49)

While the world of existence has, in a contingent way, always existed, the compositions within it, like our solar system, do have beginnings and endings.

## HOW DID THE EARTH
## COME INTO BEING?

Like the development of a fetus in the womb, the Earth developed according to natural laws appropriate to planetary bodies in the matrix (womb) of the universe:

> . . . it is clear that this terrestrial globe in its present form did not come into existence all at once, but that this universal existence gradually traversed different stages until it appeared in its present completeness. Universal existences can be likened and compared to particular ones, for both are subject to one natural order, one universal law, and one divine arrangement. For instance, you will find the smallest atoms to be similar in their general structure to the greatest entities in the universe, and it is clear that they have proceeded from one laboratory of might according to one natural order and one universal law, and can therefore be compared to one another.
>
> For example, the human embryo grows and develops gradually in the womb of its mother and assumes different forms and conditions until it reaches maturity with the utmost beauty and appears in a consummate form with the utmost grace. . . . It is likewise clear and evident that this terrestrial globe came to exist, grow, and develop in the matrix [womb] of the universe and assumed different forms and conditions until it gradually attained its present completeness, became adorned with countless beings, and appeared in such a consummate form. ('Abdu'l-Bahá, *Some Answered Questions,* no. 47.6–7)

The various compositions in the world of creation, such as our solar system and everything in it, grow, develop, and decompose over time according to natural laws.

## IS EARTH THE ONLY PLANET WITH LIFE FORMS CAPABLE OF KNOWING GOD?

'Abdu'l-Bahá stated there are other worlds than ours which are inhabited by beings capable of knowing God. (Shoghi Effendi, *The Light of Divine Guidance,* vol. II, p. 80)

## DID HUMANITY EVOLVE TO ITS CURRENT PHYSICAL FORM?

Humanity has evolved from one form to another over a long period of time as demonstrated by the physical evidence found in fossils:

> In the world of existence man has traversed successive degrees until he has attained the human kingdom. In each degree of his progression he has developed capacity for advancement to the next station and condition. While in the kingdom of the mineral he was attaining the capacity for promotion into the degree of the vegetable. In the kingdom of the vegetable he underwent preparation for the world of the animal, and from thence he has come onward to the human degree, or kingdom. Throughout this journey of progression he has ever and always been potentially man. ('Abdu'l-Bahá, *The Promulgation of Universal Peace,* p. 315)

Being "potentially man" throughout the evolutionary journey is not meant to indicate a kind of parallel evolution, but rather that, in a metaphysical sense—in the mind of God—the perfection of the human form and the capacities of the human spirit always existed potentially in creation. Parallel evolution, a theory that "proposes a separate line of biological evolution for the human species parallel to the animal kingdom since the beginning of life on earth" and other conceptions that contradict modern science are not consistent with Bahá'í belief in the harmony of science and religion (see Foreword to *Some Answered Questions,* p. xiv).

### ARE HUMANS ANIMALS?

In scientific classification, the human species (Homo Sapiens) is in the class "Mammalia" in the Kingdom "Animalia." Humans are members of the Animal Kingdom and, as this distinct species, humans have unique spiritual and intellectual capacities by which they can rise above the animal nature:

> As we have before indicated, this human reality stands between the higher and the lower in man, between the world of the animal and the world of divinity. When the animal proclivity in man becomes predominant, he sinks even lower than the brute. When the heavenly powers are triumphant in his nature, he becomes the noblest and most superior being in the world of creation. All the imperfections found in the animal are found in man. In him there is antagonism, hatred and selfish struggle for existence; in his nature lurk jealousy, revenge, ferocity, cunning, hypocrisy, greed, injustice and tyranny. So to speak, the reality of man is clad in the outer garment of the animal, the habiliments of the world of nature, the world of darkness, imperfections and unlimited baseness.
>
> On the other hand, we find in him justice, sincerity, faithfulness, knowledge, wisdom, illumination, mercy and pity coupled with intellect, comprehension, the power to grasp the realities of things and the ability to penetrate the truths of existence. All these great perfections are to be found in man. Therefore, we say that man is a reality which stands between light and darkness. From this standpoint of view, his nature is threefold, animal, human and divine. The animal nature is darkness; the heavenly is light in light. ('Abdu'l-Bahá, *The Promulgation of Universal Peace*, p. 656)

While robed in animal form, the human capacity to know God and to reflect divine attributes represents the fruit of evolution:

> Moreover, regarding the unique station of man, we read in the Writings of Bahá'u'lláh: "Having created the world and all that liveth and moveth therein, God, through the direct operation of His sovereign Will, chose to confer upon man the unique capacity to know Him and to love Him—a capacity which must be regarded as the generative impulse and the primary purpose underlying the whole of creation." 'Abdu'l-Bahá, the appointed Interpreter, has clearly stated that in God's plan of creation, man is "the culmination of all that

went before," "the crowning-point of creation," "the goal to which countless ages of existence have progressed," and God's only creation made in His "image and with potential power to attain that likeness." (From a letter of the Universal House of Justice, dated May 23, 1969, to an individual believer)

## IMAGE OF GOD

The Book of Genesis states that human beings are created in the image of God:

Then God said, "Let us make humankind in our image, according to our likeness; . . ." (Genesis 1:26)

The description of humanity as a lifeform created in God's image—capable of knowing the attributes of God—is a spiritual truth found in many Scriptures:

In the Old Testament we read that God said, "Let us make man in Our own image." In the Gospel, Christ said, "I am in the Father, and the Father in Me." In the Qur'án, God says, "Man is my Mystery and I am his." Bahá'u'lláh writes that God says, "Thy heart is My home; purify it for My descent. Thy spirit is My place of revelation; cleanse it for My manifestation."

All these sacred words show us that man is made in God's image: yet the Essence of God is incomprehensible to the human mind, for the finite understanding cannot be applied to this infinite Mystery. ('Abdu'l-Bahá, *Paris Talks,* no. 5.4–5)

### WHAT DOES IT MEAN TO BE CREATED
### IN THE IMAGE AND LIKENESS OF GOD?

To be created in the image and likeness of God has nothing to do with physical appearance; it means having the capacity to acquire spiritual attributes such as justice, truthfulness, mercy, and other characteristics of divinity:

It is recorded in the Holy Bible that God said, "Let us make man in our image, after our likeness." It is self-evident that the image and likeness mentioned do not apply to the form and semblance of a human being because the reality of Divinity is not limited to any form or figure. Nay, rather, the attributes and characteristics of God are intended. Even as God is pronounced to be just, man must likewise be just. As God is loving and kind to all men, man must likewise manifest loving-kindness to all humanity. . . . In a word, the image and likeness of God constitute the virtues of God, and man is intended to become the recipient of the effulgences of divine attributes. This is the essential foundation of all the divine religions, the reality itself, common to all. Abraham promulgated this; Moses proclaimed it. Christ and all the Prophets upheld this standard and aspect of divine religion. ('Abdu'l-Bahá, *The Promulgation of Universal Peace*, p. 569)

Becoming the image of God will forever be the goal of humanity:

As to divine education, it is the education of the Kingdom and consists in acquiring divine perfections. This is indeed true education, for by its virtue man becomes the focal centre of divine blessings and the embodiment of the verse "Let Us make man in Our image, and after Our likeness." This is the ultimate goal of the world of humanity. ('Abdu'l-Bahá, *Some Answered Questions*, no. 3.7)

Far from being either old news or a single creative act, the creation of humanity in the image and likeness of God is a continuing challenge:

Be the image and likeness of God. This is not easy. It necessitates the focalization of all heavenly virtues. It requires that we become recipients of all the perfections of God. Then we become His image and likeness. For in the Bible it is stated, "Let us make man in our image, after our likeness." The attainment of this is most difficult. ('Abdu'l-Bahá, *The Promulgation of Universal Peace*, p. 348)

Human beings have the capacity to acquire heavenly virtues and, with every individual and communal act of free will, move closer—or not—

to becoming the image of God. This makes the first chapter of Genesis a current event.

## WHAT DO THE PLURAL PRONOUNS IN GENESIS 1:26 ("THEN GOD SAID, "LET US MAKE HUMANKIND IN OUR IMAGE, ACCORDING TO OUR LIKENESS; . . .") INDICATE?

The possible meanings and implications of the plural pronouns in Genesis 1:26 are widely discussed in biblical scholarship. A majority view is that this and similar verses (Genesis 3:22; 11:7; 1 Kings 22:19; Job 1:6) refer to "the court of heavenly beings who exist to do God's bidding" (Whybray, p. 43).

In the Bahá'í Writings it is not unusual to see God or the Manifestation of God referenced with the plural pronouns "Us," "Our," or "We." However, the use of these pronouns in relation to God are specifically explained as the "royal we" or "majestic plural"—a grammatical device that indicates the supreme authority, not the plurality, of the speaker:

When Bahá'u'lláh uses the plural—"We," "Our," etc.—He is merely using a form which is regal and has greater power than the singular "I." We have this same usage in English, when the King says "we." The Pope does the same thing. (From a letter written on behalf of Shoghi Effendi, dated February 18, 1951, to an individual believer, in *Lights of Guidance,* no. 1554)

## GENDER AND SCRIPTURE

The first twenty-six verses of Genesis speak of "God." At verse twenty-seven, however, God is also referred to with the male pronouns "his" and "he":

So God created humankind in *his* image, in the image of God *he* created them; male and female *he* created them. (Genesis 1:27, emphasis added)

Thus, in the biblical text (as well as the Scriptures of other monotheistic religions), we have the traditional presentation of the one God as a male Deity; this is another example of attributing human characteristics to God.

## WHY HAVE MALE PRONOUNS MOST OFTEN BEEN USED TO REFER TO GOD IN THE SCRIPTURE OF MONOTHEISTIC RELIGIONS?

The classical rule of most European languages, as well as Hebrew, Arabic, and Persian, is that God is presented as male. This is not surprising in that all of these languages evolved in patriarchal cultures. The Bahá'í Writings, written in Persian and Arabic in the late nineteenth and early twentieth century, abide by this convention of language, although it is also clearly stated in the same Writings that the Reality of God transcends gender:

> . . . when Bahá'u'lláh was revealing His Scriptures He had to use language and forms of expression which could be understood by those whom He was addressing. . . . In Arabic and Persian, as in English and most European languages, it has been customary to refer to God as "Lord" and "Father," rather than "Lady" and "Mother." While using the conventional wording Bahá'u'lláh approached the matter on two levels. In relation to God He devoted vast numbers of Tablets to conveying the truth that God is not only neither male nor female, but is far above all human understanding. If you study deeply the Writings of Bahá'u'lláh that portray both the transcendence and immanence of God you will find that the entire question of sex in this context falls into total insignificance. On the human level, the Bahá'í Teachings stress again and again the equality of men and women. (From a letter written on behalf of the Universal House of Justice, dated October 24, 1996, to an individual)

God is neither male nor female. It is an accident of history, culture, and language that God has been traditionally represented in masculine terms. However, while an illusion, the image of a male God has caused serious justice issues; combined with a few carefully selected biblical passages it has been used to mandate sexual discrimination. In addition, as described by Jimmy Carter, "The relegation of women to an inferior or circumscribed status by many religious leaders is one of the primary reasons for the promotion and perpetuation of sexual abuse" (Carter, p.19).

## IS THE MALE GENDER SUPERIOR?

Women and men are equal in the sight of God:

Know thou, O handmaid, that in the sight of Bahá, women are accounted the same as men, and God hath created all humankind in His own image, and after His own likeness. That is, men and women alike are the revealers of His names and attributes, and from the spiritual viewpoint there is no difference between them. ('Abdu'l-Bahá, *Selections from the Writings of 'Abdu'l-Bahá*, no. 38.3)

And both genders are created in the image of God:

The truth is that all mankind are the creatures and servants of one God, and in His estimate all are human. Man is a generic term applying to all humanity. The biblical statement "Let us make man in our image, after our likeness" does not mean that woman was not created. The image and likeness of God apply to her as well. In Persian and Arabic there are two distinct words translated into English as man: one meaning man and woman collectively, the other distinguishing man as male from woman the female. The first word and its pronoun are generic, collective; the other is restricted to the male. This is the same in Hebrew. To accept and observe a distinction which God has not intended in creation is ignorance and superstition. ('Abdu'l-Bahá, *The Promulgation of Universal Peace*, pp. 104–5)

The issue of linguistic sexism in Scripture and all forms of language is a popular concern today. Traditionally, the words "man" and "mankind" have been used to refer to all of humanity, male and female; the male pronouns "he," "his," and "him" have also been used generically. A policy of inclusiveness in gender language has been among the goals of some more modern Bible translations, such as the NRSV.

## WHAT IS THE BAHÁ'Í UNDERSTANDING OF GENDER LANGUAGE IN THE BAHÁ'Í WRITINGS?

The Bahá'í perspective on gender language in its own Writings, which were all written and translated in a style determined before the 1960s, is that they be read with full consciousness of the equality of the sexes and the intended inclusive meaning of the generic terms as used in classical English:

> In the case of the generic terms in the English translations of the Bahá'í Writings, the tendency to take such terms as being applicable only to males is a reflection of the male-dominated society which has prevailed for so long, and to which there is a reaction from women who are seeking legitimate recognition and equality. Bahá'ís can well sympathize with such concerns, while pointing out that language is a living thing and that the intended meaning of the generic terms will doubtless become more readily apparent as the influence of the Bahá'í commitment to equality of the sexes permeates human society more fully. (From a letter of the Universal House of Justice, dated September 26, 1993, to a National Spiritual Assembly)

The Bahá'í community recognizes the historical milieu of the Bahá'í Writings and emphasizes the intended meanings of the gendered collective nouns.

## DOMINION OVER THE EARTH

As the fruit of creation, humanity has been given dominion over the earth:

> . . . and let them have dominion over the fish of the sea, over the birds of the air, and over the cattle, and over all the wild animals of the earth, and over every creeping thing that creeps upon the earth. (Genesis 1:26)

With seven billion people on this planet, increasing ecological degradation, and the continued advancement of technologies holding unprecedented power, questions surrounding human "dominion" over the earth have never been timelier.

## WHY DOES HUMANITY HAVE DOMINION OVER NATURE?

Mankind has dominion over nature because of uniquely human capacities such as intelligent inquiry, conscious reflection, memory, reasoning, and inventiveness:

> The phenomenal world is entirely subject to the rule and control of natural law. These myriad suns, satellites and heavenly bodies throughout endless space are all captives of nature. They cannot transgress in a single point or particular the fixed laws which govern the physical universe. The sun in its immensity, the ocean in its vastness, are incapable of violating these universal laws. All phenomenal beings—the plants in their kingdom, even the animals with their intelligence—are nature's subjects and captives. All live within the bounds of natural law, and nature is the ruler of all except man. Man is not the captive of nature, for although according to natural law he is a being of the earth, yet he guides ships over the ocean, flies through the air in airplanes, descends in submarines; therefore, he has overcome natural law and made it subservient to his wishes. . . . All the sciences, arts and discoveries were mysteries of nature, and according to natural law these mysteries should remain latent, hidden; but man has proceeded to break this law, free himself from this rule and bring them forth into the realm of the visible. Therefore, he is the ruler and commander of nature. ('Abdu'l-Bahá, *The Promulgation of Universal Peace,* p. 23)

Unlike any other earthly creation, humanity has the ability to discover the hidden laws of the universe and to use these powers in creative ways.

## WHAT IS THE SIGNIFICANCE OF HUMANITY'S DOMINION OVER NATURE?

One significant aspect of humanity wielding powers that do not exist in nature is that it indicates that humanity is a unique spiritual creation and not solely a product of the material world:

> Man hath the powers of will and understanding, but nature hath them not. Nature is constrained, man is free. Nature is bereft of understanding, man understandeth. Nature is unaware of past

events, but man is aware of them. Nature forecasteth not the future; man by his discerning power seeth that which is to come. Nature hath no consciousness of itself, man knoweth about all things.

Should any one suppose that man is but a part of the world of nature, and he being endowed with these perfections, these being but manifestations of the world of nature, and thus nature is the originator of these perfections and is not deprived therefrom, to him we make reply and say: the part dependeth upon the whole; the part cannot possess perfections whereof the whole is deprived. ('Abdu'l-Bahá, *Tablet to August Forel*, p. 10)

Wielding capacities that allow dominion over nature does not separate humanity from nature. All of creation is inter-related:

We cannot segregate the human heart from the environment outside us and say that once one of these is reformed everything will be improved. Man is organic with the world. His inner life moulds the environment and is itself deeply affected by it. The one acts upon the other and every abiding change in the life of man is the result of these mutual reactions. (From a letter written on behalf of Shoghi Effendi, dated 17 February 1933, to an individual believer, cited in *Valuing Spirituality in Development*)

### WHAT IS NECESSARY FOR HUMANITY TO ASSUME RESPONSIBLE DOMINION OVER NATURE?

In *The Prosperity of Humankind*, a statement of the Bahá'í International Community, it is noted that responsible stewardship requires a global outlook characterized by both scientific and spiritual transformation: "Only a breakthrough in understanding that is scientific and spiritual in the fullest sense of the terms will empower the human race to assume the trusteeship toward which history impels it" (paragraph V). Take, for example, the issue of climate change. In addition to a scientific problem requiring transformation in technology and industry, climate change is a moral challenge raising questions of equity and justice such as: Who is responsible for the effects of climate change? Who should pay for the harm that it has caused? Who will decide target levels of greenhouse gas concentrations in the atmosphere and how will this be determined? And how can all stakeholders be fairly represented in decision-making? With this problem, as with others, both scientific and spiritual principles will need to be applied to achieve responsible stewardship (see The Bahá'í International Community, *Seizing the Opportunity: Redefining the Challenge of Climate Change*).[5]

## BREATH OF LIFE

In what some regard as a second and independent story of creation, Genesis 2 tells how the first human being is formed from clay[6] and then, unique of all God's creatures, receives "the breath of life":

> Then the LORD God formed man from the dust of the ground, and breathed into his nostrils the breath of life; and the man became a living being. (Genesis 2:7)

### WHAT IS THE MEANING OF THE "BREATH OF LIFE"?

The breath of life symbolizes the Holy Spirit that is the source of true life:

> Observe that Adam is said to have come into being from the spirit of life. Moreover, John's utterance[7] in regard to the Apostles proves that they also proceeded from the heavenly Father. Hence it is clear and evident that the holy reality—the true existence—of every great man proceeds from God and owes its being to the breath of the Holy Spirit. ('Abdu'l-Bahá, *Some Answered Questions*, no. 18.4)

---

5. For more information on the practical application of spiritual principles to world stewardship, see additional statements and publications of the Bahá'í International Community such as: *Sustaining Societies: Towards a New "We"*; *Rethinking Prosperity: Forging Alternatives to a Culture of Consumerism;* and *Turning Point for All Nations*.

6. This formed-from-clay motif is a tradition found in earlier Near East creation stories such as the Egyptian tale of Khnum and the Sumerian Epic of Gilgamesh (see Matthews and Benjamin, p. 21; Whybray, pp. 43–44).

7. "But as many as received Him, to them gave He power to become the sons of God, even to them that believe on His name: Which were born, not of blood, nor of the will of the flesh, nor of the will of man, but of God." (John 1:12–13 cited by 'Abdu'l-Bahá in *Some Answered Questions*, no. 18.3)

It is the "breath of the Holy Spirit" that distinguishes the spiritual life of a human soul from the physical or animal nature of the human being:

> It has thus been made evident that the world of mankind is in need of the breaths of the Holy Spirit. Without the spirit the world of mankind is lifeless, and without this light the world of mankind is in utter darkness. For the world of nature is an animal world. Until man is born again from the world of nature, that is to say, becomes detached from the world of nature, he is essentially an animal, and it is the teachings of God which convert this animal into a human soul. ('Abdu'l-Bahá, *Selections from the Writings of 'Abdu'l-Bahá*, no. 227.22)

The figurative language of Genesis 2:7 captures the human condition: We are Earthlings, creatures composed of elements, evolved to a perfect form, blessed with the breath of the Spirit and adorned with a human soul—the one factor that distinguishes human beings from the rest of the Animal Kingdom.

Like many of the Bahá'í commentaries on biblical topics, this guidance on the nature of the soul is not to be understood as an explanation of the intended meanings of the ancient biblical authors. It is the opinion of many scholars that early Israelite belief did not include the concept of an immortal soul as distinct from the physical body, and that the breath of the spirit was understood as "the animating spirit lent to humans for the duration of their lifetime" (Weeks, p. 428). 'Abdu'l-Bahá confirms that the concept of eternal life was a later development:

> From the days of Adam until the time of Christ there was little mention of life eternal and of the all-embracing perfections of the Kingdom on high. ('Abdu'l-Bahá, *Some Answered Questions*, no. 30.7)

It is a testimony to the artistry of the "breath of life" Scripture that it illustrates the theological concept of the immortal soul found in the later Revelations of Zoroastrianism,[8] Christianity, Islam, and the Bahá'í Faith.

---

8. For information on the influence of Zoroastrianism on post-exilic Judaism and Christianity, see Richard C. Foltz, *Spirituality in the Land of the Noble: How*

## WHAT IS THE NATURE OF THE SOUL?

Although the soul is the essence of who and what we are, it is ultimately a mystery. However, there are things that we can know. The soul is a creation and sign of God, it has the capacity to recognize the glory of God, and it has freedom of choice:

> Thou hast asked Me concerning the nature of the soul. Know, verily, that the soul is a sign of God, a heavenly gem whose reality the most learned of men hath failed to grasp, and whose mystery no mind, however acute, can ever hope to unravel. It is the first among all created things to declare the excellence of its Creator, the first to recognize His glory, to cleave to His truth, and to bow down in adoration before Him. If it be faithful to God, it will reflect His light, and will, eventually, return unto Him. If it fail, however, in its allegiance to its Creator, it will become a victim to self and passion, and will, in the end, sink in their depths. (Bahá'u'lláh, *Gleanings from the Writings of Bahá'u'lláh,* no. 82.1)

The soul has the capacity to discover the realities of existence and creatively use the hidden powers of the material world:

> All the sciences, branches of learning, arts, inventions, institutions, undertakings, and discoveries have resulted from the comprehension of the rational soul. These were once impenetrable secrets, hidden mysteries, and unknown realities, and the rational soul gradually discovered them and brought them out of the invisible plane into the realm of the visible. This is the greatest power of comprehension in the world of nature, and the uttermost limit of its flight is to comprehend the realities, signs, and properties of contingent things. ('Abdu'l-Bahá, *Some Answered Questions,* no. 58.3)

## IS THE HUMAN SPIRIT DIFFERENT FROM THE HUMAN SOUL?

"Spirit" and "soul" are names for one entity:

---

*Iran Shaped the World's Religions; S. A. Nigosian, The Zoroastrian Faith: Tradition and Modern Research.*

The human spirit, which distinguishes man from the animal, is the rational soul, and these two terms—the human spirit and the rational soul—designate one and the same thing. ('Abdu'l-Bahá, *Some Answered Questions,* no. 55.5)

### WHEN DOES THE INDIVIDUAL SOUL COME INTO EXISTENCE?

The individual soul comes into existence at the time of conception at which time it begins its association with the physical body:

The soul or spirit of the individual comes into being with the conception of his physical body. (From a letter written on behalf of Shoghi Effendi, dated October 9, 1947, to an individual believer, in *Lights of Guidance,* no. 1699)

### DOES THE SOUL RESIDE IN THE BODY?

While the soul is associated with the body, it does not reside within it. The soul animates the body, but is not reliant upon it. In contrast, the body is reliant upon the soul:

The rational soul—the human spirit—did not descend into this body or subsist through it to begin with, that it should require some substance to depend upon after the constituent parts of the body have decomposed. On the contrary, the rational soul is the substance upon which the body depends. ('Abdu'l-Bahá, *Some Answered Questions,* no. 66.4)

### DOES SICKNESS OF THE BODY OR THE MIND
### AFFECT THE SOUL?

Sickness of the body or the mind does not affect the soul, although those sicknesses may impede its outward expression:

Know thou that the soul of man is exalted above, and is independent of all infirmities of body or mind. That a sick person showeth signs of weakness is due to the hindrances that interpose themselves between his soul and his body, for the soul itself remaineth unaffected by any bodily ailments. Consider the light of the lamp. Though an external object may interfere with its radiance, the light itself continueth to shine with undiminished power. In like manner, every malady afflicting the body of man is an impediment that preventeth the soul from manifesting its inherent might and power. (Bahá'u'lláh, *Gleanings from the Writings of Bahá'u'lláh,* no. 80.2)

## HOW CAN THE SOUL CONTINUE
## AFTER THE DEATH OF THE BODY?

Unlike the body, the soul is not a combination of physical elements subject to decomposition. It is a single indestructible element:

The whole physical creation is perishable. These material bodies are composed of atoms; when these atoms begin to separate decomposition sets in, then comes what we call death. This composition of atoms, which constitutes the body or mortal element of any created being, is temporary. When the power of attraction, which holds these atoms together, is withdrawn, the body, as such, ceases to exist.

With the soul it is different. The soul is not a combination of elements, it is not composed of many atoms, it is of one indivisible substance and therefore eternal. It is entirely out of the order of the physical creation; it is immortal.

Scientific philosophy has demonstrated that a simple element ("simple" meaning "not composed") is indestructible, eternal. The soul, not being a composition of elements, is, in character, as a simple element, and therefore cannot cease to exist. ('Abdu'l-Bahá, *Paris Talks,* no. 29.12–14)

## WHERE IS THE SPIRITUAL WORLD OF THE SOUL?

The spiritual world of the soul is right here. The world of existence is one. The spiritual worlds of God surround us, but we do not have the sensory capacity to perceive them. Like a rock that is unaware of the person standing upon it, or like a house plant that cannot engage in the human conversation happening in the same room, human beings do not have the ability to perceive the spiritual worlds of God that surround them:

. . . the souls of the children of the Kingdom, after their separation from the body, ascend unto the realm of everlasting life. But if ye ask as to the place, know ye that the world of existence is a single world, although its stations are various and distinct. For example, the mineral life occupieth its own plane, but a mineral entity is without any awareness at all of the vegetable kingdom, and indeed, with its inner tongue denieth that there is any such kingdom. In the same way, a vegetable entity knoweth nothing of the animal world, remaining completely heedless and ignorant thereof, for the stage of the animal is higher than that of the vegetable, and the vegetable is veiled from the animal world and inwardly denieth the existence of that world—all this while animal, vegetable and mineral dwell together in the one world. . . .

In the same way, the denizens of this earth are completely unaware of the world of the Kingdom and deny the existence thereof. They ask, for example: "Where is the Kingdom? Where is the Lord of the Kingdom?" These people are even as the mineral and the vegetable, who know nothing whatever of the animal and the human realm; they see it not; they find it not. Yet the mineral and vegetable, the animal and man, are all living here together in this world of existence. ('Abdu'l-Bahá, *Selections from the Writings of 'Abdu'l-Bahá,* no. 163.2–3)

## GARDEN OF EDEN

The story of the Garden of Eden is another timeless allegory:

And the LORD God planted a garden in Eden, in the east; and there he put the man whom he had formed. Out of the ground the LORD God made to grow every tree that is pleasant to the sight and good for food, the tree of life also in the midst of the garden, and the tree of knowledge of good and evil. (Genesis 2:8–9)

The story continues that eating of the "tree of life" was forbidden Adam; Eve, the first woman, was formed from one of Adam's ribs when he slept; a serpent induced Eve to eat of the forbidden tree; Adam did the same; and as a consequence they were all reproached by God:

For this the serpent was cursed, and enmity was established between the serpent and Eve and between their descendants. And God said: "The man is become like unto Us, knowing good and evil. Perhaps He will eat of the tree of life and live forever." So God guarded the tree of life. ('Abdu'l-Bahá, *Some Answered Questions,* no. 30.2)

### WHAT IS OF VALUE IN THE
### GARDEN OF EDEN STORY?

The Garden of Eden story is rich in symbolism:

If we were to take this account according to the literal meaning of the words as indicated by their common usage, it would indeed be exceedingly strange, and human minds would be excused from accepting, affirming, or imagining it. For such elaborate arrangements and details, such statements and reproaches would be implausible even coming from an intelligent person, let alone from the Divinity Himself, Who has arranged this infinite universe in the most perfect form and arrayed its countless beings in the utmost order, soundness, and perfection.

. . . The account of Adam and Eve, their eating from the tree, and their expulsion from Paradise are therefore symbols and divine mysteries. They have all-embracing meanings and marvelous interpretations, but only the intimates of the divine mysteries and the well-favoured of the all-sufficing Lord are aware of the true significance of these symbols. ('Abdu'l-Bahá, *Some Answered Questions,* no. 30.3–4)

### WHAT ARE SOME OF THE SYMBOLIC FEATURES
### OF THE GARDEN OF EDEN STORY?

Symbolism in the story includes the following:

By "the tree of good and evil" is meant the material world, for the heavenly realm of the spirit is pure goodness and absolute radiance, but in the material world light and darkness, good and evil, and all manner of opposing realities are to be found.

The meaning of the serpent is attachment to the material world. . . . By "the tree of life" is meant the highest degree of the world of existence, that is, the station of the Word of God and His universal Manifestation. That station was indeed well guarded, until it appeared and shone forth in the supreme revelation of His universal Manifestation. ('Abdu'l-Bahá, *Some Answered Questions,* no. 30.5–6)

## DID HUMANITY INHERIT
## ADAM'S SIN?

The story of Adam and Eve is a teaching parable, not history. Concerning the traditional interpretation of the sin of Adam as the source of "original sin," the Bahá'í Writings state:

> . . . the majority . . . believe that Adam sinned and transgressed by eating from the forbidden tree, that the dire and disastrous consequences of this transgression were inherited for all time by His descendants, and that Adam has thus become the cause of the death of man. This explanation is irrational and clearly mistaken, for it implies that all men, even the Prophets and Messengers of God, through no fault or sin of their own, and for no other reason than their descent from Adam, became guilty sinners and suffered the torments of hell until the day of Christ's sacrifice. This would be far from the justice of God. ('Abdu'l-Bahá, *Some Answered Questions,* no. 29.9)

Rather, the story illustrates that attachment to the material world (symbolized by the serpent) results in sin. It also reminds us in figurative language that our human condition, which includes animal inclinations, predisposes us to error:

> The child when born is far from being perfect. It is not only helpless, but actually is imperfect, and even is naturally inclined towards evil. He should be trained, his natural inclinations harmonized, adjusted and controlled, and if necessary suppressed or regulated, so as to insure his healthy physical and moral development. (From a letter written on behalf of Shoghi Effendi, dated July 9, 1939, to an individual believer, in *Lights of Guidance,* no. 510)

## THE MESSENGER

The story of Adam includes His receiving instructions directly from God and completing certain divinely ordained tasks:

> And out of the ground the LORD God formed every beast of the field, and every fowl of the air; and brought them unto Adam to see what he would call them: and whatsoever Adam called every living creature, that was the name thereof. (Genesis 2:19, KJV)

It is interesting that in the Bahá'í Writings the figure of Adam represents not only the first human being, but also the first Messenger of God in our era of civilization-building. The Messengers of God, or "Manifestations of God" as They are usually termed in the Bahá'í Writings, occupy a spiritual station higher than humanity. Manifestations of God commune with God in intimate and immediate ways, dispense laws and ordinances to the people, complete divinely ordained tasks, and serve a mystical and pivotal role in the advancement of civilization. Although the actual historical circumstances surrounding the appearance of the ancient Manifestations of God have been largely lost to time, the spiritual station of the Manifestation is a reality, as is the Manifestation's repeated appearance throughout history. The Manifestations of God in our era of civilization-building, which began about six-thousand years ago and will continue far into the future, include, but are not limited to:

| | |
|---|---|
| Adam (circa 4000 BC) | Moses (circa 1400 BC) |
| Krishna (circa 3000 BC) | Zoroaster (circa 900 BC) |
| Noah (BC date unknown) | Buddha (circa 520 BC) |
| Hud (BC date unknown) | Christ (circa 30 AD) |
| Saleh (BC date unknown) | Muhammad (622 AD) |
| Abraham (circa 1900 BC) | The Báb (1844 AD) |
| Joseph (circa 1600 BC) | Bahá'u'lláh (1863 AD) |

The above Messengers of God are mentioned in the Bahá'í Writings;[9] however, the Faith recognizes that additional Messengers have appeared throughout history:

We are taught there always have been Manifestations of God, but we do not have any record of their names. (From a letter written on behalf of Shoghi Effendi, dated October 4, 1950, to an individual believer, in *Lights of Guidance,* no. 1969*)*

## WHAT IS THE SPIRITUAL STATION
## OF A MANIFESTATION OF GOD?

The Manifestation of God is a divine Emissary—a Spiritual Reality that emanates from, but is not identical with, the essence of God. We cannot know the essence of God, but we can learn about the Will and attributes of God through the Manifestation of God. Throughout history, this divine Emissary has periodically appeared in the world of creation in all physical appearances as a human being; however, the Manifestation has a much higher spiritual station than humans, possesses innate knowledge, and serves as the Educator of humanity. It is only through the Manifestation of God that humanity can attain to the knowledge of God:

> The knowledge of the reality of the Divinity is in no wise possible, but the knowledge of the Manifestations of God is the knowledge of God, for the bounties, splendors and attributes of God are manifest in Them. Thus, whoso attains to the knowledge of the Manifestations of God attains to the knowledge of God, and whoso remains heedless of Them remains bereft of that knowledge. ('Abdu'l-Bahá, *Some Answered Questions,* no. 59.9)

While there is only one spiritual station of the Manifestation of God, there have been, and will continue to be, many different historical appearances. Therefore, it is correct to refer to the "Manifestation" (singular) as well as the "Manifestations" (plural). Many other titles for the Manifestation exist, all of which communicate something of the splendor and uniqueness of that spiritual station, such as "the Promised One," "the Sun of Truth," "Dayspring of the Spirit," and "the Face of God" (Bahá'u'lláh,

---

9. See Bahá'u'lláh, The Kitáb-i-Íqán, ¶7–13, 17–25; 146, 172, 236; 'Abdu'l-Bahá, *The Promulgation of Universal Peace,* p. 171, 346; *Selections from the Writings of the Báb,* no. 4.10.

*Gleanings from the Writings of Bahá'u'lláh*, no. 6.1, 8.4). In addition, because the Manifestations of God reflect all of the attributes of God, every name or title used to refer to God, such as "Lord," "the All Perceiving," "the All Wise," and "the Holy of Holies" (Bahá'u'lláh, *Gleanings from the Writings of Bahá'u'lláh*, no. 1.2) can be applied to the Manifestations as well:

> These Prophets and chosen Ones of God are the recipients and revealers of all the unchangeable attributes and names of God. They are the mirrors that truly and faithfully reflect the light of God. Whatsoever is applicable to Them is in reality applicable to God, Himself, Who is both the Visible and the Invisible. (Bahá'u'lláh, The Kitáb-i-Íqán, ¶151)

## WHEN DOES THE MANIFESTATION OF GOD APPEAR IN THE WORLD OF HUMANITY?

The Manifestation of God appears in the world of humanity at regular intervals, approximately every 500 to 1,000 years, creating cycles of development similar to cycles in the world of nature:

> Each of the luminous bodies of this limitless firmament has its cycle of revolution, that period wherein it completes the full circuit of its orbit before beginning a new one. The earth, for example, completes a revolution every 365 days, five hours, forty-eight minutes and a fraction, and then begins anew along the same orbit. In the same way, the entire universe, whether with respect to the realm of nature or the realm of man, proceeds through cycles of major events and occurrences.
>
> . . . Each of the Manifestations of God has likewise a cycle wherein His religion and His laws are in full force and effect. When His cycle is ended through the advent of a new Manifestation, a new cycle begins. ('Abdu'l-Bahá, *Some Answered Questions*, no. 41.3–4)

## WHAT IS THE PURPOSE OF THE MANIFESTATION OF GOD?

The purpose of the Manifestation of God is to transmit the grace of God to humanity:

. . . in the kingdoms of earth and heaven there must needs be manifested a Being, an Essence Who shall act as a Manifestation and Vehicle for the transmission of the grace of the Divinity Itself, the Sovereign Lord of all. Through the Teachings of this Daystar of Truth every man will advance and develop until he attaineth the station at which he can manifest all the potential forces with which his inmost true self hath been endowed. It is for this very purpose that in every age and dispensation the Prophets of God and His chosen Ones have appeared amongst men, and have evinced such power as is born of God and such might as only the Eternal can reveal. (Bahá'u'lláh, *Gleanings from the Writings of Bahá'u'lláh,* no. 27.5)

The Manifestation of God is like a sunbeam: while the sunbeam is not the sun, it is the vehicle for the transmission of the energy of the sun and is the cause of development on earth. In a similar sense, while the Manifestation of God is not God, the Manifestation transmits God's grace and is the cause of human development.

## FOR HOW LONG HAVE MANIFESTATIONS OF GOD GUIDED HUMANITY?

Manifestations of God have been inspiring spiritual and material advances in the evolution of civilization throughout history:

Thus there have been many holy Manifestations of God. One thousand years ago, two hundred thousand years ago, one million years ago the bounty of God was flowing, the radiance of God was shining, the dominion of God was existing. ('Abdu'l-Bahá, *The Promulgation of Universal Peace,* p. 654)

The cycle of a particular Manifestation, during which time His laws prevail, begins with the Declaration of His mission in the world and continues until the coming of the next Manifestation. Various terms refer to the cycle of a Manifestation of God. For example, the "Mosaic Cycle" may also be called the "Day of Moses," the "Mosaic Dispensation," or the "Revelation of Moses." An era of civilization-building is composed of many cycles.

## WHAT WOULD HUMAN LIFE BE LIKE
## WITHOUT THE MANIFESTATION OF GOD?

If not for the appearance of the Manifestation of God throughout history, humanity would stay in an animalistic state:

> Were it not for the coming of these holy Manifestations of God, all mankind would be found on the plane of the animal. They would remain darkened and ignorant like those who have been denied schooling and who never had a teacher or trainer. ('Abdu'l-Bahá, *The Promulgation of Universal Peace,* p. 657)

## WHAT KIND OF INFLUENCE DO THE TEACHINGS OF THE
## MANIFESTATIONS HAVE ON CIVILIZATION?

All of humanity's attainments are by virtue of these Divine Educators. More than philosophers, great teachers, or rulers, every Manifestation possesses the Power of the Holy Spirit that can regenerate souls and influence civilization for thousands of years:

> The will of every sovereign prevaileth during his reign, the will of every philosopher findeth expression in a handful of disciples during his lifetime, but the Power of the Holy Spirit shineth radiantly in the realities of the Messengers of God, and strengtheneth Their will in such wise as to influence a great nation for thousands of years and to regenerate the human soul and revive mankind. ('Abdu'l-Bahá, *Tablet to August Forel,* p. 24)

## WHY ARE REPEATED APPEARANCES
## OF THE MANIFESTATION NECESSARY?

As civilization progresses, the requirements of the age change and new teachings are necessary to heighten understandings, modify behavior, and renew humanity's social and spiritual life. In a way, religion is like a robe that clothes the body of humanity—when the robe becomes outworn, a new robe is necessary:

> And now concerning thy question regarding the nature of religion. Know thou that they who are truly wise have likened the world unto the human temple. As the body of man needeth a garment to

clothe it, so the body of mankind must needs be adorned with the mantle of justice and wisdom. Its robe is the Revelation vouchsafed unto it by God. Whenever this robe hath fulfilled its purpose, the Almighty will assuredly renew it. For every age requireth a fresh measure of the light of God. Every Divine Revelation hath been sent down in a manner that befitted the circumstances of the age in which it hath appeared. (Bahá'u'lláh, *Gleanings from the Writings of Bahá'u'lláh,* no. 34.7)

Repeated appearances of the Manifestation are necessary to direct the capacities and respond to the requirements of every age. Also, with time, man-made interpretations, dogmas, and heresies can degrade the teachings of the Manifestations, thereby creating situations that require a renewal of spiritual instruction:

In the beginning, this tree was full of vitality and laden with blossoms and fruit, but gradually it grew old, spent, and barren, until it entirely withered and decayed. That is why the True Gardener will again plant a tender sapling of the same stock, that it may grow and develop day by day, extend its sheltering shade in this heavenly garden, and yield its prized fruit. So it is with the divine religions: With the passage of time, their original precepts are altered, their underlying truth entirely vanishes, their spirit departs, doctrinal innovations spring up, and they become a body without a soul. That is why they are renewed. ('Abdu'l-Bahá, *Some Answered Questions,* no. 43.10)

### WERE THERE PROPHETS BEFORE ADAM?

There were Prophets and cycles of civilization-building before Adam, but records of those eras have been lost to time:

And now regarding thy question, "How is it that no records are to be found concerning the Prophets that have preceded Adam, the Father of Mankind, or of the kings that lived in the days of those Prophets?" Know thou that the absence of any reference to them is no proof that they did not actually exist. That no records concerning them are now available should be attributed to their extreme remoteness, as well as to the vast changes which the earth hath undergone since their time. (Bahá'u'lláh, *Gleanings from the Writings of Bahá'u'lláh*, no. 87.1)

## NOAH

In Genesis, Noah communes with God and is commissioned for certain tasks:

Then the LORD said unto Noah, "Go into the ark, you and all your household, for I have seen that you alone are righteous before me in this generation. . . ." And Noah did all that the LORD had commanded him. (Genesis 7:1,5)

### DO THE BAHÁ'Í WRITINGS CONFIRM THE LITERAL TRUTH OF THE STORIES OF NOAH AND OTHER EARLY MANIFESTATIONS OF GOD?

While the Bahá'í Writings mention elements of the accounts of Adam, Noah, Abraham, and Joseph, these references do not necessarily confirm the historical validity of the stories attributed to Them. As previously stated, the factual histories of ancient Messengers are largely lost to time:

The events that transpired at the advent of the Prophets of the past, and Their ways and works and circumstances, are not adequately set down in authoritative histories, and are referred to only in condensed form in the verses of the Qur'án, the Holy Traditions and the Torah. ('Abdu'l-Bahá, *The Secret of Divine Civilization*, ¶138)

The "traditions" of the ancient Prophets; that is, the stories that were passed down as oral tradition, later written down, and eventually adopted as Scripture convey much of the spiritual truth and impact of Their missions; however, they are not journalistic recordings in the modern sense. Nevertheless, we can refer to these potent ancient stories to benefit from and share the lessons contained therein. When the Central Figures of the Faith refer to traditions of the ancient Messengers, it is the spiritual significance of the story that is confirmed, not necessarily the story's literal accuracy:

> All the texts and teachings of the holy Testaments have intrinsic spiritual meanings. They are not to be taken literally. ('Abdu'l-Bahá, *The Promulgation of Universal Peace*, p. 648)

Although the texts may not be understood literally, they are taken seriously. The traditions attributed to Noah and other prehistoric Manifestations of God are often cited in the Bahá'í Writings for their powerful instructional value in conveying essential truths.

## HOW IS THE STORY OF NOAH CITED IN THE BAHÁ'Í WRITINGS?

In the following passage, Bahá'u'lláh acknowledges Noah's Revelation, affirms the opposition He suffered, notes various traditions related to Noah, and then invites meditation on those traditions to illuminate current circumstances and encourage personal reflection:

> Among the Prophets was Noah. For nine hundred and fifty years He prayerfully exhorted His people and summoned them to the haven of security and peace. None, however, heeded His call. Each day they inflicted on His blessed person such pain and suffering that no one believed He could survive. How frequently they denied Him, how malevolently they hinted their suspicion against Him! . . . Finally, as stated in books and traditions, there remained with Him only forty or seventy-two of His followers. At last from the depth of His being He cried aloud: "Lord! Leave not upon the land a single dweller from among the unbelievers."
>
> And now, consider and reflect a moment upon the waywardness of this people. What could have been the reason for such denial and avoidance on their part? . . . Meditate profoundly, that the secret of things unseen may be revealed unto you, that you may inhale the sweetness of a spiritual and imperishable fragrance, and that you may acknowledge the truth that from time immemorial even unto eternity the Almighty hath tried, and will continue to try, His servants, so that light may be distinguished from darkness, truth from

falsehood, right from wrong, guidance from error, happiness from misery, and roses from thorns. (Bahá'u'lláh, The Kitáb-i-Íqán, ¶7)

It is interesting that in the above quotation Bahá'u'lláh refers to two traditions that give conflicting data: one states that Noah was left with forty followers, while the other claims seventy-two. Bahá'u'lláh does not dispute the accuracy of either of the stories, He simply states, "there remained with Him only forty or seventy-two of His followers." The details are irrelevant; the traditions are cited for spiritual instruction, not historical accuracy. This is a practice of previous Messengers as well—as explained by Mírzá Abu'l-Faḍl Gulpáygání (an Apostle of Bahá'u'lláh known as the greatest Bahá'í scholar): "Finally, it is well known that neither the Prophet Muhammad nor the rest of the prophets ever engaged in disputes with the people about their historical beliefs, but addressed them according to their local traditions" (*Miracles and Metaphors,* p. 14).

### DID NOAH REALLY LIVE FOR NINE HUNDRED AND FIFTY YEARS OR DOES THIS REFER TO THE LENGTH OF HIS DISPENSATION?

Noah did not live nine hundred and fifty years as we currently measure time, nor can we interpret this as the length of His Dispensation:

The years of Noah are not years as we count them, and as our teachings do not state that this reference to year means His dispensation we cannot interpret it this way. (From a letter written on behalf of Shoghi Effendi, dated November 25, 1950, to an individual believer, in *Lights of Guidance,* no. 1659)

The unusually long life spans attributed to Noah and other biblical figures are not to be understood by modern time measurements.

### IS THE STORY OF NOAH'S ARK MENTIONED BY THE CENTRAL FIGURES OF THE BAHÁ'Í FAITH?

The story of Noah's ark is not specifically mentioned by the Central Figures of the Faith; however, They do draw on the imagery of Noah's ark as well as the Hebrews' Ark of the Covenant as symbolic of the protection inherent in the laws and teachings of God. The following passage from the Universal House of Justice explains:

> The word "ark" means, literally, a boat or ship, something that affords protection and safety, or a chest or box. It is used in two senses in the Bible. In the first sense it refers to the Ark of Noah, which He was bidden to build of gopher wood to preserve life during the Flood. In the second sense it refers to the Ark of the Covenant, the sacred chest representing to the Hebrews God's presence among them. It was constructed to hold the Tablets of the Law in Moses' time and was later placed in the Holy of Holies in the Temple of Jerusalem. The Ark, as a symbol of God's Law and the Divine Covenant that is the salvation of the people in every age and Dispensation, appears in various ways in the Bahá'í writings. Bahá'u'lláh refers to His faithful followers as "the denizens of the Crimson Ark"; He refers to the Ark of the Cause and also to the Ark of His Laws. A well-known passage in which this term is used appears in the Tablet of Carmel: "Erelong will God sail His Ark upon thee, and will manifest the people of Bahá who have been mentioned in the Book of Names." Shoghi Effendi explains that the Ark in this passage refers to the Bahá'í Administrative Centre on Mount Carmel and that the dwellers of the Ark are the members of the Universal House of Justice. (The Universal House of Justice, *Messages from the Universal House of Justice, 1963– 1986*, p. 732)

## ABRAHAM

From the announcement of His birth as Abram (meaning "exalted father"), through His name-change to Abraham (meaning "father of multitudes"), to His burial, the story of Abraham dominates the Book of Genesis:

> Now the LORD said to Abram, "Go from your country and your kindred and your father's house, to the land that I will show you. I will make of you a great nation, and I will bless you, and make

your name great so that you will be a blessing. I will bless those that bless you, and the one who curses you I will curse; and in you all the families of the earth shall be blessed." (Genesis 12:1–3)

References to Abraham and stories of His descendents extend through the rest of the Bible.

## WHAT ARE SOME OF THE MAIN POINTS
## IN THE STORY OF ABRAHAM?

The story of Abraham conveys a pattern that remains true for every Manifestation of God—the promulgation of new teachings that uplift the people; rejection by the religious and social powers of the time; banishment; and victory in the face of persecution:

Among those Who possessed this divine power and were assisted by it was Abraham. The proof is this: Abraham was born in Mesopotamia of a family that was ignorant of the oneness of God; He opposed His own people and government, and even His own kin; He rejected all their gods; and, alone and single-handed, He withstood a powerful nation. Such opposition and resistance were not simple or trivial. It is as though one were in this day to deny Christ among Christian nations who firmly cling to the Bible, or as though one were—God forbid—to blaspheme Christ in the papal court, oppose all His followers, and to act thus in the most vehement manner.

These people believed not in one God but in many gods, to whom they ascribed miracles, and hence they all rose up against Abraham. No one supported Him except His nephew Lot and one or two other individuals. . . . At last the intensity of His enemies' opposition obliged Him, utterly wronged, to forsake His native land. In reality He was banished that He might be reduced to naught and that no trace of Him might remain. Abraham then came to these regions, that is, to the Holy Land.

My point is that His enemies imagined that this exile would lead to His destruction and ruin. And indeed, if a man is banished from his native land, deprived of his rights, and oppressed from every side, he is bound—even if he be a king—to be reduced to naught. But Abraham stood fast and showed forth extraordinary constancy, and God changed His exile into abiding honour, till at last He established the oneness of God, for at that time the generality of mankind were idol worshippers. ('Abdu'l-Bahá, *Some Answered Questions,* no. 4.1–3)

### WHAT IS ABRAHAM KNOWN FOR?

Abraham is known as the "Founder of monotheism":

The Founder of monotheism was Abraham; it is to Him that this concept can be traced, and the belief was current among the Children of Israel, even in the days of Socrates.[10] ('Abdu'l-Bahá, *Selections from the Writings of 'Abdu'l-Bahá,* no. 25.3)

Abraham is also known as the Patriarch of five religions: Judaism, Christianity, Islam, the Bábí Faith, and the Bahá'í Faith (see Worthington, p. 177). The biblical story of Abraham and His progeny portrays the superhuman influence of the Manifestation of God:

This exile became the cause of the progress of Abraham's descendants. This exile resulted in their being given the Holy Land. This exile resulted in the diffusion of Abraham's teachings. This exile resulted in the appearance of a Jacob from the seed of Abraham, and of a Joseph who became ruler in Egypt. This exile resulted in the appearance of a Moses from that same seed. This exile resulted in the appearance of a being such as Christ from that lineage. This exile resulted in a Hagar being found, of whom Ishmael was begotten, and from whom Muhammad in turn descended. This exile resulted in the appearance of the Báb from the lineage of Abraham. This exile resulted in the appearance of the Prophets of Israel from the progeny of Abraham—and so it will continue forevermore. This exile resulted in the whole of Europe and most of Asia enter-

---

10. 399 BC.

ing under the shadow of the God of Israel. Behold what a power it was that enabled an emigrant to establish such a family, to found such a nation, and to promulgate such teachings. Now, can anyone claim that all this was purely fortuitous? We must be fair: Was this Man an Educator or not? ('Abdu'l-Bahá, *Some Answered Questions,* no. 4.4)

Stories of the movements, crises, victories, and prophecies of the descendants of Abraham constitute the Old Testament.

## JOSEPH

The Book of Genesis closes with the story of Joseph, popularly known as the story of Joseph and the coat of many colors. In this account, Joseph, son of Jacob, is betrayed by His brothers, sold into slavery, and transported to Egypt:

> So when Joseph came to his brothers, they stripped him of his robe, the long robe with sleeves that he wore; and they took him and threw him into a pit. The pit was empty; there was no water in it. . . . Then Judah said to his brothers, "What profit is it if we kill our brother and conceal his blood? Come, let us sell him to the Ishmaelites, and not lay our hands on him, for he is our brother, our own flesh." And his brothers agreed. When some Midianite traders passed by, they drew Joseph up, lifting him out of the pit, and sold him to the Ishmaelites for twenty pieces of silver. And they took Joseph to Egypt. (Genesis 37:23–24, 26–28)

Joseph eventually rises to a position of leadership in Egypt and then reunites His family in that land, all in the most extraordinary circumstances. There is an equivalent narrative in Surih 12 of the Qur'án, the Surih of Joseph. Both stories are highly allegorical. The story of Joseph has a special place in Bahá'í history and is alluded to in the Writings of Bahá'u'lláh.

## WHAT PART DOES THE STORY OF JOSEPH
## PLAY IN BAHÁ'Í HISTORY?

The first Sacred Writing revealed by the Báb, the Herald of the Bahá'í Faith, was a commentary on the Surih of Joseph entitled the "Qayyúmu'l-Asmá'. This commentary explains some of the symbolism in the story of Joseph, fore-tells the Báb's martyrdom, and forecasts events in Bahá'u'lláh's ministry:

> Already in Shiraz, at the earliest stage of His ministry, He [the Báb] had revealed what Bahá'u'lláh has characterized as "the first, the greatest, and mightiest of all books" in the Bábí Dispensation, the celebrated commentary on the Surih of Joseph, entitled the Qayyúmu'l-Asmá', whose fundamental purpose was to forecast what the true Joseph (Bahá'u'lláh) would, in a succeeding Dispensation, endure at the hands of one who was at once His arch-enemy and blood brother. (Shoghi Effendi, *God Passes By,* pp. 36–37)

Tahirih, a Persian poetess, had a dream about the Báb in which she heard Him reciting a portion of His commentary on the Surih of Joseph. Shortly afterwards she became one of the Báb's Letters of the Living (Apostles), translated the Báb's commentary on the Surih of Joseph into Persian, and "exerted the utmost effort for its spread and interpretation" (Shoghi Effendi, *The Dawn-Breakers,* p. 82).

### HOW IS THE STORY OF JOSEPH ALLUDED TO
### IN BAHÁ'U'LLÁH'S WRITINGS?

In His Book of Laws, Bahá'u'lláh states:

> Say: From My laws the sweet-smelling savour of My garment can be smelled, and by their aid the standards of Victory will be planted upon the highest peaks. (Bahá'u'lláh, The Kitáb-i-Aqdas, ¶4)

The above verse is an allusion to the chapter where Joseph's father, Jacob, identifies his long-lost son by the fragrance of His garment. "The metaphor of the fragrant 'garment' is frequently used in the Bahá'í Writings to refer to the recognition of the Manifestation of God and His Revelation." (From the "Notes" section of the Kitab-i-Aqdas, p. 165)

The following excerpt from a discourse on the requirements of a true spiritual seeker draws on imagery from the story of Joseph:

O My Brother! Until thou enter the Egypt of love, thou shalt never come to the Joseph of the Beauty of the Friend; and until, like Jacob, thou forsake thine outward eyes, thou shalt never open the eye of thine inward being; and until thou burn with the fire of love, thou shalt never commune with the Lover of Longing. (Bahá'u'lláh, The Seven Valleys, p. 9)


## MOSES

The Book of Exodus begins in the setting of the Israelites' enslavement in the land of Egypt where an unnamed Pharaoh, fearful of the Israelite's increasing strength and numbers, commands male infanticide. But one baby—later to be named Moses—escapes death by being placed in a basket and set adrift on a river:

Then Pharaoh commanded all his people, "Every boy that is born to the Hebrews you shall throw into the Nile, but you shall let every girl live."

Now a man from the house of Levi went and married a Levite woman. The woman conceived and bore a son; and when she saw that he was a fine baby, she hid him three months. When she could hide him no longer she got a papyrus basket for him, and plastered it with bitumen and pitch; she put the child in it and placed it among the reeds on the bank of the river. (Exodus 1:22; 2:1–3)[11]

Found by Pharaoh's daughter and raised in the Egyptian royal court (Exodus 1:9–2:10), Moses ventures out as a young man and ends up in a

---

11. A parallel to the story of the birth of Moses can be found in the birth story of Sargon of Agade (2334–2279 BC) where the motifs of a secret birth, abandoning a newborn, being drawn out of the water, and adoption by a stranger also appear (see Matthews and Benjamin, p. 89).

foreign land. Years later He is called by the voice of God in the "burning bush" to return to His home and bring the Israelites out of Egypt. Moses is the Central Figure in the Books of Exodus, Leviticus, Numbers, and Deuteronomy as the Messenger of God Who leads the Israelite tribes out of Egypt in the great Exodus, and shepherds them through the Wilderness and to the Promised Land equipped with laws.

### HAS THE HISTORICAL REALITY OF MOSES AND THE EXODUS BEEN VERIFIED BY HISTORIANS?

In his commentary on the story of the Exodus as it relates to the archaeological research of Egyptologists through the early 1900s, Mírzá Abu'l-Faḍl states, "No trace has been found of Moses' mission to the Israelites, their plea for salvation from Pharaoh's tyranny through Moses' leadership, or their emigration to the plains of Syria under his standard" (Mírzá Abu'l-Faḍl, p. 15). Today, the situation is the same. Eric H. Cline, professor of ancient history and archeology at George Washington University, states, "The story of the Exodus has become one of the most famous and enduring tales from the Hebrew Bible, still celebrated today in the Jewish holiday of Passover. Yet it is also one of the most difficult to substantiate by either ancient texts or archaeological evidence. . . . There is currently virtually nothing that sheds a specific light on the historicity of the Exodus—all is inference so far" (Cline, 2014, pp. 90, 92).

Because Moses is a giant figure in the Old Testament, it is unsettling to some that to date "no Egyptian sources mention Moses or the events of Exodus-Deuteronomy, nor has any archeological evidence been discovered in Egypt or the Sinai wilderness to support the story in which he is the central figure" (Meyers, 2005, p 3). Moses and the Exodus are, however, referenced in the New Testament, the Qur'án, and the Bahá'í Writings. Mírzá Abu'l-Faḍl explains that the Prophets refer to these stories because They often speak in compliance with traditional understandings. He states, "The Prophets have indulged the people in regard to their historical notions, folk stories, and scientific principles, and have spoken to them according to these." (Mírzá Abu'l-Faḍl, pp. 9, 14).

Before His summary of the ministry of Moses in *The Secret of Divine Civilization,* 'Abdu'l-Bahá suggests that He is accommodating the audience's historical notions of Moses when He indicates that these events "are not adequately set down in authoritative histories," are instead presented in "condensed form," and that He is commenting "conformably" to what is understood by most people:

> The events that transpired at the advent of the Prophets of the past, and Their ways and works and circumstances, are not adequately set down in authoritative histories, and are referred to only in condensed form in the verses of the Qur'án, the Holy Traditions and the Torah. . . .
>
> To preclude once and for all objections on the part of any of the world's peoples, We shall conduct Our discussion conformably to those authoritative accounts which all nations are agreed upon. ('Abdu'l-Bahá, *The Secret of Divine Civilization,* ¶138–39)

For this and other events recorded in the Bible that are not verified by sources outside of the Bible, we are reminded of 'Abdu'l-Bahá's statement that biblical events that are not recorded in history should be understood according to their "inner meaning" ('Abdu'l-Bahá, *Some Answered Questions,* no. 10.5). Whatever archaeology and other sciences uncover as to the historical facts surrounding the Dispensation of Moses, from a Bahá'í perspective the text is honored for its spiritual meanings.

## WHAT ARE SOME OF THE MAIN POINTS IN THE STORY OF MOSES?

Like the stories of Abraham and Joseph, the story of Moses conveys a pattern that remains true for every Manifestation of God. This includes the promulgation of new teachings, the attraction of a few followers, persecution by the powers-that-be, and ultimate victory:

> Moses was for a long time a shepherd in the wilderness. To outward seeming He was a man Who had been reared in the bosom of tyranny, had become reputed among men as a murderer, had taken up the shepherd's staff, and was fiercely hated and reviled by Pharaoh's government and people. It was such a man Who freed a great people from the fetters of captivity and persuaded them to leave Egypt and settle in the Holy Land.
>
> That people had sunk to the depths of degradation and were lifted up to the heights of glory. They were captives and were set

free. They were the most ignorant of peoples and became the most learned. By virtue of that which He established, they so progressed as to be singled out among all nations, and their fame spread to every land, to such a degree that when the inhabitants of neighbouring lands wanted to praise someone they would say "Surely he must be an Israelite!" Moses established laws and ordinances that conferred new life upon the people of Israel and led them to attain the highest degree of civilization at that time. ('Abdu'l-Bahá, *Some Answered Questions,* no. 5.1–2)

Accounts of Moses contain some of the most captivating images in the Old Testament, such as the burning bush (Exodus 3:2), the ten plagues of Egypt (Exodus 7–13), the parting of the Red Sea (Exodus 14), and the golden calf (Exodus 32:19). The Bahá'í Writings present a glimpse of the symbolism contained in some of these stories.

### WHAT IS THE MEANING OF THE BURNING BUSH?

The Burning Bush illustrates the moment that Moses awoke to His station as the Manifestation of God:

There the angel of the LORD appeared to him in a flame of fire out of a bush; he looked and the bush was blazing, yet it was not consumed. Then Moses said, "I must turn aside and look at this great sight, and see why the bush is not burned up." When the LORD saw that he had turned aside to see, God called to him out of the bush, "Moses, Moses!" And he said, "Here I am." (Exodus 3:2–4)

In religious Scripture, the moments that mark the awakening of the Manifestation are expressed in various symbolic images. For Zoroaster it is a sacred fire, for Moses it is a Burning Bush, for Christ it is a Dove, for Muhammad it is the Angel Gabriel, and for Bahá'u'lláh it is the Maid of Heaven:

It was on that occasion that the "Most Great Spirit," as designated by Bahá'u'lláh Himself, revealed itself to Him, in the form of a "Maiden," and bade Him "lift up" His "voice between earth and heaven"—that same Spirit which, in the Zoroastrian, the Mosaic, the Christian, and Muhammadan Dispensations, had been respectively symbolized by the "Sacred Fire," the "Burning Bush," the "Dove," and the "Angel Gabriel." (Shoghi Effendi, *Messages to America,* p. 99)

## WHAT IS THE STORY OF THE TEN PLAGUES OF EGYPT?

In the story of the Exodus, God commissions Moses to go to Pharaoh (who is not identified) to call for the release of the "children of Israel" who are under oppression in Egypt. When Pharaoh refuses to cooperate, Moses afflicts Egypt with ten plagues that are largely understood by biblical scholars to be allegorical (Harris, p. 21; Redford, p. 408; Cline, 2014, pp. 90, 92). In the first plague, the Egyptian waters turn to blood:

> The LORD said to Moses, "Say to Aaron, 'Take your staff and stretch out your hand over the waters of Egypt—over its rivers, its canals, and its ponds, and all it pools of water—so that they may become blood; and there shall be blood throughout the whole land of Egypt, even in vessels of wood and in vessels of stone.'"
>
> Moses and Aaron did just as the LORD commanded. In the sight of Pharaoh and of his officials he lifted up the staff and struck the water in the river, and all the water in the river was turned to blood, and the fish in the river died. The river stank so that the Egyptians could not drink its water, and there was blood throughout the whole land of Egypt. (Exodus 7:19–21)

## WHAT DOES THE WATER TURNING TO BLOOD SYMBOLIZE?

One meaning of the waters turning to blood is the oppression caused by holding on to outdated traditions. That is, the Nile symbolizes the traditional religion, laws, and customs that had been the basis for prosperity in Egypt that, due to the people's pride and denial of the Word of God, became the cause of their demise:

> That is, it was in their power, had they so desired, to turn the waters of the Nile into blood for the Egyptians and the deniers—or, in other words, to turn, in consequence of their ignorance and pride, that which was the source of their life into the cause of their death. Thus the sovereignty, wealth, and power of Pharaoh and of

his people, which were the source of that nation's life, became, as a result of their opposition, denial, and pride, the very cause of their death, ruin, destruction, degradation, and wretchedness. ('Abdu'l-Bahá, *Some Answered Questions,* no. 11.17)

In 'Abdu'l-Bahá's explanation, the spoiling of the river symbolizes the oppressive results of dogmatically holding on to ancestral beliefs. "Archetypal truth is expressed in figurative terms as waters turning to blood" (Borovicka, p. 19).

### WHAT ABOUT THE OTHER NINE PLAGUES?

The other nine plagues are invasions of frogs, lice, and flies; diseased livestock; boils; thunder and hail; locusts; dense darkness for three days; and death of the Egyptian firstborns (Exodus 7–11). While direct explanations for these plagues are not found in the Bahá'í Writings,[12] reflection on the plague terms may inspire personal understandings. For example, "the plague of darkness takes on fresh meaning when one considers Bahá'u'lláh's teaching that God's first purpose in sending His Prophets unto men is 'to liberate the children of men from the darkness of ignorance, and guide them to the light of true understanding.'" (Borovicka, p. 21, citing *Gleanings from the Writings of Bahá'u'lláh* no. 34.5)

After the tenth plague, the Exodus narrative continues with the Israelites departing from Egypt and approaching the Red (Reed)[13] Sea while Pharaoh's army is in pursuit. Moses parts the waters and the Israelites walk through safely on dry ground. When Pharaoh's forces follow, Moses raises His hand again, the waters close on the army, and the Israelites continue on their journey. (Exodus 14:21–22)

### WHAT IS THE MEANING OF THE CROSSING OF THE RED SEA?

Instead of a one-time miraculous event, the crossing of the Red Sea has a greater spiritual significance—it symbolizes the spiritual journey of the Israelites informed by the teachings of Moses, by which they rose above the moral corruption that surrounded them:

---

12. That is, at this time, this writer has not found direct interpretations of biblical plagues two through ten in the Bahá'í Writings that are available in English.

13. Hebrew *Yam Suph;* that is, Sea of Reeds (Exodus 15:4, NIV, note a).

The crossing of the Red Sea has a spiritual meaning. It was a spiritual journey, through and above the sea of corruption and iniquity of the Pharaoh and his people, or army. By the help of God through Moses, the Israelites were able to cross this sea safely and reach the Promised Land (a spiritual state) while Pharaoh and his people were drowned in their own corruption. The Egyptian History recorded even trifling events. Had such a wonderful thing happened as the partings of the physical sea it would also have been recorded. ('Abdu'l-Bahá, in *Lights of Guidance,* no. 1678)

In Scripture, "death" often means spiritual death. Because Pharaoh denied the Manifestation of God and opposed Him, it was as if Pharaoh and his army were dead on the shore.

## PHARAONIC OPPOSITION

The role of Pharaoh in the Exodus narrative—that is, hostile opposition of Moses at every turn—represents those forces of darkness that oppose the Manifestation of God in every age:

This dark power has always endeavoured to extinguish the light. Tyranny has ever sought to overcome justice. Ignorance has persistently tried to trample knowledge underfoot. This has, from the earliest ages, been the method of the material world. In the time of Moses, Pharaoh set himself to prevent the Mosaic Light being spread abroad. ('Abdu'l-Bahá, *Paris Talks,* no. 33.2)

### WHICH APPEARANCE OF THE MANIFESTATION
### HAS BEEN STRONGLY OPPOSED?

Strong opposition has met every appearance of the Manifestation of God:

Consider the former generations. Witness how every time the Day-star of Divine bounty hath shed the light of His Revelation upon the world, the people of His Day have arisen against Him, and repudiated His truth. They who were regarded as the leaders of men have invariably striven to hinder their followers from turning unto Him Who is the Ocean of God's limitless bounty.

Behold how the people, as a result of the verdict pronounced by the divines of His age, have cast Abraham, the Friend of God into fire; how Moses, He Who held converse with the Almighty, was denounced as liar and slanderer. Reflect how Jesus, the Spirit of God, was, notwithstanding His extreme meekness and perfect tender-heartedness, treated by His enemies. So fierce was the opposition which He, the Essence of Being and Lord of the visible and invisible, had to face, that He had nowhere to lay His head. He wandered continually from place to place, deprived of a permanent abode. (Bahá'u'lláh, *Gleanings from the Writings of Bahá'u'lláh*, no. 23.1–2)

In every Dispensation, leaders of religion deny the Divine Educator and withhold their followers from recognizing the Word of God for that day.

### WHY IS THE MANIFESTATION OF GOD OPPOSED?

The Manifestation of God teaches what is necessary for the time regardless of what the people and powers expect or desire:

Ponder a while. What is it that prompted, in every Dispensation, the peoples of the earth to shun the Manifestation of the All-Merciful? What could have impelled them to turn away from Him and to challenge His authority? . . . It is the veil of idle imaginations which, in the days of the Manifestations of the Unity of God and the Daysprings of His everlasting glory, hath intervened, and will continue to intervene, between them and the rest of mankind. For in those days, He Who is the Eternal Truth manifesteth Himself in conformity with that which He Himself hath purposed, and not according to the desires and expectations of men. Even as He hath revealed: "So oft, then, as an Apostle cometh to you with that which your souls desire not, do ye swell with pride, and treat some as impostors, and slay others." (Bahá'u'lláh, *Gleanings from the Writings of Bahá'u'lláh,* no. 35.1)

The Manifestation of God always challenges the status quo and consequently is not popularly received. In addition to outright denial, opposition may come from inside the company of believers as well, as illustrated in the Exodus episode of the golden calf.

### WHAT IS THE EPISODE OF THE GOLDEN CALF?

Moses had been gone for about forty days on Mount Sinai and the people at the foot of the mountain were getting impatient. After all, could they really be sure that Moses would return? Was He even alive? They decided to continue on their journey and they implored Aaron, Moses' brother and coworker, to make an old-fashioned god to lead them on their way. Aaron complied, collected everyone's gold jewelry, and oversaw the creation of a golden calf "god" (Exodus 32:1–8).

The picture is both shocking and ironic: Moses is on the top of the mountain receiving the Ten Commandments while His followers are at the bottom of the mountain worshipping a golden calf. When God states His intention to "consume them" for rebellion (Exodus 32:10), Moses intercedes on the people's behalf. The incident ends with the Ten Commandments broken into pieces, the golden calf powdered and force-fed to the people, the idolaters slain, and the people plagued by their own corruption (Exodus 32:19–35). Nevertheless, when it was all over everybody who was left made a tabernacle for the new Ten Commandments and continued in the direction of the Promised Land (Exodus 36–40).

### WHAT IS A SYMBOLIC MEANING OF THE GOLDEN CALF?

In the Bahá'í Writings, the term "golden calf" appears in a few passages as a symbol for spiritual rebellion. For example, speaking of spreaders of discord, Bahá'u'lláh states:

> These creatures are the same creatures who for three thousand years have worshipped idols, and bowed down before the golden calf. Now, too, they are fit for nothing better. What relation can there be between this people and Him Who is the Countenance of Glory? What ties can bind them to the One Who is the supreme embod-

iment of all that is lovable? (Bahá'u'lláh, cited in Shoghi Effendi, *God Passes By*, p. 185)

The narrative of the golden calf symbolizes the human tendency to craft idols, and the suffering caused by disobedience to the laws and teachings of the Manifestation of God.

## WHAT IS THE OUTCOME OF OPPOSING THE MANIFESTATION OF GOD?

Scripture claims, and history proves, that the forces that oppose the Word of God ultimately fail:

Regard the former times. Had the calumnies of Pharaoh any effect? . . . He declared that Moses and Aaron were fomenters of discord, that they tried to destroy the religion of Egypt and therefore must be put to death. These words of Pharaoh were vainly spoken. The light of Moses shone. The radiance of the Law of God has encircled the world! ('Abdu'l-Bahá, *Paris Talks*, no. 33.21)

Not only is it impossible to quench the fire of the Word of God, but also the opposition itself inevitably proves, in mysterious ways, to be providential in spreading the Divine Teachings:

They that are shut out as by a veil from Thee have imagined that they have the power to put out Thy light, and to quench Thy fire, and to still the winds of Thy grace. Nay, and to this Thy might beareth me witness! Had not every tribulation been made the bearer of Thy wisdom, and every ordeal the vehicle of Thy providence, no one would have dared oppose us, though the powers of earth and heaven were to be leagued against us. (Bahá'u'lláh, *Prayers and Meditations by Bahá'u'lláh*, no. 11.2)

Every opposition to the Manifestation of God ultimately serves the Cause of God.

## REBUKE OF THE PROPHETS

After years of crisis, victory, rebellion, and wandering, the Israelites are stuck in a desert, hungry and thirsty, complaining bitterly, and yearning for the days in Egypt where at least they had enough to eat. Moses turns to the Lord for guidance, is rebuked for not "believing," and then prohibited from entering the Promised Land:

> Now there was no water for the congregation; so they gathered together against Moses and against Aaron. . . . Then Moses and Aaron went away from the assembly to the entrance of the tent of meeting; they fell upon their faces, and the glory of the LORD appeared to them. . . . The LORD said to Moses and Aaron, "Because you did not trust in me to show my holiness before the eyes of the Israelites, therefore you shall not bring this assembly into the land that I have given them. (Numbers 20:2, 6, 12)

Does this rebuke mean that Moses did something wrong? Is the Exodus narrative suggesting that Moses, a Manifestation of God, actually deserved a reproach from God?

### WHAT IS THE MEANING OF THE REPRIMAND OF MOSES?

Because every Manifestation of God is the representative of the people, God's every address to the Prophet represents an address to all. A reprimand from God is addressed to the Manifestation in order to shield humanity from the heartbreaking strength of God's reproach:

> Every divine utterance that takes the form of a rebuke, though it be outwardly addressed to the Prophets of God, is in reality directed to Their followers. The wisdom of this is naught but unalloyed mercy, that the people might not be dismayed, disheartened, or burdened by such reproaches and rebukes. These words are therefore outwardly addressed to the Prophets, but, even so, they are inwardly intended for the followers and not for the Messenger.

Moreover, the mighty and sovereign monarch of a land represents all who inhabit that land; that is, whatsoever he may utter is the word of all, and whatsoever covenant he may conclude is the covenant of all, for the will and purpose of all his subjects is subsumed in his own. Likewise, every Prophet is the representative of the entire body of His followers. Therefore, the covenant that God makes with Him and the words that He addresses to Him apply to all His people. ('Abdu'l-Bahá, *Some Answered Questions,* no. 44.2–3)

Moses' atonement for the sins of the people is described in Psalm 106, which catalogues the wrongdoings of the Israelites and identifies Moses as the one Who stood between the people and God, protecting them from destruction:

Therefore he [God] said he would destroy them [the Israelites], had not Moses, his chosen one, stood in the breach before him, to turn away his wrath from destroying them. (Psalms 106:23)

Whenever in Scripture God rebukes a Manifestation of God it is understood that the Manifestation symbolizes the totality of the people. Despite the rebukes, the Manifestation is sinless and absolutely submissive to the Will of God:

Observe that is was the people of Israel who had rebelled, but the reproach was outwardly addressed to Aaron and Moses. . . .

Now, this reproach and rebuke was in reality addressed to the children of Israel, who, on account of their rebellion against the commandments of God, were made to dwell for a long period in the barren desert beyond the Jordan, until the time of Joshua. This reproach and rebuke appeared to be addressed to Moses and Aaron, but in reality it was directed to the people of Israel.

. . . In brief, our meaning is that the rebukes recorded in the Sacred Scriptures, though outwardly addressed to the Prophets— the Manifestations of God—are in reality intended for the people. Were you to peruse the Bible, this matter would become clear and evident. ('Abdu'l-Bahá, *Some Answered Questions,* no. 44.9–10, 13)

Every defect identified with the Manifestation of God is a reflection of the weaknesses of the people, not the qualities of the Manifestation.

### WHAT DEFECTS ARE MENTIONED IN REGARD TO MOSES?

When Moses first receives His commission from God He appears to arise as a reluctant Prophet in that His first and continued response is to point out His fears and failures. The following three verses are samples of His claims of inadequacy:

> But Moses said to God, "Who am I, that I should go unto Pharaoh, and bring the Israelites out of Egypt?" (Exodus 3:11)

> But Moses said to the LORD, "O my LORD, I have never been eloquent, neither in the past nor even now that you have spoken to your servant; but I am slow of speech and slow of tongue." (Exodus 4:10)

> Then Moses turned again to the LORD, and said, "O LORD, why have you mistreated this people? Why did you ever send me? (Exodus 5:22–23)

The disclaimers and questions of Moses do not sound like the confidence of a Manifestation of God—a divine Emissary and revealer of all of the attributes of God. Instead, they sound like the hesitancies of a normal person who is being severely tested.

### WHY DOES MOSES POINT OUT HIS INADEQUACIES?

This episode in the Exodus narrative illustrates themes in the utterance of every Manifestation of God. The Manifestation may confess inadequacies to serve as a model of humility toward God:

> How often have the Prophets of God and His universal Manifestations confessed in Their prayers to Their sins and shortcomings! This is only to instruct other souls, to inspire and encourage them to be humble and submissive before God, and to acknowledge their own sins and shortcomings. For these holy Souls are sanctified above every sin and freed from every fault. ('Abdu'l-Bahá, *Some Answered Questions*, no. 44.12)

It is normal for humans to experience suffering, and the Manifestation shares in the human condition. When the Manifestation of God suffers for the truth, it is demonstrated that *we* will have to suffer for the truth, and when the Manifestation shows strength and endurance under intense trials, it demonstrates that *we* will have to show strength and endurance under intense trials:

> That is, to outward seeming, the human condition of the Holy Manifestations is subjected to tests, and when Their strength and endurance have by this means been revealed in the plenitude of power, other men receive instruction therefrom, and are made aware of how great must be their own steadfastness and endurance under tests and trials. For the Divine Educator must teach by word and also by deed, thus revealing to all the straight pathway of truth. ('Abdu'l-Bahá, *Selections from the Writings of 'Abdu'l-Bahá*, no. 26.3)

The story of how Moses expressed His concerns to God and then acted in obedience presents a rolemodel for righteousness: express concerns and faults in prayer and then, despite shortcomings, act in promotion of the Word of God.[14]

## COMMANDMENTS

The Mosaic Laws traditionally known as the Ten Commandments begin:

> Then God spoke all these words: I am the LORD your God, who brought you out of the land of Egypt, out of the house of slavery, you shall have no other gods before me. (Exodus 20:1–3)

The Ten Commandments continue with: prohibitions against idol worship and "wrongful use of the name of the LORD your God"; the

---

14. See *Afraid to Speak Against Moses* by Gary L. Matthews.

requirement to "remember the Sabbath day, and keep it holy; the require-ment to "honor your father and your mother"; prohibitions against mur-der, adultery; stealing, bearing "false witness against your neighbor," and coveting "anything that belongs to your neighbor" (Exodus 20:4–17).

The Ten Commandments represent only a portion of the Mosaic Law; over six hundred laws are recorded in the Books of Exodus, Leviticus, Numbers, and Deuteronomy. Addressing procedures for matters such as personal hygiene, criminal punishments, treatment of the handicapped and strangers, diet, and sacrificial offerings, these laws present uniform practices and principles of justice for a wide range of social issues in an ancient context.

### SINCE BAHÁ'ÍS RECOGNIZE THE INTEGRITY OF JUDAISM, DO THEY HAVE TO FOLLOW THE MOSAIC LAWS?

Yes and no. The reason is because there are two kinds of religious laws: spiritual and social. Spiritual laws are eternally binding, while social laws are prescribed by the Manifestation of God specifically for the age in which they are revealed:

> The All-Knowing Physician hath His finger on the pulse of mankind. He perceiveth the disease, and prescribeth, in His unerring wisdom, the remedy. Every age hath its own problem, and every soul its par-ticular aspiration. The remedy the world needeth in its present-day afflictions can never be the same as that which a subsequent age may require. Be anxiously concerned with the needs of the age ye live in, and center your deliberations on its exigencies and requirements. (Bahá'u'lláh, *Gleanings from the Writings of Bahá'u'lláh*, no. 106.1)

The distinction between spiritual and social laws has long been rec-ognized. "Christians, from the second century on, distinguished in the Hebrew Bible between: (1) universally valid moral principles; (2) histor-ically conditioned juridical rules; and (3) ritual prescriptions for Israel" (Buss, p. 50).

### WHAT ARE THE SPIRITUAL LAWS OF RELIGION?

Spiritual laws refer to eternal truths such as the oneness of God and the cultivation of divine virtues:

The religion of God consists of two parts: One is the very foundation and belongs to the spiritual realm; that is, it pertains to spiritual virtues and divine qualities. This part suffers neither change nor alteration: It is the Holy of Holies, which constitutes the essence of the religion of Adam, Noah, Abraham, Moses, Christ, Muhammad, the Báb, and Bahá'u'lláh, and which will endure throughout all the prophetic Dispensations. It will never be abrogated for it consists in spiritual rather than material truth. . . . It is mercy to the poor, assistance to the oppressed, generosity to the needy, and upliftment of the fallen. ('Abdu'l-Bahá, *Some Answered Questions,* no. 11.7)

Spiritual laws are the same in every Dispensation; they are the essential and fundamental aspects of religion.

### WHAT ARE THE SOCIAL LAWS OF RELIGION?

Social laws have to do with the organization of the community and material affairs that change with the needs and capacities of the times. Social laws are temporary:

The second aspect of the divine religions . . . concerns human needs and undergoes change in every cycle according to the exigency of the time. For example, in the time of Moses divorce was conformable to the needs and conditions; Moses, therefore, established it. But in the time of Christ, divorces were numerous and the cause of corruption; as they were not suitable for the time, he made divorce unlawful and likewise changed other laws. These are needs and conditions which have to do with the conduct of society; therefore, they undergo change according to the exigency of the time. ('Abdu'l-Bahá, *The Promulgation of Universal Peace,* p. 233)

The social laws of one time are often not appropriate for a later Dispensation. For example the Mosaic "eye for an eye, a tooth for a tooth" law may have been appropriate for desert life in the twelfth century BC, but is not appropriate today:

Moses dwelt in the desert. As there were no penitentiaries, no means of restitution in the desert and wilderness, the laws of God were an eye for an eye, a tooth for a tooth. Could this be carried out now? If a man destroys another man's eye, are you willing to destroy the eye of the offender? If a man's teeth are broken or his ear cut off, will you demand a corresponding mutilation of his assailant? This would not be conformable to conditions of humanity at the present time. If a man steals, shall his hand be cut off? This punishment was just and right in the law of Moses, but it was applicable to the desert, where there were no prisons and reformatory institutions of later and higher forms of government. Today you have government and organization, a police system, a judge and trial by jury. The punishment and penalty is now different. Therefore, the nonessentials which deal with details of community are changed according to the exigency of the time and conditions. ('Abdu'l-Bahá, *The Promulgation of Universal Peace*, p. 234)

## WHY DOES HUMANITY NEED THE LAWS OF THE MANIFESTATION OF GOD?

The Manifestation of God knows the mysteries of reality, and therefore knows exactly what is needed for humanity's progress at any point in time:

The Prophets of God, the universal Manifestations, are even as skilled physicians; the world of being is as the body of man; and the divine religions are as the treatment and remedy. The physician must be fully aware and informed of all the parts and organs, the constitution and condition of the patient, in order to prescribe an effective remedy. Indeed, it is from the disease itself that the physician deduces the remedy, for he first diagnoses the ailment and then treats its underlying cause. Until the ailment is properly diagnosed, how can any treatment or remedy be prescribed? The physician must therefore have a thorough knowledge of the constitution, the parts, organs, and condition of the patient, and be likewise well acquainted with every disease and every remedy, in order to prescribe the appropriate cure.

Religion, then, consists in the necessary relationships deriving from the reality of things. The universal Manifestations of God, being aware of the mysteries of creation, are fully informed of these necessary relationships and establish them as the religion of God. ('Abdu'l-Bahá, *Some Answered Questions,* no. 40.8–9)

## WHICH ARE MORE IMPORTANT, THE SPIRITUAL LAWS OR THE SOCIAL LAWS?

The spiritual laws of religion are more important because they are eternal and represent the point of unity of all religious teachings:

In the former days the punishment for theft was the cutting off of the right hand; in our time this law could not be so applied. In this age, a man who curses his father is allowed to live, when formerly he would have been put to death. It is therefore evident that whilst the spiritual law never alters, the practical rules must change their application with the necessities of the time. The spiritual aspect of religion is the greater, the more important of the two, and this is the same for all time, it never changes! It is the same, yesterday, today, and for ever! "As it was the beginning, is now, and ever shall be." ('Abdu'l-Bahá, *Paris Talks,* no. 44.13)

## COVENANTS

There are several well-known Covenants with God in the Old Testament. These include: the Covenant with Abraham and His descendents, in which Abraham agreed to leave His country and go to the land designated by God and, in turn, God promised to make Abraham's descendents a great nation—the law of circumcision became a sign of this Covenant (Genesis 12:1–3; 15–17); and the Covenant with Moses and the Israelites made on Mount Sinai in which the Israelites agreed to follow God's Commandments and God promised to make the Israelites His people (Exodus 19:5–24:8). The Book of Deuteronomy contains another Covenant—a promise that God would, sometime in the future, raise up a Prophet like Moses Who would speak God's Word and to Whom the people would be accountable:

Then the LORD replied to me [Moses] "They are right in what they have said. I will raise up for them a prophet like you from among their own people; I will put my words in the mouth of the prophet, who shall speak to them everything that I command. Anyone who does not heed the words that the prophet shall speak in my name, I myself will hold accountable." (Deuteronomy 18:17–19)

## WHAT IS A COVENANT?

A religious Covenant is a binding promise between God and humanity:

> A Covenant in the religious sense is a binding agreement between God and man, whereby God requires of man certain behaviour in return for which He guarantees certain blessings, or whereby He gives man certain bounties in return for which He takes from those who accept them an undertaking to behave in a certain way. There is, for example, the Greater Covenant which every Manifestation of God makes with His followers, promising that in the fullness of time a new Manifestation will be sent, and taking from them the undertaking to accept Him when this occurs. There is also the Lesser Covenant that a Manifestation of God makes with His followers that they will accept His appointed successor after Him. If they do so, the Faith can remain united and pure. If not, the Faith becomes divided and its force spent. It is a Covenant of this kind that Bahá'u'lláh made with His followers regarding 'Abdu'l-Bahá and that 'Abdu'l-Bahá perpetuated through the Administrative Order. . . . (From the glossary of *Messages from the Universal House of Justice: 1963 to 1986, The Third Epoch of the Formative Age*, p. 737)

## WHO IS INVOLVED IN THE GREATER COVENANT?

The Greater Covenant is binding on all believers who live in the Day of the next Manifestation. For example, the Mosaic prophecy of the coming of the next Manifestation (the Messiah) established a Covenant with those souls living fourteen hundred years later at the time of Christ:

> . . . it is a basic principle of the Law of God that in every Prophetic Mission, He entereth into a Covenant with all believers—a Cove-

nant that endureth until the end of that Mission, until the promised day when the Personage stipulated at the outset of the Mission is made manifest. Consider Moses, He Who conversed with God. Verily, upon Mount Sinai, Moses entered into a Covenant regarding the Messiah, with all those souls who would live in the day of the Messiah. And those souls, although they appeared many centuries after Moses, were nevertheless—so far as the Covenant, which is outside time, was concerned—present there with Moses. ('Abdu'l-Bahá, *Selections from the Writings of 'Abdu'l-Bahá*, no. 181.2)

### WHO IS INVOLVED IN THE LESSER COVENANT?

The Lesser Covenant is binding upon the followers of a Manifestation of God during that particular Revelation. For example, in the Bahá'í Faith 'Abdu'l-Bahá is recognized as the appointed successor to Bahá'u'lláh, with a continued line of authority to the Institution of the Guardianship (Shoghi Effendi) and the Universal House of Justice:

The Lesser Covenant, in this case, refers to Bahá'u'lláh's Covenant with His followers, which establishes 'Abdu'l-Bahá as the Centre of the Covenant. It confers upon 'Abdu'l-Bahá the authority to interpret Bahá'u'lláh's Writings in order "to perpetuate the influence" of the Faith and to "insure its integrity, safeguard it from schism, and stimulate its world-wide expansion." The Lesser Covenant also establishes the Guardianship and the Universal House of Justice as the twin successors of Bahá'u'lláh and 'Abdu'l-Bahá. (From the glossary of *Messages from the Universal House of Justice: 1963 to 1986, The Third Epoch of the Formative Age*, p. 737)

### DID MOSES HAVE A LESSER COVENANT
### WITH HIS FOLLOWERS?

The Book of Deuteronomy concludes with Moses indicating that after His passing the Israelites should follow Joshua:

Joshua son of Nun was full of the spirit of wisdom, because Moses had laid his hands on him; and Israelites obeyed him, doing as the LORD had commanded Moses. (Deuteronomy 34:9)

The story of Joshua continues in the next book of the Bible, the Book of Joshua, which tells of the Israelite tribes' settlement, development, crises, and victories in the Promised Land.

# THE BOOKS OF HISTORY—OVERVIEW

The Books of History are entitled Joshua, Judges, Ruth, 1 Samuel, 2 Samuel, 1 Kings, 2 Kings, 1 Chronicles, 2 Chronicles, Ezra, Nehemiah, and Esther. They present stories related to the movements and developments of the Israelites from approximately 1300 to 400 BC. This includes: the Israelites' entry into and settlement of the Promised Land (the Land of Canaan); the creation of a united Nation of Israel; the rule of King David and King Solomon; the building of the First Temple in Jerusalem; the splitting of the nation into two rival nations (Israel in the north and Judah in the south); the Assyrian conquest of the nation of Israel; the Babylonian conquest of the nation of Judah; the Persian conquest of Assyria and Babylonia; the return of exiled Israelites to Jerusalem; and the rebuilding of the Temple.

In the broadest sense, the stories convey an outline of historical truth. The presence of the Israelites in the region of Canaan around 1300 BC is verified by the historical record outside of the Bible, as is the Davidic dynasty, the nations of Israel and Judah, the Assyrian, Babylonian, and Persian conquests, and the building and rebuilding of the Temple in Jerusalem.[15] However, like many other ancient Near Eastern writings, biblical scholars recognize that the "biblical texts are not historical documents in the modern critical sense. They do not narrate events to tell precisely what happened" (O'Connor, p. 487). These writings relay events to interpret, to persuade, to challenge, and to build community. Biblical history is "interpretative rather than descriptive" (ibid., p. 487). For example, tales of valor (stories that demonstrate that the people have

---

15. See Redford; Finkelstein and Silberman; McConville; Niditch; Jones; Dietrich; Mathys; Smith-Christopher.

"passed the test" through victory in battle, and therefore can claim divine sponsorship) fill the Books of History. However, the battles may or may not have actually happened (see Karlberg, pp. 56–57).

The Bahá'í Writings do not offer information on the exact origin or authorship of the Books of History. Biblical scholarship indicates numerous authors and sources with most of the books completed in the fifth or sixth century BC.

**Joshua** tells of the military conquest of Canaan (the "Promised Land") by the Israelites under the leadership of Joshua around 1300 BC.[16] Whether the land was actually conquered or whether it was settled by a slow process of infiltration or emergence is under debate (McConville, pp. 159–60). Credited with numerous authors and sources, the final composition of this book is generally dated to the Israelites' Exile in Babylon in the sixth century BC (see Friedman, 1997, pp. 130–46; McConville, pp. 159–60).

**Judges** tells of numerous Israelite judges (military leaders) who arose after the death of Joshua and struggled for control of portions of the Land of Canaan from the thirteenth to eleventh century BC. It presents a picture of a loosely organized confederation consisting of fragmentary groups in conflict with each other. A major theme is that Israel cannot defeat its enemies because of lack of faithfulness to the Covenant. Compared to the Book of Joshua, Judges gives a conflicting and less bloody account of conquest that is more in line with archaeological evidence (see Cline, 2014, p. 94). Credited with numerous authors and sources, the final composition of this book is generally dated to the Israelites' Exile in Babylon in the sixth century BC (see Friedman, 1977, pp. 130–46; Niditch, pp. 177–78).

**Ruth** tells a domestic story of human and divine faithfulness and the power of love to overcome ethnic prejudice. The narrative moves from loss to fulfillment through the resourcefulness of two women, Ruth and

---

16. "Archaeological evidence, in the form of pottery, architecture, and other aspects of material culture, indicates that the Israelites as an identifiable group were present in Canaan certainly by the end of the thirteenth century BC" (Cline, pp. 95–96). The first use of the term "Israel" outside of the Bible is found in a stele inscription dating to 1207 BC placed by the Egyptian pharaoh Merneptah (Cline, pp. 6–7; Matthews and Benjamin, pp. 97–98).

Naomi. The historical setting is the days of the Judges around 1100 BC. Scholars have not reached a general consensus on whether it was written before or after the Israelites' Exile in Babylon (see Emmerson, p. 192).

**1 and 2 Samuel** describe the development of Israel during the period of transition to monarchy under the guidance of the prophet Samuel. It is suggested that the setting of these books is the tenth century BC (Jones, p. 198). Saul is appointed the first king of the nation of Israel. When he falls out of favor because of disobedience, David is anointed as king. Samuel 2 closes at David's deathbed with his son Solomon appointed successor to the throne. Credited with numerous authors and sources, the final composition of these books is generally dated to the Israelites' Exile in Babylon in the sixth century BC (see Friedman, 1977, pp. 130–46; Jones, pp. 199–200).

**1 and 2 Kings** continue the history of the monarchy from Solomon in the middle of the tenth century BC through the splitting of the Kingdom of Israel into two rivaling monarchies of Israel in the north and Judah in the south. They describe the rule of twenty-three kings in Judah and eighteen kings in Israel, the fall of the northern Kingdom of Israel to the Neo-Assyrian Empire in 722 BC, and the fall of the southern Kingdom of Judah to the Babylonian Empire in 587 BC.[17] King Josiah of Judah is noted as the standard of a good king and credited with reforms upholding the worship of YHWH, the sole God of the Hebrews, and making the Temple in Jerusalem the only site of sacrificial offerings. The fall of both Israel and Judah are seen as the result of kings who tolerated idolatry (see Dietrich, p. 233). Credited with numerous authors and sources, the final composition of these books is generally dated to the Israelites' Exile in Babylon in the sixth century BC (see Friedman, 1977, pp. 130–46; Dietrich, pp. 233–34).

**1 and 2 Chronicles** encompasses the whole history of the Hebrew tribes from Adam to the fall of Judah, and closes with the proclamation of King Cyrus of Persia (536 BC) that permitted the Jews to return to

---

17. Extra-biblical records of this period are found in the "Annals of Sargon II" (713 BC), a series of cuneiform inscriptions detailing the military actions of the Assyrian ruler Sargon II between 738 and 720 BC. These tablets chronicle the days when Israel went from the status of an Assyrian ally in 738 BC to that of an Assyrian colony in 732 BC, and finally to that of an Assyrian province in 720 BC.

Jerusalem and rebuild the Temple. It contains supplemental and, at times, slightly different information than the Books of Kings. The Book of 2 Chronicles highlights the rule of King Hezekiah who is praised and credited with enforcing reforms to purify the Temple and centralize worship of YHWH in Jerusalem (see Mathys, pp. 267, 301–4). Credited with either one author (termed "the Chronicler) or numerous authors and sources, the final composition of these books is generally dated to the late fifth century BC (see Friedman, 1977, pp. 210–16; Mathys, p. 267).

**Ezra and Nehemiah** are considered by many scholars to be one work. Set in the Persian period, they describe the return of the Jews to Judah for the rebuilding of the Temple as authorized by decrees of King Cyrus (536 BC)[18] and King Darius (519 BC), and the reestablishment of Mosaic Law as authorized by two edicts of King Artaxerxes (457 and 444 BC). The completion of these books is generally dated to the late Persian period, 430–400 BC (Smith-Christopher, p. 309).[19] The prophet Ezra is considered by many scholars to be the final redactor of the Books of Moses (see Friedman, 1997, pp. 223–25; Mírzá Abu'l-Faḍl, p. 13).

**Esther** is the story of a Jewish woman who became queen of Persia during the post-exilic period, and how she risked her life to save her people from total destruction. The story is celebrated in the Jewish festival of Purim. The book is generally thought to be composed in the post-exilic period and completed by the second century BC (see Meyers, 2013, pp. 324–25).

---

18. A clay cylinder on which is inscribed the Decree of Cyrus II in Akkadian cuneiform script was recovered from the Library of Ashurbanipal and is on display in room 52 of the British Museum (item # BM 90920).

19. For studies on the Persian/Zoroastrian influence on post-exilic Judaism and Christianity regarding concepts such as angels and demons, God and Satan, heaven and hell, resurrection, everlasting life, the expectation of the Messiah, and the end of the world, see Nigosian, *The Zoroastrian Faith: Tradition and Modern Research;* Foltz, *Spirituality in the Land of the Noble.*

# TOPICS FROM
# THE BOOKS OF HISTORY

## HOLY WAR

The Book of Joshua opens with Joshua's mandate to lead the Hebrew tribes into Canaan, the Promised Land, and take possession of the land:

> After the death of Moses the servant of the LORD, t he LORD spoke to Joshua son of Nun, Moses' assistant, saying, "My servant Moses is dead. Now proceed to cross the Jordan, you and all this people, into the land that I am giving to them, to the Israelites. . . . No one shall be able to stand against you all the days of thy life. As I was with Moses, so I will be with you; I will not fail or forsake you." (Joshua 1:1–2, 5)

There follows a tale of intrigue and heroism in which the tribes win their first victory with a unique battle strategy against the heavily fortified city of Jericho (Joshua 6:1–20). The battle ends with wholesale slaughter:

> Then they devoted to destruction by the edge of the sword all in the city, both men and women, young and old, oxen, sheep, and donkeys. (Joshua 6:21)

Although there is no conclusive evidence that the Battle of Jericho actually took place, and there is mounting evidence that the settlement of the Israelites in the Land of Canaan was one of immersion or infiltration

(Cline, 2014, p. 94; McConville, p. 163; Finkelstein and Silberman, p. 82; Redford, pp. 264–65), the account of the battle of Jericho is one of many battles in the Old Testament that illustrate the ancient justification and practice of holy war.[20] The mind resists even acknowledging that these accounts are in the Bible as they are at odds with Bahá'í teachings. In the Dispensation of Bahá'u'lláh, "holy war"—that is, violence waged by religious partisans to propagate or defend their faith—is explicitly forbidden:

> The first Glad-Tidings which the Mother Book hath, in this Most Great Revelation, imparted unto all the peoples of the world is that the law of holy war hath been blotted out from the Book. (Bahá'u'lláh, *Tablets of Bahá'u'lláh*, p. 21)

### WAS HOLY WAR EVER LEGITIMATE?

Holy war was allowed in previous Dispensations to address the requirements of former times:

> In former religions such ordinances as holy war, destruction of books, the ban on association and companionship with other peoples or on reading certain books had been laid down and affirmed according to the exigencies of the time; however, in this mighty Revelation, in this momentous Announcement, the manifold bestowals and favours of God have overshadowed all men, and from the horizon of the Will of the Ever-Abiding Lord, His infallible decree hath prescribed that which We have set forth above. (Bahá'u'lláh, *Tablets of Bahá'u'lláh*, p. 27)

If religious warfare was a necessity of previous times, one can only imagine how disagreeable those times were. Understanding something of the barbaric conditions of the past—and the role of the Manifestations of God in progressively modifying those conditions—is key to coming to terms with the reality of ancestral religious war.

---

20. The peoples of the Old Testament time lived in a holy war theology in which tribal or national gods had control over military victories. Like their surrounding neighbors who attributed victory to their gods, stories of the ancient Israelites feature war victories attributed to YHWH (See McConville, p. 159).

## WHAT WERE THE CONDITIONS OF "FORMER TIMES"?

Steven Pinker's book, *The Better Angels of Our Nature,* which reports on the statistical decline of violence in the world over the past several thousand years, opens with this engaging quote: "The past is a foreign country—they do things differently there." He then states, "If the past is a foreign country, it is a shockingly violent one. It is easy to forget how dangerous life used to be. How deeply brutality was woven into the fabric of daily existence" (Pinker, p. 1). This can be applied to the period of the Old Testament.

The Old Testament era is described in the Bahá'í Writings as characterized by "barbarism" (Shoghi Effendi, *Japan Will Turn Ablaze,* p. 44). Defined as the "opposite of civilization," characteristics of barbarism include ignorance, base corruption, and savage cruelty (*The Oxford English Dictionary, Volume 1,* p. 946). In the age of the Old Testament, barbarism was not an occasional hideous event—it was embedded in daily life. The savagery of the times is evident throughout the Old Testament stories where slavery, rape, torture, and murder are common parts of the landscape. The spirit of the religion of Moses was the establishment of unity under the laws of God. Physical force for its advancement and protection was a strategy that could have taken place in accordance with the barbaric times in which it was born:

> Moses lived in the wilderness and desert of Sinai; therefore his ordinances and commandments were in conformity with those conditions. ('Abdu'l-Bahá, *The Promulgation of Universal Peace,* p. 554)

While holy war was an acceptable strategy in past Dispensations, it is now an antiquated ancestral belief.

## WHAT IS THE OUTCOME OF IMITATING ANCESTRAL BELIEFS ABOUT HOLY WAR?

Imitating ancestral beliefs—about holy war or other social teachings—is the cause of human degradation:

> Dogmatic imitations of ancestral beliefs are passing. They have been the axis around which religion revolved but now are no longer

fruitful; on the contrary, in this day they have become the cause of human degradation and hindrance. Bigotry and dogmatic adherence to ancient beliefs have become the central and fundamental source of animosity among men, the obstacle to human progress, the cause of warfare and strife, the destroyer of peace, composure and welfare in the world. . . . These conditions are the outcome of hostility and hatred between nations and peoples of religion who imitate and adhere to the forms and violate the spirit and reality of the divine teachings. ('Abdu'l-Bahá, *The Promulgation of Universal Peace*, p. 619)

Instead of holding onto ancient practices, progressive Revelation calls upon humanity to be attuned to the requirements of the current age. In the Dispensation of Bahá'u'lláh this includes the abrogation of holy war.

## IS ALL MILITARY FORCE OUTLAWED IN THE DISPENSATION OF BAHÁ'U'LLÁH?

Bahá'u'lláh abolishes "holy war," which is, distinctly, violence waged by religious partisans to propagate or defend their faith. However, for the purpose of collective security—that is, maintaining order within and between national boundaries—the use of force is not prohibited. While a military force may be required for maintaining order, it is clear in the Bahá'í Writings that force alone is not sufficient to achieve or maintain peace. A just system of law must first be established and unity in its application upheld:

The Great Being, wishing to reveal the prerequisites of the peace and tranquility of the world and the advancement of its peoples, hath written: The time must come when the imperative necessity for the holding of a vast, an all-embracing assemblage of men will be universally realized. The rulers and kings of the earth must needs attend it, and, participating in its deliberations, must consider such ways and means as will lay the foundations of the world's Great Peace amongst men. Such a peace demandeth that the Great Powers should resolve, for the sake of the tranquility of the peoples of the earth, to be fully reconciled among themselves. Should any king take up arms against another, all should unitedly arise and prevent him. If this be done, the nations of the world will no longer require any armaments, except for the purpose of preserving the security of their realms and of maintaining internal order within their territories. This will ensure the peace and composure of every people, government and nation. (Bahá'u'lláh, *The Proclamation of Bahá'u'lláh*, pp. 115–16)

### IS WAR, HOLY OR OTHERWISE, INEVITABLE IN HUMAN CIVILIZATION?

*The Promise of World Peace*, a statement by the Universal House of Justice, describes the act of war as an element of immature stages of human evolution and points to the mature capacity and promise of this age. An excerpt reads:

The Bahá'í Faith regards the current world confusion and calamitous condition in human affairs as a natural phase in an organic process leading ultimately and irresistibly to the unification of the human race in a single social order whose boundaries are those of the planet. The human race, as a distinct, organic unit, has passed through evolutionary stages analogous to the stages of infancy and childhood in the lives of its individual members, and is now in the culminating period of its turbulent adolescence approaching its long-awaited coming of age.

A candid acknowledgement that prejudice, war and exploitation have been the expression of immature stages in a vast historical process and that the human race is today experiencing the unavoidable tumult which marks its collective coming of age is not a reason for despair but a prerequisite to undertaking the stupendous enterprise of building a peaceful world. That such an enterprise is possible, that the necessary constructive forces do exist, that unifying social structures can be erected, is the theme we urge you to examine. (Universal House of Justice, *The Promise of World Peace*, p. 2)

In the past, all community pursuits have been framed as a series of contests and accomplishments. "The history of humankind as a single interdependent species, inhabiting a common homeland, is just beginning" (Karlberg, p. 51).

## KING DAVID

Some time after Joshua's death the Hebrew tribes called for a king (1 Samuel 8:20). Samuel appointed Saul who served as the first king of the United Israel. Years later, David was appointed to the throne (approximately 1003–970 BC). One of the most richly characterized figures in the Old Testament, David's long and turbulent reign is known as an era of prosperity, if not peace. In addition to his renown as an effective leader, David is known as a poet and musician. His music is noted as having special soothing properties. The Book of 1 Samuel tells how David, while still a shepherd, was summoned to King Saul who was stricken with an "evil spirit." David played the harp for Saul and the king's better nature was restored:

> And it came to pass, when the evil spirit from God was upon Saul, that David took an harp, and played with his hand: so Saul was refreshed, and was well, and the evil spirit departed from him. (1 Samuel 16:23)

David is credited for introducing and controlling the use of music in the Temple after he became king—a list of musicians and their duties extends through seven chapters of 1 Chronicles (25:1–31). Many of the poems and songs in the Book of Psalms are traditionally attributed to David (Goldhill, p. 20).

### WHAT IS THE VALUE OF MUSIC THAT IT WOULD BE OF IMPORTANCE TO A KING?

Although from a material point of view music is nothing more than vibrations, it can affect the heart and inspire receptivity in its listeners:

> Music is one of the important arts. It has great effect upon human spirit. Musical melodies are a certain something which prove to be accidental upon etheric vibrations, for voice is nothing but the expression of vibrations, which reaching the tympanum, effect the nerves of hearing. Musical melodies are, therefore, those peculiar effects produced by, or from, vibration. However, they have the keenest effect upon the spirit. In sooth, although music is a

material affair, yet its tremendous effect is spiritual, and its greatest attachment is to the realm of the spirit. If a person desires to deliver a discourse, it will prove more effectual after musical melodies. The ancient Greeks, as well as Persian philosophers, were in the habit of delivering their discourses in the following manner: first, playing a few musical melodies, and when their audience attained a certain receptivity thereby they would leave their instruments at once and begin their discourse. . . .

It was for this reason that His Holiness David sang the psalms in the Holy of Holies at Jerusalem with sweet melodies. (Attributed to 'Abdu'l-Bahá, in *The Diary of Juliet Thompson,* p. 80)

The story of David suggests that, early on, awareness of the capacity of beautiful music to arouse spiritual susceptibilities was realized.

## WHAT ACCOMPLISHMENTS ARE ATTRIBUTED TO KING DAVID?

King David is known for: ruling over and expanding the united Jewish Kingdom from 1010 to 970 BC (Goldhill, pp. 19–20);[21] bringing the Ark of the Covenant to Jerusalem (2 Samuel 6); initiating the first permanent Hebrew Temple (1 Chronicles 22); and for being rewarded with an eternal house and kingdom (2 Samuel 7:16).

## WHAT WAS THE ARK OF THE COVENANT?

The Ark of the Covenant is described as a chest constructed to hold the Tablets of the Law in the time of Moses (Exodus 25). By David's time, the Ark is reported to have survived the long journey of the Israelites to Canaan, been captured by the Philistines, returned, and temporarily housed outside of Jerusalem (1 Samuel

---

21. Evidence of the existence and fame of the Davidic dynasty has been found by the discovery of two extra-biblical inscriptions: the Tel Dan stele written in Aramaic on behalf of an Assyrian king around 835 BC found in Northern Israel; and an inscription of Meshe, king of Moab, from the ninth century BC found near the Dead Sea (See Finkelstein and Silberman, pp. 129, 142).

5–7). David's placement of the Ark in Jerusalem, the administrative center of the government, was cause for celebration. The "Ark" is found in the Bahá'í Writings as a symbol for the protection afforded by the Covenant (Universal House of Justice, *Messages from the Universal House of Justice, 1963 to 1986*, p. 732).

## WHAT WAS THE PROMISE OF AN ETERNAL KINGDOM?

After refusing David's offer to build a permanent temple for the Ark, God tells David (through a vision of the prophet Nathan) that God will build David a house, kingdom, and throne that will last forever:

> When your days are fulfilled and you lie down with your ancestors, I will raise up your offspring after you, who shall come forth from your body, and I will establish his kingdom. . . . Your house and your kingdom shall be made sure forever before me; your throne shall be established forever. (2 Samuel 7:12, 16)

The eternal throne and kingdom of David are symbolic of the spiritual Kingdom of God:

> He [Christ] shall sit upon the throne of David. . . . The Throne upon which He sat is the Eternal Throne from which Christ reigns for ever, a heavenly throne, not an earthly one, for the things of earth pass away but heavenly things pass not away. ('Abdu'l-Bahá, *Paris Talks*, no. 16.6)

The throne of David also symbolizes the high spiritual station of the Manifestation of God. For example, Isaiah prophesied that the Messiah would sit on the "throne of David" (Isaiah 9:7). This terminology is also used in the New Testament Gospels (for example, Luke 1:32). Bahá'u'lláh draws upon this traditional symbolism in stating His position as the Manifestation of God for this Day:

> The Most Great Law is come, and the Ancient Beauty ruleth upon the throne of David. Thus hath My Pen spoken that which the histories of bygone ages have related. At this time, however, David crieth aloud and saith: "O my loving Lord! Do Thou number me

with such as have stood steadfast in Thy Cause, O Thou through Whom the faces have been illumined, and the footsteps have slipped!" (Bahá'u'lláh, *The Proclamation of Bahá'u'lláh,* p. 89)

The "House of David" refers to the hereditary line of Abraham of which David is a member, and from which have appeared several Manifestations of God as well as lesser prophets (see 'Abdu'l-Bahá, *The Promulgation of Universal Peace,* p. 511).

## KING SOLOMON

After a long reign, David appointed his son Solomon as king of Israel. The reign of King Solomon (971–931 BC) is noted for peace and prosperity; his reputation for wisdom, wealth, and power was far-reaching. The legendary reign of Solomon, which was approximately four hundred years after the time of Moses, is noted as a high point in the Dispensation of Moses.

> Through the education of Moses these ignorant people attained an advanced degree of power and prestige, culminating in the glory of the reign of Solomon. ('Abdu'l-Bahá, *The Promulgation of Universal Peace,* pp. 481–82)

### WHY IS THE MOSAIC REVELATION REPRESENTED AS REACHING ITS PEAK HUNDREDS OF YEARS AFTER THE LIFE OF MOSES?

The time difference from the appearance of Moses to the peak of the Mosaic Dispensation as described in the Books of History illustrates a principle of Divine Education. While one may expect the high point of achievement to occur while the Manifestation is physically present to guide and inspire the people, His physical appearance marks only the beginning of the transforming power of the Revelation. In every Dispensation the power of the Word of God becomes apparent over time as humanity grows into the new teachings, and the spiritual forces of the Revelation expand. For example, the Bahá'í community noted the continued acceleration of spiritual forces one hundred years after the Ascension of Bahá'u'lláh:

> The swiftness of events during the past year [1992] is indicative of the acceleration, as the hundredth anniversary of Bahá'u'lláh's Ascension approaches, of the spiritual forces released with the advent of His revolutionizing mission. (The Universal House of Justice, *A Wider Horizon, Selected Letters 1983–1992*, p. 73)

The release of growing spiritual forces that happens after the passing of the physical form of the Manifestation gives greater impetus to the Revelation. The earthly limitations that the Divine Educator is subject to in the physical world fall away and the world of humanity is blessed with a greater measure of grace (see Dunbar, p. 17).

### WHAT WAS SIGNIFICANT ABOUT THE ERA OF SOLOMON?

The significance of Solomon's era is best seen in comparison to the condition of the Israelite tribes when Moses first appeared. Over the years, the discipline of the Mosaic Law transformed the tribes from a state of servility, abasement, and ignorance to a state of education, morality, and a higher expression of civilization:

> The children of Israel were in bondage and captivity in the land of Egypt four hundred years. They were in an extreme state of degradation and slavery under the tyranny and oppression of the Egyptians. While they were in the condition of abject poverty, in the lowest degree of abasement, ignorance and servility, Moses suddenly appeared among them. Although He was but a shepherd, such majesty, grandeur and efficiency became manifest in Him through the power of religion that His influence continues to this day. His Prophethood was established throughout the land, and the law of His Word became the foundation of the laws of the nations. . . . In the splendor of the reign of Solomon their sciences and arts advanced to such a degree that even the Greek philosophers journeyed to Jerusalem to sit at the feet of the Hebrew sages and acquire the basis of Israelitish law. ('Abdu'l-Bahá, *The Promulgation of Universal Peace*, p. 512)

To many, Solomon's era is revered as an idealized past—a lost era of splendor that we should strive to regain (Goldhill, p. 32).

### HAS THERE BEEN A GOLDEN AGE OF CIVILIZATION?

If all of the stories attributed to Solomon were factual, his era still would not be a golden age to which we should aspire because, since Solomon, humanity has had the bounty of repeated appearances of the Manifestation of God and almost three thousand years of practice in civilization-building. Regardless of how far civilization advances, it will always progress further:

> All men have been created to carry forward an ever-advancing civilization. (Bahá'u'lláh, *Gleanings from the Writings of Bahá'u'lláh*, no. 109.2)

# THE TEMPLE

Scripture states that the Israelites' first permanent temple was built in Jerusalem. It is called the Temple of Jerusalem, Solomon's Temple, the First Temple, and "the Temple." The First Book of Kings states that Solomon built the Temple during his reign:

> In the four hundred eightieth year after the Israelites came out of the land of Egypt, in the fourth year of Solomon's reign over Israel, in the month Ziv, which is the second month, he began to build the house of the LORD. (1 Kings 6:1)

### WHAT WAS UNIQUE ABOUT SOLOMON'S TEMPLE?

Solomon's Temple was distinctive in the ancient Near East because it held no tangible image of God. This is remarkable considering the Near Eastern temple culture that surrounded the ancient Israelites. From the earliest records of civilization to the Roman Empire and beyond, holy shrines were a regular feature of the Mediterranean landscape. The temples ranged in structure from piles of stones to colossal edifices like the Parthenon, and every one of them contained some kind of idol. The idols were typically anthropomorphic, but not always, and the people offered sacrifices to the god or gods of the temple. Solomon's Temple was unique because it was not a temple for a god—it was a temple for the *Name* of God (see Goldhill, pp. 22–24). The Book of Deuteronomy states:

> But you shall seek the place which the LORD your God shall choose out of all your tribes as his habitation to put his name there. You shall go there, bringing there your burnt offerings and your sacrifices, your tithes and your donations, your votive gifts, your freewill offerings, and the firstlings of your herds and flocks. (Deuteronomy 12:5–6)

Initially, the revered Ark of the Covenant (the chest that held the sacred Mosaic Law) was kept in the inner chambers of the Temple, but it was never visible to worshippers. After the destruction of the Temple by the Babylonians, even the Ark was gone. To the Romans and Greeks it was incomprehensible that in the Jewish Temple there was no image of a god as a material focus of worship. The Temple stood unique as a place of worship for an imperceptible, indefinable, and completely unrepresented deity (Goldhill, pp. 22–24).

### WHY WERE THERE NO IMAGES OF GOD
### IN SOLOMON'S TEMPLE?

Having no image of God in Solomon's Temple was in accord with the second of the Ten Commandments that prohibits worshipping idols (Exodus 20:4–5). This prohibition on representing the Divine in artwork in Jewish temples and synagogues is still applicable.

### WHAT IS THE SIGNIFICANCE OF TEMPLES
### IN THE BAHÁ'Í FAITH?

For Bahá'í's, all sacred structures symbolize the divinity of God, the Manifestation of God as the Collective Center, and the unity of the human race:

> Temples are symbols of the reality and divinity of God—the collective center of mankind. Consider how within a temple every

race and people is seen and represented—all in the presence of the Lord, covenanting together in a covenant of love and fellowship, all offering the same melody, prayer and supplication to God. Therefore, it is evident that the church is a collective center for mankind. For this reason there have been churches and temples in all the divine religions; but the real Collective Centers are the Manifestations of God, of Whom the church or temple is a symbol and expression. That is to say, the Manifestation of God is the real divine temple and Collective Center of which the outer church is but a symbol. ('Abdu'l-Bahá, *Promulgation of Universal Peace*, p. 226)

## DO BAHÁ'Í TEMPLES CONTAIN PORTRAYALS OF GOD?

Visual portrayals of God as well as visual portrayals of any of the Manifestations of God are forbidden in the Bahá'í Faith either in temples or in other contexts such as in one's home, in picture books, or in theatrical productions. It is understood that there are beautiful works of art of the past with religious subject matter and these may be appreciated in a spirit of reverence; however, in this Dispensation, Bahá'ís are called upon to refrain from attempting to portray God or the Manifestation of God:

The prohibition on representing the Manifestation of God in paintings and drawings or in dramatic presentations applies to all the Manifestations of God. There are, of course, great works of art of past Dispensations, many of which portrayed the Manifestations of God in a spirit of reverence and love. In this Dispensation however the greater maturity of mankind and the greater awareness of the relationship between the Supreme Manifestation and His servants enable us to realize the impossibility of representing, in any human form, whether pictorially, in sculpture or in dramatic representation, the Person of God's Manifestations. In stating the Bahá'í prohibition, the beloved Guardian pointed out this impossibility. (From a letter written on behalf of the Universal House of Justice, dated March 9, 1977, to an individual believer, in *Lights of Guidance*, no. 344)

## WHAT IS THE PURPOSE OF BAHÁ'Í TEMPLES?

Bahá'í Temples—also called Houses of Worship or Mashriqu'l-Adhkárs (Arabic for "dawning place of the mention of God")—are specifically built as places for people of all religions to join together in prayer and meditation. All of the Bahá'í Temples have certain elements in common. For example, each has a circular nine-sided shape and an open interior that is full of light and free from elaborate displays. Public programs are offered that include readings from the world's great religious traditions as well as from Writings of the Bahá'í Faith. There are no sermons, rites, prescribed ceremonies, or pulpits. Music is often included in worship programs but it is confined to the simplicity of the human voice (see Badiee, p. 12). The purpose of a Bahá'í Temple is to bring about unity in the community in which it is built.

> In brief, the original purpose of temples and houses of worship is simply that of unity—places of meeting where various peoples, different races and souls of every capacity may come together in order that love and agreement should be manifest between them. That is why Bahá'u'lláh has commanded that a place of worship be built for all the religionists of the world; that all religions, races and sects may come together within its universal shelter; that the proclamation of the oneness of mankind shall go forth from its open courts of holiness— the announcement that humanity is the servant of God and that all are submerged in the ocean of His mercy. It is the Mashriqu'l-Adhkár. ('Abdu'l-Bahá, *The Promulgation of Universal Peace,* p. 90)

While churches and temples are symbolic of the unifying power of the Manifestation of God, and Bahá'í Temples share in that symbolism and promote collective worship, from a Bahá'í perspective every spot can become sacred with the remembrance of God:

> Blessed is the spot, and the house, and the place, and the city, and the heart, and the mountain, and the refuge, and the cave, and the valley, and the land, and the sea, and the island, and the meadow where mention of God hath been made, and His praise glorified. (Bahá'u'lláh, in *Bahá'í Prayers,* p. 3)

## SPIRITUAL SEASONS

'Abdu'l-Bahá summarizes the story of the Israelite crises and victories as presented in the Books of History and beyond, through the final destruction of the Temple by Titus in the Jewish-Roman war of 70 AD:

> . . . following the decline of the glory of Solomon's era and during the reign of Jeroboam there came a great change in this nation. The high ethical standards and spiritual perfections ceased to exist. Conditions and morals became corrupt, religion was debased, and the perfect principles of the Mosaic Law were obscured in superstition and polytheism. War and strife arose among the tribes, and their unity was destroyed. The followers of Jeroboam declared themselves rightful and valid in kingly succession, and the supporters of Rehoboam made the same claim. Finally, the tribes were torn asunder by hostility and hatred, the glory of Israel was eclipsed, and so complete was the degradation that a golden calf was set up as an object of worship in the city of Tyre. Thereupon God sent Elijah, the prophet, who redeemed the people, renewed the law of God and established an era of new life for Israel.
>
> History shows a still later change and transformation when this oneness and solidarity was followed by another dispersion of the tribes. Nebuchadnezzar, King of Babylon, invaded the Holy Land and carried away captive seventy thousand Israelites to Chaldea, where the greatest reverses, trials and suffering afflicted these unfortunate people. Then the prophets of God again reformed and reestablished the law of God, and the people in their humiliation again followed it. This resulted in their liberation, and under the edict of Cyrus, King of Persia, there was a return to the Holy City. Jerusalem and the Temple of Solomon were rebuilt, and the glory of Israel was restored.
>
> This lasted but a short time; the morality of the people declined, and conditions reached an extreme degree until the Roman general Titus took Jerusalem and razed it to its foundations. Pillage and conquest completed the desolation; Palestine became a waste and

wilderness, and the Jews fled from the Holy Land of their ancestors. ('Abdu'l-Bahá, *The Promulgation of Universal Peace*, p. 573)

The stories contained in the Books of History have special value as examples of crisis and victory in the path of God:

In the onward surge of the Cause of God, crisis and victory have always alternated and have ever proven to be the staple of progress. (The Universal House of Justice, Ridván Message to the Bahá'ís of the World, 1993)

Along with the small cycles of crisis and victory that characterize growth and development, larger spiritual seasons mark the progression and regression that occur in every Dispensation.

### WHAT ARE THE CHARACTERISTICS OF SPIRITUAL SEASONS?

In spiritual spring the Manifestation of God brings new life and capacities to the world. In spiritual summer the teachings of the Manifestation reach fruition and humanity achieves great progress. In spiritual autumn growth and development slow down, souls lose connection with the foundational teachings of God, and hearts become dim. In spiritual winter the coldness of spiritual ignorance and the darkness of human error prevail:

In this material world, time has changing cycles and place is subject to varying conditions. Seasons follow one another and individuals progress, regress, and develop. At one point it is springtime and at another the autumn season; at one point it is summer and at another it is winter.

. . . The spiritual cycles associated with the Prophets of God proceed in like manner. That is, the day of the advent of the Holy Manifestations is the spiritual springtime. It is divine splendour and heavenly grace; it is the wafting of the breeze of life and the dawning of the Sun of Truth. Spirits are revived, hearts are refreshed, souls are refined, all existence is stirred into motion, and human realities are rejoiced and grow in attainments and perfections. . . .

That soul-stirring springtime then gives rise to the fruitful summer. The Word of God is proclaimed, His Law is promulgated, and all things reach a state of perfection. . . .

When that Sun reaches its zenith it begins to decline, and that summer season of the spirit is followed by autumn. Growth and development are arrested; soft breezes turn into blighting winds; and the season of dearth and want dissipates the vitality and beauty of the gardens, the fields, and the bowers. That is, spiritual attractions vanish, divine qualities decay, the radiance of the hearts is dimmed, the spirituality of the souls is dulled, virtues become vices, and sanctity and purity are no more. Of the law of God naught remains but a name, and of the divine teachings naught but an outward form. The foundations of the religion of God are destroyed and annihilated, mere customs and traditions take their place, divisions appear, and steadfastness is changed into perplexity. Spirits die away, hearts wither, and souls languish.

Winter arrives—that is, the chill of ignorance and unawareness envelopes the world, and the darkness of wayward and selfish desires prevails. Apathy and defiance ensue, with indolence and folly, baseness and animal qualities, coldness and stone-like torpor, even as in the wintertime when the terrestrial globe is deprived of the influence of the rays of the sun and becomes waste and desolate. . . .

When, however, the winter season has run its course, the spiritual springtime returns again and a new cycle reveals its splendour. The breezes of the spirit blow, the radiant morn breaks, the clouds of the Merciful rain down, the rays of the Sun of Truth shine forth, and the world of being is invested with a new life and arrayed in a wondrous robe. All the signs and bestowals of the former springtime, and perhaps even greater ones, reappear in this new season. ('Abdu'l-Bahá, *Some Answered Questions,* no. 14:1, 7–11)

## WHAT IS THE CURRENT SPIRITUAL SEASON?

Bahá'ís believe that the current spiritual season is the springtime of Bahá'u'lláh:

Bahá'u'lláh has come into this world. He has renewed that springtime. The same fragrances are wafting; the same heat of the Sun is giving life; the same cloud is pouring its rain, and with our own eyes we see that the world of existence is advancing and progressing. The human world has found new life. ('Abdu'l-Bahá, *The Promulgation of Universal Peace,* p. 13)

## WHO CAN BENEFIT FROM THE DIVINE SPRINGTIME OF THE BAHÁ'Í REVELATION?

The divine bounties that come with the springtime of the Manifestation of God shine upon the entire world:

The world's equilibrium hath been upset through the vibrating influence of this most great, this new World Order. Mankind's ordered life hath been revolutionized through the agency of this unique, this wondrous System—the like of which mortal eyes have never witnessed. (Bahá'u'lláh *Gleanings from the Writings of Bahá'u'lláh,* no. 70.1)

## IDOL WORSHIP

The Books of History tell that the commandment against idol worship was violated in many ways and always with unfortunate outcomes. For example, during the reign of King Ahaz, the Israelites engaged in idol worship by building altars in "high places" throughout the countryside at which they worshipped various gods, a common practice in the surrounding pagan cultures:

The people of Israel secretly did things that were not right against the LORD their God. They built for themselves high places at all their towns, from watchtower to fortified city; . . . they served idols, of which the Lord had said to them, "You shall not do this." (2 Kings 17:9, 12).

In addition to the worship of natural and man-made objects, idol worship can also mean ignoring the laws of God and worshiping one's selfish desires and man-made ideas. This was evident in the exploits of the kings as well.

## IS IDOL WORSHIP A CONTEMPORARY ISSUE?

Idol worship is still a characteristic of the lower nature and it continues to be a source of division, hatred, and war in this era:

> Alas! It is misguided ones like these who are the cause of division and hatred upon earth. Today there are millions of people who still worship idols, and the great religions of the world are at war among themselves. ('Abdu'l-Bahá, *Paris Talks,* no. 13.8)

## WHAT ARE THE IDOLS
## OF THE CONTEMPORARY WORLD?

Any organization, person, thing, doctrine, or lower inclination that is revered and followed in place of the laws of God could be an object of idol worship and a cause of humiliation. For example, in the past century the gods of nationalism, racism, and communism have brought spiritual calamity upon whole populations:

> God Himself has indeed been dethroned from the hearts of men, and an idolatrous world passionately and clamorously hails and worships the false gods which its own idle fancies have fatuously created, and its misguided hands so impiously exalted. The chief idols in the desecrated temple of mankind are none other than the triple gods of Nationalism, Racialism and Communism, at whose altars governments and peoples, whether democratic or totalitarian, at peace or at war, of the East or of the West, Christian or Islamic, are, in various forms and in different degrees, now worshiping. Their high priests are the politicians and the worldly-wise, the so-called sages of the age; their sacrifice, the flesh and blood of the slaughtered multitudes; their incantations outworn shibboleths and insidious and irreverent formulas; their incense, the smoke of anguish that ascends from the lacerated hearts of the bereaved, the maimed, and the homeless. (Shoghi Effendi, *The Promised Day is Come,* p. 112)

## WHAT MOTIVATES IDOL WORSHIP?

The desire to worship God is a natural impulse that springs from the heart. When this impulse is blocked the soul will try to find another center of devotion and the result is idol worship:

The yearning for belief is inextinguishable, an inherent part of what makes one human. When it is blocked or betrayed, the rational soul is driven to seek some new compass point, however inadequate or unworthy, around which it can organize experience and dare again to assume the risks that are an inescapable aspect of life. (Written under the supervision of the Universal House of Justice, *Century of Light*, p. 58)

### WHY IS IT IMPORTANT TO RECOGNIZE IDOLATRY?

It is important to recognize idolatry because it reminds us of the weakness of human nature and the necessity of training ourselves in the teachings of the Manifestation. An examination of the past century illustrates the importance of recognizing its danger and the need for divine direction:

From a Bahá'í point of view, humanity's worship of idols of its own invention [over the past century] is of importance not because of the historical events associated with these forces, however horrifying, but because of the lesson it taught. Looking back on the twilight world in which such diabolical forces loomed over humanity's future, one must ask what was the weakness in human nature that rendered it vulnerable to such influences. To have seen in someone like Benito Mussolini the figure of a "Man of Destiny," to have felt obliged to understand the racial theories of Adolf Hitler as anything other than the self-evident products of a diseased mind, to have seriously entertained the reinterpretation of human experience through dogmas that had given birth to the Soviet Union of Josef Stalin—so willful an abandonment of reason on the part of a considerable segment of the intellectual leadership of society demands an accounting to posterity. If undertaken dispassionately, such an evaluation must, sooner or later, focus attention on a truth that runs like a central strand through the Scriptures of all of humanity's religions. In the words of Bahá'u'lláh: "Upon the reality of man . . . He hath focused the radiance of all of His names and attributes, and made it a mirror of His own Self. . . . These energies . . . lie, however, latent within him, even as the flame is hidden within the candle and the rays of light are potentially present in the lamp. . . . Neither the candle nor the lamp can be lighted through their own unaided efforts, nor can it ever be possible for the mirror to free itself from its dross." (Written under the supervision of the Universal House of Justice, *Century of Light,* p. 61)

Without the foundation of divine teachings, humanity functions in the dark and it will resort to the worship of its own lower nature. When this happens, the wrath of God is not far behind.

## WRATH OF GOD

In the Old Testament, God is often presented as jealous and angry, for example:

For the LORD your God is a devouring fire, a jealous God. (Deuteronomy 4:24)

Throughout the Books of History the people are threatened with, and punished by, the wrath of God:

Because they have abandoned me and made offerings to other gods, so that they have provoked me to anger with all the work of their hands, therefore my wrath shall be kindled against this place, and it will not be quenched. (2 Kings 22:17)

In the Books of History the wrath of God is presented as punishment brought on by violation of the Covenant.

### IS THE WRATH OF GOD ONLY AN OLD TESTAMENT ISSUE?

Not just an Old Testament issue, the term "wrath of God" appears in the New Testament:

For the wrath of God is revealed from heaven against all ungodliness and wickedness of those who by their wickedness suppress truth. (Romans 1:18)

And the wrath of God is mentioned in the Bahá'í Writings:

Say: Canst thou find anyone to protect thee when the wrath of God, the All-Powerful, the Unconstrained, is visited upon thee? (Bahá'u'lláh, *The Summons of the Lord of Hosts,* no. 4.13)

### WHAT IS THE WRATH OF GOD?

In some respects, the wrath of God is similar to the wrath of physics. For example, it is our common experience that two solid objects cannot occupy the same space at the same time. This rule is self-enforcing meaning that there *will* be consequences, a small or large collision, if this rule is ignored. Early in life, humans, as well as animals, learn the natural consequences of this law and monitor movement accordingly. When a collision does happen—when the driver behind us does not stop when we do—we could say that the resulting damage and injury is a natural consequence of violating that rule of physics. We could also say that we are experiencing the wrath and jealousy of the laws of physics that insist on having their way. And because God created the laws of physics we could say we are experiencing the wrath of God. Any way we describe it, the issue is that somebody ran afoul of that particular law of the physical world and suffering ensued.

The reality is that physical laws exist and it is in everyone's best interest to know those laws and relate to them safely. Like physical laws, spiritual laws exist and running afoul of them will result in consequences:

Just as there are laws governing our physical lives, requiring that we must supply our bodies with certain foods, maintain them within a certain range of temperatures, and so forth, if we wish to avoid physical disabilities, so also there are laws governing our spiritual lives. These laws are revealed to mankind in each age by the Manifestation of God, and obedience to them is of vital importance if each human being, and mankind in general, is to develop properly and harmoniously. Moreover, these various aspects are interdependent. If an individual violates the spiritual laws for his own development he will cause injury not only to himself but to the society in which he lives. Similarly, the condition of society has a direct effect on the individuals who must live within it. (The Universal

House of Justice, *Messages from the Universal House of Justice: 1963 to 1986,* no. 126.2)

Call it the wrath of God, the vengeance of God, God's anger, God's jealousy, or God's justice; there are individual and communal natural consequences for violating spiritual laws. While we have freedom of choice, we do not have freedom from consequences.

### WHAT IS THE VALUE OF KNOWING AND OBEYING THE LAWS OF GOD?

Distinction, advancement, victory, and true happiness are some of the outcomes of aligning with the ordinances of God:

The ordinances of God have been sent down from the heaven of His most august Revelation. All must diligently observe them. Man's supreme distinction, his real advancement, his final victory, have always depended, and will continue to depend upon them. Whoso keepeth the commandments of God shall attain everlasting felicity. (Bahá'u'lláh, *Gleanings from the Writings of Bahá'u'lláh,* no. 133.1)

In the same way that adherence to physical laws ensures physical safety, obedience to the spiritual and social laws of God is in our best interest.

# THE BOOKS OF POETICAL WRITINGS— OVERVIEW

The five Books of Poetical Writings are Job, Psalms, Proverbs, Ecclesiastes, and the Song of Solomon; they represent wisdom literature, poetry, and Temple liturgy. The Bahá'í Writings do not offer information about the origin or authorship of these writings.

**Job** is an epic drama that deals with the problem of the suffering of the righteous, and is widely recognized as one of the greatest literary productions of all time. Generally dated to the post-exilic period (538–332 BC), its authorship is unknown (see Crenshaw, pp. 331–32).[22]

**Psalms** is a collection of one hundred and fifty songs and prayers of various themes including lament, thanksgiving, and praise. Dates and authors are not conclusive; however, many scholars believe the collection was compiled by the late fifth century BC (see Rodd, pp. 355–62).[23]

**Proverbs** presents parental instructions as well as short proverbial sayings, all extolling the value of wisdom while drawing on the tradition of Solomon as the model of a wise king. The book is generally understood to be a composition of separate collections from numerous authors from before and after the post-exilic period (see Aitken, pp. 405–6).

---

22. There are many parallels to the Book of Job in Ancient Near East literature including: *A Farmer and the Courts in Egypt,* 2134–2040 BC (Matthews and Benjamin, p. 231) and *A Sufferer and a Friend in Babylon,* 667–626 BC (Matthews and Benjamin, p. 239).

23. The Book of Psalms has parallels in Ugaritic literature such as *The Stories of Baal and Anat,* 1400 BC (Matthews and Benjamin, p. 263); the Sumerian *Laments for Ur,* 2026 BC (Matthews and Benjamin, p. 247); and the Egyptian *Hymn to Aten,* 1353 BC (Matthews and Benjamin, p. 275).

**Ecclesiastes**, also called "The Preacher," is a philosophical investigation of the purpose of life presented as a monologue. It is generally thought to be the work of one author sometime between the fifth and second centuries BC (see Weeks, p. 423).[24]

**The Song of Solomon** (also entitled Song of Songs) is a collection of lyrical poetry. The theme is a lover's longing for the beloved, and is generally understood to be an allegorical expression of the mystical union of the human and divine. While traditionally attributed to Solomon, authorship is not determined. The relatively late biblical Hebrew of the original text is cited as evidence that it was probably written in the Second Temple Era, around the third century BC (see Brenner, p. 429).

---

24. The Books of Ecclesiastes and Proverbs have parallels in the Egyptian *Teachings of Ptah-Hotep,* 2575–2134 BC and other Egyptian teaching manuscripts (Matthews and Benjamin, p. 283).

# TOPICS FROM THE BOOKS
# OF POETICAL WRITINGS

## SUFFERING AND DETACHMENT

The Book of Job is a study in human suffering. Its main character, Job, is presented as a righteous man whose faith is tested when all of his property is stolen, his home destroyed, and his ten children killed—all in one day and by no fault of his own. Job responds by grieving and worshipping God:

> Then Job arose, tore his robe, shaved his head, and fell on the ground and worshipped. He said, "Naked I came from my mother's womb, and naked shall I return there: the LORD gave, and the LORD has taken away; blessed be the name of the LORD." (Job 1:20–21)

Despite his piety, Job's afflictions multiply. There follows a long dialogue in which Job's friends suggest reasons for his afflictions. Job tries to answer their questions by referring to the incomprehensible wisdom of God:

> With God are wisdom and strength; he has counsel and understanding. (Job 12:13)

### WHAT IS THE "WISDOM" IN HUMAN SUFFERING?

One wisdom in human suffering is that it discloses problems and imperfections, and the work required to solve problems and address imperfections builds spiritual strengths that last eternally:

Reflect upon his holiness Job: What trials, calamities and perplexities did he not endure! But these tests were like unto the fire and his holiness Job was like unto pure gold. Assuredly gold is purified by being submitted to the fire and if it contains any alloy or imperfection, it will disappear. That is the reason why violent tests become the cause of the everlasting glory of the righteous and are conducive to the destruction and disappearance of the unrighteous. ('Abdu'l-Bahá, cited in *Fire and Gold,* p. 39)

Another wisdom is that suffering turns the heart to the Creator:

While a man is happy he may forget his God; but when grief comes and sorrows overwhelm him, then will he remember his Father who is in Heaven, and who is able to deliver him from his humiliations. ('Abdu'l-Bahá, *Paris Talks,* no. 14.8)

Suffering teaches the transitory nature of this world and the permanence of the life of the spirit:

Whenever you see tremendous personal problems in your private lives, . . . you must remember that these afflictions are part of human life; and, according to our teachings one of their wisdoms is to teach us the impermanence of this world and the permanence of the spiritual bonds that we establish with God, His Prophet, and those who are alive in the faith of God. (Shoghi Effendi, *The Unfolding Destiny of the British Bahá'í Community,* p. 459)

Suffering also cultivates detachment:

Such is this mortal abode: a storehouse of afflictions and suffering. It is ignorance that binds man to it, for no comfort can be secured by any soul in this world, from monarch down to the most humble commoner. If once this life should offer a man a sweet cup, a hundred bitter ones will follow; such is the condition of this world. The wise man, therefore, doth not attach himself to this mortal life and doth not depend upon it. ('Abdu'l-Bahá, *Selections from the Writings of 'Abdu'l-Bahá,* no. 170.1)

The Bahá'í Writings teach detachment as a virtue and an ideal condition.

### WHAT DOES "DETACHMENT" ENTAIL IN THE BAHÁ'Í FAITH?

Detachment is actually a change in attachment: one lets go of attachment to selfish and worldly desires and, instead, cultivates attachment to Divine qualities (such as patience, truthfulness, justice, forgiveness, and compassion). The outcome is pure and holy deeds that attract others to the glory of God:

> O ye the beloved of the one true God! Pass beyond the narrow retreats of your evil and corrupt desires, and advance into the vast immensity of the realm of God, and abide ye in the meads of sanctity and of detachment, that the fragrance of your deeds may lead the whole of mankind to the ocean of God's unfading glory. (Bahá'u'lláh, *Gleanings from the Writings of Bahá'u'lláh*, no. 115.2)

The following is an excerpt from guidance on how to live detached from the world and attached to the Divine:

> Soon will your swiftly-passing days be over. . . . Summon ye, then, the people to God, and invite humanity to follow the example of the Company on high. Be ye loving fathers to the orphan, and a refuge to the helpless, and a treasury for the poor, and a cure for the ailing. Be ye the helpers of every victim of oppression, the patrons of the disadvantaged. Think ye at all times of rendering some service to every member of the human race. Pay ye no heed to aversion and rejection, to disdain, hostility, injustice: act ye in the opposite way. Be ye sincerely kind, not in appearance only. Let each one of God's loved ones center his attention on this: to be the Lord's mercy to man; to be the Lord's grace. Let him do some good to every person whose path he crosseth, and be of some benefit to him. ('Abdu'l-Bahá, *Selections from the Writings of 'Abdu'l-Bahá*, no. 1.7)

From the above guidance we can see that, in the Bahá'í Writings, detachment is not indifference, withdrawal, nor apathy. Detachment is pure and holy deeds for the increase of all things good—that humanity may be relieved of injustice, illness, disadvantage, hostility, and oppression. Detachment is both a fruit of, as well as a cure for, suffering.

## MY REDEEMER LIVES

One of Job's moments of strength in his consultation with his friends is his declaration of his faith in his Redeemer despite his afflictions. He declares:

> For I know that my Redeemer lives, and that at the last he will stand upon the earth; and after my skin has been thus destroyed, then in my flesh I shall see God, whom I shall see on my side, and my eyes shall behold, and not another. (Job 19:25–27)

### WHAT IS MEANT BY THE VERSE "I KNOW THAT MY REDEEMER LIVETH, AND THAT HE SHALL STAND AT THE LATTER DAY UPON THE EARTH"?

In this verse Job is looking to the end of things, renouncing the world, relying on God, and focusing on the reality of the life of the spirit:

> As to the statement of Job . . . "I know that my Redeemer liveth, and that He shall stand at the latter day upon the earth," the meaning here is: I shall not be abased, I have a Sustainer and a Guardian, and my Helper, my Defender will in the end be made manifest. And although now my flesh be weak and clothed with worms, yet shall I be healed, and with these mine own eyes, that is, mine inner sight, I shall behold Him. This did Job say after they had reproached him, and he himself had lamented the harms that his tribulations had wreaked upon him. ('Abdu'l-Bahá, *Selections from the Writings of 'Abdu'l-Bahá*, no. 145.7)

Job's strength was that he was able to look beyond his affliction and see God and his own spiritual immortality with his inner sight.

## WHAT IS MEANT BY "INNER SIGHT"?

Inner sight is the spiritual vision that enables one to see the world of the spirit as clearly as the natural eye sees the sun:

> . . . if the human spirit be rejoiced and be attracted to the Kingdom, if the inner eye be opened and the spiritual ear attuned, and if spiritual feelings come to predominate, the immortality of the spirit will be seen as clearly as the sun, and heavenly tidings and intimations will encompass that spirit. ('Abdu'l-Bahá, *Some Answered Questions,* no. 60.7)

The inner sight is a doorway into a new consciousness that looks beyond the physical reality to the reality of the spirit:

> O Man of Two Visions! Close one eye and open the other. Close one to the world and all that is therein, and open the other to the hallowed beauty of the Beloved. (Bahá'u'lláh, The Hidden Words. Persian, no. 12)

All souls have the capacity to develop inner sight.

## WHAT IS THE VALUE OF INNER SIGHT?

When inner sight is developed, one is illumined by the light of the spirit and undisturbed by the changes and chances of the world:

> This world is even as the body of man, and the Kingdom of God is as the spirit of life. See how dark and narrow is the physical world of man's body, and what a prey it is to diseases and ills. On the other hand, how fresh and bright is the realm of the human spirit. Judge thou from this metaphor how the world of the Kingdom hath shone down, and how its laws have been made to work in this nether realm. Although the spirit is hidden from view, still its commandments shine out like rays of light upon the world of the human body. In the same way, although the Kingdom of heaven is hidden from the sight of this unwitting people, still, to him who seeth with the inner eye, it is plain as day. ('Abdu'l-Bahá, *Selections from the Writings of 'Abdu'l-Bahá,* no. 161.1)

Inner sight cultivates the spiritual power necessary for divine civilization:

> For man two wings are necessary. One wing is physical power and material civilization; the other is spiritual power and divine civilization. With one wing only, flight is impossible. Two wings are essential. Therefore, no matter how much material civilization advances, it cannot attain to perfection except through the uplift of spiritual civilization. ('Abdu'l-Bahá, *The Promulgation of Universal Peace*, p. 16)

## PRAYER

Prayer is modeled throughout the Old Testament as people, prophets, and kings express their fears, hopes, and requests to God. From Abraham's intercessory prayer for Sodom and Gomorrah (Genesis 18:23–33), to Hannah's plea for a son (1 Samuel 1:1–2:11), Samson's appeal for water (Judges 15:9–20), and Asa's petition for victory (2 Chronicles 14), the Old Testament demonstrates that it is right to pray, that God receives our prayers, and that prayers are answered according to God's wisdom. This spirit of prayer is repeated in the New Testament.[25]

The Book of Psalms, sometimes called the prayer book of the Bible (see Merten, p. 7), is one of the best-loved books of the Old Testament. The following prayer, Psalm 3, supplicates God for deliverance from enemies and expresses confidence in Divine protection, both common themes in the Old Testament. Tradition connects Psalm 3 to King David, although "it may have been written for any of the Kings of Judah" (C. S. Rodd, p. 368):

> O LORD, how many are my foes! Many are rising against me; many are saying to me, "There is no help for you in God." *Selah*

---

25. For examples of admonitions to pray and the modeling of prayer in the New Testament, see Luke 11:2–4; Mark 11:24–25; John 17; Acts 6:4; Romans 12:10–12 Timothy 2:1–4; Colossians 4:2; 1 Thessalonians 5:17.

But you, O LORD, are a shield around me, my glory, and the one who lifts up my head. I cry aloud to the LORD, and he answers me from his holy hill. *Selah*

I lie down and sleep; I wake again, for the LORD sustains me. I am not afraid of ten thousands of people who have set themselves against me all around.

Rise up, O LORD! Deliver me, O my God! For you strike all my enemies on the cheek; you break the teeth of the wicked. Deliverance belongs to the LORD; may your blessing be on your people! (Psalm 3)

### WHAT IS THE WISDOM OF PRAYER?

In prayer a connection is established between the seeker and the Beloved that engenders mindfulness, happiness, spiritual awakening, and protection in times of tests:

The wisdom of prayer is this: That it causeth a connection between the servant and the True One, because in that state man with all heart and soul turneth his face towards His Highness the Almighty, seeking His association and desiring His love and compassions. The greatest happiness for a lover is to converse with his beloved, and the greatest gift for a seeker is to become familiar with the object of his longing; that is why with every soul who is attracted to the Kingdom of God his greatest hope is to find an opportunity to entreat and supplicate before his Beloved, appeal for His mercy and grace and be immersed in the ocean of His utterance, goodness and generosity.

Beside all this, prayer and fasting is the cause of awakening and mindfulness and conducive to protection and preservation from tests. ('Abdu'l-Bahá, *Tablets of 'Abdu'l-Bahá Abbas, vol. III,* pp. 683–84)

### IF GOD IS ALL-KNOWING, THEN GOD ALREADY KNOWS OUR NEEDS. WHY SHOULD WE STATE OUR WANTS IN PRAYER?

It is appropriate for the created to beseech help from the Creator. In addition, the act of prayer has the power to strengthen, cheer, and increase capacity:

Know thou, verily, it is becoming in a weak one to supplicate to the Strong One, and it behooveth a seeker of bounty to beseech the Glorious Bountiful One. When one supplicates to his Lord, turns to Him and seeks bounty from His Ocean, this supplication brings light to his heart, illumination to his sight, life to his soul and exaltation to his being.

. . . By these attractions one's ability and capacity increase. When the vessel is enlarged the water increases, and when the thirst grows the bounty of the cloud becomes agreeable to the taste of man. This is the mystery of supplication and the wisdom of stating one's wants. ('Abdu'l-Bahá, cited in Esslemont, *Bahá'u'lláh and the New Era,* p. 104)

### DOES GOD NEED PRAYERS OF PRAISE?

God is exalted above any need. Praising the glory of God in prayer is for our instructional benefit:

Whatever duty Thou hast prescribed unto Thy servants of extolling to the utmost Thy majesty and glory is but a token of Thy grace unto them, that they may be enabled to ascend unto the station conferred upon their own inmost being, the station of the knowledge of their own selves. (Bahá'u'lláh, *Gleanings from the Writings of Bahá'u'lláh,* no. 1.5)

In a mysterious way, praising God helps us to gain knowledge about our "own selves."

### DOES PRAYING ON BEHALF OF OTHERS HELP THEM?

Praying on behalf of others; that is, intercessory prayer, is effective in helping souls to progress in this world and the next.

Thus, as souls can progress in this world through their entreaties and supplications, or through the prayers of holy souls, so too after death can they progress through their own prayers and supplications, particularly if they become the object of the intercession of the holy Manifestations. ('Abdu'l-Bahá, *Some Answered Questions,* no. 62.7)

## WHAT PRAYER IS MOST ACCEPTABLE TO GOD?

The purity of prayer, not its duration, is the measure of the prayer's acceptance before God:

> The most acceptable prayer is the one offered with the utmost spirituality and radiance; its prolongation hath not been and is not beloved by God. The more detached and the purer the prayer, the more acceptable is it in the presence of God. (The Báb, *Selections from the Writings of the Báb*, no. 3:2:4)

## HOW ARE PRAYERS ANSWERED?

Prayers are answered through meditation and action. Through our prayers we ask for guidance and through meditation we listen to the guidance that is the response to our prayer. Then we take action on that guidance and reflect on the results, paying attention to signs of confirmation and additional guidance:

> It is not sufficient to pray diligently for guidance, but this prayer must be followed by meditation as to the best methods of action and then action itself. Even if the action should not immediately produce results, or perhaps not be entirely correct, that does not make so much difference, because prayers can only be answered through action and if someone's action is wrong, God can use that method of showing the pathway which is right. (From a letter written on behalf of Shoghi Effendi, dated August 22, 1957, to an individual believer, in *Lights of Guidance*, no. 1508)

## DOES PRAYER ALWAYS REQUIRE WORDS?

Prayer can take many forms, including attitude and action. For example, work performed in a spirit of service is praise of God:

> Every individual, no matter how handicapped and limited he may be, is under the obligation of engaging in some work or profession, for work, especially when performed in the spirit of service, is according to Bahá'u'lláh, a form of worship. (Shoghi Effendi, *Directives from the Guardian*, p. 83)

## CAN PRAYER ASSIST WITH
## HEALING ILLNESSES OF THE BODY?

Matters related to the spirit greatly affect the body, and prayer can promote healing. Both material and spiritual means should be used to heal illnesses:

There are two ways of healing sickness, material means and spiritual means. The first is by the treatment of physicians; the second consisteth in prayers offered by the spiritual ones to God and in turning to Him. Both means should be used and practiced.

Illnesses which occur by reason of physical causes should be treated by doctors with medical remedies; those which are due to spiritual causes disappear through spiritual means. Thus an illness caused by affliction, fear, nervous impressions, will be healed more effectively by spiritual rather than by physical treatment. Hence, both kinds of treatment should be followed; they are not contradictory. Therefore thou shouldst also accept physical remedies inasmuch as these too have come from the mercy and favor of God, Who hath revealed and made manifest medical science so that His servants may profit from this kind of treatment also. Thou shouldst give equal attention to spiritual treatments, for they produce marvelous effects.

Now, if thou wishest to know the true remedy which will heal man from all sickness and will give him the health of the divine kingdom, know that it is the precepts and teachings of God. Focus thine attention upon them. ('Abdu'l-Bahá, *Selections from the Writings of 'Abdu'l-Bahá*, no. 133.1–3)

## ANGELS

Angels make many appearances throughout the Old Testament;[26] for example, angels led Lot and his family out of Sodom before its fiery destruction

---

26. For studies on the development of the biblical concept of angels as inspired by Zoroastrianism in the post-exilic Persian Period and the Hellenistic Age, see R.C.

(Genesis 19:15), and it was an angel that stayed Abraham's hand as He was about to sacrifice His son (Genesis 22:11). In the prayers of the Book of Psalms, angels appear as God's special assistants. Angels praise God:

Praise him, all his angels; praise him, all his hosts! (Psalms 148:2)

Angels torment people:

Let their way be dark and slippery, with the angel of the LORD pursuing them. (Psalms 35:6)

And angels protect people:

For he will command his angels concerning you to guard you in all your ways. (Psalms 91:11)

### WHO OR WHAT ARE ANGELS?

"For Bahá'ís, "angels" refer to spiritual confirmations as well to advanced spiritual beings:

The meaning of "angels" is the confirmations of God and His celestial powers. Likewise angels are blessed beings who have severed all ties with this nether world, have been released from the chains of self and the desires of the flesh, and anchored their hearts to the heavenly realms of the Lord. These are of the Kingdom, heavenly; these are of God, spiritual; these are revealers of God's abounding grace; these are dawning-points of His spiritual bestowals. ('Abdu'l-Bahá, *Selections from the Writings of 'Abdu'l-Bahá,* no. 39.3)

Angels in the form of confirmations can take many shapes such as a sense of peaceful assurance after the passing of a loved one, or a chance meeting that leads to a job offer. Angels in the form of "blessed beings" can be found in this world and the next.

---

Zaehner, *The Dawn & Twilight of Zoroastrianism* and Lawrence Heyworth Mills, *Our Own Religion in Ancient Persia.*

## HOW CAN ONE ATTAIN
## THE STATION OF A "HEAVENLY BEING"
## IN THIS MORTAL WORLD?

A person in this mortal world who reflects the qualities of the spirit could be called an angel:

> . . . the sublime achievements of man reside in those qualities and attributes that exclusively pertain to the angels of the Supreme Concourse. Therefore, when praiseworthy qualities and high morals emanate from man, he becometh a heavenly being, an angel of the Kingdom, a divine reality and a celestial effulgence. ('Abdu'l-Bahá, *Selections from the Writings of 'Abdu'l-Bahá*, no. 225.14)

The following prayer suggests that becoming an angel on earth involves spiritual inspiration, promoting the oneness of mankind, and being a cause of love and unity:

> O Divine Providence! This assemblage is composed of Thy friends who are attracted to Thy beauty and are set ablaze by the fire of Thy love. Turn these souls into heavenly angels, resuscitate them through the breath of Thy Holy Spirit, grant them eloquent tongues and resolute hearts, bestow upon them heavenly power and merciful susceptibilities, cause them to become the promulgators of the oneness of mankind and the cause of love and concord in the world of humanity, so that the perilous darkness of ignorant prejudice may vanish through the light of the Sun of Truth, this dreary world may become illumined, this material realm may absorb the rays of the world of spirit, these different colours may merge into one colour and the melody of praise may rise to the kingdom of Thy sanctity. ('Abdu'l-Bahá, *Selections from the Writings of 'Abdu'l-Bahá*, no. 68.10)

Angels, in this world and the next, assist in the work of salvation.

## COLLECTIVE SALVATION

The Old Testament often presents salvation in a very practical sense—as collective protection and victory in this world. For example, the Book of Psalms supplicates for the rescue of Israelites who were in a state of captivity and oppression:

> Oh that deliverance for Israel would come from Zion! When the Lord restores the fortunes of his people, Jacob will rejoice; Israel will be glad. (Psalms 14:7)

Salvation in terms of safeguarding the collective interests of the human race has always been one of the purposes of the Manifestation of God:

> The fundamental purpose animating the Faith of God and His Religion is to safeguard the interests and promote the unity of the human race, and to foster the spirit of love and fellowship amongst men. (Bahá'u'lláh, *Gleanings from the Writings of Bahá'u'lláh*, no. 110.1)

### HOW IS THE THEME OF COLLECTIVE SALVATION IN THE OLD TESTAMENT RELEVANT TODAY?

The Old Testament presents stories about a group of people, the Israelites, who strive for collective salvation by worshipping one God and trying to follow the Laws of Moses. Through their stories we witness the challenges of working toward unity on the scale of family, tribe, and nation. Today, the lessons in these stories can be applied to the twenty-first century challenge of widening our community of concern to include all the people and nations of the earth:

> The Great Being saith: Blessed and happy is he that ariseth to promote the best interests of the peoples and kindreds of the earth. . . . It is not for him to pride himself who loveth his own country, but rather for him who loveth the whole world. The earth is but one country, and mankind its citizens. (Bahá'u'lláh, *Gleanings from the Writings of Bahá'u'lláh*, no. 117.1)

Collective salvation is closely related to the goal of world peace.

### WHAT ARE THE PREREQUISITES OF WORLD PEACE?

Bahá'u'lláh named many prerequisites for peace including the necessity for an international tribunal of nations:

> The time must come when the imperative necessity for the holding of a vast, an all-embracing assemblage of men will be universally realized. The rulers and kings of the earth must needs attend it, and, participating in its deliberations, must consider such ways and means as will lay the foundations of the world's Great Peace amongst men. Such a peace demandeth that the Great Powers should resolve, for the sake of the tranquility of the peoples of the earth, to be fully reconciled among themselves. (Bahá'u'lláh, *Gleanings from the Writings of Bahá'u'lláh,* no. 117.1)

The abolition of racism and the realization of the oneness of mankind is a prerequisite for world peace:

> Racism, one of the most baneful and persistent evils, is a major barrier to peace. Its practice perpetrates too outrageous a violation of the dignity of human beings to be countenanced under any pretext. Racism retards the unfoldment of the boundless potentialities of its victims, corrupts its perpetrators, and blights human progress. Recognition of the oneness of mankind, implemented by appropriate legal measures, must be universally upheld if this problem is to be overcome. (The Universal House of Justice, *The Promise of World Peace,* ¶29)

The elimination of the extremes of wealth and poverty is a prerequisite for world peace:

> The inordinate disparity between rich and poor, a source of acute suffering, keeps the world in a state of instability, virtually on the brink of war. Few societies have dealt effectively with this situation. The solution calls for the combined application of spiritual, moral and practical

approaches. A fresh look at the problem is required, entailing consultation with experts from a wide spectrum of disciplines, devoid of economic and ideological polemics, and involving the people directly affected in the decisions that must urgently be made. . . . (The Universal House of Justice, *The Promise of World Peace,* ¶30)

Religious dialogue, mutual forbearance, and cooperation are prerequisites for world peace:

The challenge facing the religious leaders of mankind is to contemplate, with hearts filled with the spirit of compassion and a desire for truth, the plight of humanity, and to ask themselves whether they cannot, in humility before their Almighty Creator, submerge their theological differences in a great spirit of mutual forbearance that will enable them to work together for the advancement of human understanding and peace. (The Universal House of Justice, *The Promise of World Peace,* ¶32)

The achievement of full equality between the sexes is a prerequisite for world peace:

The emancipation of women, the achievement of full equality between the sexes, is one of the most important, though less acknowledged prerequisites of peace. The denial of such equality perpetrates an injustice against one half of the world's population and promotes in men harmful attitudes and habits that are carried from the family to the workplace, to political life, and ultimately to international relations. There are no grounds, moral, practical, or biological, upon which such denial can be justified. Only as women are welcomed into full partnership in all fields of human endeavour will the moral and psychological climate be created in which international peace can emerge. (The Universal House of Justice, *The Promise of World Peace,* ¶33)

And the adoption of an international auxiliary language is a prerequisite for world peace:

A fundamental lack of communication between peoples seriously undermines efforts towards world peace. Adopting an international auxiliary language would go far to resolving this problem and necessitates the most urgent attention. (The Universal House of Justice, *The Promise of World Peace*, ¶35)

Other prerequisites for world peace include universal education, independent investigation of truth, and realization of the harmony of science and religion. The principles and practices that will lead to world peace are also the path of salvation:

We, verily, have unfolded before your eyes that which shall profit you both in this world and in the realm of faith, and which will lead you to the path of salvation. Would that ye might turn thereunto! (Bahá'u'lláh, *The Summons of the Lord of Hosts*, no. 5.57)

### IS WORLD PEACE POSSIBLE?
World peace is not just possible—it is inevitable:

The Great Peace towards which people of good will throughout the centuries have inclined their hearts, of which seers and poets for countless generations have expressed their vision, and for which from age to age the sacred Scriptures of mankind have constantly held the promise, is now at long last within the reach of the nations. For the first time in history it is possible for everyone to view the entire planet, with all its myriad diversified peoples, in one perspective. World peace is not only possible but inevitable. It is the next stage in the evolution of this planet—in the words of one great thinker, "the planetization of mankind." (The Universal House of Justice, *The Promise of World Peace*, ¶1)

## PROGRESS

The Book of Ecclesiastes opens with a commentary on the nature of human existence in which all of life is described as vanity; that is, meaningless or futile:

Vanity of vanities, says the Teacher, vanity of vanities! All is vanity. What do people gain from all the toil at which they toil under the sun? . . . What has been is what will be, and what has been done is what will be done; there is nothing new under the sun. (Ecclesiastes 1:2–3, 9)

Maintaining an ironic tone, the book bemoans the unpredictable nature of fate, the endless circle of human drama, and the inevitability of death—making it an excellent advertisement for detachment. For our purposes, however, we will examine another one of its themes: that we exist in "a world without progress or culmination where everything has been done before, but, unremembered, will be done again" (Weeks, p. 423).

### IS HUMANITY GOING IN CIRCLES?

When one examines human affairs, a circular pattern of life, death, growth, and decay does appear; however, from the point of view of the Bahá'í Writings, the eventual outcome is not a circle—it is an upward moving spiral as it traces the continuing evolution of human achievement in areas such as science, art, industry, invention, law, ethics, community organization, and theology. As noted previously, the very purpose of creation is to "carry forward an ever-advancing civilization" (Bahá'u'lláh, *Gleanings from the Writings of Bahá'u'lláh*, no. 109.2).

The nature of this development, however, has been slow. In the fifth century BC, which was the time of the writing of Ecclesiastes, it was virtually impossible to reflect on human advancements made over thousands of years; recorded history did not exist as it does today, nor did people have the scientific skills to read the traces of history and evolution around them. One could imagine that with the relatively short range of vision available at that time, the writer of Ecclesiastes may have observed that humanity was moving in unalterable circles. However, with the accumulation of knowledge made available through developments in literacy and science, humanity's progress in every field, however slow, has become evident. This progress is inspired by progressive Revelation:

Just as the organic evolution of mankind has been slow and gradual, and involved successively the unification of the family, the tribe, the city-state, and the nation, so has the light vouchsafed by the Revelation of God, at various stages in the evolution of religion, and reflected in the successive Dispensations of the past, been slow and progressive. Indeed the measure of Divine Revelation, in every age, has been adapted to, and commensurate with, the degree of social progress achieved in that age by a constantly evolving humanity. (Shoghi Effendi, *The Promised Day is Come,* p. 118)

The past century, especially, has seen unprecedented advances in all areas of human endeavor:

All things are subject to reformation. This is a century of life and renewal. Sciences and arts, industry and invention have been reformed. Law and ethics have been reconstituted, reorganized. The world of thought has been regenerated. ('Abdu'l-Bahá, *The Promulgation of Universal Peace,* p. 191)

**WHAT IS THE EVIDENCE THAT HUMANITY HAS PROGRESSED?**

Humanity's progress is evident in that current understandings and standards have made the sciences and philosophies of the past obsolete. The problems of today's world community—themselves brought about by technological innovations and new understandings of what it means to live on this planet—require solutions different than those of the past:

Sciences of former ages and philosophies of the past are useless today. Present exigencies demand new methods of solution; world problems are without precedent. Old ideas and modes of thought are fast becoming obsolete. Ancient laws and archaic ethical systems will not meet the requirements of modern conditions, for this is clearly the century of a new life, the century of the revelation of reality and, therefore, the greatest of all centuries. Consider how the scientific developments of fifty years have surpassed and eclipsed the knowledge and achievements of all the former ages combined. Would the announcements and theories of ancient astronomers explain our present knowledge of the suns and planetary systems? Would the mask of obscurity which beclouded medieval centuries meet the demand for clear-eyed vision and understanding which characterizes the world today? Will the despotism of former governments answer the call for freedom which has risen from the heart of humanity in this cycle of illumination? It is evident that no vital results are now forthcoming from the customs, institutions and standpoints of the past. ('Abdu'l-Bahá, *The Promulgation of Universal Peace*, p. 192)

Another indicator of human progress is that the circle of moral responsibility has widened. For example, racial prejudices, once assumed as correct attitudes and often enshrined in law, are now widely understood in social discourse as morally wrong:

Racism is now tainted by its association with the horrors of the twentieth century to the degree that it has taken on something of the character of a spiritual disease. While surviving as a social attitude in many parts of the world—and as a blight on the lives of a significant segment of humankind—racial prejudice has become so universally condemned in principle that no body of people can any longer safely allow themselves to be identified with it. (The Universal House of Justice, Letter to the World's Religious Leaders, April 2002, ¶5)

When one examines the history of civilization, it is evident that humanity's progress far outweighs any seeming futility of a particular moment in time.

## FEAR OF GOD

Along with exploring the powerlessness of some aspects of the human condition, the Book of Ecclesiastes also sings the praises of wisdom and ends with acknowledging that the fear of God is the whole point of human existence:

The end of the matter; all has been heard. Fear God, and keep his commandments; for that is the whole duty of everyone. For God will bring every deed into judgment, including every secret thing, whether good or evil. (Ecclesiastes 12:13)

Similarly, the Book of Proverbs, which presents hundreds of verses full of advice and admonitions on moral behavior, points to the attainment of the fear and knowledge of God as life's greatest treasure:

If you seek it like silver, and search for it as for hidden treasures— then you will understand the fear of the LORD and find the knowledge of God. (Proverbs 2:4–5)

### WHAT IS THE FEAR OF GOD?

The fear of God, understood as awe, reverence and/or dread of God (see Shoghi Effendi, in *Lights of Guidance,* no. 789), constitutes humanity's main protection and is the cause of its preservation:

The fear of God hath ever been a sure defense and a safe stronghold for all the peoples of the world. It is the chief cause of the protection of mankind, and the supreme instrument for its preservation. (Bahá'u'lláh, Epistle to the Son of the Wolf, p. 27)

### WHY IS THE FEAR OF GOD NECESSARY?

For most people, an element of fear is required for motivation to control their actions:

You ask him about the fear of God: perhaps the friends do not realize that the majority of human beings need the element of fear in order to discipline their conduct. Only a relatively very highly evolved soul would always be disciplined by love alone. Fear of punishment, fear of the anger of God if we do evil, are needed to keep people's feet on the right path. Of course we should love God—but we must fear Him in the sense of a child fearing the righteous anger and chastisement of a parent; not cringe before Him as before a tyrant, but know His Mercy exceeds His Justice!

(From a letter written on behalf of Shoghi Effendi, dated July 26, 1946, to an individual believer, in *Lights of Guidance,* no. 794)

Cultivation of the fear of God is required because an innate sense of shame that automatically controls behaviour is strong in only a few:

Indeed, there existeth in man a faculty which deterreth him from, and guardeth him against, whatever is unworthy and unseemly, and which is known as his sense of shame. This, however, is confined to but a few; all have not possessed, and do not possess, it. (Bahá'u'lláh, Epistle to the Son of the Wolf, p. 27)

### WHAT IS THE OUTCOME OF THE FEAR OF GOD?

The fear of God results in praiseworthy character, goodly deeds, and open hearts:

Admonish men to fear God. By God! This fear is the chief commander of the army of thy Lord. Its hosts are a praiseworthy character and goodly deeds. Through it have the cities of men's hearts been opened throughout the ages and centuries, and the standards of ascendancy and triumph raised above all other standards. (Bahá'u'lláh, Epistle to the Son of the Wolf, p. 135)

The fear of God cultivates confidence in God:

From their childhood instill in their hearts the love of God so they may manifest in their lives the fear of God and have confidence in the bestowals of God. ('Abdu'l-Bahá, *The Promulgation of Universal Peace,* p. 73)

### WHAT HAPPENS WITHOUT THE FEAR OF GOD?

Lack of the fear of God results in fearfulness:

And if he feareth not God, God will make him to fear all things; whereas all things fear him who feareth God. (Bahá'u'lláh, The Four Valleys, p. 58)

## LOVE

---

The word "love" appears more times in the Books of Poetical Writings than in all of the other books of the Old Testament combined. Here is one verse from each book:

> You have granted me life and steadfast love, and your care has preserved my spirit. (Job 10:12)

> Let all who seek you rejoice and be glad in you. Let those who love your salvation say evermore, "God is great!" (Psalm 70:4)

> Hatred stirs up strife, but love covers all offenses. (Proverbs 10:12)

> Enjoy life with the wife whom you love, all the days of your vain life that are given you under the sun, because that is your portion in life and in your toil at which you toil under the sun. (Ecclesiastes 9:9)

> Many waters cannot quench love, neither can floods drown it. (Song of Solomon 8:7)

### WHAT IS LOVE?

Love is the breath of the Holy Spirit, the link between God and humanity, the essential bond inherent in the realities of things, the spirit of life, and the establisher of true civilization:

> Know thou of a certainty that Love is the secret of God's holy Dispensation, the manifestation of the All-Merciful, the fountain of spiritual outpourings. Love is heaven's kindly light, the Holy Spirit's eternal breath that vivifieth the human soul. Love is the cause of God's revelation unto man, the vital bond inherent, in accordance with the divine creation, in the realities of things. Love is the one means that ensureth true felicity both in this world and the next. Love is the light that guideth in darkness, the living link that uniteth God with man, that assureth the progress of every illu-

mined soul. Love is the most great law that ruleth this mighty and heavenly cycle, the unique power that bindeth together the divers elements of this material world, the supreme magnetic force that directeth the movements of the spheres in the celestial realms. Love revealeth with unfailing and limitless power the mysteries latent in the universe. Love is the spirit of life unto the adorned body of mankind, the establisher of true civilization in this mortal world, and the shedder of imperishable glory upon every high-aiming race and nation. ('Abdu'l-Bahá, *Selections from the Writings of 'Abdu'l-Bahá*, no. 12.1)

More than just an affinity between people, love is the most powerful force in the universe—the supreme magnetic force that directs the planets and the vital bond that holds everything together.

### HOW DOES THE FORCE OF LOVE FLOW?

Love flows in four ways—from God to man; from man to God; from God to the identity of God; and from one human being to another human being:

The first is the love that flows from God to man. It consists of the inexhaustible graces, the Divine effulgence and heavenly illumination. Through this love the world of being receives life. Through this love man is endowed with physical existence, until, through the breath of the Holy Spirit—this same love—he receives eternal life and becomes the image of the Living God. This love is the origin of all the love in the world of creation.

The second is the love that flows from man to God. This is faith, attraction to the Divine, enkindlement, progress, entrance into the Kingdom of God, receiving the Bounties of God, illumination with the lights of the Kingdom. This love is the origin of all philanthropy; this love causes the hearts of men to reflect the rays of the Sun of Reality

The third is the love of God toward the Identity of God. This is the transfiguration of His Beauty, the reflection of Himself in the mirror of His Creation. This is the reality of love, the Ancient Love, the Eternal Love. Through one ray of this Love all other love exists.

The fourth is the love of man for man. The love which exists between the hearts of believers is prompted by the ideal of the unity of spirits. This love is attained through the knowledge of God, so that men see the Divine Love reflected in the heart. Each sees in the other the Beauty of God reflected in the soul, and finding this point of similarity, they are attracted to one another in love. This love will make all men the waves of one sea, this love will make them all the stars of one heaven and the fruits of one tree. This love will bring the realization of true accord, the foundation of real unity. ('Abdu'l-Bahá, *Paris Talks,* no. 54.47)

These four kinds of love originate from God and they are all true love.

## WHAT IS NOT TRUE LOVE?

The "yielding of the hearts to the accidents of life" is not true love because it is subject to change:

But the love which sometimes exists between friends is not (true) love, because it is subject to transmutation; this is merely fascination. As the breeze blows, the slender trees yield. If the wind is in the East the tree leans to the West, and if the wind turns to the West the tree leans to the East. This kind of love is originated by the accidental conditions of life. This is not love, it is merely acquaintanceship; it is subject to change.

Today you will see two souls apparently in close friendship; tomorrow all this may be changed. Yesterday they were ready to die for one another; today they shun one another's society! This is not love; it is the yielding of the hearts to the accidents of life. When that which has caused this "love" to exist passes, the love passes also; this is not in reality love. ('Abdu'l-Bahá, *Paris Talks,* no. 58.8–9)

## WHAT IS THE HIGHEST EXPRESSION OF LOVE?

While love includes the power of attraction in the natural world, its highest expression is in the realm of the spirit:

Real love is the love that exists between God and His servants, the love which binds together holy souls. This is the love of the spiritual world, not the love of physical bodies and organisms. ('Abdu'l-Bahá, *The Promulgation of Universal Peace*, p. 357)

### HOW LONG DOES LOVE LAST?
Unlike physical attraction, spiritual love endures eternally:

. . . marriage must be a union of the body and of the spirit as well, for here both husband and wife are aglow with the same wine, both are enamoured of the same matchless Face, both live and move through the same spirit, both are illumined by the same glory. This connection between them is a spiritual one, hence it is a bond that will abide forever. Likewise do they enjoy strong and lasting ties in the physical world as well, for if the marriage is based both on the spirit and the body, that union is a true one, hence it will endure. If, however, the bond is physical and nothing more, it is sure to be only temporary, and must inexorably end in separation. ('Abdu'l-Bahá, *Selections from the Writings of 'Abdu'l-Bahá*, no. 84.3)

## MY BELOVED

The Song of Solomon is a love story that tells of a king who courts a beautiful maiden. The maiden, however, yearns for her former lover. Finally, the maiden leaves the palace to return to her beloved. Here is an excerpt:

The voice of my beloved! Look, he comes, leaping upon the mountains, bounding over the hills. My beloved is like a gazelle or a young stag. Look, there he stands behind our wall, gazing in at the windows, looking through the lattice. My beloved speaks and says to me: "Arise, my love, my fair one, and come away; for now the winter is past, the rain is over and gone." (Song of Solomon 2:8–11)

### WHAT IS THE NATURE OF THE SONG OF SOLOMON?
The Song of Solomon conveys spiritual realities to those who can unlock its mysteries:

It is difficult to comprehend even the words of a philosopher; how much more difficult it is to understand the Words of God. The divine Words are not to be taken according to their outer sense. They are symbolical and contain realities of spiritual meaning. For instance, in the book of Solomon's songs you will read about the bride and bridegroom. It is evident that the physical bride and bridegroom are not intended. Obviously, these are symbols conveying a hidden and inner significance. ('Abdu'l-Bahá, *The Promulgation of Universal Peace*, pp. 647–48)

## WHAT IS THE "HIDDEN AND INNER SIGNIFICANCE" OF THE SONG OF SOLOMON?

Although the Bahá'í Writings indicate that that Song of Solomon has inner meanings, the symbolism is not explained. Its style, however, mirrors Persian/Arabic mystic-love traditions where the soul's longing for the Divine Beloved is poetically expressed in terms of a human love relationship—the lover is attracted to the beloved, becomes sick with love and cannot endure separation from the loved one, experiences adversities in the attempt to gain the presence of the beloved, and finally comes to the realization that reunion with the beloved requires sacrifice (Hatcher, p. 56). In Bahá'u'lláh's mystical composition entitled The Seven Valleys, He draws on the mystic-love tradition of Majnun and Layli to illustrate the nature of a true seeker:

One must judge of search by the standard of the Majnun of Love. It is related that one day they came upon Majnun sifting the dust, and his tears flowing down. They said, "What doest thou?" He said, "I seek for Layli." They cried, "Alas for thee! Layli is of pure spirit, and thou seekest her in the dust!" He said, "I seek her everywhere; haply somewhere I shall find her."

Yea, although to the wise it be shameful to seek the Lord of Lords in the dust, yet this betokeneth intense ardor in searching. "Whoso seeketh out a thing with zeal shall find it." (Bahá'u'lláh, The Seven Valleys, p. 6)

Notice how the theme of the seeker who searches tirelessly for the Beloved is also found in this excerpt from the Song of Solomon:

Upon my bed at night I sought him whom my soul loves; I sought him, but found him not; I called him, but he gave no answer. "I will rise now and go about the city, in the streets and in the squares; I will seek him whom my soul loves." I sought him, but found him not. (Song of Solomon 3:1–2).

### WHAT DO THE BRIDE AND BRIDEGROOM SYMBOLIZE IN BIBLICAL SCRIPTURE?

We can look to other biblical passages for clues. For example, in Isaiah 61:10 the image of a bride and bridegroom is used to symbolize righteous qualities required for salvation. In the Gospel of Mark Christ refers to Himself as the "bridegroom" (Mark 2:19), and in the Book of Revelation the bride image symbolizes the religion of God:

Furthermore, the religion of God is likened to an adorned bride who appears with the utmost grace, as it has been said in chapter 21 of the Revelation of John: "And I John saw the holy city, new Jerusalem, coming down from God out of heaven, prepared as a bride adorned for her husband." ('Abdu'l-Bahá, *Some Answered Questions,* no. 13.4)

While the meaning of the Song of Solomon is not directly explained in the Bahá'í Writings, when read with a spiritual eye and an understanding of symbolism demonstrated in other contexts, some of the mysteries concealed in the words may unfold.

## THE VALUE OF POETICAL WRITINGS

While the Books of Poetical Writings do not add to the Revelation of Moses or report on the history of the Israelite tribes, they do celebrate a broad range of human experiences in literary excellence.

### WHAT IS THE VALUE OF POETICAL WRITINGS?

Poetry and prose can serve as keys to divine mysteries:

Treasures lie hidden beneath the throne of God; the key to those treasures is the tongue of poets. (The Báb, quoting a Persian tradition, cited in Shoghi Effendi, *The Dawn-Breakers,* p. 258)

All of the arts benefit humanity and, when prompted by the will to serve, are regarded as acts of worship:

I rejoice to hear that thou takest pains with thine art, for in this wonderful new age, art is worship. The more thou strivest to perfect it, the closer wilt thou come to God. What bestowal could be greater than this, that one's art should be even as the act of worshipping the Lord? ('Abdu'l-Bahá, cited in "The Importance of the Arts in Promoting the Faith," *Compilation of Compilations,* p. 20.)

### WHERE DOES ART COME FROM?

Artistic inspiration comes from the Holy Spirit:

All Art is a gift of the Holy Spirit. When this light shines through the mind of a musician, it manifests itself in beautiful harmonies. Again, shining through the mind of a poet, it is seen in fine poetry and poetic prose. When the Light of the Sun of Truth inspires the mind of a painter, he produces marvelous pictures. These gifts are fulfilling their highest purpose, when showing forth the praise of God. ('Abdu'l-Bahá, cited in Bloomfield, *The Chosen Highway,* p. 167)

This inspiration may be channeled through faithful souls who have passed on to the next world:

The soul that hath remained faithful to the Cause of God, and stood unwaveringly firm in His Path shall, after his ascension, be possessed of such power that all the worlds which the Almighty hath created can benefit through him. Such a soul provideth, at the bidding of the Ideal King and Divine Educator, the pure leaven that leaveneth the world of being, and furnisheth the power through which the arts and wonders of the world are made manifest. (Bahá'u'lláh, *Gleanings from the Writings of Bahá'u'lláh,* no. 82.7)

As artistic inspiration may come from spiritual worlds, the art produced may be beyond the understanding of the artist:

It is the immediate influence of the Holy Spirit that causes words such as these to stream from the tongue of poets, the significance of which they themselves are oftentimes unable to apprehend. (The Báb, cited in *The Dawn-Breakers,* p. 258)

# THE BOOKS OF PROPHECY—OVERVIEW

The final books of the Old Testament, the Books of Prophecy,[27] represent the era after David and Solomon, the tumultuous period of the split kingdoms of Judah and Israel, the fall to Assyria and Babylon and the destruction of the Temple, the return to Jerusalem, and the rebuilding of the Temple under the Persian Empire. In general, the prophets comment on national and international developments, condemn social evils, offer assurance for those who trust in God, prophesy signs of future Manifestations, and share the vision of God's long-range plan for the spiritualization of the planet. Most foretell short-term as well as long-term events. The Bahá'í Writings do not offer information concerning the origin or authorship of the Books of Prophecy. Biblical scholarship has determined that most were composed between the eighth and fourth centuries BC. The following overview includes samples of where these books are referenced in the Bahá'í Writings.

**Isaiah** is widely understood by biblical scholars as having three distinct sections: chapters 1–39, named "First" or "Proto Isaiah," was probably composed in the late seventh century BC by the prophet Isaiah ben Amoz; chapters 40–55, named "Deutero" or "Second Isaiah," were probably composed during the Babylonian exile in the 540s BC; and chapters

---

27. The Hebrew Bible groups the Prophets (Nevi'im) differently: "Latter Prophets" include the Books of Joshua, Judges, Samuel, and Kings; "Major Prophets" include Isaiah, Jeremiah, and Ezekiel; and the twelve "Minor Prophets" include Hosea, Joel, Amos, Obadiah, Jonah, Micah, Nahum, Habakkuk, Zephaniah, Haggai, Zechariah, and Malachi. The difference between "major" and "minor" prophets is not one of importance but of length; the books of the Major Prophets are much longer than the Minor Prophets. The books of Daniel and Lamentations are included in the "Writings" (Ketuvim) grouping of the Hebrew Bible (See Barton, p. 11).

56–66, named "Trito" or "Third Isaiah," were probably composed in the post-exilic period in Jerusalem (538–332 BC). The book foretells events such as Israel's fall to Assyria and the capture of Judah by the Babylonians (see Coggins, pp. 433–34). Bahá'u'lláh cites Isaiahic prophecies concerning both the Christian and Bahá'í Revelations (see Lawh-i-Aqdas, "The Tablet to the Christians"; *The Proclamation of Bahá'u'lláh,* p. 29).

**Jeremiah**, generally dated between 627 and 480 BC, foretells judgment against Judah and Jerusalem, curses those who do not heed the Covenant, laments the tragedy of invasion, and foretells ultimate salvation through the Lord of Hosts (see O'Connor, pp. 487–90). Bahá'u'lláh cites Jeremiah's prophecies about the "greatness of the Day" of the Lord (see Epistle to the Son of the Wolf, p. 144).

**Lamentations**, generally dated to about 587 BC, is a collection of five poetic laments mourning the fall of Jerusalem during the months and years following the destruction of the Temple (see Joyce, pp. 528–29).

**Ezekiel** dates itself to 593–571 BC in Babylon after the exile. It presents seven graphic visions of the prophet Ezekiel. Themes are oracles of destruction against Judah and Jerusalem caused by Judah's pride, prophecies against foreign nations, and hope for the future through the glory of God (see Galambush, pp. 533–37). Ezekiel is cited in the Bahá'í Writings as foretelling the exile travels of Bahá'u'lláh as well as the significance of 'Akká (see Shoghi Effendi, *God Passes By,* p. 291).

**Daniel** contains many independent stories that suggest a long history of composition and editorial expansion. Most scholars believe that references in the later chapters indicate it reached its present form by about 150 BC. Chapters 1–6 tell a story of the prophet Daniel surviving the siege of Jerusalem, being exiled to Babylon, and rising to a high position in the royal court. The last six chapters present prophetic visions about short-term political events as well as prophecies of the time of the end (see Davies, pp. 561–70). In the Bahá'í Writings, Daniel's end-times prophecies are noted as significant in the Christian, Islamic, and Bahá'í Revelations (see 'Abdu'l-Bahá, *Some Answered Questions,* no. 10:1–22).

**Hosea** relays prophecies regarding circumstances in the northern kingdom of Israel from about 787 to 722 BC. An allegorical story of Hosea's marriage to an unfaithful wife serves as a warning of what would come as a result of the Israelites' unfaithfulness to God. It also carries a message of repentance and restoration (see Day, pp. 571–72). The book is remembered in the Bahá'í Writings for its long-range prophecy of "a door of hope" which was identified by Shoghi Effendi as "'Akká, itself" (Shoghi Effendi, *God Passes By*, p. 291).

**Joel** is a nonhistorical document, so it is difficult to date. Theories regarding its date of composition range from 620 to 350 BC. The book notes a recent plague of locusts and equates that devastation with the destruction that precedes renewal at the coming of the day of the Lord (see Keller, p. 579). The Book of Joel is remembered in the Bahá'í Writings for prophecies concerning the day of the Lord (see Bahá'u'lláh, Epistle to the Son of the Wolf, p. 143).

**Amos** dates itself to the eighth century BC, prior to Assyria's conquest of Israel, but may be a post-exilic work (sixth to the fourth century BC). It denounces the social evils prevalent in the northern kingdom of Israel, warns of judgment to come, and gives assurance of a future salvation (see Dines, pp. 581–82). Amos is cited in the Bahá'í Writings for foretelling the appearance of the Manifestation of God on "the top of Carmel" (Bahá'u'lláh, Epistle to the Son of the Wolf, p. 145).

**Obadiah** is a nonhistorical document, so it is difficult to date. Theories regarding the date of its composition range from the ninth to the sixth century BC. It is the shortest book of the Old Testament, consisting of only twenty-one verses. In it, Obadiah chastises the nation of Edom for its superior attitude over Israel and warns of judgment to come in the day of the Lord (see Mason, pp. 590–91).

**Jonah** tells a story of the prophet Jonah, who, according to 2 Kings 14:23–27, was active in the northern kingdom of Israel at the time of Jeroboam II (786–746 BC), indicating that the text was probably written in the post-exilic period (538–332 BC). The book is unique in that, instead of proclaiming oracles, it tells a story of the prophet's adventures: upon receiving a divine mandate to go to Nineveh and preach against its corruption, Jonah tries to avoid his assignment, is swallowed by "a great fish" (1:17), and finally arises obedient to God after three days. Although successful in his mission, God rebukes Jonah for his anger (see Southwell, pp. 593–94). In His "Ode of the Dove," Bahá'u'lláh includes a poetic reference to this story when He mentions Jonah's urgent flight (see Shoghi Effendi, *God Passes By*, p. 191).

**Micah** includes writings that are generally dated from the late eighth to the sixth century BC, from the time of the fall of the northern kingdom of Israel to the Babylonian captivity. The book declares judgment on Judah and Jerusalem, condemns false prophets, and foretells restoration through the birth of a ruler out of Bethlehem (see Williamson, pp. 595–97). Bahá'í scholars have noted Micah's prophecies concerning the day of restoration—when "he shall come even to thee from Assyria, and from the fortified cities, and from the fortress even to the river, and from sea to sea, and from mountain to mountain" (Micah 7:12)—as foretelling the exile travels of Bahá'u'lláh (see Taherzadeh, p. 1).

**Nahum** celebrates the fall of the Assyrian city of Nineveh (612 BC) in a language of violent revenge. The final edited form is generally thought to be post-exilic (see O'Brien, p. 599).

**Habakkuk**, generally dated to about 600 BC, presents a dialogue between Habakkuk and God in which Habakkuk questions the suffering of the righteous. God's response to Habakkuk emphasizes the widespread consequences of corruption. The book closes with Habakkuk's prayer of praise and faith (see Gowan, pp. 601–2).

**Zephaniah** is self-dated to the time of King Josiah, about 640–609 BC, but many scholars believe that it was probably finished in post-exilic times. The book criticizes the political and religious establishment of Judah and Jerusalem, warns of God's judgment, and points to future salvation (see Mason, pp. 604–6). The book's prophecies concerning the "day of Jehovah" are mentioned in the Bahá'í Writings (see Shoghi Effendi, *God Passes By*, p. 147).

**Haggai** is self-dated to the time of Darius, about 520 BC, during the Persian Period. It focuses on ritual purification, rebuilding and rededication of the Second Temple, and the special role of the House of David in the future (Peterson, pp. 607–10). The Book of Haggai is mentioned in the Bahá'í Writings for its prophecies regarding the "Desire of all nations" (Shoghi Effendi citing Haggai 2:7, *God Passes By*, p. 146).

**Zachariah** is self-dated to the time of Darius, about 520 BC. The book is generally understood as two manuscripts: "First" or "Proto-Zachariah," including chapters 1–8, and "Second Zachariah," including chapters 9–14. It focuses on the restoration of Jerusalem, the hopes of Judah and Israel, and the cosmic day of the Lord (see Larkin, pp. 610–15). The Book of Zachariah is mentioned in the Bahá'í Writings for prophecy regarding the "Branch" Who "shall grow up out of His place," and "shall build the Temple of the Lord" (Shoghi Effendi, citing Zachariah 6:12, *God Passes By,* p. 146).

**Malachi,** commonly dated to the early fifth century BC, is a presentation of six complaints, which state the fears of the people. In response, God reproves the people, stresses His trustworthiness, and promises healing life to the faithful. The last line foretells the coming of Elijah before the day of the Lord, a prophecy that is referenced in the New Testament story of John the Baptist (see Rogerson, p. 615). The Bahá'í Writings note the fulfillment of Malachi's prophecy concerning the return of Elijah before the Messiah (see 'Abdu'l-Bahá, *Some Answered Questions,* no. 10.8) as well as the fulfillment of his prophecies concerning "the great and dreadful day of the Lord" when "the Sun of Righteousness" will "arise, with healing in His wings" (Shoghi Effendi, citing Malachi 4:2 and 4:5, *God Passes By,* p. 147).

All of the prophets represented in the Books of Prophecy are "lesser prophets."

# TOPICS FROM THE BOOKS
# OF PROPHECY

## LAMENTING THE HOLY LAND

The Book of Lamentations is a distinct book in the category of prophetic books because, instead of looking to the future, it primarily mourns the past. Its focus is the destruction of Judah, Jerusalem, and the Temple by the Babylonians in the sixth century BC, the suffering caused by that invasion, and the subsequent exile of many Israelites to Babylonia:

> The LORD gave full vent to his wrath; he poured out his hot anger, and kindled a fire in Zion that consumed its foundations. The kings of the earth did not believe, nor did any of the inhabitants of the world, that foe or enemy could enter the gates of Jerusalem. (Lamentations 4:11–12)

Concerning Jerusalem, there has been much to lament. Violence has characterized its history. Over the past four millennia there have been over 118 separate battles, "conflicts that ranged from local religious struggles to strategic military campaigns and that embraced everything in between. Jerusalem has been destroyed completely at least twice, besieged twenty-three times, attacked an additional fifty-two times, and captured and recaptured forty-four times" (Cline, 2004, p 2). Since the siege of Jerusalem by the Babylonians, the area has been under numerous rulers: the Roman, Byzantine, and Sassanian Empires; the Latin Crusader State; a succession of at least nine Muslim Dynasties; and the British Empire.

"It has been the scene of twenty revolts and innumerable riots, has had at least five separate periods of violent terrorist attacks during the past century, and has only changed hands completely peacefully twice in the past four thousand years" (Cline, 2004, p. 2).

Jerusalem contains the holy sites of three world-religions: it is an important site of Judaism's religious and political history (including Solomon's Temple); it holds one of Islam's most sacred shrines (Al-Aqsa Mosque); and it is one of the spiritual centers of Christianity (a site of Christ's ministry and the vicinity of the crucifixion). Today Jerusalem is claimed as the capital city of both the State of Israel and the State of Palestine. Conflict between Israel and Palestine continues.

### DOES JERUSALEM CONTAIN HOLY PLACES OF THE BAHÁ'Í FAITH?

Bahá'ís hold Jewish, Christian, and Muslim sites in reverence, but there are no specifically Bahá'í holy sites in Jerusalem. There are Bahá'í holy places in other locations in Israel.

### WHERE ARE THE BAHÁ'Í HOLY PLACES IN ISRAEL?

'Akká, Israel, where Bahá'u'lláh lived for twenty-four years, contains many Bahá'í holy places. The barracks in which Bahá'u'lláh was imprisoned, and the houses in which He lived after His imprisonment was eased, are all sites of pilgrimage for Bahá'ís. 'Akká is also the site of Bahá'u'lláh's burial shrine, the point to which all Bahá'ís turn when saying obligatory prayers.

Haifa, Israel contains many Bahá'í holy places and is also a center of Bahá'í pilgrimage because it is the site of the burial shrines of both the Báb, the Herald of the Bahá'í Faith, and 'Abdu'l-Bahá, the Center of the Covenant. Mount Carmel in Haifa is also the permanent seat of the Bahá'í world administrative body, the Universal House of Justice, by mandate of Bahá'u'lláh.

### HOW DO BAHÁ'ÍS RELATE TO THE POLITICAL ISSUES SURROUNDING JERUSALEM AND ISRAEL?

Being strictly nonpartisan, Bahá'ís refrain from taking sides but, instead, engage in social discourse related to principles that are attractive to all hearts and, in this way, work toward justice and peace. Shoghi Effendi explains this view in his letter to the United Nations Special Committee on Palestine. Background: In July 1947 Shoghi Effendi (the Guardian of the Faith) received a letter from the chairman of the United Nations Special Committee on Palestine requesting a statement on the relationship that the Bahá'í Faith had to the (then) British Mandate of Palestine, and the Bahá'í opinion toward any future changes in the status of the country. He responded with a letter entitled, "The Faith of Bahá'u'lláh: A World Religion." This is an excerpt:

> Your kind letter of July 9th reached me and I wish to thank you for affording me the opportunity of presenting to you and your esteemed colleagues a statement of the relationship which the Bahá'í Faith has to Palestine and our attitude towards any future changes in the status of this sacred and much disputed land. . . . .
>
> The position of the Bahá'ís in this country is in a certain measure unique; whereas Jerusalem is the spiritual center of Christendom it is not the administrative center of either the Church of Rome or any other Christian denomination. Likewise although it is regarded by Moslems as the spot where one of its most sacred shrines is situated, the Holy Sites of the Mohamedam Faith, and the center of its pilgrimages, are to be found in Arabia, not in Palestine. The Jews alone offer somewhat of a parallel to the attachment which the Bahá'ís have for this country inasmuch as Jerusalem holds the remains of their Holy Temple and was the seat of both the religious and political institutions associated with their past history. But even their case differs in one respect from that of the Bahá'ís, for it is in the soil of Palestine that the three central figures of our religion are buried, and it is not only the center of Bahá'í pilgrimages from all over the world but also the permanent seat of our Administrative Order, of which I have the honor to be the Head.
>
> The Bahá'í Faith is entirely non-political and we neither take sides in the present tragic dispute going on over the future of the Holy Land and its peoples nor have we any statement to make or advice to give as to what the nature of the political future of this country should be. Our aim is the establishment of universal peace in this world and our desire to see justice prevail in every domain of human society, including the domain of politics. As many of

the adherents of our Faith are of Jewish and Moslem extraction we have no prejudice towards either of these groups and are most anxious to reconcile them for their mutual benefit and for the good of the country.

. . . May I take this opportunity of assuring you of my deep appreciation of the spirit in which you and your colleagues have conducted your investigations into the troubled conditions of this Sacred Land. I trust and pray that the outcome of your deliberations will produce an equitable and speedy solution of the very thorny problems which have arisen in Palestine. Yours faithfully, (Signed) Shoghi Rabbani, Haifa, Palestine. (Shoghi Effendi, in *The Guardian of the Bahá'í Faith*, p. 133)

To date, the Bahá'í holy places in 'Akká and Haifa remain points of pilgrimage for Bahá'ís, and the Universal House of Justice, which is the governing body of the worldwide Bahá'í community, continues to operate from Haifa on Mount Carmel.

## LESSER PROPHETS

All of the prophets in the Books of Prophecy are "lesser prophets." In the Bahá'í Writings, "Prophet" is one of the titles for the Manifestation of God; however, there is a clear distinction between the station of a lesser prophet and that of the independent Prophets: the Manifestations of God. Although both are specially inspired, the Manifestation of God receives inspiration directly from the Reality of God, brings forth new laws, and starts a new religion. In contrast, the lesser prophets receive inspiration from the Manifestation of God (not directly from the Reality of God), do not bring forth new laws, and do not start new religions. The lesser prophets follow, and are guided by, the Manifestation:

Prophets are in general of two kinds. Some are independent Prophets Who are followed, while others are not independent and are themselves followers.

The independent Prophets are each the Author of a divine religion and the Founder of a new Dispensation. At Their advent the world is clothed in a new attire, a new religion is established, and a new Book revealed. These Prophets acquire the outpouring grace of the divine Reality without an intermediary. Their radiance is an essential radiance like that of the sun, which is luminous in and of itself and whose luminosity is an essential requirement rather than being acquired from another star: They are like the sun and not the moon. These Daysprings of the morn of Divine Unity are the fountainheads of divine grace and the mirrors of the Essence of Reality.

The other kind of Prophets are followers and promulgators, for their station is contingent rather than independent. They acquire divine grace from the independent Prophets and seek the light of guidance from the reality of universal prophethood. They are like the moon, which is not luminous and radiant in and of itself but which receives its light from the sun. ('Abdu'l-Bahá, *Some Answered Questions,* no. 43.2–4)

The lesser prophets are followers and promulgators of the Manifestation of God:

The universal Prophets Who have appeared independently include Abraham, Moses, Christ, Muhammad, the Báb and Bahá'u'lláh. The second kind, which consists of followers and promulgators, includes Solomon, David, Isaiah, Jeremiah, and Ezekiel. ('Abdu'l-Bahá, *Some Answered Questions,* no. 43.5)

### HOW MUCH DIFFERENCE IS THERE BETWEEN THE STATION OF THE MANIFESTATION OF GOD AND THE LESSER PROPHETS?

An "infinite difference" separates the Manifestations of God and the lesser prophets:

Pause then to reflect upon the difference between the virtues and perfections of Christ and the splendours and effulgences of

Bahá'u'lláh, on the one hand, and the virtues of the Prophets of the House of Israel, such as Ezekiel or Samuel, on the other. All were the recipients of divine revelation, but between them there is an immeasurable distance. ('Abdu'l-Bahá, *Some Answered Questions,* no. 37.13)

The Manifestation is to a lesser prophet as the sun is to the moon.

### CAN A LESSER PROPHET PROGRESS TO BECOME A MANIFESTATION OF GOD?

Because a lesser prophet is in an altogether different spiritual station than a Manifestation of God, a lesser prophet can never become a Manifestation of God:

> . . . every created thing has been assigned a degree which it can in no wise overpass. So he who occupies the degree of servitude, no matter how far he may progress and acquire endless perfections, can never reach the degree of divine Lordship. . . . .
>
> For example, Peter cannot become Christ. At most, he can attain infinite perfections in the degrees of servitude, for every existing reality is capable of progress. ('Abdu'l-Bahá, *Some Answered Questions,* no. 62.2–3)

### HOW DOES THE STATION OF A LESSER PROPHET COMPARE WITH THE GENERALITY OF MANKIND?

Lesser prophets occupy a different station from the generality of mankind:

> The Prophets "regarded as one and the same person" include the lesser Prophets as well, and not merely those who bring a "Book." The station is different, but They are Prophets and Their nature thus different from that of ours. (Shoghi Effendi, *Directives from the Guardian,* p. 58)

As the nature of the Manifestation of God is ultimately a mystery, so is the nature of lesser prophets. In one sense, the lesser prophets are one with the Manifestation. At the same time, the lesser prophets occupy a lower station than the Manifestations and a different station from ours.

## DID THE LESSER PROPHETS COME FROM THE RANKS OF THE LEARNED AND ACCOMPLISHED?

Worldly achievement has never been a criterion for prophethood. The lesser prophets of the Bible were often bereft of education or accomplishment. The greatness of the prophets has always been due to the power of the Holy Spirit and not attributed to worldly position:

> The Prophets of God have not all graduated in the schools of learned philosophy; indeed they were often men of humble birth, to all appearance ignorant, unknown men of no importance in the eyes of the world; sometimes even lacking the knowledge of reading and writing.
>
> That which raised these great ones above men, and by which they were able to become Teachers of the truth, was the power of the Holy Spirit. Their influence on humanity, by virtue of this mighty inspiration, was great and penetrating.
>
> . . . The prophets of Judah and Israel, Elijah, Jeremiah, Isaiah and Ezekiel, were humble men, as were also the apostles of Jesus Christ. ('Abdu'l-Bahá, *Paris Talks,* no. 51.2–3, 5)

## CORRUPTION

One of the evils that the prophets warn against is the corruption of religious leaders—those who claim the role of prophethood or priest but in reality cater to the rich, prey on their followers, and lead communities astray. For example, Ezekiel describes something of the corruption of religious leaders of his time:

> The word of the LORD came to me: Mortal, say to it: You are a land that is not cleansed, not rained upon in the day of indignation. . . . Its priests have done violence to my teaching and have profaned my

holy things; they have made no distinction between the holy and
the common, neither have they taught the difference between the
unclean and the clean, and they have disregarded my sabbaths, so
that I am profaned among them. (Ezekiel 22:23–24, 26)

Similar alarms concerning corrupt priests and prophets are voiced
by other prophets (Jeremiah 14, 23; Zechariah 10, Hosea 6; Isaiah 9),
repeated in the New Testament (Matthew 7; Mark 13; 1 John 4; 2 Peter
2; Revelation 16), and are stated anew in the Bahá'í Writings:

Some heedless souls roam the lands in the name of God, actively
engaged in ruining His Cause, and call it promoting and teaching
the Word of God. (Bahá'u'lláh, *Tablets of Bahá'u'lláh,* p. 58)

## WHAT MOTIVATES
## FALSE RELIGIOUS LEADERS?

The origin of corruption is ignorance and/or lust for power:

Leaders of religion, in every age, have hindered their people from
attaining the shores of eternal salvation, inasmuch as they held
the reins of authority in their mighty grasp. Some for the lust of
leadership, others through want of knowledge and understanding,
have been the cause of the deprivation of the people. (Bahá'u'lláh,
The Kitáb-i-Íqán, ¶15)

## HOW DOES THE OLD TESTAMENT DISTINGUISH BETWEEN
## TRUE AND FALSE PROPHETS?

According to Ezekiel 22:25–31 (cited at the beginning of this section),
characteristics of corrupt religious leaders include flattering the rich, violating the Laws of God, teaching false dogmas, profane acts, and lying.
In addition, false prophets foretell things that do not come to pass:

You may say to yourself, "How can we recognize a word that the
LORD has not spoken?" If a prophet speaks in the name of the LORD
but the thing does not take place or prove true, it is a word that the
LORD has not spoken. The prophet has spoken it presumptuously;
do not be frightened by it. (Deuteronomy 18:21–22)

## WHAT IS THE OUTCOME OF FOLLOWING
## CORRUPT RELIGIOUS LEADERS?

Following false religious leaders corrodes the foundations of religion and leads to ungodliness, chaos, and confusion:

Religion is, verily, the chief instrument for the establishment of order in the world, and of tranquility amongst its peoples. The weakening of the pillars of religion hath strengthened the foolish, and emboldened them, and made them more arrogant. Verily I say: The greater the decline of religion, the more grievous the waywardness of the ungodly. This cannot but lead in the end to chaos and confusion. (Bahá'u'lláh, Epistle to the Son of the Wolf, p. 27)

## WHAT IS A PROTECTION AGAINST RELIGIOUS CORRUPTION?

The repeated appearances of the Manifestation of God are a sure protection against religious corruption as the Manifestation corrects false beliefs that arise from human error:

The divine Manifestations have been iconoclastic in Their teachings, uprooting error, destroying false religious beliefs and summoning mankind anew to the fundamental oneness of God. ('Abdu'l-Bahá, *The Promulgation of Universal Peace*, p. 213)

Another protection against false prophets is to exercise independent investigation of truth instead of blindly following another person:

God has not intended man to imitate blindly his fathers and ancestors. He has endowed him with mind, or the faculty of reasoning, by the exercise of which he is to investigate and discover the truth, and that which he finds real and true he must accept. He must not be an imitator or blind follower of any soul. He must not rely implicitly upon the opinion of any man without investigation; nay, each soul must seek intelligently and independently, arriving at a real conclusion and bound only by that reality. The greatest cause of bereavement and disheartening in the world of humanity is ignorance based upon blind imitation. ('Abdu'l-Bahá, *The Promulgation of Universal Peace*, p. 406)

Blind imitation is the greatest cause of ignorance and the biggest promoter of false teachings.

## NATURE OF PROPHETIC VISIONS

Prophetic visions are not imaginations—they are real truths discovered in the spiritual realm:

> The visions of the Prophets are not dreams but true spiritual disclosures. Thus when they say, "I saw someone in such a form, and I spoke such words, and he gave such a reply," this vision takes place in a state of wakefulness and not in the realm of sleep. It is a spiritual discovery that is expressed in the form of a vision. ('Abdu'l-Bahá, *Some Answered Questions*, no. 71.4)

### WHERE DO PROPHETIC VISIONS COME FROM?

Prophetic visions come from spiritual interactions outside of time and place—knowledge gleaned without the use of the five senses. As scientific discoveries are made in the physical world, spiritual discoveries and communications happen in the spiritual world:

> Know, therefore, that the human reality encompasses the realities of all things and discovers their true nature, their properties, and their mysteries. For instance, all the existing crafts, inventions, sciences, and branches of learning have been discovered by the human reality. At one time they were all hidden and concealed mysteries, but the reality of man gradually discovered them and brought them forth from the invisible world into the visible realm. . . . These true disclosures which conform to reality are similar to visions—which consist in spiritual understanding, heavenly inspiration, and the close communion of human spirits—and thus the recipient will say that he saw, or said, or heard such a thing.
>
> It is therefore clear that the spirit has powerful perceptions that are not mediated by the organs of the five sense, such as the eyes and ears. ('Abdu'l-Bahá, *Some Answered Questions*, no. 71.6–7)

Like scientific discoveries, prophetic visions are hidden truths that become revealed.

## DO THE VISIONS OF THE PROPHETS CAUSE THINGS TO HAPPEN?

The visions of the prophets do not make things happen:

The knowledge of a thing is not the cause of its occurrence; for the essential knowledge of God encompasses the realities of all things both before and after they come to exist, but it is not the cause of their existence. This is an expression of the perfection of God.

As to the pronouncements which, through divine revelation, have issued from the Prophets regarding the advent of the Promised One of the Torah, these likewise were not the cause of Christ's appearance. But the hidden mysteries of the days to come were revealed to the Prophets, who thus became acquainted with future events and who proclaimed them in turn. This knowledge and proclamation were not the cause of the occurrence of these events. For instance, tonight everyone knows that in seven hours the sun will rise, but this common knowledge does not cause the appearance and rising of the sun. ('Abdu'l-Bahá, *Some Answered Questions,* no. 35.2–3)

Foreknowledge of a happening does not cause it. Because the knowledge of God encompasses the past, present, and future, those with access to some of that knowledge may tell of things to come—but this knowledge, like our expectation of a sunrise, does not make that event occur.

## LANGUAGE OF PROPHECY

Prophetic visions are communicated in the twofold language of Scripture: an "unveiled" language that states literal truths in a straightforward manner, and a "veiled" language that conveys truths embedded in symbolism.

### WHAT IS AN EXAMPLE OF AN "UNVEILED" PROPHECY?

An example of an unveiled prophecy is Jeremiah's warning of the imminent fall of Judah and the enslavement of the people:

And when your people say, "Why has the LORD our God done all these things to us?" you shall say to them, "As you have forsaken me and served foreign gods in your land, so you shall serve strangers in a land that is not yours." (Jeremiah 5:18–19)

That prophecy was literally fulfilled during Jeremiah's lifetime when Judah was invaded by Babylonia (Jeremiah 39).

### WHAT IS AN EXAMPLE OF A "VEILED" PROPHECY?

An example of a veiled prophecy is Isaiah's statement that a "rod out of the stem of Jesse" (Isaiah 11:1) would bring a reign of peace during which even the animals would cease to be at enmity:

The wolf shall live with the lamb, the leopard shall lie down with the kid, the calf and the young lion and the fatling together, and a little child shall lead them. (Isaiah 11:6)

That prophecy was fulfilled with the coming of Christ, but in a veiled or symbolic fashion: the animals symbolize disparate people and interests that came together in peace through the teachings of Christ. This is also an example of an archetypal prophecy.

### HOW ARE PROPHECIES ARCHETYPAL?

Any prophecy can be considered archetypal if it points to eternal spiritual truth. Isaiah's prophecy concerning the wolf and the lamb is archetypal because it is always true that the coming of a Manifestation of God brings a greater measure of unity to the world. In this sense, prophecies may be fulfilled numerable times.

### DO THE LESSER PROPHETS INTERPRET THEIR OWN VEILED PROPHECIES?

Although the lesser prophets experience prophetic visions, they do not necessarily interpret them. For example, consider the prophecies of Daniel about the "latter days" (Daniel 10:1–12:6). Daniel received many visions of things to come but when he inquired as to the meanings of these visions he was told that the words were "sealed till the time of the end":

I heard but I could not understand; so I said, "My LORD, what shall be the outcome of these things?" He said, "Go your way, Daniel, for the words are to remain secret and sealed until the time of the end." (Daniel 12:8–9)

In this case, as in others, the symbolic meaning is hidden even from the prophet who had the vision.

## DAY OF THE LORD

The day of the Lord is repeatedly foretold in the Books of Prophecy; for example, Zephaniah, Joel, and Malachi warn:

Hold thy peace at the presence of the LORD God: for the day of the LORD is at hand: for the LORD hath prepared a sacrifice, he hath bid his guests. (Zephaniah 1:7)

Multitudes, multitudes, in the valley of decision! For the day of the LORD is near in the valley of decision. (Joel 3:14)

Lo, I will send you the prophet Elijah before the great and terrible day of the LORD comes. (Malachi 4:5)

### WHAT IS THE DAY OF THE LORD?

In one sense, the day of the Lord refers to the entire Dispensation of any Manifestation of God. Consequently, we see references to the "day of Abraham," the "day of Moses," and so forth:

In the time of the First Manifestation the Primal Will appeared in Adam; in the day of Noah It became known in Noah; in the day of Abraham in Him; and so in the day of Moses; the day of Jesus; the day of Muhammad, the Apostle of God; the day of the "Point of the Bayán"; the day of Him Whom God shall make manifest; and the day of the One Who will appear after Him Whom God shall make manifest. (The Báb, *Selections from the Writings of the Báb,* no. 4.10.6)

And, more specific to the biblical prophecies, the coming of the day of the Lord refers to the initial stages of a Dispensation when a new Manifestation of God appears on the earth, old laws are abrogated, and new laws are established.

### WHAT DOES A NEW DAY OF THE LORD BRING?
A new day of the Lord brings spiritual revival:

When the holy, divine Manifestations or Prophets appear in the world, a cycle of radiance, an age of mercy dawns. Everything is renewed. Minds, hearts and all human forces are reformed, perfections are quickened, sciences, discoveries and investigations are stimulated afresh, and everything appertaining to the virtues of the human world is revitalized. ('Abdu'l-Bahá, *The Promulgation of Universal Peace,* p. 387)

The image of light inherent in the term "day of the Lord" is fitting because the new Manifestation of God brings a greater degree of spiritual illumination:

Then spake Jesus again unto them, saying I am the light of the world: he that followeth me shall not walk in darkness, but shall have the light of life. (John 8:12)

Although the coming of the Lord is a time of light and revitalization, most prophecies describe it as a day of oppression and darkness. For example, the prophets Joel, Ezekiel, and Zephaniah warn:

Alas for the day! For the day of the LORD is at hand, and as destruction from the Almighty it comes. (Joel 1:15)

Mortal, prophesy, and say, Thus says the LORD GOD: Wail, "Alas for the day!" For a day is near, the day of the LORD is near; it will be a day of clouds, a time of doom for the nations. (Ezekiel 30:2–3)

The great day of the LORD is near, near and hastening fast; the sound of the day of the LORD is bitter, the warrior cries aloud there.

That day will be a day of wrath, a day of distress and anguish, a day of ruin and devastation, a day of darkness and gloom, a day of clouds and thick darkness, . . . (Zephaniah 1:14–16)

## WHY IS THE COMING OF THE DAY OF THE LORD A TIME OF OPPRESSION AND DARKNESS?

The coming of the day of the Lord is a time of oppression and darkness because the human condition that calls for a return of the Manifestation is spiritual winter—a time when many souls have lost touch with the fundamental basis of religion:

> . . . when men shall become oppressed and afflicted, the time when the lingering traces of the Sun of Truth and the fruit of the Tree of knowledge and wisdom will have vanished from the midst of men, when the reins of mankind will have fallen into the grasp of the foolish and ignorant, when the portals of divine unity and understanding—the essential and highest purpose in creation—will have been closed, when certain knowledge will have given way to idle fancy, and corruption will have usurped the station of righteousness. (Bahá'u'lláh, The Kitáb-i-Íqán, ¶28)

In the darkness of spiritual winter—the condition that is *required* for the appearance of the Manifestation of God—souls do not know where to find truth and that is the greatest oppression:

> What "oppression" is more grievous than that a soul seeking the truth, and wishing to attain unto the knowledge of God, should know not where to go for it and from whom to seek it? For opinions have sorely differed, and the ways unto the attainment of God have multiplied. This "oppression" is the essential feature of every Revelation. Unless it cometh to pass, the Sun of Truth will not be made manifest. For the break of the morn of divine guidance must needs follow the darkness of the night of error. For this reason, in all chronicles and traditions reference hath been made unto these things, namely that iniquity shall cover the surface of the earth and darkness shall envelop mankind. (Bahá'u'lláh, The Kitáb-i-Íqán, ¶29)

Although the light of the new Revelation is as clear as lightning, in spiritual winter most people have their eyes closed. The result is rejection and oppression of the Manifestation:

> For as the lightning flashes and lights up the sky from one side to the other, so will the Son of Man be in his day. But first he must endure much suffering and be rejected by this generation. Just as it was in the days of Noah, so too it will be in the days of the Son of Man. (Luke 17:24–26)

The truth of the Revelation, however, becomes known over time as it shines from the steadfast followers of the Light:

> In the day of His Highness Christ, the grandeur and majesty of their Holiness the Apostles, was not known. After three-hundred years the loftiness of the station and the exaltation of their attainment became manifest. ('Abdu'l-Bahá, *Tablets of 'Abdu'l-Bahá*, vol. 3, p. 531)

## WHY IS THE COMING OF THE DAY OF THE LORD CHARACTERIZED BY WOE?

The day of the Lord is characterized by woe because it is also Judgment Day. Those who do not recognize the Light or who contend with the teachings of the Manifestation of God will, sooner or later, be called to account:

> It is therefore evident then that the day of woe is the day of the Lord; for in that day woe is upon the heedless, the sinners, and the ignorant. ('Abdu'l-Bahá, *Some Answered Questions*, no. 11.34)

## HAVE THE DAY OF THE LORD PROPHECIES BEEN FULFILLED?

From the point of view of the Bahá'í Faith, the Old Testament prophecies of the coming of the day of the Lord have been fulfilled in the Dispensations of Christ, Muhammad, the Báb, and, in this Dispensation, Bahá'u'lláh. Bahá'u'lláh states:

> Ring out the Bell, inasmuch as the Day of the Lord hath shone forth and the Beauty of the All-Glorious is established upon His

holy and resplendent Throne. (Bahá'u'lláh, cited in Taherzadeh, *The Revelation of Bahá'u'lláh, Vol. 2*, p. 19)

## SUN, MOON, AND STARS

Prophecies concerning the day of the Lord often indicate unusual celestial phenomenon such as the darkening of the sun, moon, and stars. For example:

> See, the day of the LORD comes, cruel, with wrath and fierce anger, to make the earth a desolation, and to destroy its sinners from it. For the stars of the heavens and their constellations will not give their light; the sun will be dark at its rising, and the moon will not shed its light. (Isaiah 13:9–10)

### WHAT DOES DARKENING OF THE "SUN, MOON, AND STARS" IN THE DAY OF THE LORD MEAN?

These words have numerous meanings:

> By the terms "sun" and "moon," mentioned in the Writings of the Prophets of God, is not meant solely the sun and moon of the visible universe. Nay rather, manifold are the meanings they have intended for these terms. In every instance they have attached to them a particular significance. (Bahá'u'lláh, The Kitáb-i-Íqán, ¶31)

As the sun, moon, and stars provide light and navigational guidance, they are excellent symbols for spiritual leadership. The laws of God, and the religious leaders who teach these laws, offer light in the form of spiritual direction. If religious leaders become spiritually illumined in the new Revelation, they will reflect the light of God as the moon reflects the sun, and they will shine like stars. Otherwise, they will be as if "darkened":

> . . . by these terms is intended the divines of the former Dispensation, who live in the days of the subsequent Revelations, and

who hold the reins of religion in their grasp. If these divines be illumined by the light of the latter Revelation they will be acceptable unto God, and will shine with a light everlasting. Otherwise, they will be declared as darkened, even though to outward seeming they be leaders of men, inasmuch as belief and unbelief, guidance and error, felicity and misery, light and darkness, are all dependent upon the sanction of Him Who is the Daystar of Truth. (Bahá'u'lláh, The Kitáb-i-Íqán, ¶34)

The laws of previous Manifestations can also become like darkened suns when, in spiritual winter, they cease to exert their influence:

> It is unquestionable that in every succeeding Revelation the "sun" and "moon" of the teachings, laws, commandments, and prohibitions which have been established in the preceding Dispensation, and which have overshadowed the people of that age, become darkened, that is, are exhausted, and cease to exert their influence. (Bahá'u'lláh, The Kitáb-i-Íqán, ¶42)

With the appearance of a new Manifestation, the social laws of the previous Dispensation are altered or annulled according to the requirements of the times. In this way, the social laws of the previous Manifestation of God are "darkened":

> Hence, it is clear and manifest that by the words "the sun shall be darkened, and the moon shall not give her light, and the stars shall fall from heaven" is intended . . . the annulment of laws firmly established by divine Revelation, all of which, in symbolic language, have been foreshadowed by the Manifestation of God. (Bahá'u'lláh, The Kitáb-i-Íqán, ¶41)

This intentional darkening of the no longer essential social laws of the previous Manifestation by the new Revelation is not a bad thing. It is what keeps social laws relevant.

Another meaning of darkened light is that with a new Revelation every other luminary of guidance, secular or spiritual, fades in comparison to the Word of God just as the stars fade upon the rising of the sun:

It is evident and manifest unto every discerning observer that even as the light of the star fadeth before the effulgent splendour of the sun, so doth the luminary of earthly knowledge, of wisdom, and understanding vanish into nothingness when brought face to face with the resplendent glories of the Sun of Truth, the Daystar of divine enlightenment. (Bahá'u'lláh, The Kitáb-i-Íqán, ¶35)

All of the signs of the darkening of the sun, moon, and stars—the lack of spiritual perception in religious leaders, inattention to the laws of the previous Dispensation, the annulment of past social laws, and the fading of other luminaries in comparison to the teachings of the Manifestation—accompany the day of the Lord.

## CLOUDS

Another recurring theme in prophecy regarding the day of the Lord is the appearance of dark clouds. For example:

Blow the trumpet in Zion; sound the alarm on my holy mountain! Let all the inhabitants of the land tremble, for the day of the LORD is coming, it is near—a day of darkness and gloom, a day of clouds and thick darkness! (Joel 2:1–2)

### WHAT DO "CLOUDS" SYMBOLIZE?

The clouds referred to in prophecy are often symbolic of those things that interfere with people's recognition of a new Manifestation of God, such as change. The Manifestation of God brings change, and those changes, which always challenge the comfort-zones of the times, act as "clouds" or barriers through which the people cannot see the reality of the Word of God. These changes include new social laws, corrections to man-made dogmas, and the abolishment of popular rituals and traditions. Attachments to the old ways of doing things cloud spiritual perception:

It is evident that the changes brought about in every Dispensation constitute the dark clouds that intervene between the eye of man's understanding and the divine Luminary which shineth forth from the dayspring of the divine Essence. (Bahá'u'lláh, The Kitáb-i-Íqán, ¶81)

Another factor that acts as a cloud is the humble beginning of a new Revelation.

### HOW DOES THE HUMBLE BEGINNING
### OF A NEW REVELATION ACT AS A CLOUD?

Inasmuch as the changes brought about by a new Revelation do not serve the worldly interests of established religious institutions, it is common for those in authority to ignore or oppose the new teachings. In contrast, those who do have the eyes to see the new Revelation are often those who hold no worldly authority. Because most people prefer to follow established powers with notable worldly presence, the humble nature of those who follow the new Manifestation often serves as a barrier, or cloud, to others:

By the term "clouds" is meant those things that are contrary to the ways and desires of men. . . . These "clouds" signify, in one sense, . . . the exalting of the illiterate faithful above the learned opposers of the Faith. (Bahá'u'lláh, The Kitáb-i-Íqán, ¶79)

Another "cloud" is the human condition of the Manifestation of God.

### HOW IS THE HUMAN CONDITION OF THE
### MANIFESTATION OF GOD LIKE A "CLOUD"?

While possessing a higher spiritual station, the Manifestation of God enters the world as a human being with all the physical needs and limitations of a regular person. This can be a barrier to those who are expecting a mythical superhero appearance:

In another sense, they mean the appearance of that immortal Beauty in the image of mortal man, with such human limitations as eating and drinking, poverty and riches, glory and abasement, sleeping and waking, and such other things as cast doubt in the minds of men, and cause them to turn away. All such veils are symbolically referred to as "clouds." (Bahá'u'lláh, The Kitáb-i-Íqán, ¶79)

## WHEN HAVE THESE "CLOUDS" INTERFERED WITH THE RECOGNITION OF THE MANIFESTATION?

History shows that hereditary expectations, the reluctance of individuals to leave religious comfort zones, the human condition of the Manifestation, the humble nature of His followers, and other "clouds" have intervened between humanity and the Word of God in every Dispensation:

> Consider the past. How many, both high and low, have, at all times, yearningly awaited the advent of the Manifestations of God in the sanctified persons of His chosen Ones. How often have they expected His coming, how frequently have they prayed that the breeze of divine mercy might blow, and the promised Beauty step forth from behind the veil of concealment, and be made manifest to all the world. And whensoever the portals of grace did open, and the clouds of divine bounty did rain upon mankind, and the light of the Unseen did shine above the horizon of celestial might, they all denied Him, and turned away from His face—the face of God Himself. Refer ye, to verify this truth, to that which hath been recorded in every sacred Book. (Bahá'u'lláh, The Kitáb-i-Íqán, ¶3)

Like prophecies about the darkening of the sun, moon, and stars, prophecies foretelling "clouds" in the day of the Lord are archetypal in nature—they reoccur with every Dispensation.

## MESSIANIC EXPECTATIONS

Although not universally recognized, all of the prophecies regarding the Messiah—the Manifestation of God prophesied to appear after Moses—were fulfilled with the coming of Christ. The manner of their fulfillment offers insight into the language of prophecy. For example,

Messianic expectations include that the Messiah would come from an unknown place:

> Yet we know where this man is from; but when the Messiah comes, no one will know where he is from. (John 7:27)

The Messiah would sit upon the throne of David:

> For a child has been born for us, a son given to us; authority rests upon his shoulders; and he is named Wonderful Counselor, Mighty God, Everlasting Father, Prince of Peace. His authority shall grow continually, and there shall be endless peace for the throne of David and his kingdom. (Isaiah 9:6–7)

The Messiah would slay the wicked with a rod:

> But with righteousness he shall judge the poor, and decide with equity for the meek of the earth; he shall strike the earth with the rod of his mouth, and with the breath of his lips he shall kill the wicked. (Isaiah 11:4)

The Messiah would magnify the Law:

> The LORD is well pleased for his righteousness sake; he will magnify the law, and make it honourable. (Isaiah 42:21, KJV)

The Messiah would conquer the East and the West:

> But they shall swoop down on the backs of the Philistines in the west; together they shall plunder the people of the east. (Isaiah 11:14)

The Messiah would gather and glorify the chosen people:

> Do not fear, for I am with you; I will bring your offspring from the east, and from the west I will gather you; I will say to the north, "Give them up," and to the south, "Do not withhold; bring my

sons from far away and my daughters from the end of the earth."
(Isaiah 43:5–6)

And the Messiah would bring a reign of peace:

The wolf shall live with the lamb, the leopard shall lie down with
the kid, the calf and the lion and the fatling together, and a little
child shall lead them. (Isaiah 11:6)

To examine the symbolism in these expectations we will jump ahead
briefly to the New Testament to explore why many believed, and still
believe, that the prophecies were not fulfilled.

## WHY WAS CHRIST
### INITIALLY REJECTED
### AS THE MESSIAH BY MOST OF THE JEWS?

Christ was initially rejected as the Messiah largely because of literal
interpretation of the prophecies:

Moses and the prophets of Israel announced the advent of the
Messiah but expressed it in the language of symbols. When Christ
appeared, the Jews rejected Him, although they were expecting His
manifestation and in their temples and synagogues were crying and
lamenting, saying, "O God, hasten the coming of the Messiah!"
Why did they deny Him when He announced Himself? Because
they had followed ancestral forms and interpretations and were
blind to the reality of Christ. They had not perceived the inner
significances of the Holy Bible. They voiced their objections,
saying, "We are expecting Christ, but His coming is conditioned
upon certain fulfillments and prophetic announcements. Among
the signs of His appearance is one that He shall come from an
unknown place, whereas now this claimant of Messiahship has
come from Nazareth. We know his home, and we are acquainted
with his mother.

"Second, one of the signs or Messianic conditions is that His
scepter would be an iron rod, and this Christ has not even a
wooden staff.

"Third, He was to be seated upon the throne of David, whereas this Messianic king is in the utmost state of poverty and has not even a mat.

"Fourth, He was to conquer the East and the West. This person has not even conquered a village. How can he be the Messiah?

"Fifth, He was to promulgate the laws of the Bible. This one has not only failed to promulgate the laws of the Bible, but he has broken the law of the Sabbath.

"Sixth, the Messiah was to gather together all the Jews who were scattered in Palestine and restore them to honor and prestige, but this one has degraded the Jews instead of uplifting them.

"Seventh, during His sovereignty even the animals were to enjoy blessings and comfort, for according to the prophetic texts, He should establish peace to such a universal extent that the eagle and quail would live together, the lion and deer would feed in the same meadow, the wolf and lamb would lie down in the same pasture. In the human kingdom warfare was to cease entirely; spears would be turned into pruning hooks and swords into plowshares. Now we see in the day of this would-be Messiah such injustice prevails that even he himself is sacrificed. How could he be the promised Christ?"

And so they spoke infamous words regarding Him. ('Abdu'l-Bahá, *The Promulgation of Universal Peace,* p. 278)

Christ did not fulfill the Messianic prophecies literally, but spiritually.

### HOW WERE THE PROPHECIES SPIRITUALLY FULFILLED?

Christ appeared from the invisible realm of the spirit—an unknown place; He wielded the sword of the Word of God in His utterance; He was seated upon the spiritual throne of David; He confirmed the spiritual Reality of Moses and refined the social laws for greater relevance; He conquered hate in the East and the West with His law of love; and He brought many opposing people (wolves and lambs) together through the Gospel:

The purpose of the prophetic words was not the outward or literal meaning, but the inner symbolical significance. For example, it was announced that the Messiah was to come from an unknown place. This did not refer to the birthplace of the physical body of Jesus. It has reference to the reality of the Christ—that is to say, the Christ reality was to appear from the invisible realm—for the divine reality of Christ is holy and sanctified above place.

His sword was to be a sword of iron. This signified His tongue which should separate the true from the false and by which great sword of attack He would conquer the kingdoms of hearts. He did not conquer by the physical power of an iron rod; He conquered the East and the West by the sword of His utterance.

He was seated upon the throne of David, but His sovereignty was neither a Napoleonic sovereignty nor the vanishing dominion of a Pharaoh. The Christ Kingdom was everlasting, eternal in the heaven of the divine Will.

By His promulgating the laws of the Bible the reality of the law of Moses was meant. The Sinaitic law is the foundation of the reality of Christianity. Christ promulgated it and gave it higher, spiritual expression.

He conquered and subdued the East and West. His conquest was effected through the breaths of the Holy Spirit, which eliminated all boundaries and shone from all horizons.

In His day, according to prophecy, the wolf and the lamb were to drink from the same fountain. This was realized in Christ. The fountain referred to was the Gospel, from which the water of life gushes forth. The wolf and lamb are opposed and divergent races symbolized by these animals. Their meeting and association were impossible, but having become believers in Jesus Christ those who were formerly as wolves and lambs became united through the words of the Gospel.

The purport is that all the meanings of the prophecies were fulfilled. ('Abdu'l-Bahá, *The Promulgation of Universal Peace,* pp. 279–80)

The Messianic prophecies mentioned above were spiritually fulfilled in the Revelation of Christ—and they are also archetypal.

### IN WHAT WAY ARE THE MESSIANIC PROPHECIES ARCHETYPAL?

The Messianic prophecies reviewed above are archetypal in that the Manifestation of God always comes from the invisible spiritual realm, always conquers by the sword of the Word of God, always reigns from the eternal Kingdom, always renews the spiritual laws of the previous Manifestations, always refines the previous social laws to a higher expression, and His teachings always work toward greater unity and peace.

## UNFOLDING PROPHECIES

The Messianic prophecies just examined were spiritually fulfilled in the Dispensation of Christ but outwardly fulfilled in limited ways. With subsequent Revelations, these prophecies have been, and will continue to be, fulfilled in a progressively more outward manner. In this sense, the prophecies are still unfolding as mankind grows in an ever-advancing civilization.

### WHAT IS AN EXAMPLE OF A MESSIANIC PROPHECY THAT SAW LIMITED FULFILLMENT IN THE TIME OF CHRIST?

Isaiah's vision states that wolves and lambs will live together in peace. This prophecy was spiritually fulfilled as Christ's Revelation united many who had previously been opposed. However, it has been a limited, not a universal, fulfillment:

> . . . universal peace was not established with the advent of Christ; that is, peace and well-being were not realized among the hostile and contending nations, disputes and conflicts were not resolved, and harmony and sincerity were not attained. Thus, even to this day intense enmity, hatred, and conflict prevail among the Christian peoples themselves. ('Abdu'l-Bahá, *Some Answered Questions*, no. 12.3)

The full potency of the "wolf and the lamb" prophecy, which entails the coming together in peace of all peoples and nations on Earth, was not completely realized in the Christian Dispensation. Spiritual and social evolution of that magnitude takes time; however, humanity's destiny is that the prerequisites for world peace will be accomplished and this prophecy will find complete outward fulfillment.

## WHAT WILL THE OUTWARD FULFILLMENT OF THE "WOLF AND THE LAMB" PROPHECY LOOK LIKE?

Greater outward fulfillment of the "wolf and the lamb" prophecy will look like all of the peoples and nations of the Earth coming together in political peace and spiritual harmony with full realization of the oneness of God, the oneness of religion, and the oneness of humanity:

> . . . the earth will become another earth; all existence will be renewed; the contingent world will be clothed with the robe of a new life; justice and righteousness will encompass the globe; hatred and enmity will disappear; whatever is the cause of division among peoples, races, and nations will be obliterated; and that which ensures unity, harmony, and concord will be promoted. The heedless will arise from their slumber; the blind will see; the deaf will hear; the dumb will speak; the sick will be healed; the dead will be quickened; and war will give way to peace. ('Abdu'l-Bahá, *Some Answered Questions,* no. 10.8)

## WHEN WILL THE "WOLF AND THE LAMB" PROPHECY BE OUTWARDLY FULFILLED?

The Bahá'í Writings state that the "wolf and the lamb" prophecy will be outwardly fulfilled "in this wondrous Dispensation":

> Moreover, in this wondrous Dispensation the earth will become another earth and the world of humanity will be arrayed with perfect composure and adornment. Strife, contention, and bloodshed will give way to peace, sincerity, and harmony. ('Abdu'l-Bahá, *Some Answered Questions,* no. 12.4)

Although it is recognized that some things may get worse before they get better—that is, the pain of staying the same may need to become greater than the pain of change—still, the earth and humanity have a glorious future.

## DANIEL'S DATES

Most of the prophets describe circumstances surrounding the day of the Lord; however, only the Book of Daniel provides mathematical formulas that pinpoint dates of future Manifestations, thereby foretelling the beginning of both the Christian and Bahá'í Revelations. Daniel's prophecy concerning the coming of the Messiah, hereinafter referred to as Daniel's "seventy weeks" prophecy, states:

Seventy weeks are decreed for your people and your holy city: to finish the transgression, to put an end to sin, and to atone for iniquity, to bring in everlasting righteousness, to seal both vision and prophet, and to anoint a most holy place. Know therefore and understand: from the time that the word went out to restore and rebuild Jerusalem until the time of an anointed prince, there shall be seven weeks; and for sixty-two weeks it shall be built again with streets and moat, but in a troubled time. After the sixty-two weeks, an anointed one shall be cut off and shall have nothing, and the troops of the prince who is to come shall destroy the city and the sanctuary. Its end shall come with a flood, and to the end there shall be war. Desolations are decreed. He shall make a strong covenant with many for one week, and for half of the week he shall make sacrifice and offering cease; and in their place shall be an abomination that desolates, until the decreed end is poured out upon the desolator. (Daniel 9:24–27)

### WHAT IS THE MEANING OF THE WORD "WEEKS" IN DANIEL'S "SEVENTY WEEKS" PROPHECY?

In the language of biblical prophecy, the word "week" means seven years. This is derived from the day-for-a-year formula stated in the Book of Numbers:

According to the number of the days in which you spied out the land, forty days, *for every day a year*, you shall bear your iniquity, forty years, and you shall know my displeasure. (Numbers 14:34, emphasis added)

And stated in the Book of Ezekiel:

When you have completed these, you shall lie down a second time, but on your right side, and bear the punishment of the house of Judah; forty days I assign you, *one day for each year.* (Ezekiel 4:6, emphasis added)

This day-for-a-year formula is commonly used in interpreting biblical prophecy and is confirmed by 'Abdu'l-Bahá as applicable to this prophecy (*Some Answered Questions,* no. 10.12). A week is composed of seven days. Applying the day-for-a-year formula then, a prophetic "week" is equal to seven years. Therefore, the following lengths of time mentioned in the above prophecy can be interpreted as:

70 "weeks" = 490 "days" = 490 years
7 "weeks" = 49 "days" = 49 years
62 "weeks" = 434 "days" = 434 years
1 "week" = 7 "days" = 7 years

The prophecy begins that "seventy weeks (490 years) are decreed for your people" (Daniel 9:24); however, we need to know the starting date to count *from.*

## FROM WHAT POINT
## ARE THESE TIME PERIODS
## TO BE MEASURED?

Daniel's prophecy indicates one point to count from—"from the time that the word went out to restore and rebuild Jerusalem":

Know therefore and understand: *from the time that the word went out to restore and rebuild Jerusalem* until the time of an anointed prince, there shall be seven weeks; and for sixty-two weeks it shall be built again with streets and moat, but in a troubled time. (Daniel 9:25, emphasis added)

The word, or command, to "restore and rebuild Jerusalem" is the point in time from which to start counting the 490 years. This command is the Edict of Artaxerxes I dated 457 BC.

## WHAT IS THE EDICT OF ARTAXERXES I, AND WHY IS IT CHOSEN AS THE COMMAND IN DANIEL'S "SEVENTY WEEKS" PROPHECY?

In 586 BC the Neo-Babylonian Empire conquered Judah and exiled many Jews to Babylonia. Forty-seven years later, the Persian Empire conquered the Babylonian Empire and consequently became ruler over Judah. Over the next ninety-five years, during this Persian rule, a sequence of four royal edicts (dated 536 BC, 519 BC, 457 BC, and 444 BC) authorized the Israelites to return to Judah to rebuild the city of Jerusalem and the Temple. The third proclamation, the Edict of Artaxerxes I (dated 457 BC), is singled out as the command referred to in Daniel's "seventy weeks" prophecy because, in addition to calling for the rebuilding of Jerusalem and the Temple, it also called for the restoration of the Mosaic Law in Jerusalem—the only edict to do so. The following is an excerpt from that edict:

> Artaxerxes, king of kings, to the priest Ezra, the scribe of the law of the God of heaven: Peace. And now I decree that any of the people of Israel or their priests or Levites in my kingdom who freely offers to go to Jerusalem may go with you. . . . And you, Ezra, according to the God-given wisdom you possess, appoint magistrates and judges who may judge all the people in the province Beyond the River who know the laws of your God; and you shall teach those who do not know them. (Ezra 7:12–13, 25)

'Abdu'l-Bahá confirms that it is the 457 BC Edict of Artaxerxes that fits Daniel's prophecy:

> The first was by Cyrus in 536 BC, and this is recorded in the first chapter of the Book of Ezra. The second edict regarding the rebuilding of Jerusalem was issued by Darius of Persia in 519 BC, and this is recorded in the sixth chapter of Ezra. The third was issued by Artaxerxes in the seventh year of his reign, that is, in 457 BC, and this is recorded in the seventh chapter of Ezra. The fourth edict was issued by Artaxerxes in 444 BC, and this is recorded in the second chapter of Nehemiah.

What Daniel intended is the third edict, which was issued in 457 BC. ('Abdu'l-Bahá, *Some Answered Questions,* no. 10.11)

### GIVEN THIS INFORMATION, WHAT IS THE MEANING OF DANIEL'S "SEVENTY WEEKS" PROPHECY?

Inserting the "day-for-a-year" conversions into the "seventy weeks" prophecy, as well as the date of the Edict of Artaxerxes (457 BC), makes the prophecy more intelligible:

Seventy weeks [490 years] are decreed[28] for your people and your holy city: . . . Know therefore and understand: from the time that the word went out to restore and rebuild Jerusalem [457 BC] until the time of an anointed prince, there shall be seven weeks [49 years]; and for sixty-two weeks [434 years]: it shall be built again with streets and moat, but in a troubled time. After the sixty-two weeks [434 years], an anointed one shall be cut off and shall have nothing, . . . Desolations are decreed. He shall make a strong covenant with many for one week [7 years], and for half of the week [3 ½ years] he shall make sacrifice and offering cease; and in their place shall be an abomination that desolates, until the decreed end is poured out upon the desolator. (Daniel 9:24–27, footnote added)

Now it is just a matter of addition and we have the following events foretold:

457 BC + 49 years = 408 BC:
the date of the rebuilding of the Second Temple.
408 BC + 34 years = 27 AD:[29] the date of the Declaration of Christ.
27 AD + 7 years = 34 AD: the date of the crucifixion of Christ.

---

28. Decreed (or determined): The original Hebrew "chathak" means "cut off" or "divided" (*Strong's Exhaustive Concordance of the Bible)* in this context conveying a sense of a time interval that opens a longer period in which it is included. In this prophecy, the 490 years that pertain especially to the Jews is the initial subset of years that opens the 2,300 year period. That is, the 490 years is "cut off" from the 2,300 year period (Communication with Gary Matthews, 2013).

29. 408 BC + 434 years = 27 AD instead of 26 AD because a year has to be added to compensate for the fact that there is no year "0."

'Abdu'l-Bahá explains the "seventy weeks" prophecy this way:

What Daniel intended is the third edict, which was issued in 457 BC. Seventy weeks makes 490 days. Each day, according to the text of the Bible, is one year, for in the Torah it is said: "The day of the Lord is one year." Therefore, 490 days is 490 years. The third edict of Artaxerxes was issued 457 years before the birth of Christ, and Christ was thirty-three years old at the time of His martyrdom and ascension. Thirty-three added to 457 is 490, which is the time announced by Daniel for the advent of Christ. ('Abdu'l-Bahá, *Some Answered Questions,* no. 10.12)

In addition to foretelling critical dates of the Christian Dispensation, the Book of Daniel also foretells the Bahá'í Dispensation.

### HOW DOES THE BOOK OF DANIEL FORETELL THE BAHÁ'Í DISPENSATION?

The Bahá'í Dispensation is foretold in an oracle concerning the cleansing "time of the end":

Then I heard a holy one speaking, and another holy one said to the one that spoke, "For how long is this vision concerning the regular burnt offering, the transgression that makes desolate, and the giving over of the sanctuary and host to be trampled?" And he answered him, "For two thousand three hundred evenings and mornings; then the sanctuary shall be restored to its rightful state." . . . So he came near where I stood; and when he came, I became frightened and fell prostrate. But he said to me, "Understand, O mortal, that the vision is for the time of the end." (Daniel 8:13–14, 17)

This prophecy finds greater definition in the New Testament when it is referenced as a clue disclosing the appearance of the "Son of man" to come sometime after Christ:

But when ye shall see the abomination of desolation, spoken of by Daniel the prophet, standing where it ought not, (let him that readeth understand,) then let them that be in Judaea flee to the mountains: . . . And then shall they see the Son of man coming in the clouds with great power and glory. (Mark 13:14, 26, also found in Matthew 24:15)

The "time of the end" mentioned in Daniel 8:17 refers to the coming of the Manifestation of God sometime after the Christian Revelation.

## HOW DOES THE MATH WORK IN THE "TIME OF THE END" PROPHECY?

Daniel's prophecy for the "time of the end" states one time period: "For two thousand three hundred evenings and mornings; then the sanctuary shall be restored to its rightful state." (Daniel 8:14) Using the day-for-a-year formula, that time period becomes 2,300 years. Using the starting date of the "commandment to restore and build Jerusalem"[30] the prophetic equation points to 1844 AD.

$$457 \text{ BC} + 2,300 \text{ years} = 1844 \text{ AD}^{31}$$

For Bahá'ís, the "time of the end" indicates the Bahá'í Dispensation that began in 1844 with the Declaration of the Báb. 'Abdu'l-Bahá, quoting the King James Version of the Bible, explains the mathematics of Daniel's prophecy this way:

In Daniel 8:13 it is said: "Then I heard one saint speaking, and another saint said unto that certain saint which spake, How long shall be the vision concerning the daily sacrifice, and the transgression of desolation, to give both the sanctuary and the host to be trodden under foot?" And he said unto me, Unto two thousand

---

30. The 457 BC starting date is appropriate for the "time of the end" prophecy as well as the Messianic prophecy because both occur in the same context. The vision of the 2,300 year "time of the end" prophecy was received first with no starting point to count from (Daniel 8:14) and Daniel bemoans the fact that he can't understand it (Daniel 8:27). After a lot of prayer he receives more visions, which include the instructions to start "from the commandment to restore and build Jerusalem" (Daniel 9:25).

31. 457 BC + 2,300 years = 1844 (not 1843) because a year has to be added to compensate for the fact that there is no year "0."

and three hundred days; then shall the sanctuary be cleansed," until it says: "at the time of the end shall be the vision." That is to say, how long shall this misfortune, this ruin, this abasement and degradation endure? Or, when will the morn of Revelation dawn? Then he said, "two thousand and three hundred days; then shall the sanctuary be cleansed". Briefly, the point is that he fixes a period of 2,300 years, for according to the text of the Torah each day is one year. Therefore, from the date of the edict of Artaxerxes to rebuild Jerusalem until the day of the birth of Christ there are 456 years, and from the birth of Christ until the day of the advent of the Báb there are 1,844 years, and if 456 years are added to this number it makes 2,300 years. That is to say, the fulfilment of the vision of Daniel took place in A.D. 1844, and this is the year of the advent of the Báb. Examine the text of the Book of Daniel and observe how clearly he fixes the year of His advent! There could indeed be no clearer prophecy for a Manifestation than this. ('Abdu'l-Bahá, *Some Answered Questions,* no. 10.16)

# Daniel's Prophecy of "2300 Days" (years)

"I have appointed thee each day for a year" – Eze. 4:6

(Graphic from Gary L. Matthews, *He Cometh With Clouds,* p. 109.)

## WHY WAS 1844, THE BEGINNING OF THE BAHÁ'Í DISPENSATION, INDICATED AS "THE TIME OF THE END"?

Like all Scripture, this phrase has multiple meanings. In one sense, the "time of the end" is every coming of the "day of the Lord" in that the beginning of each Revelation marks the "time of the end" of the previous

Revelation. The coming of spring always marks the end of winter. In another sense, and specific to Daniel's prophecy, the "time of the end" marks the end of the Prophetic Cycle and the Beginning of the Cycle of Fulfillment.

## END OF THE PROPHETIC CYCLE

The Prophetic Cycle (also called the Adamic Cycle) started with humanity in its infancy about eight thousand years ago and continued through the Dispensation of Muhammad:

> . . . the Adamic, or Prophetic, Cycle began with Adam and ended with the Dispensation of Muhammad. (*Messages from the Universal House of Justice: 1963 to 1986*, Glossary, p. 738)

Bahá'ís understand this age as "the time of the end" prophesied in the Book of Daniel—the end of the Prophetic Cycle and a growing into the Cycle of Fulfillment:

> [Bahá'u'lláh's] mission is to proclaim that the ages of the infancy and of the childhood of the human race are past, that the convulsions associated with the present stage of its adolescence are slowly and painfully preparing it to attain the stage of manhood, and are heralding the approach of that Age of Ages when swords will be beaten into plowshares, when the Kingdom promised by Jesus Christ will have been established, and the peace of the planet definitely and permanently ensured. (Shoghi Effendi, *The Promised Day is Come*, p. v)

That Muhammad was the last appearance of the Manifestation of God in the Prophetic Cycle is one of the significances of His title "Seal of the Prophets":

> It is evident that every age in which a Manifestation of God hath lived is divinely ordained, and may, in a sense, be characterized as

God's appointed Day. This Day, however, is unique, and is to be distinguished from those that have preceded it. The designation "Seal of the Prophets" fully revealeth its high station. The Prophetic Cycle hath, verily, ended. The Eternal Truth is now come. He hath lifted up the Ensign of Power, and is now shedding upon the world the unclouded splendor of His Revelation. (Bahá'u'lláh, *Gleanings from the Writings of Bahá'u'lláh*, no. 25.1)

## WHY DOES BAHÁ'U'LLÁH HAVE THE TITLE "PROPHET" WHEN THE AGE OF PROPHECY HAS ENDED?

The definition of "prophet" includes: "One who speaks for God," "the inspired revealer or interpreter of his will," and "One who predicts or foretells what is going to happen" (*The Oxford English Dictionary, Vol. 12*, pp. 642–43). Every Manifestation of God proclaims the will of God and foretells what will happen in the future. Therefore, every Manifestation of God can be described as a "Prophet." Although the Cycle of Prophecy has come to a close, the Manifestation of God will continue to guide humanity and, with each new appearance, will prophesy of Revelations to come:

> . . . all the Prophets of God, whenever made manifest unto the peoples of the world, have invariably foretold the coming of yet another Prophet after them, and have established such signs as would herald the advent of the future Dispensation. To this the records of all sacred books bear witness. (Bahá'u'lláh, The Kitáb-i-Íqán, ¶13)

Every appearance of the Manifestation of God is a Prophet and more than a Prophet. No one title that can capture the essence of the Manifestation.

## WHAT ARE SOME OF BAHÁ'U'LLÁH'S PROPHECIES?

Bahá'u'lláh foretold the next appearance of the Manifestation of God Who would appear sometime after one thousand years:

> Whoso layeth claim to a Revelation direct from God, ere the expiration of a full thousand years, such a man is assuredly a lying impostor. (Bahá'u'lláh, The Kitáb-i-Aqdas, ¶37)

Bahá'u'lláh also prophesied world events, scientific developments, and certain achievements of the human race, many of which have already been fulfilled.[32]

## CYCLE OF FULFILLMENT

Throughout biblical history, prophets have foretold the coming of the Kingdom of God on the earth. It is voiced in many different ways, such as a time when swords will be beaten into plowshares:

> And it shall come to pass in the last days, that the mountain of the LORD's house shall be established in the top of the mountains, and shall be exalted above the hills; and all nations shall flow unto it.
>
> And many people shall go and say, Come ye, and let us go up to the mountain of the LORD, to the house of the God of Jacob; and he will teach us of his ways, and we will walk in his paths: for out of Zion shall go forth the law, and the word of the Lord from Jerusalem.
>
> And he shall judge among the nations, and shall rebuke many people: and they shall beat their swords into plowshares, and their spears into pruninghooks; nation shall not lift up sword against nation, neither shall they learn war any more. (Isaiah 2:2–4)

These and other "time of the end" prophecies are seeing fulfillment as humanity "slowly and painfully" moves through its contentious adolescence and approaches maturity (Shoghi Effendi, *The Promised Day is Come*, p. v).

---

32. For information regarding prophecies of Bahá'u'lláh, see Matthews' *The Challenge of Bahá'u'lláh*, chapters 4–6.

**WHAT IS THE DURATION OF THE CYCLE OF FULFILLMENT?**

The Cycle of Fulfillment began with the Dispensation of the Báb (the Herald of the Bahá'í Faith) in 1844, will continue through the Dispensation of Bahá'u'lláh (which will last at least one thousand years), and will continue through future Dispensations for no less than five thousand centuries. Shoghi Effendi describes the Bahá'í Dispensation as:

A Revelation, hailed as the promise and crowning glory of past ages and centuries, as the consummation of all the Dispensations within the Adamic Cycle, inaugurating an era of at least a thousand years' duration, and a cycle destined to last no less than five thousand centuries, signalizing the end of the Prophetic Era and the beginning of the Era of Fulfillment, . . . (Shoghi Effendi, *God Passes By*, p. 155)

The Cycle of Fulfillment (Bahá'í Cycle)
The Báb (1844 AD)
Bahá'u'lláh (1863 AD)
The next Manifestation of God (after one thousand years)
Succeeding Manifestations of God (through five thousand centuries)

**WHAT MAKES THE CYCLE OF FULFILLMENT
DIFFERENT FROM PREVIOUS AGES?**

It is all about the capacity of the human race, which has been building for thousands of years. Humanity has progressed through infancy and childhood, and is now in the throes of a turbulent adolescence that will bloom into a spiritual maturity. Bahá'u'lláh states:

Verily I say, this is the Day in which mankind can behold the Face, and hear the Voice, of the Promised One. (Bahá'u'lláh, *Gleanings from the Writings of Bahá'u'lláh*, no. 7.1)

The human race has achieved a long-cultivated capacity to recognize the Word of God on a level never before possible. This is the capacity that the Prophets and Messengers have "thirsted for":

Great indeed is this Day! The allusions made to it in all the sacred Scriptures as the Day of God attest its greatness. The soul of every Prophet of God, of every Divine Messenger, hath thirsted for this wondrous Day. (Bahá'u'lláh, *Gleanings from the Writings of Bahá'u'lláh,* no. 7.2)

At this stage in humanity's development, spiritual acuity, social maturity, and technological advancement make universal connection with the Word of God possible:

Therefore, in this age of splendors, teachings once limited to the few are made available to all, that the mercy of the Lord may embrace both east and west, that the oneness of the world of humanity may appear in its full beauty, and that the dazzling rays of reality may flood the realm of the mind with light. ('Abdu'l-Bahá, *Selections from the Writings of 'Abdu'l-Bahá,* no. 29.6)

The Cycle of Fulfillment—the next five hundred thousand years—will see the coming of age of humanity and an era of universal peace.

## NAMES AND TITLES

There are many biblical prophecies of a new day to be ushered in by a great Personage Who is referred to by various names including: "Wonderful Counselor, Mighty God, Everlasting Father, Prince of Peace" (Isaiah 9:6); the "Lord of Hosts" (Zechariah 6:12), "a rod out of the stem of Jesse" and the "Branch" (Isaiah 11:1–2). The Baha'i Writings state that these prophecies and more have been fulfilled in the Baha'i Dispensation. Therefore, to Baha'is, all of these names refer to Bahá'u'lláh:

To Israel He was neither more nor less than the incarnation of the "Everlasting Father," the "Lord of Hosts" come down "with ten thousands of saints"; . . . To Him Isaiah, the greatest of the Jewish prophets, had alluded as the "Glory of the Lord," the "Everlasting Father," the "Prince of Peace," the "Wonderful," the "Counsellor," the "Rod come forth out of the stem of Jesse" and the "Branch grown out of His roots," Who "shall be established upon the throne of David," Who "will come with strong hand," Who "shall judge among the nations," Who "shall smite the earth with the rod of His mouth, and with the breath of His lips slay the wicked," and Who "shall assemble the outcasts of Israel, and gather together the dispersed of Judah from the four corners of the earth." Of Him David had sung in his Psalms, acclaiming Him as the "Lord of Hosts" and the "King of Glory." To Him Haggai had referred as the "Desire of all nations," and Zachariah as the "Branch" Who "shall grow up out of His place," and "shall build the Temple of the Lord." Ezekiel had extolled Him as the "Lord" Who "shall be king over all the earth," while to His day Joel and Zephaniah had both referred as the "day of Jehovah," the latter describing it as "a day of wrath, a day of trouble and distress, a day of wasteness and desolation, a day of darkness and gloominess, a day of clouds and thick darkness, a day of the trumpet and alarm against the fenced cities, and against the high towers." His Day Ezekiel and Daniel had, moreover, both acclaimed as the "day of the Lord," and Malachi described as "the great and dreadful day of the Lord" when "the Sun of Righteousness" will "arise, with healing in His wings," whilst Daniel had pronounced His advent as signalizing the end of the "abomination that maketh desolate." (Shoghi Effendi, *God Passes By*, p. 171)[33]

Bahá'u'lláh's claim is tremendous. However, the above names are not restricted to Bahá'u'lláh. For example, Christ is also known as the "Prince of Peace," the "King of Glory," and the "Lord of Hosts."

## HOW CAN BOTH BAHÁ'U'LLÁH AND CHRIST BE CALLED BY THE SAME NAMES?

Because of Their essential unity as the Word of God, all of the Manifestations can be called by the same names:

---

33. For additional prophecies fulfilled by Bahá'u'lláh, see Shoghi Effendi, *God Passes By*, pp. 144–52.

. . . if thou callest Them all by one name, and dost ascribe to Them the same attribute, thou hast not erred from the truth. (Bahá'u'lláh, The Kitáb-i-Íqán, ¶161)

The unity of the Manifestations of God will always be a mystery to human beings, but let's look at the explanation anyway. Every Manifestation of God has two stations: the station of the "voice of God" and the "human station":

He hath, moreover, conferred upon Him a double station. The first station, which is related to His innermost reality, representeth Him as One Whose voice is the voice of God Himself. The second station is the human station, exemplified by the following verses: "I am but a man like you." (Bahá'u'lláh, The Kitab-i-Aqdas, notes, p. 233)

In the human station, every appearance of the Manifestation of God has a rational soul and a physical body, consequently every Manifestation has a historical identity and personality. But the Manifestation of God is more than human. In the station of the "voice of God," every appearance of the Manifestation is one with God and therefore one with every other Manifestation:

These Manifestations of God have each a twofold station. One is the station of pure abstraction and essential unity. In this respect, if thou callest them all by one name, and dost ascribe to them the same attribute, thou hast not erred from the truth. . . . For they one and all summon the people of the earth to acknowledge the Unity of God. . . . If thou wilt observe with discriminating eyes, thou wilt behold them all abiding in the same tabernacle, soaring in the same heaven, seated upon the same throne, uttering the same speech, and proclaiming the same Faith. Such is the unity of those Essences of being. (Bahá'u'lláh, The Kitáb-i-Íqán, ¶161)

As an illustration, consider the calendar. Every day has a unique designation such as December 26, 1941 or August 2, 1975. These are specific days with particular histories. But from the point of view of the sun, there are no distinct days—the sun shines continuously with no time boundaries. The sun of yesterday is the sun of today. In the same way, there is no distinction in the shining of the Word of God:

> The transcendent Word of God is sanctified beyond time. The past, the present, and the future are all equal in relation to God. Yesterday, today, and tomorrow do not exist in the sun. ('Abdu'l-Bahá, *Some Answered Questions,* no. 28.3)

In the second "station of distinction," the Manifestations carry names and attributes relevant to their specific historical appearances, but in the first station of essential unity these names apply to all.

### WHAT IS THE GREATEST NAME?

An Islamic tradition states that among all the numerous names of God, one is the greatest, but this Most Great Name is hidden from mankind. To Bahá'ís, the Greatest Name of God has been revealed and it is "Bahá," meaning Glory, Splendor, or Light. Bahá is a reference to Bahá'u'lláh, the "Glory of God." Bahá'u'lláh states:

> This is His Most Great Name, His Most Exalted Word, and the Dayspring of His Most Excellent Titles, if ye could understand. (Bahá'u'lláh, The Kitáb-i-Aqdas, ¶143)

### CAN THE MOST GREAT NAME BE APPLIED TO OTHER MANIFESTATIONS OF GOD IN ADDITION TO BAHÁ'U'LLÁH?

The Most Great Name is a title that is historically specific to the Bahá'í Revelation in this Age of Fulfillment. However, in the station of essential unity, the Most Great Name, like other titles, can be applied to all of the Manifestations of God. Indeed, the Báb addresses Jesus Christ as "Thy Most Great Name" (*Selections from the Writings of the Báb,* no. 2.35.2). Whereas this title evokes an image of "there can be only one"—which is characteristic of many of titles of the Manifestations of God—this is not a challenge to other Manifestations. Rather, it communicates something of the greatness of the station of the Word of God and the greatness of this Day. To interpret it otherwise is to take its meaning out of context (Sours, p. 105). The different historical appearances of the Manifestation of God are not in competition with each other—They are one in Spirit and Reality.

## WHY IS THE ONENESS OF THE MANIFESTATIONS OF GOD AN IMPORTANT CONCEPT?

World peace depends on it. The spiritual oneness of the Manifestation of God is essential to understanding the oneness of God, the oneness of religion, and the oneness of mankind. When taken to heart, these principles will bring an end to religious and sectarian divisions that foster domination and hostilities. Humanity's new capacity to "get" the principle of the oneness of religion is one of the things that make this era the Cycle of Fulfillment:

> The gift of God to this enlightened age is the knowledge of the oneness of mankind and of the fundamental oneness of religion. War shall cease between nations, and by the will of God the Most Great Peace shall come; the world will be seen as a new world, and all men will live as brothers. ('Abdu'l-Bahá, *'Abdu'l-Bahá in London*, p. 19)

## ARMY OF THE LORD

Prophecies concerning the day of the Lord include references to "a great and powerful army" who will, with extraordinary powers, arise to serve God:

> Blow the trumpet in Zion; sound the alarm on my holy mountain! Let all the inhabitants of the land tremble, for the day of the LORD is coming, . . . Like blackness spread upon the mountains a great and powerful army comes; their like has never been from of old, nor will be again after them in ages to come. Fire devours in front of them, and behind them a flame burns. Before them the land is like the garden of Eden, but after them a desolate wilderness, and nothing escapes them. They have the appearance of horses, and like war-horses they charge. . . . The LORD utters his

voice at the head of his army; how vast is his host! Numberless are those who obey his command. (Joel 2:1–4, 11)

The description of the army of the Lord carries the "destruction," "wrath," "anger," and "desolation" (Isaiah 13:6, 9) images that are characteristic of ancient prophecies concerning the day of the Lord. As discussed previously, these images suggest the darkness of spiritual winter, the turmoil caused by the falling away of the old, and the woe of judgment. The other side of the picture is rebirth, revival, and renewal.

### WHAT DOES IT MEAN TO SERVE IN THE ARMY OF THE LORD IN THIS DISPENSATION?

To serve in the army of the Lord in this Dispensation means to live one's life equipped with certain qualities of the spirit such as pure intentions, spiritual virtues, and goodly deeds—and to teach the Word of God:

To do battle, as stated in the sacred verse, doth not, in this greatest of all dispensations, mean to go forth with sword and spear, with lance and piercing arrow—but rather weaponed with pure intent, with righteous motives, with counsels helpful and effective, with godly attributes, with deeds pleasing to the Almighty, with the qualities of heaven. It signifieth education for all mankind, guidance for all men, the spreading far and wide of the sweet savours of the spirit, the promulgation of God's proofs, the setting forth of arguments conclusive and divine, the doing of charitable deeds. ('Abdu'l-Bahá, *Selections from the Writings of 'Abdu'l-Bahá*, no. 207.2)

### HOW DOES THE MANIFESTATION OF GOD DIRECT THE ARMY OF THE LORD?

The Manifestation of God directs the army of the Lord through word and example. In the following passage, 'Abdu'l-Bahá offers some personal observations on Bahá'u'lláh's selfless service:

During His [Bahá'u'lláh's] lifetime He was intensely active. His energy was unlimited. Scarcely one night was passed in restful sleep. He bore these ordeals, suffered these calamities and difficulties in order that a manifestation of selflessness and service might become apparent in the world of humanity; that the Most Great Peace should become a reality; that human souls might appear as the angels of heaven; that heavenly miracles would be wrought among men; that human faith should be strengthened and perfected; that the precious, priceless bestowal of God—the human mind—might be developed to its fullest capacity in the temple of the body; and that man might become the reflection and likeness of God, even as it hath been revealed in the Bible, "Let us make man in our image." ('Abdu'l-Bahá, *The Promulgation of Universal Peace,* p. 38)

When people follow the example of the Manifestation and arise in unity to serve the laws and teachings of God with qualities of the spirit, the purpose of the Word of God is achieved and humanity gets closer to the ultimate goal stated in the first chapter of Genesis: to shine forth in the image and likeness of God.

# REFLECTIONS ON THE OLD TESTAMENT— WATER FROM A ROCK

If I had to choose one verse to represent the essence of the Old Testament, I would pick a verse from the Book of Numbers that we have not yet examined. In the story leading up to this verse, Moses and Aaron were exhausted from trying to turn the hungry, thirsty, and miserable tribes from chaotic rebellion to ordered obedience, and the two men fell on their faces in prayer. The Lord appeared and gave them instructions to pick up a rod, assemble the people, and speak to a certain rock. They were promised that water would then flow from the rock. They were to offer the water to the people and the beasts. Moses and Aaron did what they were told: they gathered the people, Moses "spoke" to the rock by slashing it twice, the water flowed from the rock, and everyone drank:

> And Moses lifted up his hand, and with his rod he smote the rock twice: and the water came out abundantly, and the congregation drank, and their beasts also. (Numbers 20:11)

I do not know of an authoritative Bahá'í interpretation of Numbers 20:11, but considering symbolic interpretation offered for other Scripture, I offer this personal interpretation:

*And Moses* – And the Word of God
*lifted up His hand* – announced His presence in the world
*and with His rod* – and with the Teachings of God
*He smote* – He awakened
*the rock* – the spiritually lifeless bodies

***twice*** – through reward and punishment.[34]
***and the water*** – and knowledge and wisdom
***came out abundantly*** – were expressed in all endeavors.
***and the congregation*** – and the people, in unity,
***drank*** – voluntarily sought the Word of God
***and their beasts also*** – as did the rulers of the earth.[35]

To me, Numbers 20:11 symbolizes the factors revisited in every Dispensation: the power of the Word of God, the drama of change, the capacity of humanity, and our glorious future.

Now that we are at the end of the Old Testament, I would love to start at the beginning and do it all over again—this time looking at different Scripture. But like the process of progressive Revelation, it's good to keep moving. Now it's on to the New Testament.

---

34. "O people of God! That which traineth the world is Justice, for it is upheld by two pillars, reward and punishment. These two pillars are the sources of life to the world" (Bahá'u'lláh, *Tablets of Bahá'u'lláh,* p. 27).

35. In the Book of Revelation, "beast" is interpreted as governmental or religious rulers (see Bauckham, pp. 1296–98).

# THE NEW TESTAMENT

The Books of the New Testament tell of the life, ministry, and teachings of Jesus Christ, the teaching work of His followers after His ascension, and an apocalyptic vision related to the Return of Christ. The books are presented in this sequence:

| The Gospels | The Pauline Epistles | The General Epistles |
|---|---|---|
| Matthew | Romans | 1 Timothy |
| Mark | Romans | 2 Timothy |
| Luke | 1 Corinthians | Titus |
| John | 2 Corinthians | Philemon |
| | Galatians | Hebrews |
| **A Sequel to the** | Ephesians | James |
| **Gospels** | Colossians | 1 Peter |
| Acts of the Apostles | 1 Thessalonians | 2 Peter |
| | 2 Thessalonians | 1 John |
| | | 2 John |
| | | 3 John |
| | | Jude |

The Bahá'í Faith unhesitatingly acknowledges the spiritual integrity of the New Testament:

> As to the position of Christianity, let it be stated without any hesitation or equivocation that its Divine origin is unconditionally acknowledged, that the Sonship and Divinity of Jesus Christ are fearlessly asserted, that the Divine inspiration of the Gospel is fully recognized, that the reality of the mystery of the Immaculacy of

the Virgin Mary is confessed, and the primacy of Peter, the Prince of the Apostles, is upheld and defended. The Founder of the Christian Faith is designated by Bahá'u'lláh as the "Spirit of God," is proclaimed as the One Who "appeared out of the breath of the Holy Ghost," and is even extolled as the "Essence of the Spirit." His mother is described as "that veiled and immortal, that most beauteous countenance," and the station of her Son eulogized as a "station which hath been exalted above the imaginings of all that dwell on earth," whilst Peter is recognized as one whom God has caused "the mysteries of wisdom and of utterance of flow out of his mouth." (Shoghi Effendi. *The Promised Day is Come,* p. 109)

# THE BOOKS OF THE GOSPELS—
## OVERVIEW

The word "gospel" comes from the Old English word "godspel": "god," meaning "good," plus "spell," meaning "news" or "a story." Thus the Gospels tell the "good news" of the Revelation of Jesus Christ. The texts were originally written in Greek with a few words from Hebrew and Aramaic, and they are anonymous—"none of the four gospels originally included an attribution to an author" (Wansbrough, p. 1001). They are named after the disciples to whom they are traditionally credited: Matthew, Mark, Luke, and John. Bahá'u'lláh mentions these same disciples as writers of the Gospels:

> Four Gospels were written after Him. John, Luke, Mark and Matthew—these four wrote after Christ what they remembered of His utterances. (Bahá'u'lláh, cited in "The Resurrection of Christ Memorandum," Research Department of the Universal House of Justice, September, 14, 1987)

Whether Bahá'u'lláh was speaking to traditional understandings or confirming authorship may be made clear with future research. A main point of the above quotation, however, is that the Gospels were written sometime after the Ascension of Jesus Christ and were based on human memory of what was spoken. The Bahá'í Writings do not offer specific information on the exact origins of the Gospels. Biblical scholarship has determined that most of the books were written between 70 and 100 AD, long before they came together as the Christian Canon at the Third Council of Carthage in 397 AD (see Houlden, p. 831).

**The Gospel according to Matthew** provides a bridge between the Old and New Testaments as it frequently relates the Revelation of Christ to

Hebrew Scripture and points to a process of differentiation between the early church and Judaism. The content implies a Jewish-Christian audience and author. The majority opinion of biblical scholars is that Matthew was written sometime between 75 and 100 AD (see Allison, pp. 844–45).

**The Gospel according to Mark** presents the life of Jesus in dramatic episodes. A key theme is the suffering of Christ and the centrality of sacrifice in discipleship. Generally considered to be the oldest of the Gospels, the prevailing academic model dates its writing to shortly after 70 AD (see Tuckett, p. 886).

**The Gospel according to Luke** opens with a preface, the only example of its kind in the New Testament, in which the author explains that his account is based upon information received from eyewitnesses. Tradition attributes authorship to Luke, Paul's "beloved physician" (Colossians 4:14), who is also credited with the Book of Acts. The current majority opinion is that Luke was probably written by 80 to 85 AD (see Franklin, pp. 923–24).

**The Gospel according to John** is unique in that it focuses on the divinity of Christ and the preexistence of the Son of God. While tradition attributes its authorship to John the son of Zebedee (one of the twelve Apostles), many scholars see indications that different authors composed it in two or three layers and that it reached its final form about 90 to 100 AD (see Harris, p. 302; Kieffer, pp. 960–61).

### DO THE GOSPELS PRESENT A COMPLETE RECORD OF THE CHRISTIAN REVELATION?

The Gospels present information about the Christian Revelation from four different points of view, but even these together do not present a complete record of the teachings of Christ:

Our knowledge of Jesus' life and teachings is rather fragmentary. . . . There may be other teachings and ordinances too, of which no record is left. (From a letter written on behalf of Shoghi Effendi, dated November 12, 1933, to an individual believer, in *Lights of Guidance,* no. 1645)

The degree to which the Gospels accurately present the exact utterances of Christ is not measurable. Bahá'ís can, however, be sure that the Gospel passages quoted by Bahá'u'lláh and 'Abdu'l-Bahá represent authentic teachings of Christ:

> We cannot be sure how much or how little of the four Gospels are accurate and include the words of Christ and His undiluted teachings, all we can be sure of, as Bahá'ís, is that what has been quoted by Bahá'u'lláh and the Master must be absolutely authentic. (From a letter written on behalf of Shoghi Effendi, dated January 23, 1944, to an individual believer, cited in a collection compiled under the supervision of the Universal House of Justice, January 1, 1981, entitled "Other Holy Scriptures")

# TOPICS FROM THE GOSPELS

## THE WORD

The first few verses of the Gospel of John take us back to "the beginning":

> In the beginning was the Word, and the Word was with God, and the Word was God. He was in the beginning with God. All things came into being through him, and without him not one thing came into being. (John 1:1–3)

The above verses are full of meanings, mysteries, and limitless applications:

> Consider the statement recorded in the first chapter of the book of John: "In the beginning was the Word, and the Word was with God, and the Word was God." This statement is brief but replete with the greatest meanings. Its applications are illimitable and beyond the power of books or words to contain and express. ('Abdu'l-Bahá, *The Promulgation of Universal Peace*, p. 213)

### WHAT IS "THE WORD"?

"The Word" is a title for the Manifestation of God—the eternal station of Christhood. The imagery of "the Word" suggests a completeness that is unique to the Manifestation. As individual letters are meaningless in themselves and it is only when they are put together as words that they convey meaning, so the Manifestation of God is a complete expression of divine reality, while all phenomenal beings are incomplete—like letters:

In the universe of creation all phenomenal beings are as letters. Letters in themselves are meaningless and express nothing of thought or ideal—as, for instance, a, b, etc. Likewise, all phenomenal beings are without independent meaning. But a word is composed of letters and has independent sense and meaning. Therefore, as Christ conveyed the perfect meaning of divine reality and embodied independent significance, He was the Word. . . . The reality of Jesus was the perfect meaning, the Christhood in Him which in the Holy Books is symbolized as the Word. ('Abdu'l-Bahá, *The Promulgation of Universal Peace,* p. 214)

### JOHN 1:1 STATES, "IN THE BEGINNING WAS THE WORD." IN WHAT WAY WAS THE WORD (THE MANIFESTATION OF GOD) "IN THE BEGINNING"?

The Word of God precedes creation:

. . . the reality of Christ, Who is the Word of God, undoubtedly precedes all created things in essence, in attributes, and in distinction. Before appearing in human form, the Word of God was in a state of utmost sanctity and glory, abiding in perfect beauty and splendour in the height of its majesty. ('Abdu'l-Bahá, *Some Answered Questions,* no. 28.4)

The Word (the Manifestation of God) is the appearance of preexistent Reality that is the source of everlasting life:

As to the Holy Manifestations of God, They are the focal points where the signs, tokens and perfections of that sacred, preexistent Reality appear in all their splendor. They are an eternal grace, a heavenly glory, and on Them dependeth the everlasting life of humankind. ('Abdu'l-Bahá, *Selections from the Writings of 'Abdu'l-Bahá,* no. 21.12)

### JOHN 1:1 SAYS "THE WORD WAS WITH GOD." WHAT DOES IT MEAN FOR THE WORD (THE MANIFESTATION OF GOD) TO BE "WITH GOD"?

That the Manifestation of God is "with God" is another way of saying that the Manifestation embodies the attributes of God:

"And the Word was with God." . . . This does not imply separation from God, even as it is not possible to separate the rays of the sun from the sun. The reality of Christ was the embodiment of divine virtues and attributes of God. ('Abdu'l-Bahá, *The Promulgation of Universal Peace*, p. 214)

All of the acts, laws, and doings of the Manifestation of God can be regarded as "with" or identical to God's Will:

The essence of belief in Divine unity consisteth in regarding Him Who is the Manifestation of God and Him Who is the invisible, the inaccessible, the unknowable Essence as one and the same. By this is meant that whatever pertaineth to the former, all His acts and doings, whatever He ordaineth or forbiddeth, should be considered, in all their aspects, and under all circumstances, and without any reservation, as identical with the Will of God Himself. (Bahá'u'lláh, *Gleanings from the Writings of Bahá'u'lláh*, no. 84.4)

### JOHN 1:1 SAYS "THE WORD WAS GOD."
### IS THE WORD (THE MANIFESTATION OF GOD)
### ACTUALLY GOD?

The answer to this question depends on one's perspective. From one point of view the Manifestation of God *is* God because the Manifestation has a certain oneness with God that humanity does not have, and only by the Manifestation can humanity obtain the attributes of God:

Were any of the all-embracing Manifestations of God to declare: "I am God!" He verily speaketh the truth, and no doubt attacheth thereto. For it hath been repeatedly demonstrated that through their Revelation, their attributes and names, the Revelation of God, His name and His attributes, are made manifest in the world. (Bahá'u'lláh, The Kitáb-i-Íqán, ¶196)

This oneness is sometimes expressed as the Manifestation being the image of God, such as in this verse from the Gospel of John:

Whoever has seen Me has seen the Father. (John 14:9)

At the same time, however, the Manifestation of God is *not* the essence of God, as indicated in the following verse, as well as others like it, that emphasizes the distinction between the Manifestation and God:

And the Father who sent me has himself testified on my behalf. You have never heard his voice or seen his form, (John 5:37)

Therefore, depending on one's point of view, the Manifestation of God *is* God, and the Manifestation of God *is not* God. Bahá'u'lláh expresses His experience of this unique station in these words:

When I contemplate, O my God, the relationship that bindeth me to Thee, I am moved to proclaim to all created things "verily I am God." And when I consider my own self, lo, I find it coarser than clay. (Bahá'u'lláh, The Kitáb-i-Aqdas, Notes, p. 234)

The relationship between the sun and a sunbeam is a helpful analogy when reflecting on the relationship between God and the Manifestation of God. You might step outside to "get some sun." From your point of view, the sunbeam that touches your skin is the sun because it has a certain oneness with the sun that you do not have, and only by the sunbeam can you obtain the attributes of the sun. At the same time, the sunbeam is not the essence of the sun. As the sunbeam is to the sun, so the Manifestation of God is to God.

## THE BIRTH OF JESUS

Old Testament prophecies state that the Messiah ("the Anointed One") would be born of a virgin (Isaiah 7:14). A little over two thousand years ago, Mary of Nazareth became apprised of her role:

In the sixth month the angel Gabriel was sent by God to a town in Galilee called Nazareth, to a virgin engaged to a man whose name was Joseph, of the house of David. The virgin's name was Mary. And he came to her and said, "Greetings, favored one! The Lord is with you." But she was much perplexed by his words and pondered what sort of greeting this might be. The angel said to her, "Do not be afraid, Mary, for you have found favor with God. And now, you will conceive in your womb and bear a son, and you will name him Jesus." (Luke 1:26–31)

### WAS JESUS BORN OF A VIRGIN?

The Bahá'í Writings state that Jesus was conceived of the Holy Spirit in a miraculous birth:

First regarding the birth of Jesus Christ. In the light of what Bahá'u'lláh and 'Abdu'l-Bahá have stated concerning this subject it is evident that Jesus came into this world through the direct intervention of the Holy Spirit, and that consequently His birth was quite miraculous. (From a letter written on behalf of Shoghi Effendi, dated December 31, 1937, to an individual believer, in *Lights of Guidance,* no. 1637)

### HOW CAN A MIRACLE BE ACCEPTED AS TRUTH WHEN IT APPEARS TO BREAK THE LAWS OF NATURE?

The Author of the universe and the Creator of all of its laws can manipulate the laws of nature at any time:

Again with regard to your question relative to the birth of Jesus; . . . miracles are always possible, even though they do not constitute a regular channel whereby God reveals His power to mankind. . . . God Who is the Author of the universe can, in His Wisdom and Omnipotence, bring any change, no matter how temporary, in the operation of the laws which He Himself has created. (From a letter written on behalf of Shoghi Effendi, dated February 27, 1928, to an individual believer, in *Lights of Guidance,* no. 1638)

### HOW DOES THE MIRACLE OF JESUS' BIRTH RECONCILE WITH THE HARMONY OF SCIENCE AND RELIGION?

The harmony of religion and science does not discount the possibility of miracles:

. . . the principle of harmony between religion and science, while it enables us, with the help of reason, to see through the falsity of superstitions, does not imply that truth is limited to what can be explained by current scientific concepts. Not only do all religions have their miracles and mysteries, but religion itself, and certain fundamental religious concepts, such as the nature of the Manifestations of God, are far from being explicable by present-day scientific theories. (From a letter of the Universal House of Justice, dated February 16, 1996)

### IS EVERY MANIFESTATION OF GOD
### CONCEIVED BY THE HOLY SPIRIT?
No other miraculous births are mentioned in the Bahá'í Writings:

The Teachings do not tell us of any miraculous birth besides that of Jesus. (From a letter written on behalf of Shoghi Effendi, dated February 27, 1938, to an individual believer, in *Lights of Guidance,* no. 1638)

### IS CHRIST GREAT BECAUSE HE WAS CONCEIVED
### OF THE HOLY SPIRIT?
Christ's greatness is due to His spiritual perfections in His eternal station as the Manifestation of God, not due to the miraculous circumstances of His physical birth:

The honor and greatness of Christ reside not in His being without a father, but rather in His divine perfections, outpourings, and splendours. ('Abdu'l-Bahá, *Some Answered Questions,* no. 18.3)

In the timeless spiritual station of the Word, the greatness of Christ exists before, during, and after the physical conception of Jesus of Nazareth.

### WHAT WAS MARY'S REACTION TO HER SITUATION?
Surely, no one felt the mystery of a child conceived by the Holy Spirit more than Mary. Bahá'u'lláh gives a tender account of her condition:

Likewise, reflect upon the state and condition of Mary. So deep was the perplexity of that most beauteous countenance, so grievous her case, that she bitterly regretted she had ever been born. To this beareth witness the text of the sacred verse wherein it is mentioned that after Mary had given birth to Jesus, she bemoaned her plight and cried out: "O would that I had died ere this, and been a thing forgotten, forgotten quite!" I swear by God! Such lamenting consumeth the heart and shaketh the being. . . . Reflect, what answer could Mary have given to the people around her? How could she claim that a Babe Whose father was unknown had been conceived of the Holy Ghost? Therefore did Mary, that veiled and immortal Countenance, take up her Child and return unto her home. No sooner had the eyes of the people fallen upon her than they raised their voice saying: "O sister of Aaron! Thy father was not a man of wickedness, nor unchaste thy mother."

And now, meditate upon this most great convulsion, this grievous test. Notwithstanding all these things, God conferred upon that essence of the Spirit, Who was known amongst the people as fatherless, the glory of Prophethood, and made Him His testimony unto all that are in heaven and on earth. (Bahá'u'lláh, The Kitáb-i-Íqán, ¶60–59)

The above passage reminds us that the miraculous nature of the conception of Jesus of Nazareth was no social advantage to Jesus or Mary.

### WHAT IS THE VIRGIN MARY'S SPIRITUAL STATION?

The Virgin Mary's spiritual station is unsurpassed and comparable to such heroines as the Greatest Holy Leaf (Bahíyyih Khánum, daughter of Bahá'u'lláh), Ásíyih (wife of Bahá'u'lláh), Fatimih (daughter of Muhammad), Táhirih (one of the eighteen Letters of the Living), and Sarah (wife of Abraham). This high station is described in the following passage where Shoghi Effendi depicts Bahíyyih Khánum as one of these "immortal heroines":

. . . the Greatest Holy Leaf, the "well-beloved" sister of 'Abdu'l-Bahá, the "Leaf that hath sprung" from the "Pre-existent Root," the "fragrance" of Bahá'u'lláh's "shining robe," elevated by Him to a "station such as none other woman hath surpassed," and comparable in rank to those immortal heroines such as Sarah, Ásíyih, the Virgin Mary, Fátimih and Táhirih. . . . (Shoghi Effendi, *God Passes By,* p. 551)

## THE WISE MEN AND THE STAR

The Gospel of Matthew states that "wise men from the East"[36] followed a star to Bethlehem in search of the King of the Jews:

In the time of King Herod, after Jesus was born in Bethlehem of Judea, wise men from the East came to Jerusalem, asking, "Where is the child who has been born king of the Jews? For we observed his star at its rising, and have come to pay him homage." When King Herod heard this, he was frightened, and all Jerusalem with him. (Matthew 2:1–3)

The Scripture continues that Herod, jealous of power, sought to destroy the child that would be "King of the Jews." The wise men eventually found Jesus and worshipped Him.

### DID A VISIBLE STAR IN THE SKY MARK THE BIRTH OF JESUS?

At the coming of every Manifestation of God a sign appears (1) in the visible heaven as an astronomical occurrence, and (2) in the invisible heaven as a spiritually advanced soul who acts as a herald of the new Revelation:

---

36. "Wise men," from the original Greek "magoi," is often interpreted "magi." Bahá'u'lláh uses the term "magi" in His reference to this Scripture (The Kitáb-i-Íqán,¶69). In Persian, "magi" would refer to Zoroastrian priests: "Magi; the Wise Men of the New Testament. Persian mugh and majus, English Magus, defined as a priestly caste or order of ancient Media and Persia. Zoroaster may have been a Magus; Persians use the term to mean Zoroastrian" (Marzieh Gail, *Bahá'í Glossary,* p. 30).

By "heaven" is meant the visible heaven, inasmuch as when the hour draweth nigh on which the Daystar of the heaven of justice shall be made manifest, and the Ark of divine guidance shall sail upon the sea of glory, a star will appear in the heaven, heralding unto its people the advent of that most great light. In like manner, in the invisible heaven a star shall be made manifest who, unto the peoples of the earth, shall act as a harbinger of the break of that true and exalted Morn. These twofold signs, in the visible and the invisible heaven, have announced the Revelation of each of the Prophets of God, as is commonly believed. (Bahá'u'lláh, The Kitáb-i-Íqán, ¶68)

The star in the invisible (spiritual) heaven that heralded the coming of Christ was John the Baptist. A literal star in the visible heaven also marked the coming of Christ:

. . . when the hour of the Revelation of Jesus drew nigh, a few of the Magi aware that the star of Jesus had appeared in heaven, sought and followed it, till they came unto the city which was the seat of the Kingdom of Herod. The sway of his sovereignty in those days embraced the whole of that land.

These Magi said: "Where is He that is born King of the Jews? for we have seen His star in the east and are come to worship Him!" When they had searched, they found out that in Bethlehem, in the land of Judea, the Child had been born. This was the sign that was manifested in the visible heaven. (Bahá'u'lláh, The Kitáb-i-Íqán, ¶69–70)

## HOW DID THE HOLY FAMILY
### ESCAPE THE THREAT OF HEROD?

The Gospel of Matthew tells that Joseph was inspired to get the Holy Family out of Bethlehem and quietly seek refuge in Egypt (2:13–15). This Scripture teaches that God's Will prevails even in the midst of intense opposition:

Consider and call thou to mind the days whereon the Spirit of God (Jesus Christ) appeared, and Herod gave judgment against

Him. God, however, aided Him with the hosts of the unseen, and protected Him with truth, and sent Him down unto another land, according to His promise. He, verily, ordaineth what He pleaseth. Thy Lord truly preserveth whom He willeth, be he in the midst of the seas or in the maw of the serpent, or beneath the sword of the oppressor." (Bahá'u'lláh, Epistle to the Son of the Wolf, p. 57)

## THE YOUNG JESUS

The Gospel of Luke tells a brief story of the young Jesus and His extraordinary knowledge and understanding. It begins with Mary, Joseph, and Jesus going to Jerusalem for Passover. As they set out on the trip home, His parents assumed He was with their group, but after a day of traveling they discovered He was missing. They returned to Jerusalem, searched for three days, and finally found the young Jesus conversing with the teachers in the Temple and amazing them with His knowledge:

> After three days they found him in the temple, sitting among the teachers, listening to them and asking them questions. And all who heard him were amazed at his understanding and his answers. (Luke 2:46)

This story harmonizes with the Bahá'í observation that the Manifestations of God are, even in childhood, renowned for Their extraordinary wisdom, inherent knowledge, and eloquence.

### ARE THERE CHILDHOOD ACCOUNTS OF GREATNESS IN THE LIVES OF OTHER MANIFESTATIONS OF GOD?

Signs of greatness are found in accounts of the early lives of Bahá'u'lláh and the Báb.[37] One lesson in these stories is that even before the Manifestation of God awakens to His mission, He possesses an exalted station.

---

37. See Esslemont, *Bahá'u'lláh and the New Era*, p. 23; and Lambden, *"An Episode in the Childhood of the Báb."*

Announced or not, in the station of divine unity, the Manifestation of God is always the Manifestation:

> God and His Manifestation can, under no circumstances, be dissociated from the loftiness and sublimity which They inherently possess. (Bahá'u'lláh, *Gleanings from the Writings of Bahá'u'lláh,* no. 29.7)

### AS A CHILD, IS THE MANIFESTATION OF GOD AWARE OF THE GREATNESS OF HIS STATION?

On some level, the Manifestation of God is conscious of His own station, even as a child:

> From the beginning, that sanctified Reality is undoubtedly aware of the secret of existence, and from childhood the signs of greatness are clearly manifested in Him. How then could He fail, in spite of such bounties and perfections, to be conscious of His own station? ('Abdu'l-Bahá, *Some Answered Questions,* no. 39.5)

## THE RETURN OF ELIJAH

In the last verses of the Old Testament, Malachi prophesied the return of the prophet Elijah, a lesser prophet in Israel around the ninth century BC whose return was to herald the coming of the Messiah:

> Lo, I will send you the prophet Elijah before the great and terrible day of the LORD comes. He will turn the hearts of parents to their children and the hearts of children to their parents, so that I will not come and strike the land with a curse. (Malachi 4:5–6)

In the New Testament we hear of Elijah's return through the story of a vision that came to Zechariah, the future father of John the Baptist:

> Then there appeared to him an angel of the LORD, standing at the right side of the altar of incense. When Zechariah saw him, he was

terrified; and fear overwhelmed him. But the angel said to him, "Do not be afraid, Zechariah, for your prayer has been heard. Your wife Elizabeth will bear you a son, and you will name him John. . . . He will turn many of the people of Israel to the Lord their God. With the spirit and power of Elijah he will go before him, to turn the hearts of parents to their children, and the disobedient to the wisdom of the righteous, to make ready a people prepared for the LORD." (Luke 1:11–13, 16–17)

This Scripture connects John the Baptist to the "spirit and power of Elijah."

### WAS JOHN THE BAPTIST THE RETURN OF ELIJAH?

Biblically, we have two answers to this question: John said, "No" and Jesus said, "Yes." When the Pharisees confronted John the Baptist about his identity, he said that he *was not* Elijah:

This is the testimony given by John when the Jews sent priests and Levites from Jerusalem to ask him, "Who are you?" He confessed and did not deny it, but confessed, "I am not the Messiah." And they asked him, "What then? Are you Elijah?" He said, "I am not." "Are you the prophet?" He answered, "No." (John 1:19, 21)

Nevertheless, Jesus proclaimed that John the Baptist *was* Elijah:

Truly I tell you, among those born of women no one has arisen greater than John the Baptist; . . . and if you are willing to accept it, he is Elijah who is to come. Let anyone with ears listen! (Matthew 11:11, 14–15)

In short, John the Baptist said that he *was not* Elijah while Jesus said that John the Baptist *was* Elijah. Both were correct.

### IN WHAT WAY WAS JOHN THE BAPTIST BOTH ELIJAH
### AND NOT ELIJAH?

The answer lies in point of view. When John the Baptist denied being Elijah, he was speaking from a physical point of view—he was not the return of the physical body and personality of Elijah. However, Christ was speaking from a spiritual point of view. Because John was the return of the spiritual qualities and perfections of Elijah, John was Elijah. 'Abdu'l-Bahá explains this using the Greek and Latin form of Elijah, "Elias," for "Elijah"—consistent with the King James Version of the Bible:

> Now, they asked John the Baptist, "Art thou Elias [Elijah]?" and he answered, "I am not," whereas it is said in the Gospel that John was the promised Elias himself, and Christ clearly stated this as well. If John was Elias, why did he say he was not, and if he was not Elias, why did Christ say he was?
>
> The reason is that we consider here not the individuality of the person but the reality of his perfections—that is to say, the very same perfections that Elias possessed were realized in John the Baptist as well. Thus John the Baptist was the promised Elias. What is being considered here is not the essence but the attributes.
>
> For example, last year there was a flower, and this year there has also appeared a flower. When I say that the flower of last year has returned, I do not mean that the same flower has returned with the selfsame identity. But since this flower is endowed with the same attributes as last year's flower—as it possesses the same fragrance, delicacy, colour, and form—it is said that last year's flower has returned, and that this is that same flower. Likewise, when spring comes we say that last year's spring has returned, since all that was found in the former is to be found again in the latter. This is why Christ said, "Ye will witness all that came to pass in the days of the former Prophets."
>
> . . . In the same way, if we consider the individual, it is a different one, but if we consider the attributes and perfections, the same have returned. Thus when Christ said, "This is Elias," He meant: This person is a manifestation of the grace, the perfections, the qualities, the attributes, and the virtues of Elias. And when John the Baptist said, "I am not Elias," He meant: "I am not the same person as Elias." Christ considered their attributes, perfections, qualities, and virtues, and John referred to his own substance and individuality. ('Abdu'l-Bahá, *Some Answered Questions*, no. 33.5–7, 9)

The explanation of the return of Elijah in the person of John the Baptist offers biblical guidance on the spiritual meaning of "return" in prophecy. The "return" of a prophet refers to the return of the "spirit and power" of that prophet, not a return of the physical body or individual personality.

### WHAT WAS THE ROLE OF
### JOHN THE BAPTIST?

John the Baptist was "the Herald or Gate of the Christ" (George Townsend, Introduction to *The Dawn-Breakers,* p. xxx). In every Dispensation a Herald or Gate educates and prepares the faithful for the imminent coming of the Manifestation of God. This is the star in the "invisible heaven" that is a counterpart of the literal star in the sky:

> The sign of the invisible heaven must needs be revealed in the person of that perfect man who, before each Manifestation appeareth, educateth, and prepareth the souls of men for the advent of the divine Luminary, the Light of the unity of God amongst men. (Bahá'u'lláh, The Kitáb-i-Íqán, ¶73)

John the Baptist was the spiritual star who proclaimed the coming of the "divine Luminary" in the person of Jesus of Nazareth.

## BAPTISM

As Herald, John the Baptist called the people to purify their hearts, repent their sins, and prepare for the imminent coming of Christ. With their repentance, John baptized the people in a water submersion ritual:

> The beginning of the good news of Jesus Christ, the Son of God. As it is written in the prophet Isaiah, "See, I am sending my messenger ahead of you, who will prepare your way; the voice of one crying out in the wilderness: 'Prepare the way of the Lord, make his paths straight.'" (Mark 1:1–3)

### WHAT IS THE MEANING OF THE BAPTISM RITUAL?

The meaning of the baptism ritual is repentance from sin and purification of the heart:

> The essence of baptism is purification by repentance. John admonished and exhorted the people, caused them to repent, and then baptized them. It is evident then that this purification is a symbol of repentance from all sin, as though one were saying: "O God! Just as my body has been cleansed and purified from material defilements, so cleanse and purify my spirit from the defilements of the world of nature, which are unworthy of Thy divine threshold." Repentance is the return from rebelliousness to obedience. It is after experiencing remoteness and deprivation from God that man repents and purifies himself. Thus, this purification is a symbol saying, "O God! Render my heart goodly and pure, and cleanse and sanctify it from all save Thy love." ('Abdu'l-Bahá, *Some Answered Questions,* no. 19.3)

Jesus approached John the Baptist and requested to be baptized. John, recognizing Jesus' station, declined. Jesus persisted, and John finally baptized Jesus in the Jordan River:

> Then Jesus came from Galilee to John at the Jordan, to be baptized by him. John would have prevented him, saying, "I need to be baptized by you, and do you come to me?" (Matthew 3:13–14)

### DID CHRIST NEED TO BE BAPTIZED?

Christ did not need to be baptized. He modeled repentance and participated in this symbolic rite to confirm its importance at that time and to encourage others to repent and turn to God:

> As Christ desired that this custom instituted by John be practiced by all at that time, He Himself submitted to it, that souls might be awakened and that the law which had issued from the former religion might be fulfilled. For even though this custom was instituted by John, it represented in reality the purification of repentance which has been practiced an all the divine religions.

It is not that Christ was in need of baptism; but He submitted to it because at that time this action was praiseworthy and acceptable before God and presaged the glad tidings of the Kingdom. ('Abdu'l-Bahá, *Some Answered Questions,* no. 19.4–5)

John the Baptist baptized with water, but he foretold that Christ would baptize "with the Holy Spirit and fire":

John answered all of them by saying, "I baptize you with water; but one who is more powerful than I is coming; I am not worthy to untie the thong of his sandals. He will baptize you with the Holy Spirit and fire." (Luke 3:16)

### WHAT DOES BAPTISM WITH WATER, THE HOLY SPIRIT, AND FIRE MEAN?

Water symbolizes knowledge and life, the Holy Spirit symbolizes the bounty of God, and fire symbolizes the love of God:

Therefore, by "spirit" is meant divine grace; by "water," knowledge and life; and by "fire," the love of God. For material water cleanses not the heart of man but his body. Rather, the heavenly water and spirit, which are knowledge and life, cleanse and purify the heart of man. In other words, the heart that partakes of the outpouring grace of the Holy Spirit and becomes sanctified is made goodly and pure. The purpose is that the reality of man be purified and sanctified from the defilements of the world of nature, which are vile attributes such as anger, lust, worldliness, pride, dishonesty, hypocrisy, deceit, self-love, and so on.

Man cannot free himself from the onslaught of vain and selfish desires save through the confirming grace of the Holy Spirit. That is why it is said that baptism must be with the spirit, with water and with fire—that is, with the spirit of divine grace, the water of knowledge and life, and the fire of the love of God. It is with this spirit, this water, and this fire that man must be baptized, that he may partake of everlasting grace. For otherwise, of what avail is it to be baptized with material water? No, this baptism with water was a symbol of repentance and of seeking remission of sins. ('Abdu'l-Bahá, *Some Answered Questions,* no. 19.6–7)

## IS THE RITE OF BAPTISM AN INSTITUTION IN THE BAHÁ'Í FAITH?

The rite of baptism is not an institution in the Bahá'í Faith:

. . . in the Dispensation of Bahá'u'lláh this symbol is no longer required, for its reality, which is to be baptized with the spirit and the love of God, has been established and realized. ('Abdu'l-Bahá, *Some Answered Questions,* no. 19.8)

## LIKE A DOVE

The Gospels relate that at the baptism of Jesus the Holy Spirit descended upon Jesus in a "form like a dove," and a voice from heaven claimed Jesus as "Son":

Now when all the people were baptized, and when Jesus also had been baptized and was praying, the heaven was opened, and the Holy Spirit descended upon him in bodily form like a dove. And a voice came from heaven, "You are my Son, the Beloved; with you I am well pleased." (Luke 3:21–22)

### DID AN ACTUAL DOVE DESCEND UPON CHRIST?

The story of the descent of the dove is symbolic of Christ's spiritual condition, His oneness with the Holy Spirit:

Thus it is evident that the dove which descended upon Christ was not a physical dove but a spiritual condition expressed, for the sake of comprehension, by a sensible figure. ('Abdu'l-Bahá, *Some Answered Questions,* no. 16.6)

As noted in this book's section on Moses, various symbols in the world's Scriptures mark the awakening of the Manifestations. For Moses it is a

"Burning Bush," for Zoroaster a "Sacred Fire," for Christ "the Dove," for Muhammad the "Angel Gabriel," and for Bahá'u'lláh a "Maiden" (see Shoghi Effendi, *Messages to America,* p. 99).

### WHAT IS THE MEANING OF THE VOICE FROM HEAVEN SAYING, "YOU ARE MY SON, THE BELOVED; WITH YOU I AM WELL PLEASED" (LUKE 3:22)?

The voice from heaven claiming Jesus as "Son" is a scriptural proclamation of the reality of Jesus of Nazareth as the appearance of the Manifestation of God. The Jews at the time of Christ would have been familiar with the term "son of God" because in the Old Testament all of Israel is designated as the firstborn son of God:

> Then you shall say to Pharaoh, "Thus says the LORD: Israel is my firstborn son." (Exodus 4:22)

Proclaiming Jesus as the "Son of God" embraces all of Jewish history, and establishes Jesus as the fruit of the people's spiritual heritage and their Divine Representative. The title may also be an allusion to the fulfillment of prophecy in the unusual nature of His birth. While the title "Son of God" suggests the greatness of Jesus' station, it does not indicate any physical relationship with God:

> It is true that Jesus referred to Himself as the Son of God, but this, as explained by Bahá'u'lláh in the Íqán, does not indicate any physical relationship whatever. Its meaning is entirely spiritual and points to the close relationship existing between Him and the Almighty God. (From a letter written on behalf of Shoghi Effendi, dated November 29, 1937, to an individual believer, in *Lights of Guidance,* no. 1644)

### WHY DOES THE MANIFESTATION OF GOD, A PREEXISTENT REALITY, NEED AN AWAKENING?

In the spiritual station of the eternal Word of God, the Manifestation does not need an awakening; the awakening happens only in the Manifestation's human station involving His human body (the corporeal form) and His human rational soul:

The holy Manifestations have three stations: the corporeal station, the station of the rational soul, and the station of perfect divine manifestation and heavenly splendour. Their bodies perceive things only according to the capacity of the material world, and so it is that They have at certain times expressed physical weakness. For example: "I was asleep and unconscious; the breeze of God wafted over Me, awoke Me and summoned Me to voice His call"; or when Christ was baptized in His thirtieth year and the Holy Spirit descended upon Him, having not manifested itself in Him before this time. All these things refer to the corporeal station of the Manifestations, but Their heavenly station encompasses all things, is aware of all mysteries, is informed of all signs, and rules supreme over all things. And this is equally true both before and after the intimation of Their mission. That is why Christ said: "I am Alpha and Omega, the first and the last" [Rev 22:13]—that is, there has never been, nor shall there ever be, any change or alteration in Me. ('Abdu'l-Bahá, *Some Answered Questions,* no. 58.5)

While the physical human plane of Christ experienced an awakening, the spiritual Reality of Christ as the Word of God was the same before and after His awakening. This is true for the awakening experience of every Manifestation of God.

### WHAT IS IT LIKE FOR THE MANIFESTATION OF GOD, IN THE HUMAN CONDITION, TO EXPERIENCE THE FIRST MOMENTS OF REVELATION?

To help us understand something of this experience we can read the firsthand account of Bahá'u'lláh's awakening:

I was but a man like others, asleep upon My couch, when lo, the breezes of the All-Glorious were wafted over Me, and taught Me the knowledge of all that hath been. This thing is not from Me, but from One Who is Almighty and All-Knowing. And He bade Me lift up My voice between earth and heaven, and for this there befell Me what hath caused the tears of every man of understanding to flow. (Bahá'u'lláh, *The Summons of the Lord of Hosts,* no. 1.192)

The metaphorical nature of Bahá'u'lláh's description is apparent because this awakening occurred during His imprisonment in the Síyáh Chál (the dreaded Black Pit of Tehran, Persia)—a disease-infested subterranean dungeon where He was chained and shackled in the most inhumane of conditions. There was no "couch" and there was very little sleep.

Bahá'u'lláh continues to describe His awakening through the symbolism of a Maid of Heaven:

> While engulfed in tribulations I heard a most wondrous, a most sweet voice, calling above My head. Turning My face, I beheld a Maiden—the embodiment of the remembrance of the name of My Lord—suspended in the air before Me. So rejoiced was she in her very soul that her countenance shone with the ornament of the good pleasure of God, and her cheeks glowed with the brightness of the All-Merciful. Betwixt earth and heaven she was raising a call which captivated the hearts and minds of men. She was imparting to both My inward and outer being tidings which rejoiced My soul, and the souls of God's honored servants.
>
> Pointing with her finger unto My head, she addressed all who are in heaven and all who are on earth, saying: By God! This is the Best-Beloved of the worlds, and yet ye comprehend not. This is the Beauty of God amongst you, and the power of His sovereignty within you, could ye but understand. This is the Mystery of God and His Treasure, the Cause of God and His glory unto all who are in the kingdoms of Revelation and of creation, if ye be of them that perceive. (Bahá'u'lláh, *The Summons of the Lord of Hosts*, no. 1.6)

## THE WORD MADE FLESH

The exalted spiritual station of the Manifestation of God—the Word of God through which all of creation has its being—periodically enters the earthly dimensions of time and space and appears as a flesh and blood human being on the earth:

And the Word became flesh and lived among us, and we have seen his glory, the glory as of a father's only son, full of grace and truth. (John 1:14)

### WHEN THE MANIFESTATION OF GOD APPEARS IN THE WORLD, DOES THAT MAKE HIM "GOD INCARNATE"?

The appearance of the Manifestation of God in human form is the incarnation of all of the names and attributes of God—not God incarnate. To return to the analogy of the sun: a sunbeam possesses the attributes of the sun, but the sun does not incarnate its essence into the sunbeam. In like manner, the divinity of the Manifestation is "entirely distinguished" from the essence of God:

The divinity attributed to so great a Being [the Manifestation] and the complete incarnation of the names and attributes of God in so exalted a Person should, under no circumstances, be misconceived or misinterpreted. The human temple that has been made the vehicle of so overpowering a Revelation must, if we be faithful to the tenets of our Faith, ever remain entirely distinguished from that "innermost Spirit of Spirits" and "eternal Essence of Essences"— that invisible yet rational God Who, however much we extol the divinity of His Manifestations on earth, can in no wise incarnate His infinite, His unknowable, His incorruptible and all-embracing Reality in the concrete and limited frame of a mortal being. Indeed, the God Who could so incarnate His own reality would, in the light of the teachings of Bahá'u'lláh, cease immediately to be God. (Shoghi Effendi, *The World Order of Bahá'u'lláh,* p. 112)

### DOES THE ESSENCE OF GOD DESCEND INTO THE HUMAN REALM IN THE PERSON OF THE MANIFESTATION OF GOD?

God does not come and go. The essence of God is above ascent and descent into the human plane:

To every discerning and illumined heart it is evident that God, the unknowable Essence, the Divine Being, is immeasurably exalted beyond every human attribute such as corporeal existence, ascent and descent, egress and regress. . . . He is, and hath ever been, veiled in the ancient eternity of His Essence, and will remain in His Reality everlastingly hidden from the sight of men. (Bahá'u'lláh, The Kitáb-i-Íqán, ¶104)

It is in the spiritual station of oneness with God, not the physical human station, that the Manifestation of God is God:

The Christhood means not the body of Jesus but the perfection of divine virtues manifest in Him. Therefore, it is written, "He is God." ('Abdu'l-Bahá, *The Promulgation of Universal Peace*, p. 214)

## IS THE MANIFESTATION OF GOD DIVINE OR HUMAN?

The Manifestation has a double station—both divine and human. Although fully engaged in human life, the Manifestation maintains the spiritual reality of "One Whose voice is the voice of God Himself":

And since there can be no tie of direct intercourse to bind the one true God with His creation, and no resemblance whatever can exist between the transient and the Eternal, the contingent and the Absolute, He hath ordained that in every age and dispensation a pure and stainless Soul be made manifest in the kingdoms of earth and heaven. Unto this subtle, this mysterious and ethereal Being He hath assigned a twofold nature; the physical, pertaining to the world of matter, and the spiritual, which is born of the substance of God Himself. He hath, moreover, conferred upon Him a double station. The first station which is related to His innermost reality, representeth Him as One Whose voice is the voice of God Himself.
. . .
The second station is the human station, exemplified by the following verses: "I am but a man like you." (Bahá'u'lláh, *Gleanings from the Writings of Bahá'u'lláh*, no. 27.4)

Although there are some things we can know, the station and condition of the Manifestation of God will forever be a mystery to human beings.

## INTO THE WILDERNESS

After His baptism, Jesus went into the wilderness and fasted for forty days. During this time He was tempted by the devil. One temptation was to perform a miracle to make food appear:

> Jesus, full of the Holy Spirit, returned from the Jordan and was led by the Spirit in the wilderness, where for forty days he was tempted by the devil. He ate nothing at all during those days, and when they were over, he was famished. The devil said to him, "If you are the Son of God, command this stone to become a loaf of bread." Jesus answered him, "It is written, 'One does not live by bread alone.'" (Luke 4:1–4)

Two more temptations followed: glory and authority over all the kingdoms in the world if He would worship the devil; and being physically rescued by angels because of His importance. Jesus declined all the temptations.

### WHAT IS THE SIGNIFICANCE OF THE
### TEMPTATION OF CHRIST?

Every account of the Manifestation of God overcoming temptation and demonstrating endurance is a lesson and source of strength to those with eyes to see:

> . . . to outward seeming, the human condition of the Holy Manifestations is subjected to tests, and when Their strength and endurance have by this means been revealed in the plenitude of power, other men receive instruction therefrom, and are made aware of how great must be their own steadfastness and endurance under tests and trials. For the Divine Educator must teach by word and also by deed. ('Abdu'l-Bahá, *Selections from the Writings of 'Abdu'l-Bahá*, no. 26.3)

And, in a mystical sense, what the Manifestation endures brings strength and capacity to the human soul. Bahá'u'lláh states:

My body hath endured imprisonment that ye may be released from the bondage of self. (Bahá'u'lláh, *Tablets of Bahá'u'lláh,* p. 12)

Everything that the Manifestation of God experiences is for the empowerment of humanity. Therefore, we can look upon the Temptation of Christ, and everything He endured, as mystically endowing humanity with new capacities.

### WAS CHRIST THE ONLY MANIFESTATION OF GOD TO GO INTO A PERIOD OF WITHDRAWAL FROM THE WORLD?

Scripture shows that, sometime after awakening to Their Revelation, every Manifestation of God goes into one or more seclusions: Abraham dwelt in the wilderness of Paran (Genesis 21:21); Moses retreated to Mount Sinai (Exodus 34:28); Muhammad spent time in the caves of Mount Hira (Hadith, Bukhari, vol. 1); and Bahá'u'lláh retreated to the remote uplands of Kurdistan ('Abdu'l-Bahá, *A Travelers Narrative,* p. 38). These self-imposed isolations are regarded as periods of preparation for the Manifestations' world-reforming tasks.

## DOWN FROM HEAVEN

In a claim surprising to some, Christ stated that He came from heaven, was in heaven, and had ascended up to heaven:

No one has ascended into heaven except the one who descended from heaven, the Son of Man. (John 3:13)

Many wondered how Christ could have "descended from heaven" when He had been born from the womb of Mary:

They were saying, "Is not this Jesus, the son of Joseph, whose father and mother we know? How can he now say, 'I have come down from heaven'?" (John 6:42)

## IN WHAT WAY DID CHRIST COME DOWN FROM HEAVEN?

Heaven is the condition of spiritual oneness with God. Being the Word of God and therefore in perfect unity with God, Christ rightfully claimed to have come from heaven, to be in heaven, and to have ascended to heaven—all as He was standing on the earth in a human body born of a woman:

> It is evident that the body of Christ did not descend from heaven but came from the womb of Mary: What descended from the heaven of God was the spirit of Christ. ('Abdu'l-Bahá, *Some Answered Questions,* no. 21.3)

Christ continued to expand people's understanding of heaven with more new teachings.

## WHAT WERE CHRIST'S NEW TEACHINGS ABOUT HEAVEN?

Christ enlarged heaven—the Kingdom of God—to a place not just for God, angels, and prophets. The heaven of Christ is an eternal home (2 Corinthians 5:1) accessible to human souls and particularly available to those who humbly do God's Will:

> Not everyone who says to me, "LORD, LORD," will enter the kingdom of heaven, but only the one who does the will of my Father in heaven. (Matthew 7:21)

Christ's teachings about heaven are part of the good news of the Gospel, for in 30 AD the eternal life of the soul was, for many, a novel concept:

> For from the days of Adam until the time of Christ there was little mention of life eternal and of the all-embracing perfections of the Kingdom on high. ('Abdu'l-Bahá, *Some Answered Questions,* no. 30.7)

The possibility of heaven as an eternal home of the soul expanded people's understanding of their own spiritual potential.

**WHAT IS HEAVEN?**

Heaven, like its counterpart hell, is not a final destination. It is a condition of the soul:

> Heaven and hell are conditions within our own beings. (From a letter written on behalf of Shoghi Effendi, dated November 14, 1947, to an individual believer, *High Endeavors: Messages to Alaska,* p. 49)

To attain a heavenly condition is to develop divine qualities such as love, forgiveness, justice, selfless service, and patience. This is nearness to God and progress on the path to salvation. Heaven may be experienced in this world and in the life of the soul after the passing of the body:

> For just as the effects and the fruitage of the uterine life are not to be found in that dark and narrow place, and only when the child is transferred to this wide earth do the benefits and uses of growth and development in that previous world become revealed—so likewise reward and punishment, heaven and hell, requital and retribution for actions done in this present life, will stand revealed in that other world beyond. ('Abdu'l-Bahá, *Selections from the Writings of 'Abdu'l-Bahá,* no. 156.11)

## HELL FIRE

Hell as a place of fiery misery is a frequent image in the New Testament:

> If your hand causes you to stumble, cut it off; it is better for you to enter life maimed than to have two hands and to go to hell, to the unquenchable fire. (Mark 9:43)

The Bahá'í Writings use the word hell in a similar way, often in contrast to Paradise:

> Paradise is decked with mystic roses, and hell hath been made to blaze with the fire of the impious. (Bahá'u'lláh, Epistle to the Son of the Wolf, p. 133)

## WHAT IS HELL?

Hell is the condition of ungodliness within our own selves:

Think ye of love and good fellowship as the delights of heaven, think ye of hostility and hatred as the torments of hell. ('Abdu'l-Bahá, *Selections from the Writings of 'Abdu'l-Bahá,* no. 200.8)

## IS HELL EXPERIENCED IN THIS LIFE
## OR IN THE LIFE HEREAFTER?

Both. The heaven and hell of existence are experiences of the soul in our physical life as well as in the spiritual worlds:

In the heavenly Books, mention is made of the immortality of the spirit, which is the very foundation of the divine religions. For rewards and punishments are said to be of two kinds—one being existential rewards and punishments and the other, ultimate rewards and punishments. Existential paradise and hell are to be found in all the worlds of God, whether in this world or in the heavenly realms of the spirit, and to gain these rewards is to attain life eternal. ('Abdu'l-Bahá, *Some Answered Questions,* no. 60.2)

## WHAT ARE THE PUNISHMENTS OF HELL?

The punishments of hell are to be distant from God and to be submerged in the qualities of the lower nature:

When these souls are delivered from the darkness of these vices through the light of faith, when they are illumined by the rays of the Sun of Truth and endowed with every human virtue, they reckon this as the greatest reward and regard it as the true paradise. In like manner, they consider spiritual punishment—that is, existential torment and chastisement—to consist in subjection to the world of nature; in being veiled from God; in ignorance and unawareness; in engrossment with covetous desires; in absorption in animal vices; in being marked by evil attributes, such as falsehood, tyranny, and iniquity; in attachment to worldly things; and in immersion in satanic fancies—all of which they reckon to be the greatest of torments and punishments. ('Abdu'l-Bahá, *Some Answered Questions,* no. 60.3)

## WHAT DO THE PUNISHMENTS OF HELL LOOK LIKE IN THE MATERIAL WORLD?

As the experience of hell is a condition of the soul, it has no particular outward appearance. Ease of life and material benefits, if they cause the soul to forget about God, could be a condition of hell:

> . . . shouldst Thou ordain evil for a servant by reason of that which his hands have unjustly wrought before Thy face, Thou wouldst test him with the benefits of this world and of the next that he might become preoccupied therewith and forget Thy remembrance. (The Báb, *Selections from the Writings of the Báb*, 7.22.4)

## WHAT IS THE UNDERLYING CAUSE OF HELL?

Spiritual ignorance is the underlying cause of hell:

> The root cause of wrongdoing is ignorance, and we must therefore hold fast to the tools of perception and knowledge. Good character must be taught. Light must be spread afar, so that, in the school of humanity, all may acquire the heavenly characteristics of the spirit, and see for themselves beyond any doubt that there is no fiercer hell, no more fiery abyss, than to possess a character that is evil and unsound; no more darksome pit nor loathsome torment than to show forth qualities which deserve to be condemned. ('Abdu'l-Bahá, *Selections from the Writings of 'Abdu'l-Bahá*, no. 111.1)

## BORN AGAIN

As we have seen, the Gospels often convey Christ's teachings in the form of parables, stories, and dialogues. The following dialogue between Christ and Nicodemus presents the concept of being "born again":

> Jesus answered him, "Very truly, I tell you, no one can see the kingdom of God without being born from above." Nicodemus said to him, "How can anyone be born after having grown old? Can one enter a second time into the mother's womb and be born?" Jesus

answered, "Very truly, I tell you, no one can enter the kingdom of God without being born of water and Spirit. What is born of the flesh is flesh, and what is born of the Spirit is spirit." (John 3:3–6)

## WHAT IS THE MEANING OF "BORN AGAIN"?

Being born again is awakening to the life of the spirit through the power of the Word of God—it is opening a door to a higher consciousness. As a child in the womb is born into a larger life outside of the mother, the soul inspired by the Holy Spirit awakens to the eternal life of its own higher self:

> Christ announced, "That which is born of the flesh is flesh; and that which is born of the Spirit is spirit," meaning that man must be born again. As the babe is born into the light of this physical world, so must the physical and intellectual man be born into the light of the world of Divinity. In the matrix [womb] of the mother the unborn child was deprived and unconscious of the world of material existence, but after its birth it beheld the wonders and beauties of a new realm of life and being. In the world of the matrix it was utterly ignorant and unable to conceive of these new conditions, but after its transformation it discovers the radiant sun, trees, flowers and an infinite range of blessings and bounties awaiting it. In the human plane and kingdom man is a captive of nature and ignorant of the divine world until born of the breaths of the Holy Spirit out of physical conditions of limitation and deprivation. Then he beholds the reality of the spiritual realm and Kingdom, realizes the narrow restrictions of the mere human world of existence and becomes conscious of the unlimited and infinite glories of the world of God. ('Abdu'l-Bahá, *The Promulgation of Universal Peace,* p. 403)

When born into the life of the spirit, the soul feels its worth.

## HOW CAN ONE BE BORN AGAIN?

One can be born again by opening one's heart to the Word of God in any Dispensation:

Even as Jesus said: "Ye must be born again." . . . The purport of these words is that whosoever in every dispensation is born of the Spirit and is quickened by the breath of the Manifestation of Holiness, he verily is of those that have attained unto "life" and "resurrection" and have entered into the "paradise" of the love of God. (Bahá'u'lláh, The Kitáb-i-Íqán, ¶125)

In addition to introducing the concept of being spiritually born again, the dialogue between Christ and Nicodemus is a commentary on the hazards of the literal interpretation of Scripture.

### WHAT DOES THE "BORN AGAIN" STORY TEACH ABOUT LITERAL INTERPRETATION OF SCRIPTURE?

The "born again" story exposes the inadequacy of literalism when dealing with spiritual realities. The life of the spirit is not of this dimension, therefore symbolism and poetry are required to point to spiritual truths. Symbolism is capable of great explanations, but understanding its meanings demands certain capacities:

Consider how the parable makes attainment dependent upon capacity. Unless capacity is developed, the summons of the Kingdom cannot reach the ear, the light of the Sun of Truth will not be observed, and the fragrances of the rose garden of inner significance will be lost. ('Abdu'l-Bahá, *The Promulgation of Universal Peace,* p. 206)

Spiritual capacity is a quality of the heart that is not dependent on human learning. In the dialogue between Christ and Nicodemus, we see that even though Nicodemus was a "teacher of Israel," (John 3:10) his attachment to literalism at that moment blinded him to the significance of being spiritually reborn.

## A NEW DEFINITION OF DEAD

It is one of the most provocative passages in the Gospels:

To another he said, "Follow me." But he said, "Lord, first let me go and bury my father." But Jesus said to him, "Let the dead bury their own dead; but as for you, go and proclaim the kingdom of God." (Luke 9:59–60)

Physically dead people can't bury physically dead people. Therefore, this passage needs to be interpreted symbolically. The meaning involves a new definition of life (spiritually alive with recognition of the Word of God) and death (spiritually dead with denial of the Word of God):

. . . we must understand the interpretation of Christ's words concerning the dead. A certain disciple came to Christ and asked permission to go and bury his father. He answered, "Let the dead bury their dead." Therefore, Christ designated as dead some who were still living—that is, let the living dead, the spiritually dead, bury your father. They were dead because they were not believers in Christ. Although physically alive, they were dead spiritually. This is the meaning of Christ's words, "That which is born of flesh is flesh; and that which is born of Spirit is spirit." He meant that those who were simply born of the human body were dead spiritually, while those quickened by the breaths of the Holy Spirit were living and eternally alive. These are the interpretations of Christ Himself. Reflect upon them, and the meanings of the Holy Books will become clear as the sun at midday. ('Abdu'l-Bahá, *The Promulgation of Universal Peace,* p. 344)

Spiritual death is being without the "presence of the Holy Spirit" and being a stranger to the divine virtues:

Material development may be likened to the glass of a lamp, whereas divine virtues and spiritual susceptibilities are the light within the glass. The lamp chimney is worthless without the light; likewise, man in his material condition requires the radiance and vivification of the divine graces and merciful attributes. Without the presence of the Holy Spirit he is lifeless. Although physically and mentally alive, he is spiritually dead. ('Abdu'l-Bahá, *The Promulgation of Universal Peace,* p. 402)

The metaphor of death meaning "without the presence of the Holy Spirit" is repeated throughout the Gospels in stories of bringing the "dead" back to life. One example is the story of the resurrection of Lazarus of Bethany.

### WHAT IS THE STORY OF LAZARUS OF BETHANY?

Christ's friend Lazarus is described as being sick. Later, from a distant location, Christ confirms that Lazarus is dead. Jesus and a few disciples then travel to Bethany and find that Lazarus has been dead for four days. Jesus consoles Lazarus' sister Martha, assures her that her brother shall "rise again" (John 11:23), and inquires as to Martha's faith:

> Jesus said to her, "I am the resurrection and the life. Those who believe in me, even though they die, will live, and everyone who lives and believes in me will never die. Do you believe this?" She said to him, "Yes, LORD, I believe that you are the Messiah, the Son of God, the one coming into the world." (John 11:25–27)

Then they go to the cave gravesite, roll away the stone blocking the entrance, Christ calls out to Lazarus, and Lazarus gets up and walks out of the tomb.

### WHAT IS THE MEANING OF THE STORY OF LAZARUS?

This and other accounts of raising the dead are allegorical stories indicating real spiritual resurrections—the spiritual awakening of those who were physically alive but spiritually dead:

> Consider that Christ reckoned as dead those who were nonetheless outwardly and physically alive; for true life is life eternal and true existence is spiritual existence. Thus if the Sacred Scriptures speak of raising the dead, the meaning is that they attained everlasting life. . . . ('Abdu'l-Bahá, *Some Answered Questions*, no. 22.7)

### WOULD IT BE POSSIBLE FOR THE MANIFESTATIONS OF GOD TO LITERALLY RAISE THE PHYSICALLY DEAD TO LIFE?

The Manifestation of God is capable of performing any physical miracle, but this is not a problem-solving strategy generally put to use or advertised. The Manifestation teaches the reality of the eternal life of the spirit through spiritual means, not through temporary physical marvels:

> Our meaning is not that the Manifestations of God are unable to perform miracles, for this indeed lies within Their power. But that which is of import and consequence in Their eyes is inner sight, spiritual hearing, and eternal life. ('Abdu'l-Bahá, *Some Answered Questions,* no. 22.8)

The spiritual interpretation of the raising of Lazarus is consistent with the story of the Temptation of Christ in which He chooses not to use superhuman powers to force or prove His mission.

### WHY WOULD BRINGING SOMEONE PHYSICALLY BACK TO LIFE BE LESS IMPORTANT THAN SPIRITUAL HEALING?

When we are confronted with physical death it feels monumentally important. The loss, grief, and fear can be unbearable. But in this physical world, death is, sooner or later, inevitable, and our only safety is not a temporary resurrection of the body that is bound to die another time, but knowledge of the eternal life of the spirit. The pain of death and the supremacy of the life of the spirit is expressed in this letter from 'Abdu'l-Bahá addressed to a grieving mother:

> O thou beloved maidservant of God, although the loss of a son is indeed heart-breaking and beyond the limits of human endurance, yet one who knoweth and understandeth is assured that the son hath not been lost but, rather, hath stepped from this world into another, and she will find him in the divine realm. That reunion shall be for eternity, while in this world separation is inevitable and bringeth with it a burning grief.
>
> Praise be unto God that thou hast faith, art turning thy face toward the everlasting Kingdom and believest in the existence of a heavenly world. Therefore be thou not disconsolate, do not languish, do not sigh, neither wail nor weep; for agitation and mourning deeply affect his soul in the divine realm.
>
> That beloved child addresseth thee from the hidden world: "O thou kind Mother, thank divine Providence that I have been freed

from a small and gloomy cage and, like the birds of the meadows, have soared to the divine world—a world which is spacious, illumined, and ever gay and jubilant. Therefore, lament not, O Mother, and be not grieved; I am not of the lost, nor have I been obliterated and destroyed. I have shaken off the mortal form and have raised my banner in this spiritual world. Following this separation is everlasting companionship. Thou shalt find me in the heaven of the Lord, immersed in an ocean of light." ('Abdu'l-Bahá, *Selections from the Writings of 'Abdu'l-Bahá,* no. 171.1–3)

The lasting blessing and the real miracle is the awakening of the soul to the eternal life of the spirit—that is the real life in this world and the next.

### CAN A SOUL BE CONSIDERED SPIRITUALLY DEAD EVEN AFTER THE DEATH OF THE BODY?

Spiritual death is a condition in this world and in the next:

Similarly, ultimate retributions and punishments consist in being deprived of the special bounties and unfailing bestowals of God and sinking to the lowest degrees of existence. And whoso is deprived of these favours, though he continue to exist after death, is accounted as dead in the eyes of the people of truth. ('Abdu'l-Bahá, *Some Answered Questions,* no. 60.4)

## MIRACLE HEALINGS

Accounts of miracle healings occur throughout the Gospels. For example, Christ healed lepers:

He stretched out his hand and touched him, saying, "I do choose. Be made clean!" Immediately his leprosy was cleansed. (Matthew 8:3)

Christ healed the deaf:

They brought to him a deaf man who had an impediment in his speech; and they begged him to lay his hand on him. . . . Then looking up to heaven, he sighed and said to him, "Ephphatha," that is, "Be opened." And immediately his ears were opened, his tongue was released, and he spoke plainly. (Mark 7:32, 34–35)

And Christ healed the blind:

He took the blind man by the hand and led him out of the village; and when he had put saliva on his eyes and laid his hands on him, he asked him, "Can you see anything?" And the man looked up and said, "I can see people, but they look like trees, walking." Then Jesus laid his hands on his eyes again; and he looked intently and his sight was restored, and he saw everything clearly. (Mark 8:23–25)

## HOW ARE WE TO UNDERSTAND THE MIRACLE HEALINGS IN THE GOSPELS?

These miracle healings have greater meanings beyond temporary physical repairs. Like the raising of the dead, the healing of the deaf and blind symbolize eternal spiritual healings:

. . . if they say that one who was blind was made to see, the meaning of this seeing is true insight; if they say that one who was deaf was made to hear, the meaning is that he acquired an inner ear and attained spiritual hearing. This is established by the very text of the Gospel where Christ says that they are like those of whom Isaiah once said, "They have eyes and see not, they have ears and hear not; and I healed them." ('Abdu'l-Bahá, *Some Answered Questions*, no. 22.7; Matthew 13:14 cited)

The healing of the soul is a reality of the spiritual world and difficult to describe in common language. Therefore, in the poetry of Scripture, the healing of the soul is expressed as being cured of leprosy, seeing after being blind, and hearing after being deaf. Through these symbolic accounts of transformation, something of the magnitude of spiritual healing can be understood even by those with little awareness of the life of the spirit. The miracle stories are important instructional tools that convey real spiritual truths to be understood in various degrees depending upon the capacity of the hearers.

### WHAT IS THE IMPORTANCE OF OUTWARD MIRACLES?

Outward (physical) miracles are of little importance because they represent only temporary changes in circumstances:

> These outward miracles are of no importance to the followers of truth. For example, if a blind man is made to see, in the end he will again lose his sight, for he will die and be deprived of all his senses and faculties. Thus, causing the blind to see is of no lasting importance, since the faculty of sight is bound to be lost again in the end. And if a dead body be revived, what is gained thereby, since it must die again? What is important is to bestow true insight and everlasting life, that is, a spiritual and divine life; for this material life will not endure and its existence is tantamount to non-existence. ('Abdu'l-Bahá, *Some Answered Questions,* no. 22.6)

### ARE PHYSICAL MIRACLES PROOFS OF DIVINITY?

Physical marvels are not proofs of divinity for three reasons: those who are not witnesses can dispute them, stories of miracles can be found in many traditions, and even magicians can perform physical marvels:

> I will not mention the miracles of Bahá'u'lláh, for the hearer might say that these are merely traditions which may or may not be true. Such, too, is the case with the Gospel, where the accounts of the miracles of Christ come down to us from the Apostles and not from other observers, and are denied by the Jews. Were I nonetheless to mention the supernatural feats of Bahá'u'lláh, they are numerous and unequivocally acknowledged in the East, even by some of the non-believers. But these accounts cannot be a decisive proof and testimony for all, since the hearer might say that they are not factually true, as the followers of other denominations also recount miracles from their leaders. For instance, Hindus recount certain miracles of Brahma. How can we know that those are false and that these are true? If these are reported accounts, so too are those; if these are widely attested, then the same holds true of

those. Thus such accounts do not constitute a sufficient proof. Of course, a miracle may be a proof for the eyewitness, but even then he might not be sure whether what he beheld was a true miracle or mere sorcery. Indeed, extraordinary feats have also been attributed to certain magicians. ('Abdu'l-Bahá, *Some Answered Questions,* no. 10.3)

### IF OUTWARD MIRACLES ARE NOT SIGNIFICANT, WHAT IS THE PROOF OF THE TRUTH OF CHRIST?

The greatest miracle of Christ and proof of His divinity is the outcome of His Revelation:

However, in the day of God's Manifestation, they that are endued with insight will find all things pertaining to Him to be miraculous. For these things are distinguished above all else, and this distinction is in itself an absolute miracle. Consider how Christ, alone and single-handed, with no helper or protector, with no legions or armies, and with the utmost meekness, raised aloft the banner of God before all the peoples of the world; how He withstood them; and how at last He subdued them all, even though outwardly He was crucified. Now, this is an absolute miracle which can in no wise be denied. Indeed, the truth of Christ stands in no need of further proof. ('Abdu'l-Bahá, *Some Answered Questions,* no. 22.5)

The outcome of Christ's Revelation is the greatest miracle. His proofs are the same as the proofs of Abraham, Moses, and every Manifestation. Although bereft of worldly power and persecuted by those with worldly power, Christ's new teachings persevered and souls became educated. His life, teachings, and the results of His ministry are demonstrations of the power of the Holy Spirit and the real proofs of His station.

## THE LAW FULFILLED

One purpose of the Revelation of Christ was to fulfill the laws and teachings of Moses:

Do not think that I have come to abolish the law or the prophets; I have come not to abolish but to fulfill. For truly I tell you, until heaven and earth pass away, not one letter, not one stroke of a letter, will pass from the law until all is accomplished. (Matthew 5:17–18)

It is interesting that in the course of fulfilling the Mosaic Laws, Christ changed or abolished many of those laws.

### IN WHAT WAY DID CHRIST CHANGE
### THE LAWS AND TEACHINGS OF MOSES?

A few examples of how Christ changed the laws of Moses are that He added anger and insult to the list of those sins that would put one "in liable to judgment":

You have heard that it was said to those of ancient times, "You shall not murder"; and "whoever murders shall be liable to judgment." But I say to you that if you are angry with a brother or sister, you will be liable to judgment; and if you insult a brother or sister, you will be liable to the council; and if you say, "You fool," you will be liable to the hell of fire. (Matthew 5:21–22)

Christ abolished the law of divorce:

It was also said, "Whoever divorces his wife, let him give her a certificate of divorce." But I say to you that anyone who divorces his wife, except on the ground of unchastity, causes her to commit adultery; and whoever marries a divorced woman commits adultery. (Matthew 5:31–32)

In the eyes of the Pharisees, Christ broke the law of the Sabbath:

Some of the Pharisees said, "This man is not from God, for he does not observe the Sabbath." (John 9:16)

After the crucifixion, Christ's disciples changed the application of the laws of Moses concerning diet, male circumcision, and sacrificial offerings (See *Some Answered Questions*, no. 20.2).

## BY WHAT AUTHORITY DID CHRIST CHANGE
## THE LAWS OF MOSES?

Christ had the authority to change the laws of Moses because every Manifestation of God is the ultimate authority, the Divine Physician, for that Dispensation:

> Briefly, Bahá'u'lláh says that "He Who is the Dawning-place of God's Cause" is the manifestation of "He doeth whatsoever He willeth," that this station is reserved to that sanctified Being, and that others receive no share of this essential perfection. That is, since the essential infallibility of the universal Manifestations of God has been established, whatsoever proceeds from Them is identical with the truth and conformable to reality. They are not under the shadow of the former religion. Whatsoever They say is the utterance of God, and whatsoever They do is a righteous deed. . . . Therefore, whatsoever the universal Manifestation of God says and does is the very essence of wisdom and conformable to reality.
>
> Thus Christ—may my soul be a sacrifice for His sake!—was the embodiment of the words, "He doeth whatsoever He willeth . . . ." ('Abdu'l-Bahá, *Some Answered Questions,* no. 45.5, 10)

The Divine Physician has perfect knowledge of what is required for the progress of humanity. To adjust the social laws is to continue the work and fulfill the purpose of the preceding Manifestation, and therefore to glorify Moses. This is one of the meanings of Christ's statement: "I have not come to abolish, but to fulfill" (Matthew 5:18).

## HOW DID CHRIST ACQUIRE PERFECT KNOWLEDGE
## OF THE NEEDS OF THE TIME?

Christ's knowledge was innate, not acquired. The Manifestation of God is the source of all knowledge, and therefore is never in need of acquiring learning like a regular human being:

> The sun emanates from itself and does not draw its light from other sources. The divine teachers have the innate light; they have knowledge and understanding of all things in the universe; the rest

of the world receives its light from them and through them the arts and sciences are revived in each age.

Abraham and Moses went to no school; Jesus had neither school nor master; Mohammed never had a lesson; the Báb and Bahá'u'lláh had no professors. ('Abdu'l-Bahá, cited in Lample, *The Proofs of Bahá'u'lláh's Mission,* p. 94)

## HOW WERE THE CHANGES IN THE LAWS OF MOSES RECEIVED BY THE GENERAL POPULATION?

Like the changes brought by every appearance of the Manifestation of God, Christ's adjustments of the Mosaic Laws were received with hostility and He was considered by many to be the enemy of Moses:

> Among other objections, they said, "We are promised through the tongue of the prophets that His Holiness Christ at the time of his coming would proclaim the law of the Torah whereas now we see this person abrogating the commands of the Pentateuch, disturbing our blessed sabbath and abolishing the law of divorce. He has left nothing of the ancient law of Moses, therefore he is the enemy of Moses." ('Abdu'l-Bahá, *The Promulgation of Universal Peace,* p. 408)

## FORGIVENESS

In the story of the crucifixion as presented in the Gospel of Luke, Christ modeled forgiveness when He forgave those responsible for His death:

> Then Jesus said, "Father, forgive them; for they do not know what they are doing." And they cast lots to divide his clothing. (Luke 23:34)

### HOW SHOULD THE LAW OF FORGIVENESS BE APPLIED?

Christ's law of forgiveness abolishes the right of personal vengeance, but it does not forfeit the community's right of chastisement:

There are two sorts of retributive actions: One is revenge and retaliation, and the other—punishment and requital. An individual has no right to seek revenge, but the body politic has the right to punish the criminal. Such punishment is intended to dissuade and deter others from committing similar crimes. It is for the protection of the rights of man and does not constitute revenge, for revenge is that inner gratification that results from returning like for like. This is not permissible, for no one has been given the right to seek revenge. And yet, if criminals were entirely left to their own devices, the order of the world would be disrupted. So while punishment is one of the essential requirements of the body politic, the wronged and aggrieved party has no right to seek revenge. On the contrary, he should show forgiveness and magnanimity, for this is that which befits the human world ('Abdu'l-Bahá, *Some Answered Questions,* no. 77.2)

It is the responsibility of the individual to forgive. It is the responsibility of the community to chastise. Punishment is a necessary element of maintaining order:

Some men are like bloodthirsty wolves: If they were to see no punishment ahead, they would kill others solely for the sake of their own pleasure and diversion. ('Abdu'l-Bahá, *Some Answered Questions,* no. 77.9)

Punishment, along with reward, is required for the establishment of Justice:

O people of God! That which traineth the world is Justice, for it is upheld by two pillars, reward and punishment. These two pillars are the sources of life to the world. (Bahá'u'lláh, *Tablets of Bahá'u'lláh,* p. 27)

### WHAT IS THE PROBLEM WITH PERSONAL VENGEANCE?

The problem with personal vengeance is that both actions are injurious. The healing action is to forgive:

For example, if someone wrongs, injures, and assaults another, and the latter retaliates in kind, this constitutes revenge and is blameworthy. If Peter kills the son of Paul, Paul has no right to kill the son of Peter. Were he to do so, it would be an act of vengeance and blameworthy in the extreme. Rather, he must act in the opposite manner and show forgiveness, and, if possible, even be of some assistance to his aggressor. This indeed is that which is worthy of man; for what advantage does one gain from revenge? The two actions are indeed one and the same: If one is reprehensible, so too is the other. The only difference is that one preceded the other. ('Abdu'l-Bahá, *Some Answered Questions,* no. 77.5)

## THE LAW OF LOVE

When Christ was asked which of the Mosaic commandments was most important, His response was "love"—love of God then love of one's neighbor:

Jesus answered, "The first is, 'Hear, O Israel: the LORD our God, the LORD is one; you shall love the LORD your God with all your heart, and with all your soul, and with all your mind, and with all your strength." The second is this, "You shall love your neighbor as yourself." There is no other commandment greater than these." (Mark 12:29–31)

Later, Christ proclaimed a "new commandment" about love:

I give you a new commandment, that you love one another. Just as I have loved you, you also should love one another. By this everyone will know that you are my disciples, if you have love for one another. (John 13:34–35)

### WHAT MAKES "LOVE ONE ANOTHER; AS I HAVE LOVED YOU" A "NEW COMMANDMENT"?
Previous Dispensations commanded love in a limited sense:

In every dispensation, there hath been the commandment of fellowship and love, but it was a commandment limited to the community of those in mutual agreement, not to the dissident foe. ('Abdu'l-Bahá, *Selections from the Writings of 'Abdu'l-Bahá*, no. 7.4)

Christ's law to love "as I have loved you" brought a new standard that opened the circle of love to include "others" such as those deemed undesirable and one's enemies:

When the Messianic star of Jesus Christ dawned, He declared He had come to gather together the lost tribes or scattered sheep of Moses. He not only shepherded the flock of Israel, but brought together people of Chaldea, Egypt, Syria, ancient Assyria and Phoenicia. These people were in a state of utmost hostility, thirsting for the blood of each other with the ferocity of animals; but Jesus Christ brought them together, cemented and united them in His cause and established such a bond of love among them that enmity and warfare were abandoned. It is evident therefore that the divine teachings are intended to create a bond of unity in the human world and establish the foundations of love and fellowship among mankind. ('Abdu'l-Bahá, *The Promulgation of Universal Peace*, p. 162)

The commandment of love was initially somewhat limited because human learning is progressive and cumulative—we have to walk before we can run:

. . . peace must first be established among individuals, until it leadeth in the end to peace among nations. ('Abdu'l-Bahá, *Selections from the Writings of 'Abdu'l-Bahá*, no. 201.2)

The Dispensations before Christ had accomplished the integration of family units, tribes, city-states, and, to some degree, nations—progressively larger units cultivated with a strong sense of exclusivity. This was necessary to establish certain foundations of society (see Shoghi Effendi, *The Promised Day is Come*, p. 117). Christ's law of love was a progression toward love that encompasses the entire world.

# YOU CANNOT BEAR IT NOW

The Gospel of John states that there was more that Christ wanted to teach, but that He had to hold back:

> I still have many things to say to you, but you cannot bear them now. When the Spirit of truth comes, he will guide you into all the truth; for he will not speak on his own, but will speak whatever he hears, and he will declare to you the things that are to come. (John 16:12–13)

### WHY DID CHRIST HOLD BACK CERTAIN TEACHINGS?

Christ determined that humanity had reached its capacity for new teachings for a while, but promised that the Spirit of Truth—the next appearance of the Manifestation of God—would reveal more truth:

> Briefly, in the sayings of Him Who is the Spirit (Jesus) unnumbered significances lie concealed. Unto many things did He refer, but as He found none possessed of a hearing ear or a seeing eye He chose to conceal most of these things. Even as He saith: "But ye cannot bear them now." That Dawning-Place of Revelation saith that on that Day He Who is the Promised One will reveal the things which are to come. (Bahá'u'lláh, Epistle to the Son of the Wolf, p. 147)

### WHAT ABOUT THE TEACHINGS THAT CHRIST CONCEALED?

Bahá'u'lláh's claim is that He has brought the Word that Christ concealed. He states:

> The Father is come, and that which ye were promised in the Kingdom is fulfilled! This is the Word which the Son concealed, when to those around Him He said: "Ye cannot bear it now." (Bahá'u'lláh, *Tablets of Bahá'u'lláh*, p. 11)

The Bahá'í Writings contain teachings that could not have been understood at the time of Christ, such as the oneness of religion, the oneness of mankind, the unity of the races, the equality of women and men, and the requisites for world peace.

## DID BAHÁ'U'LLÁH WITHHOLD KNOWLEDGE IN HIS REVELATION?

In the process of teaching according to humanity's capacity, every Manifestation of God withholds knowledge. Bahá'u'lláh indicates that there is much that He could have revealed that remains undisclosed:

Other knowledges We do as well possess, not a single letter of which We can disclose, nor do We find humanity able to hear even the barest reference to their meaning. Thus have We informed you of the knowledge of God, the All-Knowing, the All-Wise. Were We to find worthy vessels, We would deposit within them the treasures of hidden meanings. (Bahá'u'lláh, cited in Shoghi Effendi, *The World Order of Bahá'u'lláh*, p. 25)

## THE TRANSFIGURATION

As Christ was teaching with His disciples, He took Peter, James, and John to a certain area where His disciples saw a vision of Christ in the full glory of His station as the Word of God talking with Moses and Elijah:

Jesus took with him Peter and James and his brother John and led them up a high mountain, by themselves. And he was transfigured before them, and his face shone like the sun, and his clothes became dazzling white. Suddenly there appeared to them Moses and Elijah, talking with him. Then Peter said to Jesus, "LORD, it is good for us to be here; if you wish, I will make three dwellings here, one for you, one for Moses, and one for Elijah." While he was still speaking, suddenly a bright cloud overshadowed them, and from the cloud a voice said, "This is my Son, the Beloved; with him I am well pleased; listen to him!" When the disciples heard this, they fell to the ground and were overcome by fear. (Matthew 17:1–6)

## WHAT HAPPENED AT THE TRANSFIGURATION?

The Transfiguration describes a real spiritual experience:

> Thou didst ask as to the transfiguration of Jesus, with Moses and
> Elias [Elijah] and the Heavenly Father on Mount Tabor, as referred
> to in the Bible. This occurrence was perceived by the disciples with
> their inner eye, wherefore it was a secret hidden away, and was a
> spiritual discovery of theirs. ('Abdu'l-Bahá, *Selections from the Writings of 'Abdu'l-Bahá,* no. 140.1)

A spiritual vision is not an imagination. Like the visions of the lesser
prophets that foretold future events, spiritual visions are authentic experiences in the spiritual world:

> . . . with respect to spiritual understandings and inner disclosures,
> there exists among spiritual souls a unity that surpasses all imagination and comparison and a communion that transcends time and
> place. So, for example, when it is written in the Gospel that Moses
> and Elijah came to Christ on Mount Tabor, it is clear that this was
> not a material communion but a spiritual condition that has been
> expressed as a physical meeting. ('Abdu'l-Bahá, *Some Answered Questions,* no. 71.7)

## BLASPHEMY AGAINST THE HOLY SPIRIT

The sayings of Christ offer forgiveness from blasphemy, including speaking against the Son of Man Himself. However, speaking against the Holy
Spirit is described as eternally unforgivable:

> Therefore I tell you, people will be forgiven for every sin and
> blasphemy, but blasphemy against the Spirit will not be forgiven.
> Whoever speaks a word against the Son of Man will be forgiven,
> but whoever speaks against the Holy Spirit will not be forgiven,
> either in this age or in the age to come. (Matthew 12:31–32)

## WHY IS IT FORGIVABLE TO SPEAK AGAINST THE SON OF MAN (THE MANIFESTATION OF GOD)?

One may love light but have an aversion to a particular lamp. In the same way, a soul may be attracted to the light of the Holy Spirit (that is, the divine perfections) but have an aversion to, or not recognize, the Manifestation of God Who brings that light. In this case the soul can still be awakened because of its fundamental love of the light:

> If a soul distances himself from the Manifestation, he may yet be awakened, for he may have failed to know Him and to recognize Him as the Embodiment of the divine perfections.
>
> . . . That is why there have been many souls who opposed the Manifestations of God, not realizing that They were Manifestations, but who became Their friends once they had recognized Them. Thus, enmity towards the Manifestation of God was not the cause of eternal deprivation, for they were enemies of the candleholder and knew not that it was the seat of God's effulgent light. They were not the enemies of the light itself, and once they understood that the candleholder was the seat of the light, they became true friends. ('Abdu'l-Bahá, *Some Answered Questions,* no. 31.3, 6)

## WHY IS DENIAL OF THE HOLY SPIRIT UNFORGIVABLE?

For a soul to hate the Holy Spirit is to hate the divine perfections—to have an aversion to all things good. One cannot be illumined by the light if one hates and hides from the light:

> But if he loathes the divine perfections themselves, which are the Holy Spirit, this shows that, bat-like, he is a hater of the light.
>
> This hatred of the light itself is irremediable and unforgivable; that is, it is impossible for such a soul to draw near to God. This lamp here is a lamp because of its light; without the light it would not be a lamp. A soul that abhors the light of the lamp is, at it were, blind and cannot perceive the light, and this blindness is the cause of eternal deprivation.
>
> It is evident that souls receive grace from the outpourings of the Holy Spirit which are apparent in the Manifestations of God, and

not from the individual personality of the Manifestation. It follows that if a soul fails to partake of the outpourings of the Holy Spirit, it remains deprived of God's grace, and this deprivation itself is equivalent to the denial of divine forgiveness. ('Abdu'l-Bahá, *Some Answered Questions,* no. 31.3–5)

The Manifestation of God shines on everyone. Souls who do not recognize the appearance of the Manifestation are still recipients of the bounties of the Holy Spirit that shine from that realm. However, if one is an enemy of the divine perfections themselves, that soul turns away from the Holy Spirit, thereby banishing him or herself from the heavenly bounties.

## PERSECUTION

From the beginning of Christ's teaching He was opposed and persecuted. For example, He was persecuted for His teachings regarding the Sabbath and His claim of oneness with God:

For this reason the Jews were seeking all the more to kill him, because he was not only breaking the sabbath, but was also calling God his own Father, thereby making himself equal to God. (John 5:18)

Christ's teachings challenged the status quo, were interpreted as threats, and exposed Him to constant danger (John 7:1). This dynamic is repeated in every Dispensation.

### WHY DOES THE MANIFESTATION OF GOD ENDURE PERSECUTION?

The Manifestation endures hardships for the purpose of teaching love and unity:

Moses was persecuted and driven out into the desert, Abraham was banished, Muhammad took refuge in caves, the Báb was killed and

Bahá'u'lláh was exiled and imprisoned forty years. Yet all of Them desired fellowship and love among men. They endured hardships, suffered persecution and death for our sakes that we might be taught to love one another and be united and affiliated instead of discordant and at variance. ('Abdu'l-Bahá, *The Promulgation of Universal Peace,* p. 328)

The Manifestation endures hardships to free humanity from sin:

This is the meaning of Christ's words that I gave My blood for the life of the world.[38] That is, I chose to bear all these trials, afflictions, and calamities, even the most great martyrdom, to attain this ultimate objective and to ensure the remission of sin—that is, the detachment of spirits from the material world and their attraction to the divine realm—that souls may arise who will be the very essence of guidance and the manifestations of the perfections of the Kingdom on high. ('Abdu'l-Bahá, *Some Answered Questions,* no. 30.9)

### WHAT IS THE MOTIVATION FOR THE MANIFESTATION OF GOD TO TEACH MANKIND DESPITE PERSECUTION?

The motivation is love:

What an infinite degree of love is reflected by the divine Manifestations toward mankind! For the sake of guiding the people They have willingly forfeited Their lives to resuscitate human hearts. They have accepted the cross. To enable human souls to attain the supreme degree of advancement, They have suffered during Their limited years extreme ordeals and difficulties. If Jesus Christ had not possessed love for the world of humanity, surely He would not have welcomed the cross. He was crucified for the love of mankind. Consider the infinite degree of that love. Without love for humanity John the Baptist would not have offered his life. It has been likewise with all the Prophets and Holy Souls. If the Báb had not

---

38. John 6:51.

manifested love for mankind, surely He would not have offered His breast for a thousand bullets. If Bahá'u'lláh had not been aflame with love for humanity, He would not have willingly accepted forty years' imprisonment . . . all the divine Manifestations suffered, offered Their lives and blood, sacrificed Their existence, comfort and all They possessed for the sake of mankind. ('Abdu'l-Bahá, *The Promulgation of Universal Peace*, p. 359)

## BREAD AND BLOOD

In the story of the Lord's Supper—the final meal that Christ had with His Apostles in Jerusalem before His crucifixion—Christ blessed bread and wine and then offered these to His Apostles with the invitation to eat his flesh and drink his blood:

While they were eating, Jesus took a loaf of bread, and after blessing it he broke it, gave it to the disciples, and said, "Take, eat; this is my body." Then he took a cup, and after giving thanks he gave it to them, saying, "Drink from it, all of you; for this is my blood of the covenant, which is poured out for many for the forgiveness of sins." (Matthew 26:26–28)

### WHAT IS THE MEANING OF THE BREAD AND WINE
### AT THE LAST SUPPER?

The bread and wine at the Last Supper are symbolic of the divine bounties and perfections of Christ:

It is therefore clear that the bread and wine were symbols, meaning: My grace and My perfections have been given you, and since you have partaken of this manifold grace, you have attained everlasting life and received your share and portion of the heavenly sustenance. ('Abdu'l-Bahá, *Some Answered Questions*, no. 21.10)

In some religious traditions it is taught that Christ miraculously changed the bread and wine into His flesh and blood (transubstantiation), and that this mystery can be repeated through certain priestly rituals; this is the doctrine of the Eucharist, or sacrament of Holy Communion.

### CAN BAHÁ'ÍS PARTICIPATE IN HOLY COMMUNION?

First it would depend on whether or not the Bahá'ís were invited to participate in Holy Communion by the church they were visiting, because in many churches participation is restricted to baptized Christians. It would also depend on the Bahá'í's personal choice. Participation in the ritual is not forbidden, and if a Bahá'í chose to partake it would be with the understanding that Holy Communion does not represent a miracle of transubstantiation, but that it:

> . . . is symbolical of the truth that Christ is the food from heaven, the eating of which produces eternal life. ('Abdu'l-Bahá, *The Promulgation of Universal Peace,* p. 297)

### IS THERE A BAHÁ'Í RITUAL COMMEMORATING THE LORD'S SUPPER?

The Lord's Supper is not commemorated ritualistically in the Bahá'í Faith; however, 'Abdu'l-Bahá states that meetings of a Spiritual Assembly (elected administrative body of a Bahá'í community) should reflect the spirit of the Lord's Supper:

> O ye dear friends of mine! Light up this Assembly with the splendour of God's love. Make it ring out with the joyous music of the hallowed spheres, make it thrive on those foods that are served at the Lord's Supper, at the heavenly banquet table of God. ('Abdu'l-Bahá, *Selections from the Writings of 'Abdu'l-Bahá,* no. 37.4)

'Abdu'l-Bahá also states that the meetings of the Bahá'í community (the Nineteen Day spiritual Feasts) should be held in the spirit of the Lord's Supper:

> The beloved and the maid-servants of the Merciful must inaugurate the feast in such wise as to resurrect the feast of the ancients—namely, the "Lord's supper." ('Abdu'l-Bahá, *Tablets of 'Abdu'l-Bahá,* vol. 1, p. 149)

## PROMISE TO RETURN

Christ prophesies the return of the Son of Man and warns His followers to keep alert:

> Beware, keep alert; for you do not know when the time will come. It is like a man going on a journey, when he leaves home and puts his slaves in charge, each with his work, and commands the door-keeper to be on the watch. Therefore, keep awake—for you do not know when the master of the house will come, in the evening, or at midnight, or at cockcrow, or at dawn, or else he may find you asleep when he comes suddenly. And what I say to you I say to all: Keep awake." (Mark 13:33–37)

The return of the Son of Man—the Manifestation of God—is prophesied in every Dispensation.

### WHAT IS THE MEANING OF THE RETURN OF THE MANIFESTATION OF GOD?

The return of a Manifestation of God refers to the return of the "spirit and power" of the Manifestation, not a return of the physical body or individual personality. We have already seen how Jesus demonstrated the spiritual meaning of return when He recognized John the Baptist as the return of Elijah. As the spirit and power of Elijah returned in the person of John, the spirit and power of the Manifestation of God returns periodically as different historical persons:

> Know that the return of Christ for a second time doth not mean what the people believe, but, rather, signifieth the One promised to come after Him. He shall come with the Kingdom of God and His power which hath surrounded the world. ('Abdu'l-Bahá, cited in Esslemont, *Bahá'u'lláh and the New Era*, p. 247)

This spiritual meaning of the return of the Manifestation of God is demonstrated in the Gospels when Christ refers to both His return and the coming of another.

## IN WHAT WAY DOES CHRIST PROMISE THE RETURN
## OF BOTH HIMSELF AND ANOTHER?

Christ promises His return:

You heard me say to you, "I am going away, and I am coming to you." If you loved me, you would rejoice that I am going to the Father, because the Father is greater than I. (John 14:28)

Christ also promises that the Advocate will come:

Nevertheless I tell you the truth: it is to your advantage that I go away, for if I do not go away, the Advocate will not come to you; but if I go, I will send him to you. (John 16:7)

He also promises the Spirit of truth will come:

When the Spirit of truth comes, he will guide you into all the truth; for he will not speak on his own, but will speak whatever he hears, and he will declare to you the things that are to come. (John 16:13)

## WHO ARE "THE ADVOCATE" AND THE
## "SPIRIT OF TRUTH"?

The "Advocate" and the "Spirit of Truth" are titles for the Manifestation of God. Christ's prophecies concerning His Return and the Coming of the Advocate and the Spirit of Truth are the same prophecy:

To them that are endowed with understanding, it is clear and manifest that, when the fire of the love of Jesus . . . was made apparent and partially enforced, He, . . . addressing one day His disciples, referred unto His passing, and . . . said unto them: "I go away and come again unto you." And in another place He said: "I go and another will come, Who will tell you all that I have not told you, and will fulfill all that I have said." Both these sayings have but one meaning, were ye to ponder upon the Manifestations of the Unity of God with Divine insight. (Bahá'u'lláh, *Gleanings from the Writings of Bahá'u'lláh*, no. 13.5)

## HOW CAN CHRIST RETURN AS SOMEONE DIFFERENT
## AND ALSO AS HIMSELF?

This question takes us back to the double station of the Manifestation of God. In the first station of unity with God, all of the appearances of the Manifestation are spiritually One. In the second station of distinction, each appearance of the Manifestation has a different body and personality:

> Thus it is that Jesus, Himself, declared: "I go away and come again unto you." Consider the sun. Were it to say now, "I am the sun of yesterday," it would speak the truth. And should it, bearing the sequence of time in mind, claim to be other than that sun, it still would speak the truth. In like manner, if it be said that all the days are but one and the same, it is correct and true. And if it be said, with respect to their particular names and designations, that they differ, that again is true. For though they are the same, yet one doth recognize in each a separate designation, a specific attribute, a particular character. Conceive accordingly the distinction, variation, and unity characteristic of the various Manifestations of holiness, that thou mayest comprehend the allusions made by the Creator of all names and attributes to the mysteries of distinction and unity, and discover the answer to thy question as to why that everlasting Beauty should have, at sundry times, called Himself by different names and titles. (Bahá'u'lláh, *Gleanings from the Writings of Bahá'u'lláh*, no. 13.6)

Christ's prophecies concerning His return, the coming of the Advocate, and the coming of the Spirit of Truth all refer to the return of the spirit and power of the Manifestation of God.

## STARS AND CLOUDS

In addition to His return, Christ prophesied certain signs such as a darkened sun and falling stars that would mark the coming of the next appearance of the Manifestation of God:

Immediately after the suffering of those days the sun will be darkened, and the moon will not give its light; the stars will fall from heaven, and the powers of heaven will be shaken. Then the sign of the Son of Man will appear in heaven, and then all the tribes of the earth will mourn, and they will see 'the Son of Man coming on the clouds of heaven' with power and great glory. (Matthew 24:29–30)

### WHAT IS THE SIGNIFICANCE OF THE DARKENED SUN AND THE FALLING STARS?

Like the Bahá'í interpretation of similar Old Testament prophecies (see "Sun, Moon, and Stars"), New Testament prophecies about darkened and falling celestial lights symbolize the inadequacy of other guidance compared to the new Revelation, old religious laws that have become outdated, and the abrogation of previous laws by the new appearance of the Manifestation of God. In a symbolic sense, leaders of religion who do not recognize the Word of God in a new Revelation become like fallen stars. Referring to Christ's prophecy, Bahá'u'lláh states:

O concourse of bishops! Ye are the stars of the heaven of My knowledge. My mercy desireth not that ye should fall upon the earth. My justice, however, declareth: "This is that which the Son hath decreed." And whatsoever hath proceeded out of His blameless, His truth-speaking, trustworthy mouth, can never be altered. (Bahá'u'lláh, *Tablets of Bahá'u'lláh*, p. 13)

### DO STARS LITERALLY FALL FROM THE SKY UPON THE RETURN OF THE MANIFESTATION?

While literal astronomical signs marking the Return of the Manifestation of God do occur (Bahá'u'lláh, The Kitáb-i-Íqán, ¶72), catastrophic star events have not accompanied the appearance of the Manifestation in the past and are not expected in the future:

All the signs and conditions that have been indicated have inner meanings and are not to be taken literally. For otherwise it is said, among other things, that the stars will fall upon the earth. Yet the stars are endless and innumerable, and modern mathematicians have established and proven that the mass of the sun is approximately one and a half million times greater than that of the earth, and that each one of the fixed stars is a thousand times larger than the sun. If these stars were to fall upon the surface of the earth, how could there be room for them? It would be as though a thousand million mountains as mighty as the Himalayas were to fall upon a grain of mustard seed. Such a thing is, by reason and by science (and indeed as a matter of simple common sense), utterly impossible. And yet even more astonishing is that Christ said: Perchance I shall come when you are sleeping, for the coming of the Son of man is like the coming of a thief. Perhaps the thief will be in the house and the owner will be unaware.

It is therefore clear and evident that these signs have inner meanings and should not be taken literally. ('Abdu'l-Bahá, *Some Answered Questions*, no. 26.5–6)

## WHAT ARE THE "CLOUDS OF HEAVEN"?

As noted in the section entitled "Clouds," clouds refer to factors that act as barriers to peoples' recognition of a new Revelation. These include the annulment of former social religious laws, the abolishment of old rituals and customs, the appearance of the Manifestation of God in mortal form, the humble nature of His followers, and other things contrary to human desires and expectations.

## WHY WOULDN'T THE MANIFESTATION OF GOD LITERALLY DESCEND FROM THE CLOUDS IN THE VISIBLE HEAVEN?

A fantastic worldly phenomenon is of little value in the process of Divine Revelation that is, among other things, a spiritual testing ground of the souls:

Were the prophecies recorded in the Gospel to be literally fulfilled; were Jesus, Son of Mary, accompanied by angels, to descend from the visible heaven upon the clouds; who would dare to disbelieve, who would dare to reject the truth, and wax disdainful? Nay, such consternation would immediately seize all the dwellers of the earth that no soul would feel able to utter a word, much less to reject or accept the truth. (Bahá'u'lláh, The Kitáb-i-Íqán, ¶88)

## HAS THE SON OF MAN
## COME UPON THE CLOUDS OF HEAVEN AGAIN
## AS PROPHESIED?

The Son of Man has come upon the clouds of heaven since the Christian Revelation. Speaking of Bahá'u'lláh's station as the return of the Manifestation of God for this age, 'Abdu'l-Bahá points out that all of these prophecies have been fulfilled:

O people who are inhaling the scent of life from the Spirit of God! . . . the powers of heaven have been shaken, the corners of the earth have quaked, the sun has been darkened, the moon ceased to give light, the stars have fallen, the nations of the earth have lamented, and the Son of Man hath come upon the clouds of heaven with power and great glory. ('Abdu'l-Bahá, *Tablets of 'Abdu'l-Bahá*, vol. 1, p. 145)

# THE
# CRUCIFIXION

The Gospel of John relates that after Jesus' arrest He was taken before Pontius Pilate, the magistrate of the Roman province of Judaea. Many people called for Jesus' death with the reasoning that His claim to be King of the Jews was a challenge to the authority of the Roman Empire. Finally, Christ was crucified:

They cried out, "Away with him! Away with him! Crucify him!" Pilate asked them, "Shall I crucify your King?" The chief priests answered, "We have no king but the emperor." Then he handed him over to them to be crucified. So they took Jesus; and carrying the cross by himself, he went out to what is called The Place of the Skull, which in Hebrew is called Golgotha. There they crucified him, and with him two others, one on either side, with Jesus between them. (John 19:15–18)

Some hours later, the physical body of Jesus Christ died on the cross.

### WAS JESUS CHRIST REALLY CRUCIFIED?

The Bahá'í Writings state that it is a historical fact that Jesus Christ was crucified.

The crucifixion as recounted in the New Testament is correct. (From a letter written on behalf of Shoghi Effendi, dated July 14, 1943, to an individual believer, in *Lights of Guidance,* no. 1646)

The specific details of the stories of the crucifixion as related in the Gospels may or may not be historically accurate, but the Bahá'í Writings confirm that the spiritual integrity of these stories has been protected by Providence (see letter of the Universal House of Justice, dated August 9, 1984, to an individual believer, as cited in "Resurrection of Christ" Memorandum from the Research Department, September 14, 1987).

### DOES THE QUR'ÁN STATE THAT CHRIST WAS NOT CRUCIFIED?

A passage in the Qur'án states that Christ's enemies only had His "likeness":

Yet they slew him not, and they crucified him not, but they had only his likeness. (Sura 4)

However, these verses mean that only Christ's physical body ("His likeness") was killed, but the eternal Spirit of Christ lives on. Muhammad, like Christ, considered the true life to be the life of the spirit, not the life of the body:

The meaning of the Qur'ánic version is that the spirit of Christ was not Crucified. There is no conflict between the two. (From a letter written on behalf of Shoghi Effendi, dated July 14, 1943, to an individual believer, in *Lights of Guidance,* no. 1646)

### WHAT ARE SOME OF THE SYMBOLIC VERSES IN THE STORY OF THE CRUCIFIXION?

The Gospels of Matthew, Mark, and Luke include the splitting of the veil of the temple, a shaking of the earth, and the coming forth of the dead out of their tombs at the time of Christ's death. Matthew states:

Then Jesus cried again with a loud voice and breathed his last. At that moment the curtain of the temple was torn in two, from top to bottom. The earth shook, and the rocks were split. The tombs also were opened, and many bodies of the saints who had fallen asleep were raised. After his resurrection they came out of the tombs and entered the holy city and appeared to many. (Matthew 27:50–53)

The above verses are symbolic of spiritual truths:

. . . it is recorded in the Gospel that upon the martyrdom of Christ darkness fell, the earth shook, the veil of the Temple was rent in twain, and the dead arose from their graves. If this had outwardly come to pass, it would have been a stupendous thing. Such an event would have undoubtedly been recorded in the chronicles of the time and would have seized with dismay the hearts of men. At the very least the soldiers would have removed Christ from the cross or would have fled. But as these events have not been recorded in any history, it is evident that they are not to be understood literally but according to their inner meaning. Our purpose is not to deny, but merely to say that these accounts do not constitute a decisive proof, and that they have an inner meaning—nothing more. ('Abdu'l-Bahá, *Some Answered Questions,* no. 10.5)

### WHAT IS THE INNER SIGNIFICANCE OF THE DEAD RISING, THE RENDING OF THE TEMPLE VEIL, AND THE SHAKING OF THE EARTH?

We have already seen that "dead" means spiritually dead, so the dead coming from their graves could indicate that many realized the divinity of Christ and became, in a spiritual sense, alive. As for the symbolism of veils, they are often used in the Bahá'í Writings to represent spiritual blindness:

The bestowals of God which are manifest in all phenomenal life are sometimes hidden by intervening veils of mental and mortal vision which render man spiritually blind and incapable, but when those scales are removed and the veils rent asunder, then the great signs of God will become visible, and he will witness the eternal light filling the world. ('Abdu'l-Bahá, *The Promulgation of Universal Peace*, p. 124)

With this symbolism in mind, the splitting of the veils of the Temple might indicate the power of the sacrifice of Christ to remove the veils of ignorance and give spiritual sight to the spiritually blind. Regarding the shaking of the earth: while interpreting another Scripture, 'Abdu'l-Bahá refers to the "tremor of doubt" that shook the earth upon the passing of Bahá'u'lláh. (*Some Answered Questions*, no. 11.45).

If we use the above interpretations to inform our personal understanding of the splitting of the veil, the raising of the dead, and the shaking of the earth in the crucifixion Scripture, then perhaps we could say that Christ and His sacrifice split the veils of ignorance and raised the spiritually dead from their tombs of disbelief, while His death caused many to shake with doubt and fear.

## HOW DID CHRIST'S INFLUENCE CHANGE AFTER THE CRUCIFIXION?

Christ's sacrifice infused new capacity into the whole of creation, and this capacity bloomed in human wisdom, learning, arts, and sciences throughout the world:

Know thou that when the Son of Man yielded up His breath to God, the whole creation wept with a great weeping. By sacrificing Himself, however, a fresh capacity was infused into all created things. Its evidences, as witnessed in all the peoples of the earth, are now manifest before thee. The deepest wisdom which the sages have uttered, the profoundest learning which any mind hath unfolded, the arts which the ablest hands have produced, the influence exerted by the most potent of rulers, are but manifestations of the quickening power released by His transcendent, His all-pervasive, and resplendent Spirit.

We testify that when He came into the world, He shed the splendor of His glory upon all created things. Through Him the leper recovered from the leprosy of perversity and ignorance. Through Him, the unchaste and wayward were healed. Through His power, born of Almighty God, the eyes of the blind were opened, and the soul of the sinner sanctified.

Leprosy may be interpreted as any veil that interveneth between man and the recognition of the Lord, his God. Whoso alloweth himself to be shut out from Him is indeed a leper, who shall not be remembered in the Kingdom of God, the Mighty, the All-Praised. We bear witness that through the power of the Word of God every leper was cleansed, every sickness was healed, every human infirmity was banished. He it is Who purified the world. Blessed is the man who, with a face beaming with light, hath turned towards Him. (Bahá'u'lláh, *Gleanings from the Writings of Bahá'u'lláh,* no. 36.1–3)

If the world of creation is like a body, then the appearance and sacrifice of the Manifestation of God is like an intravenous feeding of life-giving nutrients to that body. The Manifestation infuses new abilities and competencies for humanity to grow into. The educative and spiritualizing powers of the appearance of the Word of God in the world of creation is one of the mysteries of Divine Revelation.

## HOW WAS THE INFLUENCE OF CHRIST CHANGED AFTER THE CRUCIFIXION?

The splendor, grace, and powers of Christ were intensified after the crucifixion:

As to the influence of holy Beings and the continuance of Their grace to mankind after They have put away Their human form, this is, to Bahá'ís, an indisputable fact. Indeed, the flooding grace, the streaming splendours of the holy Manifestations appear after Their ascension from this world. The exaltation of the Word, the revelation of the power of God, the conversion of God-fearing souls, the bestowal of everlasting life—it was following the Messiah's martyrdom that all these were increased and intensified. ('Abdu'l-Bahá, *Selections from the Writings of 'Abdu'l-Bahá,* no. 31.9)

## WHAT ARE SOME OF THE LESSONS OF THE CRUCIFIXION?

The lessons of the crucifixion are illimitable. We will examine three.

First, the crucifixion demonstrates that spiritual truth is often in opposition to worldly powers. Therefore, to guide people to the truth one must be willing to endure opposition, to suffer, and to sacrifice:

> In order to understand the reality of sacrifice let us consider the crucifixion and death of Jesus Christ. It is true that He sacrificed Himself for our sake. What is the meaning of this? When Christ appeared, He knew that He must proclaim Himself in opposition to all the nations and peoples of the earth. He knew that mankind would arise against Him and inflict upon Him all manner of tribulations. There is no doubt that one who put forth such a claim as Christ announced would arouse the hostility of the world and be subjected to personal abuse. He realized that His blood would be shed and His body rent by violence. Notwithstanding His knowledge of what would befall Him, He arose to proclaim His message, suffered all tribulation and hardships from the people and finally offered His life as a sacrifice in order to illumine humanity—gave His blood in order to guide the world of mankind. He accepted every calamity and suffering in order to guide men to the truth. Had He desired to save His own life, and were He without wish to offer Himself in sacrifice, He would not have been able to guide a single soul. There was no doubt that His blessed blood would be shed and His body broken. Nevertheless, that Holy Soul accepted calamity and death in His love for mankind. This is one of the meanings of sacrifice. ('Abdu'l-Bahá, *The Promulgation of Universal Peace*, p. 634)

Second, we learn from Christ's example that when we sacrifice our personal attachments and worldly reality for a higher reality, we become a greater manifestation of the Holy Spirit. It is only though a willingness to lose ourselves in service to others that we truly find our lives:

> If you plant a seed in the ground, a tree will become manifest from that seed. The seed sacrifices itself to the tree that will come from it. The seed is outwardly lost, destroyed; but the same seed which is sacrificed will be absorbed and embodied in the tree, its blossoms, fruit and branches. If the identity of that seed had not been

sacrificed to the tree which became manifest from it, no branches, blossoms or fruits would have been forthcoming. Christ outwardly disappeared. His personal identity became hidden from the eyes, even as the identity of the seed disappeared; but the bounties, divine qualities and perfections of Christ became manifest in the Christian community which Christ founded through sacrificing Himself. ('Abdu'l-Bahá, *The Promulgation of Universal Peace*, pp. 635–36)

Third, through the crucifixion, Christ modeled the perfect expression of forgiveness and mercy. Like Christ, followers of the Word of God are called upon to forgive those who persecute them:

You must follow the example and footprints of Jesus Christ. Read the Gospels. Jesus Christ was mercy itself, was love itself. He even prayed in behalf of His executioners—for those who crucified Him—saying, "Father, forgive them; for they know not what they do." If they knew what they were doing, they would not have done it. Consider how kind Jesus Christ was, that even upon the cross He prayed for His oppressors. We must follow His example. We must emulate the Prophets of God. We must follow Jesus Christ. We must free ourselves from all these imitations which are the source of darkness in the world. ('Abdu'l-Bahá, *The Promulgation of Universal Peace*, p. 57)

## THE RISEN CHRIST

After the crucifixion and burial, the Gospels tell of Christ's Resurrection and appearance to His disciples. Mary Magdalene, Mary the mother of James, and Salome went to the gravesite to anoint the body of Jesus but found the sepulcher open and empty:

As they entered the tomb, they saw a young man, dressed in a white robe, sitting on the right side; and they were alarmed. But he said to them, "Do not be alarmed; you are looking for Jesus of

Nazareth, who was crucified. He has been raised; he is not here. Look, there is the place they laid him." (Mark 16:5–6)

They fled. Later, Christ appeared to Mary Magdalene and others:

> Later he appeared to the eleven themselves as they were sitting at the table; and he upbraided them for their lack of faith and stubbornness, because they had not believed those who saw him after he had risen. (Mark 16:14)

## WHAT IS THE MEANING OF
## CHRIST'S RESURRECTION?

After the crucifixion, Christ's followers were troubled. Their Lord, Who had taught of everlasting life, was dead and buried. Discouragement prevailed. However, after two or three days, as their certitude in His teachings strengthened and they felt the Reality of Christ in their hearts, His Spirit became apparent to His followers once more. This was a true spiritual Resurrection:

> We explain, therefore, the meaning of Christ's resurrection in the following way: After the martyrdom of Christ, the Apostles were perplexed and dismayed. The reality of Christ, which consists in His teachings, His bounties, His perfections, and His spiritual power, was hidden and concealed for two or three days after His martyrdom, and had no outward appearance or manifestation— indeed, it was as though it were entirely lost. For those who truly believed were few in number, and even those few were perplexed and dismayed. The Cause of Christ was thus as a lifeless body. After three days the Apostles became firm and steadfast, arose to aid the Cause of Christ, resolved to promote the divine teachings and practice their Lord's admonitions, and endeavoured to serve Him. Then did the reality of Christ become resplendent, His grace shine forth, His religion find new life, and His teachings and admonitions become manifest and visible. In other words, the Cause of Christ, which was like unto a lifeless body, was quickened to life and surrounded by the grace of the Holy Spirit.

Such is the meaning of the resurrection of Christ, and this was a true resurrection. ('Abdu'l-Bahá, *Some Answered Questions,* no. 23.6–7)

Without the Resurrection, there would have been no Christianity: "If those who accepted Jesus during his earthly life had not continued to follow, believe and experience his continuing presence after the crucifixion, all would have been over. That *is* the meaning of resurrection, the continuing presence in a continuing community of the past Jesus in a radically new and transcendental mode of present and future existence" (Crossan, p. 404).

**WAS CHRIST'S PHYSICAL BODY RESURRECTED FROM THE DEAD?**

From a Bahá'í perspective, Christ's Resurrection was a real Resurrection of the Spirit of Christ in the hearts of His followers, not a physical resuscitation:

From a Bahá'í point of view the belief that the Resurrection was the return to life of a body of flesh and blood, which later rose from the earth into the sky is not reasonable, nor is it necessary to the essential truth of the disciples' experience, which is that Jesus did not cease to exist when He was crucified (as would have been the belief of many Jews of that period), but that His Spirit, released from the body, ascended to the presence of God and continued to inspire and guide His followers and preside over the destinies of His dispensation. (From a letter written on behalf of the Universal House of Justice, dated May 28, 1984, to an individual, cited in a memorandum of the Research Department, dated September 14, 1987)

**WHAT IS THE "RISEN CHRIST"?**

The "Risen Christ" is the spiritual realization that Christ is an eternal living Reality:

The "Risen Christ" is the consciousness that came to His disciples, grieving over His death, of His living reality; it was not a physical thing but a spiritual realization. (Shoghi Effendi, *Messages to the Antipodes*, p. 256)

## WHAT WAS MARY MAGDALENE'S ROLE
## IN THE RESURRECTION?

Mary Magdalene's spiritual perceptiveness enabled her to grasp the fact of the living Spirit of Christ:

When Jesus Christ died upon the cross, the disciples who witnessed His crucifixion were disturbed and shaken. Even Peter, one of the greatest of His followers, denied Him thrice. Mary Magdalene brought them together and confirmed their faith, saying, "Why are ye doubting? Why have ye feared? O thou Peter! Why didst thou deny Him? For Christ was not crucified. The reality of Christ is ever-living, everlasting, eternal. For that divine reality there is no beginning, no ending, and, therefore, there can be no death. At most, only the body of Jesus has suffered death." In brief, this woman, singly and alone, was instrumental in transforming the disciples and making them steadfast. ('Abdu'l-Bahá, *The Promulgation of Universal Peace*, p. 556)

## WHY DID IT TAKE A WHILE FOR THE DISCIPLES TO FEEL THE
## RESURRECTION OF CHRIST IN THEIR HEARTS?

The account of the Resurrection presents a time lapse for some of the disciples between coming into contact with and actually accepting the Resurrected Christ. This delay represents a process of spiritual growth. The light of Christ shines on everyone, but it takes a while to develop the capacity to receive the light and reflect it back:

Know thou that the Messianic Spirit and the outpouring of the Holy Spirit is always manifest, but capacity and ability (to receive it) is more in some and less in others. After the crucifixion the apostles had not in the beginning the capacity and ability of witnessing the Messianic reality. For they were agitated. But when they found firmness and steadfastness, their inner sight became opened, and they saw the reality of the Messiah as manifest. For the body of

Christ was crucified and vanished, but the Spirit of Christ is always pouring upon the contingent world, and is manifest before the insight of the people of assurance. ('Abdu'l-Bahá, cited in memorandum of the Research Department of the Universal House of Justice, dated September 14, 1987)

## IF CHRIST WAS NOT PHYSICALLY RESURRECTED FROM THE DEAD, WHAT IS THE PROOF OF HIS DIVINITY?

Proofs of the Divinity of Christ are the potency of His Word, the sublimity of His example, and the efficacy of His teachings:

Christ, single and alone, without schooling or outward education and trained to labor in the shop of a carpenter, appeared in the world at the time when the Jewish nation was in the greatest abasement. This radiant Youth, without wealth, power of armies or prestige, rescued the Jews who believed on Him from tyranny and degradation and lifted them to the highest plane of development and glory. Peter, His disciple, was a fisherman. Through the power of Christ he shed light upon all the horizons of the world. Furthermore, various people of the Greek, Roman, Egyptian and Assyrian nations were brought together in unity and agreement; where warfare and bloodshed had existed, humility and love were manifest, and the foundations of divine religion were established, never to be destroyed. This proves that Christ was a heavenly Teacher and Educator of the world of humanity, for such evidences are historical and irrefutable, not based upon tradition and circumstantial report. The power of His Word in cementing these nations together is as clear and evident as the sun at midday. There is no need of further demonstration.

The proof of the validity of a Manifestation of God is the penetration and potency of His Word, the cultivation of heavenly attributes in the hearts and lives of His followers and the bestowal of divine education upon the world of humanity. This is absolute proof. The world is a school in which there must be Teachers of the Word of God. The evidence of the ability of these Teachers is efficient education of the graduating classes. ('Abdu'l-Bahá, *The Promulgation of Universal Peace*, pp. 482–83)

## WHAT CAN WE LEARN FROM THE RESURRECTION?

One thing we are to learn from the Resurrection is that, like Christ, mankind's true reality is not the physical body, but the immortal soul:

Concerning the resurrection of Christ, he wishes to call your attention to the fact that in this as well as in practically all the so-called miraculous events recorded in the Gospel we should, as Bahá'ís, seek to find a spiritual meaning and to entirely discard the physical interpretation attached to them by many of the Christian sects. The resurrection of Christ was, indeed, not physical but essentially spiritual, and is symbolic of the truth that the reality of man is to be found not in his physical constitution, but in his soul. (From a letter written on behalf of Shoghi Effendi, dated August 14, 1934, to an individual believer, in *Lights of Guidance,* no. 1649)

# THE BOOK OF THE
# ACTS OF THE APOSTLES—OVERVIEW

**The Book of the Acts of the Apostles** narrates the steps by which the message of Christ moved from rural Palestine to the urban areas of the Roman Empire through the teaching work of the Apostles. While the Gospels focus on Jesus, the Book of Acts focuses on people teaching about Jesus. The Bahá'í Writings do not offer information on the origin or authorship of the Book of Acts. Biblical scholarship has determined that its language, style, and theological interests identify it as the work of the same author who wrote the Gospel of Luke—this is "one of the few virtually unchallenged conclusions of New Testament scholarship" (Alexander, p. 1028). Some of the topics addressed are the Ascension of Christ, the descent of the Holy Spirit upon the Apostles at Pentecost, and accounts of the Apostles' teaching.

# TOPICS FROM THE BOOK OF THE ACTS
# OF THE APOSTLES

## TRUE CONSULTATION

Acts begins with the apostles communing with the resurrected Christ, then watching as Christ was lifted up in a cloud to heaven:

> When he had said this, as they were watching, he was lifted up, and a cloud took him out of their sight. While he was going and they were gazing up toward heaven, suddenly two men in white robes stood by them. They said, "Men of Galilee, why do you stand looking up toward heaven? This Jesus, who has been taken up from you into heaven, will come in the same way as you saw him go into heaven." (Acts 1:9–11)

### WHAT IS THE MEANING OF CHRIST BEING LIFTED UP
### IN A CLOUD TO HEAVEN?

The Scripture describing the ascension of Christ symbolizes the continuation of Christ's spiritual Reality after the passing of His elemental body:

> The individual realities of the holy Manifestations cannot be separated from divine grace and revelation any more than the corporeal mass of the sun can be separated from its light. Thus the ascension of the holy Manifestations is simply the abandonment of Their elemental bodies. ('Abdu'l-Bahá, *Some Answered Questions*, no. 39.4)

The spiritual meaning of Christ's disciples watching His form being lifted up into heaven, like the symbolism of the Resurrection, is that their vision of Christ as the Word of God was restored.

## WHAT DID CHRIST'S DISCIPLES DO WHEN THEIR FAITH WAS RESURRECTED?

When the spirit of His Faith was resurrected in His disciples, they gathered to consult on how they should proceed:

Then they returned to Jerusalem from the mount called Olivet, which is near Jerusalem, a sabbath day's journey away. When they had entered the city, they went to the room upstairs where they were staying, Peter, and John, and James, and Andrew, Philip and Thomas, Bartholomew and Matthew, James son of Alphaeus, and Simon the Zealot, and Judas son of James. All these were constantly devoting themselves to prayer, together with certain women, including Mary the mother of Jesus, as well as his brothers. (Acts 12–14)

'Abdu'l-Bahá extols this meeting of the disciples as true "spiritual consultation":

The most memorable instance of spiritual consultation was the meeting of the disciples of Jesus Christ . . . after His ascension. They said, "Jesus Christ has been crucified, and we have no longer association with Him in His physical body; therefore, we must be loyal and faithful to Him, we must be grateful and appreciate Him, for He has raised us from the dead, He made us wise, He has given us eternal life. What shall we do to be faithful to Him?" And so they held council. One of them said, "We must detach ourselves from the chains and fetters of the world; otherwise, we cannot be faithful." The others replied, "That is so." Another said, "Either we must be married and faithful to our wives and children or serve our Lord free from these ties. We cannot be occupied with the care and provision for families and at the same time herald the Kingdom in the wilderness. Therefore, let those who are unmarried remain so, and those who have married provide means of sustenance and comfort for their families and then go forth to spread the message of glad tidings." There were no dissenting voices; all agreed, saying, "That is right." A third disciple said, "To perform worthy deeds in the Kingdom we must be further self-sacrificing. From now on we should forgo ease and bodily comfort, accept every difficulty, forget self and teach the Cause of God." This found acceptance and approval by all the others. Finally a fourth disciple said, "There is still another aspect to our faith and unity. For Jesus' sake we shall be beaten, imprisoned and exiled. They may kill us. Let us receive this lesson now. Let us realize and resolve that though we are beaten, banished, cursed, spat upon and led forth to be killed, we shall accept all this joyfully, loving those who hate and wound us." All the disciples replied, "Surely we will—it is agreed; this is right." Then . . . each went forth in a different direction upon his divine mission.

This was true consultation. This was spiritual consultation and not the mere voicing of personal views in parliamentary opposition and debate. ('Abdu'l-Bahá, *The Promulgation of Universal Peace,* p. 101)

### HOW MANY DISCIPLES
### DID CHRIST HAVE?

Christ had only a few disciples at the time of His ascension:

It was not until many years after His ascension that they knew who He was, and at the time of His ascension He had only a very few disciples; only a comparatively small following believed His precepts and followed His laws. The ignorant said, "Who is this individual; He has only a few disciples!" But those who knew said: "He is the Sun who will shine in the East and in the West, He is the Manifestation who shall give life to the world."

What the first disciples had seen the world realized later. ('Abdu'l-Bahá, *Paris Talks,* no. 38.7)

This is a pattern that is repeated in every Dispensation.

## PENTECOST

Pentecost, the Greek name for the Feast of Weeks, was the ancient Jewish festival that commemorated the receipt of the Mosaic Laws on Sinai; it is still celebrated in Judaism as Shavuot. In the Christian calendar, Pentecost became a commemoration of the descent of the Holy Spirit upon the Apostles after the crucifixion of Christ. As the Scripture describes, the Apostles were gathered together in celebration of the Jewish Pentecost when they became filled with the Holy Spirit and enabled to speak "with other tongues":

> When the day of Pentecost had come, they were all together in one place. And suddenly from heaven there came a sound like the rush of a violent wind, and it filled the entire house where they were sitting. Divided tongues, as of fire, appeared among them, and a tongue rested on each of them. All of them were filled with the Holy Spirit and began to speak in other languages, as the Spirit gave them ability. (Acts 2:1–4)

### WHAT IS THE HOLY SPIRIT?

As sunbeams are the bounty that emanate from the sun, the Holy Spirit is the Bounty of God that radiates from the Manifestation of God:

> By "the Holy Spirit" is meant the outpouring grace of God and the effulgent rays that emanate from His Manifestation. Thus Christ was the focal centre of the rays of the Sun of Truth, and from this mighty centre—the reality of Christ—the grace of God shone upon the other mirrors which were the realities of the Apostles. ('Abdu'l-Bahá, *Some Answered Questions*, no. 25.2)

### WHAT IS MEANT BY THE DESCENT OF THE HOLY SPIRIT AS FIRE UPON THE DISCIPLES?

The descent of the Holy Spirit as tongues of fire is symbolic of the real spiritual transformation of the disciples as they were attracted to the Holy Spirit, came together in unity, and felt the power of the Spirit of Christ manifesting through them:

After the death of Christ, the Apostles were troubled and diverged in their thoughts and opinions; later they became steadfast and united. At Pentecost they gathered together, detached themselves from the world, forsook their own desires, renounced all earthly comfort and happiness, sacrificed body and soul to their Beloved, left their homes, took leave of all their cares and belongings, and even forgot their own existence. Then was divine assistance vouchsafed and the power of the Holy Spirit manifested. The spirituality of Christ triumphed, and the love of God took hold. On that day, they received divine confirmations, and each departed in a different direction to teach the Cause of God and unloosed his tongue to set forth the proofs and testimonies.

Thus the descent of the Holy Spirit means that the Apostles were attracted by the messianic Spirit, attained constancy and steadfastness, found a new life through the spirit of God's love, and saw Christ to be their ever-living helper and protector. They were mere drops and became the ocean; they were feeble gnats and became soaring eagles; they were all weakness and became endowed with strength. ('Abdu'l-Bahá, *Some Answered Questions,* no. 24.3–4)

### WHAT DOES IT MEAN THAT THE DISCIPLES WERE ABLE TO "SPEAK WITH OTHER TONGUES"?

That the disciples spoke "with other tongues" means that they were able to communicate "celestial meanings and divine mysteries" across language barriers and to adapt those teachings to the capacities of their listeners:

The disciples of Christ taught His Faith with the language of the Kingdom. That language conformeth to all languages, for it consisteth of celestial meanings and divine mysteries. For the one who becometh conversant with that language the realities and secrets of creation stand unveiled before him. Divine truths are common to all languages. The Holy Spirit, therefore, taught the disciples the language of the Kingdom, and they thus were able to converse with the people of all nations. Whenever they spoke to those of other nations of the world, it was as if they conversed in their tongues. ('Abdu'l-Bahá, from a previously untranslated Tablet, cited in memorandum of the Research Department of the Universal House of Justice, dated September 14, 1987)

## WAS THE SPIRITUAL PERCEPTION OF THE DISCIPLES A PRODUCT OF PREVIOUS RELIGIOUS TRAINING OR DUE TO SCHOLARLY CAPACITY?

The spiritual perception of the disciples was not the product of previous religious training, nor was it due to scholarly capacity. They were common people—unlikely heroes—whose hearts were illumined by the Holy Spirit and who reflected the Light of God:

> Peter was a fisherman and Mary Magdalene a peasant, but as they were specially favoured with the blessings of Christ, the horizon of their faith became illumined, and down to the present day they are shining from the horizon of everlasting glory. In this station, merit and capacity are not to be considered; nay rather, the resplendent rays of the Sun of Truth, which have illumined these mirrors, must be taken into account. ('Abdu'l-Bahá, *Selections from the Writings of 'Abdu'l-Bahá,* no. 68.8)

Conversely, the "learned," for the most part, rejected Christ:

> Consider those who rejected the Spirit [Jesus] when He came unto them with manifest dominion. How numerous the Pharisees who had secluded themselves in synagogues in His name, lamenting over their separation from Him, and yet when the portals of reunion were flung open and the divine Luminary shone resplendent from the Dayspring of Beauty, they disbelieved in God, the Exalted, the Mighty. They failed to attain His presence, notwithstanding that His advent had been promised them in the Book of Isaiah as well as in the Books of the Prophets and the Messengers. No one from among them turned his face towards the Dayspring of divine bounty except such as were destitute of any power amongst men. . . . Moreover, call thou to mind the one who sentenced Jesus to death [Caiaphus]. He was the most learned of his age in his own country, whilst he who was only a fisherman believed in Him. Take

good heed and be of them that observe the warning. (Bahá'u'lláh, *Tablets of Bahá'u'lláh,* p. 9)

---

## MARTYRDOM

The Book of Acts presents Stephen as the first Christian martyr. Like Christ, Stephen was accused of heresy. In the account of his trial he defends his beliefs with a review of progressive Revelation as seen through the Dispensations of Abraham, Joseph, and Moses (Acts 7:2–44), and makes the point that each "Righteous One" was initially met with opposition:

> You stiff-necked people, uncircumcised in heart and ears, you are forever opposing the Holy Spirit, just as your ancestors used to do. Which of the prophets did your ancestors not persecute? They killed those who foretold the coming of the Righteous One, and now you have become his betrayers and murderers. (Acts 7:51–52)

The council responded by casting Stephen out of Jerusalem and having him stoned to death. Steven is described as remaining calm, having a vision of "the glory of God," and forgiving his murderers:

> While they were stoning Stephen, he prayed, "LORD Jesus, receive my spirit." Then he knelt down and cried out in a loud voice, "Lord, do not hold this sin against them." When he had said this, he died. (Acts 7:59–60)

Steadfastness and imperturbable dignity at the time of death are qualities found repeatedly in accounts of the martyrs.

### WHAT WERE THE FATES OF CHRIST'S OTHER DISCIPLES?

All of Christ's disciples, except for Judas, were martyred:

> In the days of Jesus only a few individuals turned their faces toward God; in fact only the twelve disciples and a few women truly

became believers, and one of the disciples, Judas Iscariot apostatized from his Faith, leaving eleven. After the ascension of Jesus to the Realm of Glory, these few souls stood up with their spiritual qualities and with deeds that were pure and holy, and they arose by the power of God and the life-giving breaths of the Messiah to save all the peoples of the earth. Then all the idolatrous nations as well as the Jews rose up in their might to kill the Divine fire that had been lit in the lamp of Jerusalem. "Fain would they put out God's light with their mouths: but God hath willed to perfect His light, albeit the infidels abhor it" [2 Qur'án 9:33]. Under the fiercest tortures, they did every one of these holy souls to death; with butchers' cleavers, they chopped the pure and undefiled bodies of some of them to pieces and burned them in furnaces, and they stretched some of the followers on the rack and then buried them alive. In spite of this agonizing requital, the Christians continued to teach the Cause of God, and they never drew a sword from its scabbard or even so much as grazed a cheek. Then in the end the Faith of Christ encompassed the whole earth. ('Abdu'l-Bahá, *The Secret of Divine Civilization*, ¶81)

The earliest days of Christianity, as well as the earliest days of the Bahá'í Faith, saw intense martyrdom with periods of wholesale massacre of early believers, such as the slaughter of Christians in Rome in 64 AD (Borg and Crossan, pp. 220–21), and the massacre of Bábís in Iran in 1852 (Shoghi Effendi, *God Passes By*, pp. 313–21, 469–74).[39]

### WHAT IS THE ESSENCE OF MARTYRDOM?

Martyrdom is the sacrifice of the self for the propagation of greater spiritual truths:

The martyr's field is the place of detachment from self, that the anthems of eternity may be upraised. ('Abdu'l-Bahá, *Selections from the Writings of 'Abdu'l-Bahá*, no. 36.5)

---

39. For detailed accounts of martyrs in the Bahá'í Faith, see 'Abdu'l-Bahá, *A Traveler's Narrative;* and Shoghi Effendi, *The Dawn-Breakers*, pp. 430–464.

"In one of His Tablets Bahá'u'lláh explains that 'martyrdom is not confined to the shedding of blood,' that it is possible to live and still be counted as a martyr in the sight of God. . . . Bahá'u'lláh has further ordained that teaching the Cause is as meritorious as dying for the Cause" (Momen, p. 147).

## IS IT DESIRABLE TO SEEK OUT MARTYRDOM?

One should teach the Cause of God with wisdom and not volunteer for martyrdom:

Martyrdom in the path of God is undoubtedly the greatest bounty provided it takes place through circumstances beyond one's control. (Summary of a passage from the Mu'assisiy-i-Ayadiy-i-Amrullah Tablet written by Bahá'u'lláh for Ibn-i-Abhar, Adib Taherzadeh, *The Revelation of Bahá'u'lláh,* vol. 4, p. 305)

## PAUL

The account of Stephen's martyrdom in the Book of Acts mentions Saul of Tarsus as an approving witness (Acts 7:58). Acts later describes that Saul had a powerful vision in which he was struck with the truth of Christ as the Word of God and became a devoted follower:

Now as he was going along and approaching Damascus, suddenly a light from heaven flashed around him. He fell to the ground and heard a voice saying to him, "Saul, Saul, why do you persecute me?" He asked, "Who are you, Lord?" The reply came, "I am Jesus, whom you are persecuting. But get up and enter the city, and you will be told what you are to do." . . . For several days he was with the disciples in Damascus, and immediately he began to proclaim Jesus in the synagogues, saying, "He is the Son of God." (Acts 9:6, 19–20)

Saul, who is later known as Paul, became one of the greatest teachers in the early Jesus movement. The details of his vision on the road to Damascus as it appears in the Book of Acts are not verified in his authenticated letters, but his dramatic transformation is. From a persecutor of the Jesus movement, Paul became a persecuted follower of Christ (2 Corinthians 12).

### HOW IS PAUL'S STORY MENTIONED IN THE BAHÁ'Í WRITINGS?

Paul's transformation is referenced by 'Abdu'l-Bahá as an example of the fact that we are never in a position to judge others:

> Who are we that we should judge? How shall we know who, in the sight of God, is the most upright man? God's thoughts are not like our thoughts! How many men who have seemed saint-like to their friends have fallen into the greatest humiliation. Think of Judas Iscariot; he began well, but remember his end! On the other hand, Paul, the Apostle, was in his early life an enemy of Christ, whilst later he became His most faithful servant. How then can we flatter ourselves and despise others? ('Abdu'l-Bahá, *Paris Talks,* no. 45.7)

'Abdu'l-Bahá also mentions Paul as an example to show that remoteness from the physical body of the Manifestation of God is not a barrier to a close spiritual connection with the Manifestation:

> Physical nearness or remoteness is of no importance; the essential fact is the spiritual affinity and ideal nearness. Judas Iscariot was for a long time favored in the holy court of His Holiness Christ, yet he was entirely far and remote; while Paul, the apostle, was in close embrace with His Holiness. . . . Consequently, it is evident that one can certainly and surely inhale the perfume of affinity even from a far distance. ('Abdu'l-Bahá, *Tablets of 'Abdu'l-Bahá,* vol. 3, p. 719)

Paul's integrity is acknowledged even though he had some differences with Peter concerning the application of Mosaic Laws. Paul's letter to the Galatians presents a situation in which he disagrees with Peter's hesitancy to associate with Gentile followers of Christ who did not abide by the Mosaic dietary laws and the law of male circumcision:

> But when Cephas [Paul] came to Antioch, I opposed him to his face, because he stood self-condemned; for until certain people

came from James, he used to eat with the Gentiles. But after they
came, he drew back and kept himself separate for fear of the circumcision faction. And the other Jews joined him in this hypocrisy,
so that even Barnabas was led astray by their hypocrisy. But when
I saw that they were not acting consistently with the truth of the
gospel, I said to Cephas [Paul] before them all, "If you, though a
Jew, live like a Gentile and not like a Jew, how can you compel the
Gentiles to live like Jews?" (Galatians 2: 11–14)

### HOW IS THE RELATIONSHIP BETWEEN PAUL AND PETER UNDERSTOOD IN THE BAHÁ'Í WRITINGS?

In the Bahá'í Writings the legitimacy of the primacy of Peter is recognized (*The Promised Day is Come*, p. 110), both Apostles are noted as
having part in decisions regarding applicability of the laws of the Torah
to early followers of Christ, and Paul's later abrogation of some of those
laws initially agreed upon in consultation with Peter is also mentioned
(*Some Answered Questions*, 20:2). Regardless of what may have been their
differences, both Apostles are honored in the Bahá'í Writings:

That St. Paul on occasion disputed with St. Peter is seen from St.
Paul's own words in the Epistle to the Galatians 2:11–14. It is also
St. Paul who mentions early divisions among the Christians, which
he endeavours to heal, in I Corinthians 1:11–13. St. Peter's attitude
to St. Paul appears in II Peter 3:15–18. In considering the relationship between St. Peter and St. Paul, one needs to bear in mind all
of these various factors. High praise is accorded to them both in the
Bahá'í Writings. A particularly pertinent statement by 'Abdu'l-Bahá
appears on page 223 [no. 189.5] of the new publication *Selections
from the Writings of 'Abdu'l-Bahá*: "One's conduct must be like the
conduct of Paul, and one's faith similar to that of Peter." (From a
letter written on behalf of the Universal House of Justice, dated
February 25, 1980, to an individual, cited in the "Station of Paul"
Memo from the Research Department of the Universal House of
Justice, dated February 22, 1998)

# THE BOOKS OF THE EPISTLES— OVERVIEW

After the Book of Acts, the next twenty-one books of the New Testament are the Epistles (letters or essays) written by several disciples of Christ to communities and individuals early in the Jesus movement. The first thirteen letters have the name "Paul" as the first word in the title; consequently, they are traditionally grouped as the Pauline Epistles. The remaining eight letters are traditionally grouped as the General Epistles. The Bahá'í Writings do not offer commentary on the exact origin or authorship of either the Pauline or General Epistles.

## THE PAULINE EPISTLES

Although thirteen of the Epistles are attributed to Paul, only seven are accepted by most New Testament scholars as being authentic (composed by Paul himself). The other six Epistles are either generally believed to be written in Paul's name by someone after Paul's martyrdom (pseudonymous), or the authorship is highly disputed (see Dunn, p. 1166). The current majority opinion on the authenticity of each of the Pauline Epistles will be noted below.

**The Epistle of Paul to the Romans** is widely thought to be authentic and written in the mid-50s AD. It is the longest of the Pauline Epistles and "commonly regarded as Paul's supreme work, the consummate expression of his mature theology" (Hill, p. 1083).

**The First Epistle of Paul to the Corinthians** is widely thought to be authentic and written between 52 and 55 AD. It encourages the Corinthians to distinguish themselves from the surrounding pagan culture, and admonishes them for practices that create disunity (see Barclay, pp. 1108–10).

**The Second Epistle of Paul to the Corinthians** is widely thought to be authentic. It addresses the situation in Corinth that had deteriorated since Paul's last correspondence, encourages forgiveness, implores believers to rise above their problems through grace, and defends Paul's apostolic authority (see MacDonald, pp. 1134–35).

**The Epistle of Paul to the Galatians**, also widely thought to be authentic, denounces the false teachings of agitators who had caused confusion, preaches the inclusion of Jews and Gentiles in one community, and addresses the position of the Mosaic Law in the community of Christ. Theories on dating range from 49 to 58 AD (see Stanton, pp. 1152–53).

**The Epistle of Paul to the Ephesians** is widely thought to be pseudonymous. It relays a spirit of absolute confidence in God as well as a vision of a united church as the Body of Christ. Theories on the date of its writing range from the early 60s to the 80s AD (see Dunn, pp. 1165–67).

**The Epistle of Paul to the Philippians** is widely thought to be authentic and written when Paul was imprisoned either in Rome in the early 60s AD or Ephesia in the mid-50s AD. He stoically describes unexpected benefits of imprisonment, addresses the position of Mosaic Laws in the community of Christ, and makes appeals for unity (see Murray, p. 1179).

**The Epistle of Paul to the Colossians**, the authorship of which is widely disputed, is thought by some scholars to have been written by both Paul and Timothy and dated to the early 50s AD. Major themes are the supremacy of Christ, Paul's work for the church, warnings to reject false teachers, and the importance of becoming risen with Christ through the Word (see Murphy-O'Connor, p. 1191).

**The First Epistle of Paul to the Thessalonians** is widely thought to be authentic and written approximately 50 AD. The Thessalonians are praised for their fidelity to Christ and their rejection of idolatry, and encouraged to persevere despite persecution (see Esler, p. 1200).

**The Second Epistle of Paul to the Thessalonians**, the authorship of which is widely disputed, offers encouragement and thanksgiving, advises avoidance of those who live in a disorderly way, and cautions against being deceived before the coming day of the Lord. Theories on dating range from the early 50s to 100 AD (see Esler, pp. 1213–14).

**The Pastoral Epistles: the First and Second Epistles of Paul to Timothy and the Epistle of Paul to Titus**, widely thought to be pseudonymous and possibly written as late as the second century AD, address topics such as church organization, behavior of women, virtues expected of community leaders, and Paul as the exemplar of Christian behavior (see Drury, pp. 1220–21).

**The Epistle of Paul to Philemon** is widely thought to be authentic and written from prison in Rome, Ephesus, Philippi, or elsewhere. The letter offers no clues to its dating other than sometime during Paul's ministry. Paul thanks Philemon and the Philippians for their support, speaks of his imminent return with Philemon's slave (Onesimus), and appeals to Philemon to receive Onesimus back as a brother in the Lord (see Wansink, pp. 1233–34).

## THE GENERAL EPISTLES

Except for the Epistle to the Hebrews, the General Epistles are named for those who are traditionally identified as the writers: James, Peter, John and Jude.

**The Epistle to the Hebrews** addresses the dilemma of Jewish believers who struggled with their perception of having to choose between Christ and Moses. The central theme is the doctrine of Christ and His role as mediator between God and humanity. Generally dated to 55 to 90 AD, authorship has been attributed, at various times, to Paul, Barnabus, Apollos, and Sylvanus (see Attridge, pp. 1236–37).

**The Epistle of James** is addressed to "the twelve tribes scattered abroad" (1:1) referring either to Christians in general or to scattered Jewish-Christian communities who lived outside of Palestine. Believers are counseled on how to respond to religious persecution. Some theories place its writing as early as the mid-40s AD. The prescript presents "James" as the author; perhaps the brother, stepbrother, or cousin of Jesus (see Riesner, pp. 1253–54).

**The First Epistle of Peter** urges believers to hold fast to their faith despite hostile persecutions by reminding them of what they have already received as followers of Christ, assures them of future reward, and enjoins them to excel in good conduct even when provoked. Its composition is generally dated between 70 and 100 AD. While ascribed to Peter, authorship is contested primarily because of the highly cultured Greek that characterizes the writing (see Eve, pp. 1263–64).

**The Second Epistle of Peter** differs from 1 Peter in style and terminology, which is seen by some scholars as evidence that the two letters do not share a common author. It is hypothesized that 2 Peter was either written by Peter, written by someone else under his authority, or written by a disciple after Peter's death. It presents the nature of true knowledge, warns of exploitation by false prophets and teachers, and urges the believers to prepare themselves for the day of God. Proposed dates range from 60 to 130 AD (see Duff, pp. 1270–71).

**The First, Second, and Third Epistles of John,** generally dated to the second half of the first century AD, are traditionally grouped together, although only the Second and Third Epistles claim a common authorship by "the elder." The First and Second Epistles address the problem of certain former church members (termed "antichrist") who taught heretical doctrines that created schisms in the church. The Third Epistle is a letter of encouragement as well as caution to Gaius, a believer who hosted traveling missionaries (see Lieu, pp. 1274, 1282).

**The Epistle of Jude**, generally dated to the late first century AD, describes the writer as a "servant" and as a brother of James. The purpose of the letter is to encourage moral purity, to warn of God's judgment, and to extol the mercy of God for the faithful. Jude is especially of interest due to "its use of non-canonical scripture" (Rowland, pp. 1284–86); that is, references to Christian writings that are outside of the New Testament collection.

# TOPICS FROM THE BOOKS
# OF THE EPISTLES

## RAISING THE DEAD

In Paul's Epistles, the raising of the dead is presented as a promise and a mystery:

> Listen, I will tell you a mystery! We will not all die, but we will all be changed, in a moment, in the twinkling of an eye, at the last trumpet. For the trumpet will sound, and the dead will be raised imperishable, and we will be changed. For this perishable body must put on imperishability, and this mortal body must put on immortality. (I Corinthians 15:51–53)

The raising (or resurrection) of the dead is described as a transition from perishable bodies to imperishable bodies:

> So it is with the resurrection of the dead. What is sown is perishable, what is raised is imperishable. (1 Corinthians 15:42, 44)

### HOW DO BAHÁ'ÍS UNDERSTAND THE RAISING OF THE DEAD?

As in similar New Testament passages, true life is understood to be the attainment of divine knowledge and the realization of the immortal life of the spirit. The raising of the dead indicates spiritual awakening, not the restoration of the life of the flesh after physical death. The purpose of all the Prophets of God is to convey that true life is the life of the spirit:

In every age and century, the purpose of the Prophets of God and their chosen ones hath been no other but to affirm the spiritual significance of the terms "life," "resurrection," and "judgment." . . . Behold, all the people are imprisoned within the tomb of self, and lie buried beneath the nethermost depths of worldly desire! Wert thou to attain to but a dewdrop of the crystal waters of divine knowledge, thou wouldst readily realize that true life is not the life of the flesh but the life of the spirit. For the life of the flesh is common to both men and animals, whereas the life of the spirit is possessed only by the pure in heart who have quaffed from the ocean of faith and partaken of the fruit of certitude. This life knoweth no death, and this existence is crowned by immortality. Even as it hath been said: "He who is a true believer liveth both in this world and in the world to come." If by "life" be meant this earthly life, it is evident that death must needs overtake it. (Bahá'u'lláh, The Kitáb-i-Íqán, ¶128)

The resurrection of the believers from the dead, like the resurrection of Christ, does not have to do with a revival of the physical body. Upon the death of the body, the physical form decomposes and those elements never reassemble into the same form. True resurrection is the transformation of the individual to spiritual life through the Holy Spirit. The "tomb" from which the "dead" arise is the tomb of ignorance of God. The sleep from which the "dead" awaken is the condition of spiritual blindness. The body that is raised up after physical death is a spiritual reality suitable to the spiritual worlds:

The world beyond is as different from this world as this world is different from that of the child while still in the womb of its mother. When the soul attaineth the Presence of God, it will assume the form that best befitteth its immortality and is worthy of its celestial habitation. (Bahá'u'lláh, *Gleanings from the Writings of Bahá'u'lláh*, no. 81.1)

## CAN THE SOULS OF THOSE WHO ARE PHYSICALLY DEAD ALSO BENEFIT FROM THE BOUNTY OF THE MANIFESTATION OF GOD?

Paul's First Epistle to the Thessalonians promises that "the dead in Christ will rise first" (1 Thessalonians 4:16). David G. Horrell and other biblical scholars understand this verse as assurance that, when Christ returns, those believers who are physically dead will, along with the physically living believers, be included in the salvation that comes in the day of the Lord: "the dead are not lost but will rise first" (Horrell, p. 2074). The potential for continued progress of the soul after the death of the body is confirmed in the Bahá'í Writings:

> And now concerning thy question regarding the soul of man and its survival after death. Know thou of a truth that the soul, after its separation from the body, will continue to progress until it attaineth the presence of God, in a state and condition which neither the revolution of ages and centuries, nor the changes and chances of this world, can alter. It will endure as long as the Kingdom of God, His sovereignty, His dominion and power will endure. (Bahá'u'lláh, *Gleanings from the Writings of Bahá'u'lláh*, no. 81.1)

## HOW CAN SOULS PROGRESS
## AFTER THE DEATH OF THE BODY?

The progress of souls may come by virtue of their own supplications, the supplications of others on their behalf, and by the bounty of the Manifestation of God:

> It is even possible for those who have died in sin and unbelief to be transformed, that is, to become the object of divine forgiveness. This is through the grace of God and not through His justice, for grace is to bestow without desert, and justice is to give that which is deserved. As we have the power to pray for those souls here, so too will we have the same power in the next world, the world of the Kingdom. Are not all the creatures in that world the creation of God? They must therefore be able to progress in that world as well. And just as they can seek illumination here through supplication, so too can they plead there for forgiveness and seek illumination through prayer and supplication. Thus, as souls can progress in this world through their entreaties and supplications, or through the prayers of holy souls, so too after death can they progress through their own prayers and supplications, particularly if they become the object of the intercession of the holy Manifestations. ('Abdu'l-Bahá, *Some Answered Questions*, no. 62.7)

## SATAN

In the Bible, the name "Satan" first appears in the Book of Job in reference to a supernatural entity who walks the earth, has God's ear, and does God's bidding (1:6–22).[40] We do not hear much about Satan again until the New Testament story of Christ's temptation in the wilderness (Matthew 4). From then on, Satan, or the devil, is presented as a powerful, deceptive, and lawless adversary:

The coming of the lawless one is apparent in the working of Satan, who uses all power, signs, lying wonders. (2 Thessalonians 2:9)

. . . a monster who devours souls:

Discipline yourselves, keep alert. Like a roaring lion your adversary the devil prowls around, looking for someone to devour. (1 Peter 5:8)

. . . and a constant threat of temptation:

Do not deprive one another except perhaps by agreement for a set time, to devote yourselves to prayer, and then come together again, so that Satan may not tempt you because of your lack of self-control. (1 Corinthians 7:5)

The New Testament Satan is the personification of evil. The term Satan is used in the same sense—the opposite of good and the enemy of God—in the Bahá'í Writings. For example, Bahá'u'lláh states,

---

40. For studies on the development of the biblical concept of Satan, especially as influenced by Zoroastrianism in the post-exilic Persian Period and the Hellenistic Age, see R.C. Zaehner, *The Dawn & Twilight of Zoroastrianism*; Lawrence Heyworth Mills, *Our Own Religion in Ancient Persia*; and Matthew Black, *Peake's Commentary on the Bible,* section 607.

Only those will attain to the knowledge of the Word of God that have turned unto Him, and repudiated the manifestations of Satan. (Bahá'u'lláh, The Kitáb-i-Íqán, ¶130)

However, in the Bahá'í Writings the symbolic meaning of the term "Satan" is clearly defined.

### WHAT IS SATAN?

The scriptural figure of Satan is symbolic of humanity's lower nature:

The reality underlying this question is that the evil spirit, Satan or whatever is interpreted as evil, refers to the lower nature in man. This baser nature is symbolized in various ways. ('Abdu'l-Bahá, *The Promulgation of Universal Peace,* p. 411)

Rather than a character external to humanity, "Satan" is symbolic of the evil within. Christ demonstrates this meaning of the term when He refers to an erring Peter as "Satan":

But turning and looking at his disciples, he rebuked Peter and said, "Get behind me, Satan! For you are setting your mind not on divine things but on human things." (Mark 8:33)

The good news is that there is no literal larger-than-life, external, super-powerful God-nemesis with horns named "Satan" walking the earth. The bad news is that "Satanic" power, with all the chilling attributes ascribed to it in Scripture, is real and ready within the lower nature of every human being on the planet:

This lower nature in man is symbolized as Satan—the evil ego within us, not an evil personality outside. ('Abdu'l-Bahá, *The Promulgation of Universal Peace,* p. 400)

### WHAT IS THE LOWER NATURE?

The lower nature—also referred to as the baser nature, animal nature, or material nature—is the spiritually uneducated animal-like human disposition characterized by vices such as hate, envy, and cruelty. This is in contrast to the higher or spiritual human nature that is characterized by virtues such as love, generosity, and kindness. As Adam was created from both the dust of the earth and the breath of the Spirit, so to be human is to experience the full continuum of a lower nature and a higher nature:

> In man there are two natures: his spiritual or higher nature and his material or lower nature. In one he approaches God, in the other he lives for the world alone. Signs of both these natures are to be found in men. In his material aspect he expresses untruth, cruelty and injustice; all these are the outcome of his lower nature. The attributes of his Divine nature are shown forth in love, mercy, kindness, truth and justice, one and all being expressions of his higher nature. Every good habit, every noble quality belongs to man's spiritual nature, whereas all his imperfections and sinful actions are born of his material nature. ('Abdu'l-Bahá, *Paris Talks*, no. 18.2)

Triumph over one's lower nature results in nobilities of the spirit—virtues. Succumbing to one's lower nature results in degradations of the spirit—vices:

> If his morals become spiritual in character, his aspirations heavenly and his actions conformable to the will of God, man has attained the image and likeness of his Creator; otherwise, he is the image and likeness of Satan. Therefore, Christ hath said, "Ye shall know them by their fruits." ('Abdu'l-Bahá, *The Promulgation of Universal Peace*, p. 475)

Although this concept is presented like a dichotomy—higher nature/lower nature—the human condition is not either/or. At any moment, in many dimensions, and to many degrees, a person stands between spiritual darkness and light.

### WHAT IS THE NATURE OF EVIL?

Evil is the absence of good. For example, hate is the absence of love, greed is the absence of generosity, and cruelty is the absence of kindness. In this sense, evil has a "negative existence." Although evil is defined by being the absence of something else, its existence is a fact and a real spiritual danger:

> We know absence of light is darkness, but no one would assert darkness was not a fact. It exists even though it is only the absence of something else. So evil exists too, and we cannot close our eyes to it, even though it is a negative existence. We must seek to supplant it by good, and if we see an evil person is not influenceable by us, then we should shun his company for it is unhealthy. (Shoghi Effendi, *The Unfolding Destiny of the British Bahá'í Community*, p. 457)

The "negative existence" of evil does not lessen its damaging power. For example, consider that a vacuum, which is the absence of matter (a negative reality), pulls the center of a tornado causing it to suck up and destroy everything in its path. Anyone who has experienced a tornado or seen its aftermath can testify to the destructive power of a negative reality. In the same way, when evil human forces build—when there is large-scale absence of good in a person or in a community—the effects are devastating:

> A world in which naught can be perceived save strife, quarrels and corruption is bound to become the seat of the throne, the very metropolis, of Satan. (Bahá'u'lláh, *Tablets of Bahá'u'lláh*, p. 176)

## DOES "LOWER AND HIGHER NATURE" INDICATE THAT THE SOUL HAS A DOUBLE REALITY WITH TWO DISTINCT DISPOSITIONS?

A human soul is not dualistic—it is one soul that is capable of development toward higher and lower expressions:

> According to the Bahá'í conception, the soul of man, or in other words his inner spiritual self or reality, is not dualistic. There is no such thing . . . as a double reality in man, a definite higher self and lower self. The latter is capable of development in either way. All depends fundamentally on the training or education which man receives. Human nature is made up of possibilities for both good and evil. True religion can enable it to soar in the highest realm

of the spirit, while its absence can, as we already witness around us, cause it to fall to the lowest depth of degradation and misery. (From a letter written on behalf of Shoghi Effendi, dated 1936, to Alfred Lunt, in *Lights of Guidance,* no. 698)

A human being does not have two isolated competing natures. However, because a multifaceted, multidimensional, higher/lower nature continuum is difficult to visualize, the "angel on one shoulder and the devil on the other" image may remain a helpful symbol of the struggle inherent in the human condition.

## SIN

The Apostle Paul presents sin as a universal human condition:

> What then? Are we any better off? No, not at all; for we have already charged that all, both Jews and Greeks, are under the power of sin, as it is written: "There is no one who is righteous, not even one; there is no one who has understanding, there is no one who seeks God." (Romans 3:9–11)

### WHAT IS SIN?

Sin is another word for actions characterized by the lower nature:

> Sin is the state of man in the world of the baser nature, for in nature exist defects such as injustice, tyranny, hatred, hostility, strife: these are characteristics of the lower plane of nature. ('Abdu'l-Bahá, *Paris Talks,* no. 56.1)

All sinful inclinations come from the material world.

### IS THE MATERIAL WORLD EVIL?

Because sin comes from the material world it might seem as though the world itself is evil, but this is not the case. The material world is neither good nor evil—it just is. However, humanity, which has a material (or animal) nature *and* a spiritual nature, is called to a standard higher than its animal form:

> All sin is prompted by the dictates of nature. These dictates of nature, which are among the hallmarks of corporeal existence, are not sins with respect to the animal but are sins with regard to man. The animal is the source of imperfections such as anger, lust, envy, greed, cruelty, and pride. All these blameworthy qualities are found in the nature of the animal, and do not constitute sins with regard to the animal, whereas they are sins with regard to man. ('Abdu'l-Bahá, *Some Answered Questions,* no. 29.6)

Humanity's task and ultimate destiny is to combine divine attributes with the material world, both individually and communally.

### HOW CAN WE FREE OURSELVES FROM SIN?

Spiritual education—that is, education in the eternal verities of all religions, such as love, service, unity, and the sacrifice of what is lower for what is higher—is required in order to dominate our own lower nature and free us from sin:

> Through education we must free ourselves from these imperfections. The Prophets of God have been sent, the Holy Books have been written, so that man may be made free. Just as he is born into this world of imperfection from the womb of his earthly mother, so is he born into the world of spirit through divine education. ('Abdu'l-Bahá, *Paris Talks,* no. 56.1)

Spiritual education trains us to become living sacrifices, a teaching that is found in the Epistles:

> I beseech you therefore, brethren, by the mercies of God, that ye present your bodies a living sacrifice, holy, acceptable unto God, which is your reasonable service. (Romans 12:1)

. . . and the Bahá'í Writings:

O Thou divine Providence, . . . strengthen us that we may arise to help Thy Cause and offer ourselves as a living sacrifice in the pathway of guidance. ('Abdu'l-Bahá, *Selections from the Writings of 'Abdu'l-Bahá*, no. 233.17)

### WHAT DOES IT MEAN TO BE A "LIVING SACRIFICE"?

To be a "living sacrifice" is to sacrifice one's lower nature, and rise above worldly attachments. It means choosing to act on spiritual principles rather than only materialistic, self-serving ones. The spiritual, mental, and often physical challenges required in such a life find fruition in attributes like selfless service, discipline, generosity, moderation, truthfulness, and perseverance. It is through this moment-to-moment living sacrifice of the lower nature that "the radiance of the living God" shines forth:

Until a being setteth his foot in the plane of sacrifice, he is bereft of every favour and grace; and this plane of sacrifice is the realm of dying to the self, that the radiance of the living God may then shine forth. . . . Do all ye can to become wholly weary of self, and bind yourselves to that Countenance of Splendors; and once ye have reached such heights of servitude, ye will find, gathered within your shadow, all created things. This is boundless grace; this is the highest sovereignty; this is the life that dieth not. All else save this is at the last but manifest perdition and great loss. ('Abdu'l-Bahá, *Selections from the Writings of 'Abdu'l-Bahá*, no. 36.5)

### IS IT POSSIBLE TO BECOME A PERFECT LIVING SACRIFICE?

To be human is to be imperfect. Consequently, it is not possible to live a sinless life or to expect others to do so. Regardless of our conditions, we are all works in progress. We can help others and ourselves by not focusing on imperfections and, instead, being proactive about seeing the good in others:

Humanity is not perfect. There are imperfections in every human being, and you will always become unhappy if you look toward the people themselves. But if you look toward God, you will love them and be kind to them, for the world of God is the world of perfection and complete mercy. Therefore, do not look at the shortcomings of anybody; see with the sight of forgiveness. The imperfect eye beholds imperfections. The eye that covers faults looks toward the Creator of souls. ('Abdu'l-Bahá, *The Promulgation of Universal Peace,* p. 128)

## SALVATION

The purpose of the Epistles is to lead people to salvation through Christ:

> But since we belong to the day, let us be sober, and put on the breastplate of faith and love, and for a helmet the hope of salvation. For God has destined us not for wrath but for obtaining salvation through our Lord Jesus Christ, who died for us, so that whether we are awake or asleep we may live with him. (1 Thessalonians 5:8–10)

### FROM WHAT DO WE NEED TO BE SAVED?

We need to be saved from our lower nature and our ignorance of our own spiritual reality—from spiritual blindness, spiritual deafness, and darkened hearts:

> . . . although the people possess external eyes, yet the insight or perception of the soul is blind; although the outer ear hears, the spiritual hearing is deaf; although they possess conscious hearts they are without illumination; and the bounties of His Holiness Christ save souls from these conditions. ('Abdu'l-Bahá, *The Promulgation of Universal Peace,* p. 626)

Those who are spiritually aware develop a moral compass informed by spiritual laws and thereby better themselves, as well as society at large, through pure deeds.

### IS SALVATION A ONE-TIME EVENT?

Far from being a one-time event, salvation is a path and many paths that continue eternally:

May your deeds proclaim your faith and enable you to lead the erring into the paths of eternal salvation. (Bahá'u'lláh, cited in Shoghi
Effendi, *The Dawn-Breakers*, p. 586)

Salvation is a never-ending path moving ever closer to the presence
of God.

### WHAT IS REQUIRED TO PROGRESS ALONG THE
### PATHS OF SALVATION?

Progress along the paths of salvation is dependent on both knowledge
of God through His Revelation and obedience to His laws. These are the
"twin duties" of every soul:

The first duty prescribed by God for His servants is the recognition
of Him Who is the Dayspring of His Revelation and the Fountain
of His laws, Who representeth the Godhead in both the Kingdom
of His Cause and the world of creation. Whoso achieveth this duty
hath attained unto all good; and whoso is deprived thereof hath gone
astray, though he be the author of every righteous deed. It behoveth
every one who reacheth this most sublime station, this summit of
transcendent glory, to observe every ordinance of Him Who is the
Desire of the world. These twin duties are inseparable. Neither is
acceptable without the other. (Bahá'u'lláh, The Kitáb-i-Aqdas, ¶1)

Faith that is not expressed in action, is dead:

What good is it, my brothers and sisters, if you say you have faith
but do not have works? Can faith save you? If a brother or sister
is naked and lacks daily food, and one of you says to them, "Go
in peace; keep warm and eat your fill," and yet you do not supply
their bodily needs, what is the good of that? So faith by itself, if it
has no works, is dead. (James 2:14–17, 19–20, 26)

And good works alone, without faith, is not enough for salvation:

. . . good deeds alone, without the recognition of God, cannot
lead to eternal redemption, to everlasting success and salvation,

and to admittance into the Kingdom of God. ('Abdu'l-Bahá, *Some Answered Questions,* no. 65.4)

## WHY DOES A PERSON WHO HAS PRAISEWORTHY CHARACTERISTICS AND PERFORMS GOOD DEEDS NEED THE KNOWLEDGE OF THE MANIFESTATION OF GOD?

Good actions without the knowledge of the Revelation of God are commendable; however, they do not bring about the spiritual progress and illumination required for the exaltation of humanity and the building of a divine civilization:

Know that such ways, words, and deeds are to be lauded and approved, and they redound to the glory of the human world. But these actions alone are not sufficient. They are a body of the greatest beauty, but without a spirit. No, that which leads to everlasting life, eternal honour, universal enlightenment, and true success and salvation is, first and foremost, the knowledge of God. It is clear that this knowledge takes precedence over every other knowledge and constitutes the greatest virtue of the human world. For the understanding of the reality of things confers a material advantage in the realm of being and brings about the progress of outward civilization, but the knowledge of God is the cause of spiritual progress and attraction, true vision and insight, the exaltation of humanity, the appearance of divine civilization, the rectification of morals, and the illumination of the conscience. ('Abdu'l-Bahá, *Some Answered Questions,* no. 84.2)

Whether one acknowledges the appearance of the Manifestation of God or not, the origin of all good deeds is still found in the teachings of God as revealed by the Manifestations throughout history:

. . . if you consider the matter with fairness you will see that these good deeds of the non-believers also have their origin in the divine teachings. That is, the Prophets of old exhorted men to perform them, explained their advantages, and expounded their positive effects; these teachings then spread among mankind, successively reaching the non-believing souls and inclining their hearts towards these perfections; and when they found these actions to be laudable and to bring about joy and happiness among men, they too conformed to them. Thus these actions also arise from the divine teachings. But to see this, a measure of fair-mindedness is called for and not dispute and controversy. (Abdu'l-Bahá, *Some Answered Questions*, no. 84.11)

## THE WAY

The First Epistle to Timothy proclaims Christ as the one mediator between God and humanity:

> This is right and is acceptable in the sight of God our Savior, who desires everyone to be saved and to come to the knowledge of the truth. For there is one God; there is also one mediator between God and humankind, Christ Jesus, himself human, who gave himself a ransom for all. (1 Timothy 2:4-6)

The unique station of Christ as the mediator between God and humanity is also proclaimed in the Gospels:

> Jesus said to him, "I am the way, and the truth, and the life. No one comes to the Father except through me." (John 14:6)

. . . and the Book of Acts:

> Be it known unto you all, and to all the people of Israel, that by the name of Jesus Christ of Nazareth, whom ye crucified, whom God raised from the dead, even by him doth this man stand here before you whole. . . . Neither is there salvation in any other: for there is none other name under heaven given among men, whereby we must be saved. (Acts 4:10, 12)

Similar proclamations of the "only way to salvation" are voiced in the Scripture of all the world's religions, for example:

Hinduism: Abandoning all duties, come unto Me alone for shelter. (Bhagavad Gita 18:66)

Judaism: Moses alone shall come near the LORD. (Exodus 24:2)

Buddhism: This is the path. There is no other that leads to vision. (Dhammapada 20:274)

Islam: The only true faith in God's sight is Islam. (Qur'án 3:19)

Bahá'í Faith: Be thou content with Me and seek no other helper. For none but Me can ever suffice thee. (Bahá'u'lláh, The Hidden Words, Arabic, no. 17)

### WHAT IS THE BAHÁ'Í UNDERSTANDING OF NUMEROUS RELIGIOUS CLAIMS OF THE "ONLY WAY TO SALVATION"?

For Bahá'ís, the above quotations are not dogmatic challenges between religions; They are different statements of the fundamental truth that knowledge of the purpose of our existence can be attained only through awakening to the divine enlightenment emanating from the Manifestation of God:

> There is equal agreement in these texts [the world's Scripture] that the soul's ability to attain to an understanding of its Creator's purpose is the product not merely of its own effort, but of interventions of the Divine that open the way. The point was made with memorable clarity by Jesus: "I am the way, the truth, and the life: no man cometh unto the Father, but by me." If one is not to see in this assertion merely a dogmatic challenge to other stages of the one ongoing process of Divine guidance, it is obviously the expression of the central truth of revealed religion: that access to the unknowable Reality that creates and sustains existence is possible only through awakening to the illumination shed from that Realm. (Written under the supervision of, and commissioned by, the Universal House of Justice, *Century of Light*, p. 31)

Just as there is one sun and many days of sunlight, there is one spiritual station of the Manifestation of God and many historical appearances:

And know thou that He indeed resembleth the sun. Were the risings of the sun to continue till the end that hath no end, yet there hath not been nor ever will be more than one sun; and were its settings to endure for evermore, still there hath not been nor ever will be more than one sun. It is this Primal Will which appeareth resplendent in every Prophet and speaketh forth in every revealed Book. It knoweth no beginning, inasmuch as the First deriveth its firstness from It; and knoweth no end, for the Last oweth its lastness unto It. . . . Hence the inner meaning of the words uttered by the Apostle of God, 'I am all the Prophets', inasmuch as what shineth resplendent in each one of Them hath been and will ever remain the one and the same sun. (The Báb, *Selections from the Writings of the Báb*, no. 4.10.5)

### WHAT ABOUT THE CLAIM OF ETERNAL SOVEREIGNTY?

Every appearance of the Manifestation of God claims eternal sovereignty. This relates to the first station of the Word of God in which the Manifestation is one with God and represents spiritual laws that are unchanging. For example, consider this statement of the eternal station of Christ:

Jesus Christ is the same yesterday, today, and forever. (Hebrews 13:8)

Christ is unchanging in that His spiritual station and the spiritual laws He represents are eternal. As the sun is the same regardless of earthly perceptions of yesterday and today, the appearances of the Manifestations of God are one, "eternal and everlasting":

Now, the reality of prophethood, which is the Word of God and the state of perfect divine manifestation, has neither beginning nor end, but its radiance varies like that of the sun. For example, it dawned above the sign of Christ with the utmost splendour and radiance, and this is eternal and everlasting. See how many world-conquering kings, how many wise ministers and rulers have come and gone, each and all fading into oblivion—whereas even now the breezes of Christ still waft, His light still shines, His call is still upraised, His banner is still unfurled, His armies still do battle, His voice still rings sweetly, His clouds still rain down life-giving showers, His lightning still streaks forth, His glory is still clear and indisputable, His splendour is still radiant and luminous; and the same holds true of every soul that abides beneath His shade and partakes of His light. ('Abdu'l-Bahá, *Some Answered Questions,* no. 38.7)

## IS SALVATION RESTRICTED TO THE FOLLOWERS
## OF A CERTAIN RELIGION?

Salvation is not restricted to the followers of a certain religion. Every appearance of the Manifestation of God is the way to God:

The door of the knowledge of the Ancient Being hath ever been, and will continue forever to be, closed in the face of men. No man's understanding shall ever gain access unto His holy court. As a token of His mercy, however, and as a proof of His loving-kindness, He hath manifested unto men the Daystars of His divine guidance, the Symbols of His divine unity, and hath ordained the knowledge of these sanctified Beings to be identical with the knowledge of His own Self. . . . *Every one of them is the Way of God that connecteth this world with the realms above,* and the Standard of His Truth unto every one in the kingdoms of earth and heaven. They are the Manifestations of God amidst men, the evidences of His Truth, and the signs of His glory. (Bahá'u'lláh, *Gleanings from the Writings of Bahá'u'lláh,* no. 21.1, emphasis added)

The Book of God has many chapters. Each chapter leads to the next. A soul can open the Book and progress along the journey through any chapter.

These Prophets and chosen Ones of God are the recipients and revealers of all the unchangeable attributes and names of God. They are the mirrors that truly and faithfully reflect the light of God. . . . Therefore, whosoever, and in whatever Dispensation, hath recognized and attained unto the presence of these glorious, these resplendent and most excellent Luminaries, hath verily attained unto the "Presence of God" Himself, and entered the city of eternal and immortal life. (Bahá'u'lláh, The Kitáb-i-Íqán, ¶151)

### HOW DO THE PURPOSES OF THE DIFFERENT APPEARANCES OF THE MANIFESTATION OF GOD COMPARE?

The Manifestations of God are united in purpose:

The holy Manifestations Who have been the Sources or Founders of the various religious systems were united and agreed in purpose and teaching. Abraham, Moses, Zoroaster, Buddha, Jesus, Muhammad, the Báb and Bahá'u'lláh are one in spirit and reality. Moreover, each Prophet fulfilled the promise of the One Who came before Him and, likewise, Each announced the One Who would follow. . . . It is evident, therefore, that the Holy Manifestations Who founded the religious systems are united and agreed; there is no differentiation possible in Their mission and teachings; all are reflectors of reality, and all are promulgators of the religion of God. The divine religion is reality, and reality is not multiple; it is one. Therefore, the foundations of the religious systems are one because all proceed from the indivisible reality. ('Abdu'l-Bahá, *The Promulgation of Universal Peace*, p. 276)

Evolutionary stages in the advancement of civilization require different social laws, but the Divine purpose has always been greater expression of love and unity.

## A BETTER COVENANT

One of the disciples' challenges was how to explain that Christ fulfilled the Mosaic Law even though He changed some of those laws. Addressing this point, the Epistle to the Hebrews notes that Christ, as the new mediator, brought a new covenant:

But Jesus has now obtained a more excellent ministry, and to that degree he is the mediator of a better covenant, which has been enacted through better promises. (Hebrews 8:6)

This new covenant was prophesied in the Old Testament:

"The days are surely coming," saith the LORD, "when I will make a new covenant with the house of Israel and with the house of Judah." (Jeremiah 31:31)

### IN WHAT WAY DID CHRIST OFFER A
### "BETTER" COVENANT THAN MOSES?

Every new appearance of the Manifestation of God offers a "better covenant" than the previous Dispensation because the growing maturity of humanity allows for the Manifestation to dispense more knowledge, more insights, and more capacity as well as updated social laws. The teachings of the old Covenant become like darkened stars as their authority vanishes:

In speaking of "a new covenant," he has made the first one obsolete. And what is obsolete and growing old will soon disappear. (Hebrews 8:13)

As the Covenant of every Manifestation of God is fulfilled by the appearance of the next appearance of the Manifestation, the previous Covenant is like a seed that sacrifices itself in the process of germination. Another way that the comparative potency of the Revelations of Moses and Christ is expressed in Scripture is that Christ is "worthy of more glory than Moses" (Hebrews 3:3).

### IN WHAT WAY IS CHRIST
### "WORTHY OF MORE GLORY THAN MOSES"?

The comparative greatness of Christ is due to the potency of His Revelation and the results achieved:

Likewise, must we set aside prejudice in considering other Divine Educators by investigating reality. For instance, let us take Christ.

He achieved results greater than Moses. ('Abdu'l-Bahá, *The Promulgation of Universal Peace,* p. 488)

But it is the *Revelation* of Christ that is "worthy of more glory than Moses," not Christ Himself:

Any variations in the splendor which each of these Manifestations of the Light of God has shed upon the world should be ascribed not to any inherent superiority involved in the essential character of any one of them, but rather to the progressive capacity, the ever-increasing spiritual receptiveness, which mankind, in its progress towards maturity, has invariably manifested. (Shoghi Effendi, *The World Order of Bahá'u'lláh,* p. 165)

No difference exists in the capacities of the Manifestations of God. A college math teacher may reveal a greater amount of information about mathematics than a third grade teacher, and college students may accomplish more than third grade students, but that does not mean that the third grade teacher is bereft of that knowledge or that the elementary math books are in any way inadequate. In each case, instruction is appropriate to the students. In like manner, the Manifestation of God dispenses knowledge appropriate to humanity's capacity at the time. The process of increasingly greater dispensation of the Word of God will continue, but the intrinsic powers and attributes of all of the religious systems are the same.

## HOW DOES THE
## REVELATION OF BAHÁ'U'LLÁH
## COMPARE TO PREVIOUS DISPENSATIONS?

The Revelation of Bahá'u'lláh is "distinguished above all other ages":

The time hath come for the effects and perfections of the Most Great Name to be made manifest in this excellent age, so as to establish, beyond any doubt, that this era is the era of Bahá'u'lláh, and this age is distinguished above all other ages. ('Abdu'l-Bahá, *Selections from the Writings of 'Abdu'l-Bahá,* no. 35.6)

Although what has been revealed in the Bahá'í Revelation is greater than previous Revelations, Bahá'u'lláh draws on the same Source available to all the Prophets:

> Bahá'u'lláh's claims are much greater because humanity is more mature and can afford to hear them. But He draws on the same Source that was accessible to all the Prophets; it is we who can now receive more. (Shoghi Effendi, *Unfolding Destiny*, p. 406)

## WOMEN

In the Gospels we see Christ ministering to women as He did to men. He healed women (Luke 13:12); He forgave women (Luke 7:47); and He protected women by abrogating what had been, for men, easy laws of divorce (Mark 10:11). In *A Call to Action: Women, Religion, Violence, and Power*, Jimmy Carter states, "There is one incontrovertible fact concerning the relationship between Jesus Christ and women: he treated them as equal to men, which was dramatically different from the prevailing custom of the times" (p. 23). For the most part, the Epistles attributed to Paul demonstrate the same egalitarian spirit. The Epistle to the Galatians states:

> Because all of you are one in the Messiah Jesus, a person is no longer a Jew or a Greek, a slave or a free person, a male or a female. (Galatians 3:28)

In addition, many prominent women who had leadership roles in the early churches are celebrated in Pauline Epistles. These include: Junia, who is praised as an apostle of Christ (Romans 16:1); Priscilla, who is praised as a missionary partner (Romans 16:3); and Phoebe, who is noted as a deacon (Romans 16:7). Therefore, verses in some of the Pauline epistles that suggest that women should take subservient roles to men seem "strangely inconsistent" (Barclay, p. 1130), such as the guidance in First Corinthians that states that women should not talk in church:

Women should be silent in the churches. For they are not permitted to speak, but should be subordinate, as the law also says. If there is anything they desire to know, let them ask their husbands at home. For it is shameful for a woman to speak in church. (1 Corinthians 14:34–35)

The above verses are inconsistent with the leadership roles that Paul ascribed to women.

### WHY IS 1 CORINTHIANS 14:34–35 INCONSISTENT WITH THE MORE EQUITABLE GENDER ROLES DEMONSTRATED IN THE GOSPELS AND THE EPISTLES?

This question has been the subject of intense debate. New Testament scholar John Barclay suggests two possibilities: either Paul was "truly inconsistent" in his guidance offered to the Corinthians, or this guidance is "an interpolation into the letter by a later editor" (Barclay, p. 1130). Many scholars support the latter opinion. The argument that this passage was written by someone other than Paul is strengthened by the fact that similar teachings involving strict gender hierarchy are found in those Pauline Epistles that are now largely believed to be pseudonymous (Barclay, p. 1130).[41] Whatever the reason, the fact that a restrictive ethos of gender is found in the Epistles is not surprising because the subjugation of women was characteristic of that historical period.

### WHAT HAS BEEN THE STATUS OF WOMEN HISTORICALLY?

In the Bahá'í Writings the status of women in the past is described as "deplorable":

---

41. Examples include: "But I suffer not a woman to teach, nor to usurp authority over the man, but to be in silence." (1 Timothy 2:12); "That they may teach the young women to be . . . discreet, chaste, keepers at home, good, obedient to their own husbands, that the word of God be not blasphemed." (Titus 2:4–5); "Therefore as the church is subject unto Christ, so let the wives be to their own husbands in every thing" (Ephesians 5:24).

The status of woman in former time was exceedingly deplorable, for it was the belief of the Orient that it was best for woman to be ignorant. It was considered preferable that she should not know reading or writing in order that she might not be informed of the events in the world. Woman was considered to be created for rearing children and attending to the duties of the household. If she pursued educational courses, it was deemed contrary to chastity; hence women were made prisoners of the household. The house did not even have window opening upon the outside world. Bahá'u'lláh destroyed these ideas and proclaimed the equality of man and woman. He made woman respected by commanding that all women be educated, that there be no difference in the education of the two sexes and that the man and woman share all rights. ('Abdu'l-Bahá, *The Promulgation of Universal Peace,* p. 230)

## WHY HAS THE OPPRESSION OF WOMEN BEEN A PROMINENT FEATURE OF HUMAN HISTORY?

Early in the development of civilization, the rule of "might makes right" was a fact of life. In eras when greater physical size, strength, and aggression ruled, men ruled. Those rules are changing:

The world in the past has been ruled by force, and man has dominated over women by reason of his more forceful and aggressive qualities both of body and mind. ('Abdu'l-Bahá, cited in Esslemont, *Bahá'u'lláh and the New Era,* p. 164)

Also, in the past, women were not allowed all of the educational opportunities afforded to men:

It is not to be denied that in various directions woman at present [1911] is more backward than man, also that this temporary inferiority is due to the lack of educational opportunity. ('Abdu'l-Bahá, *Paris Talks,* no. 50.7)

Full access to education for girls as well as boys is one of the requirements for progress in this age.

## WHY IS THE EDUCATION OF GIRLS
## SO IMPORTANT TO PROGRESS?

The education of girls is most important to progress because they grow up to be mothers, and mothers are the first educators of the children:

> For mothers are the first educators, the first mentors; and truly it is the mothers who determine the happiness, the future greatness, the courteous ways and learning and judgment, the understanding and the faith of their little ones. ('Abdu'l-Bahá, *Selections from the Writings of 'Abdu'l-Bahá*, no. 96.2)

Today, it is widely recognized that the education of girls is the biggest factor in social development. Kofi Annan, Former Secretary General of the United Nations, states: "To educate girls is to reduce poverty." He adds, "Study after study has taught us that there is no tool for development more effective than the education of girls. No other policy is as likely to raise economic productivity, lower infant and maternal mortality, improve nutrition and promote health" (Kofi Annan, Message to Global Education Campaign Event, 9 April 2003, United Nations Meetings Coverage and Press Releases. http://www.un.org/press/en/2003/sgsm8662.doc.htm).

### DOES THE EQUALITY OF THE SEXES MEAN THAT WOMEN
### AND MEN ARE THE SAME?

Women and men are equal in capacity and importance while different in certain characteristics and functions. In "mercy and sympathy," women may inherently excel men:

> Erelong the days shall come when the men addressing the women, shall say: "Blessed are ye! Blessed are ye! Verily ye are worthy of every gift. Verily ye deserve to adorn your heads with the crown of everlasting glory, because in sciences and arts, in virtues and perfections ye shall become equal to man, and as regards tenderness of heart and the abundance of mercy and sympathy ye are superior." ('Abdu'l-Bahá, *Paris Talks*, no. 59.8)

Physiological differences may also indicate difference in function:

Equality between men and women does not, indeed physiologically it cannot, mean identity of functions. In some things women excel men, for others men are better fitted than women, while in very many things the difference of sex is of no effect at all. The differences of function are most apparent in family life. The capacity for motherhood has many far-reaching implications which are recognized in Bahá'í Law. For example, when it is not possible to educate all one's children, daughters receive preference over sons, as mothers are the first educators of the next generation. Again, for physiological reasons, women are granted certain exemptions from fasting that are not applicable to men. (The Universal House of Justice, *Messages from the Universal House of Justice, 1963 to 1986*, no. 145.5)

## WHY ARE THE QUALITIES OF WOMEN ESPECIALLY VALUED IN THIS AGE?

The evolution of civilization has brought the planet to a point where physical strength and aggressive qualities are no longer the most important tools for survival; the qualities inherent in women are "gaining ascendance":

But the balance is already shifting—force is losing its weight and mental alertness, intuition, and the spiritual qualities of love and service, in which woman is strong, are gaining ascendancy. Hence the new age will be an age less masculine and more permeated with the feminine ideals—or, to speak more exactly, will be an age in which the masculine and feminine elements of civilization will be more evenly balanced. ('Abdu'l-Bahá, cited in Esslemont, *Bahá'u'lláh and the New Era*, p. 164)

## THREE ARE ONE

In the First Epistle of John, the Father, the Word, and the Holy Spirit are proclaimed as "one":

For there are three witnesses in heaven—the Father, the Word, and the Holy Spirit, and these three are one. (1 John 5:7, ISV)

Scripture that extols the oneness of the Father, the Word, and the Holy Spirit (sometimes voiced as the Father, the Son, and the Holy Ghost) is the inspiration of the doctrine of the Holy Trinity that is held in some faith traditions.

### HOW DO BAHÁ'ÍS UNDERSTAND THE ONENESS OF THE FATHER, THE WORD, AND THE HOLY SPIRIT?

For Bahá'ís, the "three are one" Scripture points to the mystical relationship between God and the Manifestation of God. A way to visualize this mystery is through the analogy of a perfect solar mirror. In this analogy: (1) the Sun represents God, (2) a perfect solar mirror represents the Manifestation of God, and (3) the bounty of the Sun (the light and heat that emanate from the Sun) represents the Holy Spirit. The solar mirror perfectly reflects the image of the Sun while it receives, focuses, and dispenses the energy of the Sun (the bounty of the sun) in a way that perfectly meets the needs of the community for that day. Similarly, the Manifestation of God perfectly reflects the image of God while receiving, focusing, and dispensing the Holy Spirit (the Bounty of God) in a way that perfectly meets the needs of humanity for that Day:

> The purport of our words is that the reality of Christ was a clear mirror wherein the Sun of Truth—that is, the divine Essence—appeared and shone forth with infinite perfections and attributes. It is not that the Sun, which is the Essence of the Divinity, was ever divided or multiplied—for it remains one—but it became manifest in the mirror. That is why Christ said, "The Father is in the Son," meaning that that Sun is manifest and visible in this mirror. ('Abdu'l-Bahá, *Some Answered Questions*, no. 27.7)

### DOES GOD DESCEND INTO THE WORLD OF CREATION IN THE PERSON OF THE MANIFESTATION OF GOD?

The essence of God does not ascend or descend. The Manifestation of God reflects the Bounty of God in the world of creation, but is not God:

> God is pure perfection and the creation is absolute imperfection. For God to descend into the degrees of existence would be the greatest of imperfections; rather, His manifestation, dawning, and

effulgence are even as the appearance of the sun in a clear, bright, and polished mirror.

All created things are resplendent signs of God. For instance, the rays of the sun shine upon all earthly things, yet the light that falls upon the plains, the mountains, the trees and fruits is only in such measure as to make them visible, to ensure their growth, and to cause them to attain the object of their existence. The Perfect Man, however, is even as a clear mirror in which the Sun of Truth is revealed and manifested in the fullness of its attributes and perfections. Thus the reality of Christ was a bright and polished mirror of the greatest purity and clarity. The Sun of Truth, the Essence of the Divinity, appeared in that mirror and manifested its light and heat therein, yet it did not descend from the heights of holiness and the heaven of sanctity to reside within it. No, it continues to abide in its loftiness and sublimity, but has been revealed and manifested in the mirror in all its beauty and perfection. ('Abdu'l-Bahá, *Some Answered Questions,* no. 27.4–5)

## IS GOD DIVISIBLE?

Although the Holy Spirit and the Manifestation of God are signs of the Bounty of God, God is not divisible:

The reality of the Divinity is sanctified and exalted beyond the comprehension of all created things, can in no wise be imagined by mortal mind and understanding, and transcends all human conception. That reality admits of no division, for division and multiplicity are among the characteristics of created and hence contingent things, and not accidents impinging upon the Necessary Being.

The reality of the Divinity is sanctified above singleness, then how much more above plurality. For that divine reality to descend into stations and degrees would be tantamount to deficiency, contrary to perfection, and utterly impossible. It has ever been, and will ever remain, in the loftiest heights of sanctity and purity. All that is mentioned regarding the manifestation and revelation of God pertains to the effulgence of His light and not to a descent into the degrees of existence. ('Abdu'l-Bahá, *Some Answered Questions,* no. 27.2–3)

## HOW MANY "PERFECT MIRRORS" ARE THERE?

Many "Perfect Mirrors" (Manifestations of God) have appeared in the world and all of Them have perfectly reflected the image of the One God:

> The Sun of Divinity and of Reality has revealed itself in various mirrors. Though these mirrors are many, yet the Sun is one. The bestowals of God are one; the reality of the divine religion is one. Consider how one and the same light has reflected itself in the different mirrors or manifestations of it. There are certain souls who are lovers of the Sun; they perceive the effulgence of the Sun from every mirror. They are not fettered or attached to the mirrors; they are attached to the Sun itself and adore it, no matter from what point it may shine. But those who adore the mirror and are attached to it become deprived of witnessing the light of the Sun when it shines forth from another mirror. For instance, the Sun of Reality revealed itself from the Mosaic mirror. The people who were sincere accepted and believed in it. When the same Sun shone from the Messianic mirror, the Jews who were not lovers of the Sun and who were fettered by their adoration of the mirror of Moses did not perceive the lights and effulgences of the Sun of Reality resplendent in Jesus; therefore, they were deprived of its bestowals. Yet the Sun of Reality, the Word of God, shone from the Messianic mirror through the wonderful channel of Jesus Christ more fully and more wonderfully. ('Abdu'l-Bahá, *The Promulgation of Universal Peace*, p. 159)

## WHAT BOUNTIES OF GOD ARE REFLECTED
## IN THE MANIFESTATION OF GOD?

The names and attributes of God are reflected in the Manifestation of God:

> These Tabernacles of Holiness, these Primal Mirrors which reflect the light of unfading glory, are but expressions of Him Who is the Invisible of the Invisibles. By the revelation of these Gems of Divine virtue all the names and attributes of God, such as knowledge and power, sovereignty and dominion, mercy and wisdom,

glory, bounty, and grace, are made manifest. (Bahá'u'lláh, The Kitáb-i-Íqán, ¶109)

### IN WHAT WAY CAN A PERSON BECOME LIKE A
### MIRROR OF DIVINITY?

Everyone can, in her or his own way, reflect something of the qualities and perfections of divinity:

To be a real Christian is to be a servant in His Cause and Kingdom, to go forth under His banner of peace and love toward all mankind, to be self-sacrificing and obedient, to become quickened by the breaths of the Holy Spirit, to be mirrors reflecting the radiance of the divinity of Christ, to be fruitful trees in the garden of His planting, to refresh the world by the water of life of His teachings—in all things to be like Him and filled with the spirit of His love. ('Abdu'l-Bahá, *The Promulgation of Universal Peace*, p. 8)

## FALSE PROPHETS

Like the Old Testament Books of Prophecy (see "Corruption"), the Epistles warn against the dangers of false prophets:

But false prophets also arose among the people, just as there will be false teachers among you, who will secretly bring in destructive opinions. They will even deny the Master who bought them— bringing swift destruction on themselves. Even so, many will follow their licentious ways, and because of these teachers the way of truth will be maligned. (2 Peter 2:1–2)

### SINCE FALSE PROPHETS ARE DANGEROUS, SHOULD ALL
### CLAIMS OF PROPHETHOOD BE IGNORED OR DENIED?

Although false prophets are serious dangers from which the people of God must protect themselves, the New Testament advises not to ignore or to deny all claims of prophecy but to investigate these claims and "hold fast to what is good":

Do not quench the Spirit. Do not despise the words of prophets, but test everything; hold fast to what is good. (1 Thessalonians 5:19–21)

## WHAT ARE THE NEW TESTAMENT CRITERIA FOR DISTINGUISHING BETWEEN FALSE AND TRUE PROPHETS?

False and true prophets can be distinguished by their fruits:

Beware of false prophets, which come to you in sheep's clothing, but inwardly they are ravening wolves. Ye shall know them by their fruits. Do men gather grapes of thorns, or figs of thistles? Even so every good tree bringeth forth good fruit; but a corrupt tree bringeth forth evil fruit. A good tree cannot bring forth evil fruit, neither can a corrupt tree bring forth good fruit. Every tree that bringeth not forth good fruit is hewn down, and cast into the fire. Wherefore by their fruits ye shall know them." (Matthew 7:15–20)

## WHAT ARE THE GOOD FRUITS?

The good fruits are higher qualities of the spirit—"love, joy, peace, patience, kindness, generosity, faithfulness, gentleness, and self-control." These are contrasted with the "works of the flesh" which are qualities of the lower nature:

Now the works of the flesh are obvious: fornication, impurity, licentiousness, idolatry, sorcery, enmities, strife, jealousy, anger, quarrels, dissensions, factions, envy, drunkenness, carousing, and things like these. I am warning you, as I warned you before: those who do such things will not inherit the kingdom of God.

By contrast, the fruit of the Spirit is love, joy, peace, patience, kindness, generosity, faithfulness, gentleness, and self-control. There is no law against such things. (Galatians 5:19–23)

Seekers can distinguish between true and false prophets by investigating the lives, teachings, and results of those claiming prophethood—as measured by the biblical standard of the fruits of the spirit and the works of the flesh. The same standard can be used to evaluate the integrity of religious leaders on all levels. The pain caused by false religious leaders remains an important and painful issue, often turning people away from religion altogether.

### WHO IS TO BLAME
### FOR FALSE RELIGIOUS TEACHERS?

Corruption of religious leaders is not the fault of the Manifestation of God Who founded the religion. False teachings come from human failings. For example, Christ taught peace, yet many have waged war in the name of Christ:

> Look at the Gospel of the Lord Christ and see how glorious it is! Yet even today men fail to understand its priceless beauty, and misinterpret its words of wisdom.
>
> Christ forbade war! When the disciple Peter, thinking to defend his Lord, cut off the ear of the servant of the High Priest, Christ said to him: "Put up thy sword into the sheath." Yet, in spite of the direct command of the Lord they profess to serve, men still dispute, make war, and kill one another, and His counsels and teaching seem quite forgotten.
>
> But do not therefore attribute to the Masters and Prophets the evil deeds of their followers. If the priests, teachers and people, lead lives which are contrary to the religion they profess to follow, is that the fault of Christ or the other Teachers? ('Abdu'l-Bahá, *Paris Talks*, no. 13.13–15)

Misdeeds in the name of religion that defy the laws of the Manifestation of God are not of that religion—they are human error.

## ANTICHRIST

Only four verses in the New Testament mention "antichrist" and these are all found in the first and second Epistles of John (1 John 2:18, 22; 4:3; 2 John 1:7). We will look at all of these verses.

## WHO OR WHAT
## IS ANTICHRIST?

The First Epistle of John describes antichrist as former believers who denied that Jesus was the Christ, denied the Father and the Son, and also left the community of believers:

> Children, it is the last hour! As you have heard that antichrist is coming, so now many antichrists have come. From this we know that it is the last hour. They went out from us, but they did not belong to us; for if they had belonged to us, they would have remained with us. But by going out they made it plain that none of them belongs to us. But you have been anointed by the Holy One, and all of you have knowledge. I write to you, not because you do not know the truth, but because you know it, and you know that no lie comes from the truth. Who is the liar but the one who denies that Jesus is the Christ? This is the antichrist, the one who denies the Father and the Son. (1 John 2:18–22)

Antichrist is also equated with false prophets who were active at the time of the writing of the Epistles of John:

> Beloved, do not believe every spirit, but test the spirits to see whether they are from God; for many false prophets have gone out into the world. By this you know the Spirit of God: every spirit that confesses that Jesus Christ has come in the flesh is from God, and every spirit that does not confess Jesus is not from God. And this is the spirit of the antichrist, of which you have heard that it is coming; and now it is already in the world. (1 John 4:1–3)

It is also stated that at that time there were many people who could be termed antichrist:

> Many deceivers have gone out into the world, those who do not confess that Jesus Christ has come in the flesh; any such person is the deceiver and the antichrist! (2 John 1:7).

## IS ANTICHRIST A PROBLEM TODAY?

Today, many people deny and speak against the divinity of Christ. Therefore, according to the definition of antichrist in the Epistles, antichrist still exists. In addition, the Bahá'í Writings use the term antichrist to refer to actions that are against the teachings of Christ, such as hostility and war:

> Therefore, these wars and cruelties, this bloodshed and sorrow are Antichrist, not Christ. These are the forces of death and Satan, not the hosts of the Supreme Concourse of heaven. ('Abdu'l-Bahá, *The Promulgation of Universal Peace,* p. 7)

### CAN ANTICHRIST BECOME MANIFEST WITHIN A RELIGION?

In the Bahá'í Writings, the scope of antichrist includes any bitter conflicts, regardless of the setting. Hatred and antagonism between denominations can be described as antichrist:

> No less bitter is the conflict between sects and denominations. Christ was a divine Center of unity and love. Whenever discord prevails instead of unity, wherever hatred and antagonism take the place of love and spiritual fellowship, Antichrist reigns instead of Christ. ('Abdu'l-Baha, *The Promulgation of Universal Peace,* p. 7)

### IS ANY ONE PERSON DESIGNATED AS
### "THE ANTICHRIST" IN THE BAHÁ'Í ERA?

In addition to hatred and antagonism in a general sense, any person who aggressively works against the Manifestation of God could be termed antichrist:

> Anyone who violently and determinedly sought to oppose the Manifestation could be called an "anti-Christ," such as the Vazir in the Báb's day, Hájí Mírzá Áqásí. (Shoghi Effendi, *High Endeavors,* p. 69)

The Bahá'í Writings specifically refer to two people in Baha'í history as antichrist: Hájí Mírzá Áqásí, the antichrist of the Bábí Revelation, and

Siyyid Muhammad, the antichrist of the Bahá'í Revelation (see Shoghi Effendi, *God Passes By,* p. 260).

# THE BOOK OF THE REVELATION
# TO JOHN—OVERVIEW

**The Book of the Revelation to John** (Revelation) is the last book of the New Testament. From a literary perspective, Revelation belongs in the "apocalyptic" category along with the Book of Daniel. Apocalyptic literature features: visions received by a seer; concern with the problem of evil;[42] the hope of good born out of evil taking shape in a new creation; and the use of symbolism and fantastic imagery to reconceptualize the past, present, and future in an otherworldly perspective. Revelation is the culminating prophecy of the entire biblical tradition. The author of Revelation is named in the text as John, a believer in Christ, who was exiled on the island of Patmos at the time of the book's writing, which is generally dated between 81 and 96 AD (see Bauckham, pp. 1287–88).

In Revelation, John describes a vision he received of "what must soon take place" (1:1). Like a dream and sometimes like a nightmare, his vision's extravagant imagery—including a beast rising from out of a bottomless pit, a seven-horned dragon, and a woman crowned with stars—has led to a variety of interpretations, speculations, and often disappointments as many of the fantastic scenarios contained within its verses seemed to have failed to come to pass. In considering the Revelation to John and all prophecy, it is helpful to remember that the apparent lack of fulfillment of prophecy is often, rather, a lack of understanding:

These things We mention only that the people may not be dismayed because of certain traditions and utterances, which have

---

42. The problem of evil: the tension of God's rule over creation concurrent with the apparent dominance of evil.

315

not yet been literally fulfilled, that they may rather attribute their perplexity to their own lack of understanding, and not to the non-fulfilment of the promises in the traditions, . . . The people, therefore, must not allow such utterances to deprive them of the divine bounties, but should rather seek enlightenment from them who are the recognized Expounders thereof, so that the hidden mysteries may be unravelled, and be made manifest unto them. (Bahá'u'lláh, The Kitáb-i-Íqán, ¶284)

Like other biblical literature, a key to connecting with John's visions is to look for their inner meanings:

. . . the Revelations of St. John are not to be taken literally, but spiritually. These are the mysteries of God. It is not the reading of the words that profits you; it is the understanding of their meanings. Therefore, pray God that you may be enabled to comprehend the mysteries of the divine Testaments. ('Abdu'l-Bahá, *The Promulgation of Universal Peace,* p. 648)

The Book of the Revelation to John has twenty-two chapters. 'Abdu'l-Bahá, a "recognized Expounder" in the Bahá'í Faith, gave a detailed commentary of one of those chapters, chapter eleven, as well as commentary on some additional verses. His explanations of the symbolisms contained in these ancient images places the significance of Revelation in the past, present, and future. Although 'Abdu'l-Bahá unfolds many of the mysteries in the Book of Revelation, it is understood that the meanings are not exhausted. With 'Abdu'l-Bahá's guidance we can examine the Revelation to John with a spiritual eye, and continue to marvel at its mysteries.

## OUTLINE OF THE REVELATION TO JOHN

If you are not familiar with the Revelation to John, it may be helpful to familiarize yourself with its story through the following outline before examining the Bahá'í interpretations.

Chapter 1: John announces himself and his commission to relay prophetic messages to the seven Asian churches: Ephesus, Smyrna, Pergamos, Thyatira, Sardis, Philadelphia, and Laodicea. He also introduces his vision of the Son of Man,

Chapters 2 and 3: In the vision, the Son of Man speaks to each of the seven churches addressing their individual strengths and failings. Victory is promised to the faithful.

Chapters 4 and 5: John sees a vision of the Creator surrounded by worshippers who hold a book "sealed up with seven seals" (5:1). None are found worthy to open the book until the Lamb appears.

Chapters 6 and 7: The Lamb breaks the first four seals and four horsemen come out representing conquest, war, famine, and death.[43] The breaking of the fifth seal discloses martyrs. The sixth reveals terror "for the great day of their wrath has come" (6:17). Servants of God from the tribe of Israel, as well as believers from all nations, are marked for protection.

Chapter 8: The Lamb breaks the seventh seal, and seven angels appear with trumpets. When the first trumpet is sounded, hail, fire, and blood are "thrown to the earth; and a third of the earth was burned up" (8:7). At the second trumpet blast "something like a great mountain burning with fire was thrown into the sea" (8:8). The third blast brings down a star into a third of the waters, causing death. The fourth trumpet darkens a third of the sun, moon, and stars.

Chapter 9 and 10: With the fifth trumpet blast, a bottomless pit opens and locusts with faces of men and teeth like lions emerge, tormenting anyone unmarked by the seal of God. The sixth trumpet unleashes two hundred million horsemen who kill "a third of humankind" (9:18). Survivors continue to worship idols. An angel announces the coming fulfillment of "the mystery of God" (10:7), and gives John a book that is sweet to the taste but bitter to swallow.

Chapter 11: John is told that "two witnesses" will prophecy until they are killed by "the beast that comes up from the bottomless pit" (11:7). Their bodies will lie in the streets and be reviled until raised by God

---

43. These are often referred to as the Four Horsemen of the Apocalypse.

"after three and a half days" (11:11). With the seventh trumpet, the eternal Kingdom of God is proclaimed amidst a great storm.

Chapter 12: A woman "clothed with the sun" (12:1) gives birth to a child who is almost eaten by a dragon. As the child is "caught up unto God" (12:5) the woman flees into the wilderness for "one thousand two hundred and sixty days" (12:6). Angels wage war on the dragon and throw him down to earth. The dragon continues to pursue the woman and makes war on her children.

Chapters 13 and 14: The dragon delegates his power to a beast from the sea that makes war on the saints, blasphemes God, and is given authority over every nation. Another beast arises from the land, and with great signs convinces people to worship the first beast. John sees Jesus and 144,000 righteous followers on Mount Zion singing "a new song" (14:3). Angels announce the coming of the hour of judgment, that Babylon has fallen, and that the worshippers of the beast will be tormented.

Chapters 15 and 16: While the righteous praise Moses and the Lamb, seven angels empty seven bowls of plagues across the Earth bringing destruction to the wicked. The suffering people do not repent. With the pouring out of the seventh bowl a voice from the temple says, "It is done" (16:17).

Chapters 17 and 18: Babylon the harlot appears sitting on a beast that has seven heads and ten horns; these are explained to be mountains and kings that wage war against the Lamb and devour the harlot. The city of Babylon falls and there are lamentations.

Chapters 19 and 20: Voices from heaven celebrate, the marriage of the Lamb is announced, and the Word of God appears named "King of Kings, and Lord of Lords" (19:16). The beast, the false prophet, and their worshippers are thrown into the fire. Satan is bound for a thousand years while the faithful reign with Christ. Souls are judged according to their deeds written in the book of life.

Chapters 21 and 22: John sees "a new heaven and a new earth" (21:1); God declares that all things are made new; Jerusalem is prepared as a bride for the Lamb; and the river of life flows with clear waters. The final message includes, "Behold I am coming quickly, and My reward is with Me, to render to every man according to what he has done. I am the Alpha and the Omega, the first and the last, the beginning and the end" (22:12–13).

# TOPICS FROM THE BOOK OF REVELATION TO JOHN

For an examination of topics from the Revelation to John, we will start with a verse-by-verse interpretive commentary of the eleventh chapter by 'Abdu'l-Bahá. The King James Version of the Bible will be used in this section because that is the translation quoted by 'Abdu'l-Bahá in His commentary.

## A REED LIKE A ROD

The eleventh chapter of Revelation begins by introducing "a reed like unto a rod" and the inner and outer courts of the "temple of God":

> And there was given me a reed like unto a rod: and the angel stood, saying, Rise, and measure the temple of God, and the altar, and them that worship therein. But the court which is without the temple leave out, and measure it not; for it is given unto the Gentiles: and the holy city shall they tread under foot forty and two months. (Revelation 11:1–2, KJV)

### WHAT DOES THE "REED" SYMBOLIZE?
The "reed" refers to the Manifestation of God—the "Perfect Man"—as a clear channel for the transmission of divine bounty:

> By this reed is meant the Perfect Man, and the reason for His being likened to a reed is that when the latter is entirely freed and emptied of its pith, it becomes capable of producing wondrous melodies.

Moreover, these songs and airs proceed not from the reed itself but from the player who blows into it. In the same way, the sanctified heart of that blessed Being is free and empty of all save God, is averse to and exempt from attachment to every selfish inclination, and is intimately acquainted with the breath of the Divine Spirit. That which He utters proceeds not from Himself but from the ideal Player and from divine revelation. Hence He is likened to a reed, and that reed is like a rod; that is, it is the succour of the weak and the support of every mortal soul. It is the rod of the True Shepherd by which He guards His flock and leads it about in the pastures of the Kingdom. ('Abdu'l-Bahá, *Some Answered Questions*, no. 11.2)

Like a rod, cane, or staff, the Manifestation is the supporter and helper.

### WHAT DOES IT MEAN TO MEASURE THE WORSHIPPERS IN THE TEMPLE?

To measure the worshippers in the temple means to evaluate the conditions of the souls who are striving to follow the spiritual Laws of God:

Thus the angel said: Weigh the Holy of Holies, and the altar, and them that are worshipping therein—that is, investigate their true condition; discover their rank and station, their attainments, their perfections, their conduct, and their attributes; and acquaint thyself with the mysteries of those holy souls who abide in the station of purity and sanctity in the Holy of Holies. ('Abdu'l-Bahá, *Some Answered Questions*, no. 11.3)

### WHAT IS THE SIGNIFICANCE OF THE AREAS WITHIN THE TEMPLE AND THE HOLY CITY OUTSIDE OF THE TEMPLE?

The area within the temple is symbolic of the spiritual laws of God— the Holy of Holies—that never change. The outer court and Holy City (Jerusalem) are symbolic of the religious social laws that are altered with each Dispensation:

Briefly, what is meant by the term "Holy of Holies" is that spiritual law which can never be changed or abrogated, and what is meant by the "Holy City" is the material law which may indeed be abrogated. . . . ('Abdu'l-Bahá, *Some Answered Questions,* no. 11.11)

## WHAT IS THE MEANING OF
## THE OUTER COURT OF THE TEMPLE BEING
## "GIVEN UNTO THE GENTILES"?

The outer court being "given over to the Gentiles" symbolizes spiritual winter—the spiritual devastation that characterizes the end time of every Dispensation when people lose touch with the spiritual foundations of religion and only the outward forms remain:

> Thus, at the end of the Mosaic Dispensation, which coincided with the advent of Christ, the true religion of God vanished from among the Jews, leaving behind a form without a spirit. The Holy of Holies was no more, but the outer court of the Temple—which signifies the outward form of the religion—fell into the hands of the Gentiles. In the same way, the very heart of the religion of Christ, which consists in the greatest human virtues, is no more, but its outward form has remained in the hands of the priests and monks. Likewise, the foundation of the religion of Muhammad is no more, but its outward form remains in the hands of the Muslim divines. ('Abdu'l-Bahá, *Some Answered Questions,* no. 11.8)

## WHAT DOES IT MEAN THAT
## THE HOLY CITY WILL BE TRODDEN
## "UNDER FOOT FORTY AND TWO MONTHS"?

This verse contains two prophecies: the duration of the Dispensation of Islam and the date of the beginning of the Bahá'í era. "Forty and two months" equals twelve hundred and sixty days. In biblical prophecy each day equals a year. Therefore, the time indicated is twelve hundred and sixty years. That is both the duration of Islam, and, in the Islamic calendar, the year of the beginning of the Bahá'í era that came with the Manifestation of the Báb:

> "And the holy city shall they tread under foot forty and two months"; that is, the Gentiles will seize and subdue Jerusalem for forty-two months, or 1,260 days, or—each day being equivalent

to a year—1,260 years, which is the duration of the Qur'ánic Dispensation.[44]

. . . This 1,260 years is a prophecy concerning the advent of the Báb, the "Gate" leading to Bahá'u'lláh, which took place in the year A.H. 1260.[45] As the period of 1,260 years has been completed, the Holy City of Jerusalem is now beginning to prosper and flourish again. ('Abdu'l-Bahá, *Some Answered Questions,* no. 11.6–7)

## TWO WITNESSES

Revelation continues with the promised appearance of "two witnesses":

And I will give power unto my two witnesses, and they shall prophesy a thousand two hundred and threescore days, clothed in sackcloth. These are the two olive trees, and the two candlesticks standing before the God of the earth. (Revelation 11:3–4, KJV)

### WHO ARE THE "TWO WITNESSES"?

The "two witnesses" are Muhammad, the Founder of Islam, and His Disciple, Ali. In the Qur'án, "Witness" is one of Muhammad's titles:

By these two witnesses are intended Muhammad the Messenger of God and Alí the son of Abú Talíb. In the Qur'án it is said that God addressed Muhammad saying, "We made You a Witness, a Herald, and a Warner";[46] that is, We have established Thee as one Who

---

44. The biblical formula of a prophetic day representing a year is applied here: "For according to the text of the Bible each day is a year, as it is said in Ezekiel 4:6 'thou shalt bear the iniquity of the house of Judah forty days: I have appointed thee each day for a year'" ('Abdu'l-Bahá, *Some Answered Questions,* no. 11.6–7).

45. 1844 AD.

46. Qur'án 48:8.

bears witness, Who imparts the glad-tidings of that which is to come, and Who warns of the wrath of God. A "witness" means one by whose affirmation matters are ascertained. The commandments of these two witnesses were to be followed for 1,260 days, each day corresponding to a year. ('Abdu'l-Bahá, *Some Answered Questions,* no. 11.12)

### WHY ARE MUHAMMAD AND ALI "CLOTHED IN SACKCLOTH"?

Being "clothed in sackcloth" (old clothes) indicates that the religion of Muhammad would not appear new because the laws of Islam repeated those of previous Dispensations:

> It is said they were "clothed in sackcloth," meaning that they appeared to wear not a new raiment but an old one. In other words, they would initially appear to be of no consequence in the eyes of other peoples and their Cause would not seem new. For the spiritual principles of the religion of Muhammad correspond to those of Christ in the Gospel, and His material commandments correspond for the most part to those of the Torah. This is the symbolism of the old raiment. ('Abdu'l-Bahá, *Some Answered Questions,* no. 11.12)

Muhammad's social laws were harsh like those of Moses, because the Arab tribes to whom He appeared had many of the same barbaric characteristics of the Israelite tribes at the time of Moses.

### WHY ARE MUHAMMAD AND ALI DESCRIBED AS "OLIVE TREES" AND "CANDLESTICKS"?

Olive oil fueled the lamps of that time and furnished light, as did candles. In these verses, olive trees and candlesticks symbolize spiritual illumination:

> These two Souls have been likened to olive trees, since all the lamps of that time were lit at night with olive oil. In other words, these are two Souls from whom the oil of divine wisdom—which is the cause of the illumination of the world—will appear, and through whom the lights of God will shine bright and resplendent. Thus have they

also been likened to candlesticks. The candlestick is the locus of the light and the place from whence it emanates. In the same way, the light of guidance would shine resplendent from these luminous Countenances. ('Abdu'l-Bahá, *Some Answered Questions,* no. 11.13)

### IN WHAT WAY WERE MUHAMMAD AND ALI "STANDING BEFORE GOD"?

"Standing before God" means that Muhammad and Ali would serve God:

They are "standing before God,"—that is, they have arisen in His service and are educating His creatures. For instance, they so educated the barbarous, desert-dwelling tribes of the Arabian Peninsula as to cause them to attain the loftiest heights of human civilization at the time and to spread their fame and renown throughout the world. ('Abdu'l-Bahá, *Some Answered Questions,* no. 11.14)

## RIVERS TO BLOOD

The next two verses state that the Witnesses were protected by fire that proceeded out of their mouths, they had the power over rain and the waters, and they possessed the ability to smite the earth with "plagues":

And if any man will hurt them, fire proceedeth out of their mouth, and devoureth their enemies: and if any man will hurt them, he must in this manner be killed. These have power to shut heaven, that it rain not in the days of their prophecy: and have power over waters to turn them to blood, and to smite the earth with all plagues, as often as they will. (Revelation 11:5–6, KJV)

### WHAT DOES IT MEAN THAT FIRE WOULD COME OUT OF THEIR MOUTHS AND DEVOUR THEIR ENEMIES?

This verse indicates that the divine laws and teachings proclaimed by their mouths would defeat many enemies:

"And if any man would hurt them, fire proceedeth out of their mouth, and devoureth their enemies." This means that no soul would be able to withstand their might. That is, should anyone seek to subvert their teachings or their law, he would be overcome and defeated by virtue of that law which proceeds, whether in brief or in full, from their mouth. In other words, they would issue a command that would destroy any enemy that would attempt to harm or oppose them. And so it came to pass, for their opponents were all vanquished, dispersed, and destroyed, and these two witnesses were outwardly assisted by the power of God. ('Abdu'l-Bahá, *Some Answered Questions,* no. 11.15)

## WHAT IS THE MEANING OF
## "RAIN" IN THESE VERSES?

In these verses, "rain" means the heavenly teachings that Muhammad and Ali could shower upon people if they wished to do so:

"These have power to shut heaven, that it rain not in the days of their prophecy," This means that they would rule supreme in that age. In other words, the law and teachings of Muhammad, and the exposition and commentaries of 'Alí, are a heavenly grace. Should they wish to bestow this grace, it is in their power to do so, and should they wish otherwise, no rain will fall, and by "rain" is meant here the outpouring grace. ('Abdu'l-Bahá, *Some Answered Questions,* no. 11.16)

## WHAT DOES WATER TURNING TO BLOOD SYMBOLIZE?

This verse is another allusion to the Dispensation of Moses. In the Exodus story, the Egyptians in their pride did not accept Moses and Joshua as Messengers of God. Therefore, that which was the source of the Egyptians' pride—their traditions and easy livelihood, symbolized by the term "waters"—became the source of their spiritual death. In this way, the Egyptians' life-giving "water" (traditions and confidence in material riches) was turned to "blood" (spiritual death and destruction). This prophecy states that the same would happen at the time of Muhammad and Ali:

"And have power over waters to turn them to blood." This means that the prophethood of Muhammad was similar to that of Moses, and the power of ʿAlí like that of Joshua. That is, it was in their power, had they so desired, to turn the waters of the Nile into blood for the Egyptians and the deniers—or, in other words, to turn, in consequence of their ignorance and pride, that which was the source of their life into the cause of their death. Thus the sovereignty, wealth, and power of Pharaoh and of his people, which were the source of that nation's life, became, as a result of their opposition, denial, and pride, the very cause of their death, ruin, destruction, degradation, and wretchedness. Hence these two witnesses have power to destroy nations. (ʿAbduʾl-Bahá, *Some Answered Questions,* no. 11.17)

### WHAT DOES IT MEAN THAT THE TWO WITNESSES COULD "SMITE THE EARTH WITH ALL PLAGUES"?

This is another allusion to the Mosaic Dispensation. To "smite the earth with all plagues" means that Muhammad and Ali would possess the power to correct even the most bloodthirsty oppressors:

"And to smite the earth with all plagues, as often as they will." This means that they would also be endowed with outward power and ascendancy, that they might school the workers of iniquity and the embodiments of oppression and tyranny. For God had granted these two witnesses both outward might and inward power, and so it is that they reformed and educated the wicked, bloodthirsty, and iniquitous Arabs of the desert who were like ravening wolves and beasts. (ʿAbduʾl-Baha, *Some Answered Questions,* no. 11.18)

## THE BEAST

The next verses have a beast coming out of a bottomless pit, overpowering the two Witnesses, and leaving their bodies on display in a city that is the spiritual equivalent of the site of the crucifixion:

And when they shall have finished their testimony, the beast that ascendeth out of the bottomless pit shall make war against them, and shall overcome them, and kill them. And their dead bodies shall lie in the street of the great city, which spiritually is called Sodom and Egypt, where also our LORD was crucified. (Revelation 11:7–8, KJV)

### WHAT DOES IT MEAN THAT THE TWO WITNESSES WOULD FINISH THEIR TESTIMONY?

To have "finished their testimony" means that Muhammad and Ali would have completed the mission of proclaiming the heavenly teachings they were ordained to bring:

"And when they shall have finished their testimony"—that is, when they have accomplished that which they were bidden, and have delivered the divine message, and promoted the religion of God, and spread abroad His heavenly teachings, so that the signs of spiritual life might be manifested in the souls of men, the light of human virtues might shine forth, and these desert tribes might achieve substantive progress. ('Abdu'l-Bahá, *Some Answered Questions,* no. 11.19)

### WHAT IS THE "BEAST" THAT COMES "OUT OF THE BOTTOMLESS PIT"?

The beast represents the Umayyads:

"The beast that ascendeth out of the bottomless pit shall make war against them, and shall overcome them, and kill them." By this beast is meant the Umayyads, who assailed these witnesses from the pit of error. And indeed it came to pass that the Umayyads assailed the religion of Muhammad and the truth of 'Alí, which consist in the love of God. ('Abdu'l-Bahá, *Some Answered Questions,* no. 11.20)

### WHO WERE THE UMAYYADS?

The Umayyads refer to people of the Umayyad clan of the Quraish tribe of Mecca. The Quraish of Mecca were aristocrats, merchants, and managers of the lucrative Kaaba shrine—a site of idol worship and other pagan practices.

At the time of Muhammad, the Quraish tribe was divided into two rivaling clans: one led by the rich merchant and philanthropist Hashim (this clan was called the Hashimites); the other by Hashim's jealous nephew Umayya (this clan was called Umayyads). Muhammad was born into the Hashimite clan. When Muhammad began preaching monotheism and urging his fellow Meccans to stop worshipping idols—a teaching that was a threat to the economy—He was met with violent opposition, particularly from the Umayyads. After Muhammad's passing, the Umayyad clan eventually usurped control of Islam, using the power and charisma of the religion for selfish purposes (see Durant, pp. 62, 166, 195–96).

## HOW DID THE UMAYYADS MAKE "WAR AGAINST THE TWO WITNESSES"?

The war against Muhammad and Ali was a spiritual war in which the power-mongering desires of the Umayyads darkened the divine laws and teachings of Islam, essentially destroying the spiritual essence of the religion:

"The beast made war against these two witnesses." By this is intended a spiritual war, meaning that the beast would act in complete opposition to the teachings, conduct, and character of these two witnesses, to such an extent that the virtues and perfections that had been diffused among the peoples and nations by virtue of their power would entirely vanish, and animal qualities and carnal desires would predominate. Therefore, this beast would wage war against them and would gain ascendancy, meaning that the darkness of the error propagated by this beast would prevail throughout the world and slay those two witnesses—that is, it would extinguish their spiritual life amidst the people, obliterate their divine laws and teachings, and trample underfoot the religion of God, leaving behind naught but a dead and soulless body. ('Abdu'l-Bahá, *Some Answered Questions*, no. 11.21)

### WHAT IS THE SIGNIFICANCE OF THE "DEAD BODIES" LYING IN THE STREET OF "SODOM AND EGYPT"?

The "dead bodies" lying in "the street" of "Sodom and Egypt" symbolize the religion of Muhammad being practiced without its original spirit:

> By "their bodies" is meant the religion of God and by "the street," exposure to public view. "Sodom and Egypt, where also our Lord was crucified" refers to the land of Syria and especially to Jerusalem, for the Umayyads had their seat of power in this land and it was here that the religion of God and the divine teachings first disappeared, leaving behind a soulless body. "Their bodies" refers to the religion of God, which remained as a dead and soulless body. ('Abdu'l-Bahá, *Some Answered Questions,* no. 11.22)

## THREE DAYS AND A HALF

John's vision continues with the dead bodies of the two Witnesses on display for three and a half days while others rejoice over the spectacle:

> And they of the people and kindreds and tongues and nations shall see their dead bodies three days and a half, and shall not suffer their dead bodies to be put in graves. And they that dwell upon the earth shall rejoice over them, and make merry, and shall send gifts one to another; because these two prophets tormented them that dwelt on the earth. (Revelation 11:9–10, KJV)

### WHAT DOES THE THREE AND A HALF DAYS SIGNIFY?

Three and a half days signifies 1,260 years. This is determined by using the "day for a year" formula twice: 3.5 prophetic days = 3.5 prophetic years = 42 months = 1,260 days = 1,260 years:

> As was already explained, in the terminology of the Sacred Scriptures three days and a half signifies three years and a half, and

three years and a half represents forty-two months, and forty-two months—1,260 days. Since according to the explicit text of the Bible each day is equivalent to a year, this means that for 1,260 years, which is the duration of the Qur'ánic Dispensation, the nations, tribes, and peoples would behold their bodies; that is, they would keep the religion of God before their eyes but would not act in accordance with it. ('Abdu'l-Bahá, *Some Answered Questions,* no. 11.23)

### WHY IS THE "DAY FOR A YEAR" FORMULA USED TWICE ON "THREE DAYS AND A HALF"?

The twelfth chapter of the Book of Revelation adds this twist to the formula when it equates "a thousand two hundred and threescore days" (Revelation 12:6) with three and a half ("time, times, and half a time," Revelation 12:14). Both of these numbers are indicated as the same duration of time—the time that the "woman" (the religion of Muhammad) spent in the "wilderness." Thus, the Book of Revelation uses four indicators for 1,260 years:

"a thousand two hundred and threescore days" = 1,260 years (Revelation 11:3, 12:6)

"forty and two months" x 30 days each = 1,260 days = 1,260 years (Revelation 11:2)

"three days and a half" = 3 ½ years = 42 months = 1,260 days = 1,260 years (Revelation 11:9)

"time [1], times [2], and half time [½]" = 3 ½ days = 3 ½ years = 42 months = 1,260 days = 1,260 years (Revelation 12:14)

### WHAT DOES IT MEAN THAT THE "DEAD BODIES" WOULD NOT "BE PUT IN GRAVES"?

That the "dead bodies" would not "be put in graves" means that many people would cling to the form of the religion of Islam without its spiritual foundation:

Yet they would not suffer these bodies—the religion of God—to be laid to rest in the grave. That is, they would hold fast to its outward form and not let it entirely vanish from their midst nor allow the body to be wholly destroyed and annihilated. Rather, they would forsake its reality while outwardly preserving its name and remembrance. ('Abdu'l-Bahá, *Some Answered Questions,* no. 11.23)

### WHO ARE THE "KINDREDS, PEOPLE, AND NATIONS"?

The "kindreds, people, and nations" indicate followers who continued the religious habits of Islam without its original spirituality:

That which is intended here are such kindreds, peoples, and nations as were gathered beneath the shadow of the Qur'án. These are they who would not allow the Cause and religion of God to be destroyed and annihilated outwardly as well. Thus, some manner of prayer and fasting was practiced among them, but the very foundations of the religion of God, which are goodly character, upright conduct, and the knowledge of the divine mysteries, had disappeared; the light of human virtues, which proceeds from the love and knowledge of God, had been extinguished; the darkness of oppression and tyranny, of carnal desires and satanic attributes, prevailed; and the body of the religion of God, like unto a corpse, was exposed to public view. ('Abdu'l-Bahá, *Some Answered Questions,* no. 11.24)

### WHO ARE "THOSE THAT DWELT UPON THE EARTH" AND WHY WOULD THEY REJOICE?

"Those who dwelt upon the earth" are non-Islamic nations who, upon seeing moral corruption in some of the followers of that religion, would rejoice over the possibility of overcoming those weakened peoples:

By "them that dwelt on the earth" is meant other peoples and nations, such as those of Europe and of distant Asian lands, who, seeing that the character of Islam had entirely changed; that the religion of God had been forsaken; that virtue, decency, and honour had vanished; and that characters had been subverted, rejoiced that the morals of the Muslims had been corrupted and that they stood therefore to be vanquished by other nations. And this indeed came to pass in a most conspicuous manner. ('Abdu'l-Bahá, *Some Answered Questions,* no. 11.26)

### IN WHAT WAY DID THE TWO WITNESSES TORMENT PEOPLES OF THE EARTH AND WHY WOULD THE OTHER NATIONS "SEND GIFTS TO ONE ANOTHER"?

The two Witnesses, Muhammad and Ali, "tormented" other nations by overcoming them with their new teachings; the other nations sent "gifts" in solidarity with one another:

The other nations "shall send gifts to one another," meaning that they would help each other, for "these two prophets tormented them that dwelt upon the earth"; that is, they subdued and subjugated the other peoples and nations of the earth. ('Abdu'l-Bahá, *Some Answered Questions,* no. 11.27)

## ASCENDED TO HEAVEN

After three days and a half, the two Witnesses stood upon their feet and ascended into heaven:

And after three days and a half the spirit of life from God entered into them, and they stood upon their feet; and great fear fell upon them which saw them. And they heard a great voice from heaven saying unto them, Come up hither. And they ascended up to heaven in a cloud; and their enemies beheld them. (Revelation 11:11–12, KJV)

### IN WHAT WAY DID THE TWO WITNESSES STAND "UPON THEIR FEET" AFTER THREE AND A HALF DAYS?

After three and half days (that is, after 1,260 years) in the year 1260 of the Hejira (1844 AD), the spiritual realities of Muhammad and Ali were resurrected in the Manifestation of the Báb and His disciple, Quddús:

"And after three days and a half the Spirit of life from God entered into them, and they stood upon their feet; and great fear fell upon them which saw them." Three days and a half, as we explained earlier, is 1,260 years. These two Persons whose bodies were lying soulless—that is, the teachings and the religion that Muhammad had established and that 'Alí had promoted, whose reality had vanished, and of which only an empty form had remained—were again endowed with spirit. That is, the spirituality of the religion of God that had become materiality, the virtues that had become vices, the love of God that had become hatred, the light that had become darkness, the divine qualities that had become satanic attributes, the justice that had become tyranny, the mercy that had become malice, the sincerity that had become hypocrisy, the guidance that had become error, the purity that had become carnality—all these divine teachings, heavenly virtues and perfections, and spiritual bounties—were, after three and a half days (which by the terminology of the Sacred Scriptures is 1,260 years) renewed by the advent of the Báb and by the allegiance of Quddús. ('Abdu'l-Bahá, *Some Answered Questions,* no. 11.28)

## IN WHAT WAY DID THE BÁB AND QUDDÚS ASCEND "UP TO HEAVEN"?

After promulgating the religion of God, both the Báb and Quddús were martyred and ascended to the spiritual world:

"And they heard a great voice from heaven saying unto them, Come up hither. And they ascended up to heaven in a cloud," meaning that from the invisible heaven they heard the voice of God, saying: You have accomplished all that was called for with regard to educating the people and conveying the glad-tidings of that which is to come. You have delivered My message to the people, raised the call of Truth, and fulfilled your every obligation. Now, even as Christ, you must lay down your lives in the path of the Beloved and suffer a martyr's death. And so that Sun of Reality and that Moon of Guidance both set, Christ-like, beneath the horizon of the supreme sacrifice and ascended to the realm of Heaven. ('Abdu'l-Bahá, *Some Answered Questions,* no. 11.30)

### WHAT IS MEANT BY "THEIR ENEMIES BEHELD THEM"?

This verse indicates that, after the martyrdom of the Báb and Quddús, many people who had previously been their enemies became transformed and realized the truth of their teachings:

"And their enemies beheld them." That is, many of their enemies realized after their martyrdom the sublimity of their station and the excellence of their virtues, and testified to their greatness and their perfections. ('Abdu'l-Bahá, *Some Answered Questions*, no. 11.31)

## WOES

After the ascension there was an earthquake and thousands perished. A second "woe" was "past" and a third "woe" was coming quickly:

And the same hour was there a great earthquake, and the tenth part of the city fell, and in the earthquake were slain of men seven thousand: and the remnant were affrighted, and gave glory to the God of heaven. The second woe is past; and, behold, the third woe cometh quickly. (Revelation 11:13–14, KJV)

### WHAT IS THE SIGNIFICANCE OF THE EARTHQUAKE?

In one sense, these verses refer to an actual earthquake that happened in Shiraz, Persia, immediately after the Báb was martyred. The devastation was such that many people turned to God:

This earthquake occurred in Shíráz after the martyrdom of the Báb. The city was plunged into turmoil, and many people were killed. Great agitation ensued, moreover, from diseases, cholera, scarcity, famine, starvation, and other afflictions—an agitation the like of which had never before been witnessed. ('Abdu'l-Bahá, *Some Answered Questions*, no. 11.32)

In another sense, the earthquake could symbolize the tremors of doubt and fear that overcame many of the believers upon the martyrdom of the

Báb. 'Abdu'l-Bahá refers to the "tremor of doubt" that shook the earth upon the passing of Bahá'u'lláh. (*Some Answered Questions*, no. 11.45).

**WHAT ARE
THE THREE "WOES"?**

The three woes are three Manifestations. The first is Muhammad, the second is the Báb, and the third is Bahá'u'lláh:

> The first woe was the advent of the Apostle of God, Muhammad the son of 'Abdu'lláh—peace be upon Him. The second woe is that of the Báb, upon Him be glory and praise. The third woe is the great day of the advent of the Lord of Hosts and the revelation of the promised Beauty. The explanation of matter is explained in the thirtieth chapter of Ezekiel, where it is said: "The word of the Lord came again unto me, saying, Son of man, prophesy and say, Thus saith the Lord God; Howl ye, Woe worth the day! For the day is near, even the day of the Lord is near." It is therefore evident then that the day of woe is the day of the Lord; for in that day woe is upon the heedless, the sinners, and the ignorant. That is why it is said, "The second woe is past; and, behold, the third woe cometh quickly." This third woe is the day of the manifestation of Bahá'u'lláh, the Day of God, and it is near to the day of the appearance of the Báb. ('Abdu'l-Bahá, *Some Answered Questions,* no. 11.34)

## TWENTY-FOUR ELDERS

With the appearance of the third woe came "the seventh angel" and twenty-four elders:

> And the seventh angel sounded; and there were great voices in heaven, saying, The kingdoms of this world are become the kingdoms of our Lord, and of his Christ; and he shall reign for ever and ever. And the four and twenty elders, which sat before God on their seats, fell upon their faces, and worshipped God, Saying, We give thee thanks, O Lord God Almighty, which art, and wast, and

335

art to come; because thou hast taken to thee thy great power, and hast reigned. (Revelation 11:15–17, KJV)

### WHO IS THE SEVENTH ANGEL AND WHAT ARE THE VOICES?

The seventh angel refers to human beings with the qualities and character of heaven. The voices are those with eyes to see and ears to hear who will proclaim the teachings of the Manifestation of God:

That angel refers to human souls who have been endowed with heavenly attributes and invested with an angelic nature and disposition. Voices will be lifted up and the appearance of the divine Manifestation will be proclaimed and noised abroad. ('Abdu'l-Bahá, *Some Answered Questions*, no. 11.35)

### WHAT IS THE "KINGDOM OF OUR LORD"?

The kingdom of our Lord is the spiritual civilization of the earth that is promised in all of the Holy Books. It is the culmination of previous cycles and the maturity of the human race when unity, love, and fellowship will be universally realized:

It has been promised and recorded in all the Sacred Books and Scriptures that in this Day of God His divine and spiritual sovereignty will be established, the world will be renewed, a fresh spirit will be breathed into the body of creation, the divine springtime will be ushered in, the clouds of mercy will rain down, the Sun of Truth will shine forth, the life-giving breezes will blow: The world of humanity will be arrayed in a new garment; the face of the earth will become even as the highest paradise; humanity will be educated; war, dissension, strife and contention will vanish; truthfulness, uprightness, peace and godliness will prevail; love, concord, and union will encompass the world; and God will rule forevermore—that is, a spiritual and everlasting sovereignty will be established. Such is the Day of God. For all the days which have come and gone were the days of Abraham, Moses, Christ, or of the other Prophets, but this day is the Day of God, inasmuch as the Sun of Truth will shine forth therein with the utmost intensity and radiance. ('Abdu'l-Bahá, *Some Answered Questions*, no. 11.35)

### WHO ARE THE "FOUR AND TWENTY ELDERS"?

The twenty-four elders are holy souls who are guardians and promulgators of the Faith of Bahá'u'lláh:

> In every Dispensation there have been twelve chosen ones: In the time of Joseph there were twelve brothers; in the time of Moses there were twelve heads or chiefs of the tribes; in the time of Christ there were twelve Apostles; and in the time of Muhammad there were twelve Imáms. But in this glorious Revelation there are twenty-four such souls, double the number of all the others, for so does its greatness require.[47] These holy souls are in the presence of God seated upon their thrones, meaning that they reign eternally. ('Abdu'l-Bahá, *Some Answered Questions,* no. 11.36)

## WRATH AND REWARD

The third woe—the Revelation of Bahá'u'lláh—is followed by crisis and victory as both the dead in spirit and the servants of God face judgment:

> And the nations were angry, and thy wrath is come, and the time of the dead, that they should be judged, and that thou shouldest give reward unto thy servants the prophets, and to the saints, and them that fear thy name, small and great; and shouldest destroy them which destroy the earth. (Revelation 11.18, KJV)

The Day of Judgment is also known as the Day of Resurrection:

> The Day of Resurrection, according to Bahá'í interpretation, is the Judgment Day, the Day when unbelievers will be called upon to

---

47. "Regarding the four and twenty elders: The Master, in a Tablet, stated that they are the Báb, the 18 Letters of the Living and five others who would be known in the future" (From a letter written on behalf of Shoghi Effendi to an individual believer, dated July 22, 1943).

give account of their actions, and whether the world has prevented them from acknowledging the new Revelation. (Shoghi Effendi, *Dawn of a New Day,* p. 79)

### WHY WILL THE NATIONS BE "ANGRY"?

The nations will be angry because those who follow their own passions and neglect the teachings of the Bahá'í Revelation will be at a loss:

"And the nations were angry," for Thy teachings ran counter to the selfish desires of the other nations, "and Thy wrath is come," meaning that all suffered grievous loss for failing to follow Thy counsels, admonitions, and teachings; were deprived of grace everlasting; and were veiled from the light of the Sun of Truth. ('Abdu'l-Bahá, *Some Answered Questions,* no. 11.38)

### HOW CAN THE DEAD BE JUDGED?

In these verses, "dead" is used in the same way that Christ used the term: dead means spiritually dead. Judgment indicates that the low degree of existence of the spiritually dead will be made outwardly apparent. At the same time, the bounty of being spiritually alive and engaged in service for the love of God will also be made manifest:

"And the time of the dead, that they should be judged" means that the time has come that the dead—that is, those who are deprived of the spirit of the love of God and bereft of that life which is holy and everlasting—should be judged with equity, meaning that each should be raised up according to their worthiness and capacity, and that the truth should be fully divulged as to what depths of degradation they occupy in this world of existence and how they should, in reality, be accounted among the dead. ('Abdu'l-Bahá, *Some Answered Questions,* no. 11.39)

### HOW WILL "THEM WHICH DESTROY THE EARTH" BE DESTROYED?

The difference between the poverty of spiritual blindness and the richness of spiritual sight will be universally recognized. Darkness will be destroyed by love of the Light:

"And shouldest destroy them which destroy the earth." That is, Thou wilt entirely deprive the heedless; for the blindness of the blind will be exposed and the sight of them that see will become evident; the ignorance and folly of the exponents of error will be recognized and the knowledge and wisdom of the rightly guided will be manifested; and thus the destroyers will be destroyed. ('Abdu'l-Bahá, *Some Answered Questions,* no. 11.41)

## THE TEMPLE OPENED

Finally, the temple of God containing the "ark of his testament" was opened and accompanied by much tribulation:

And the temple of God was opened in heaven, and there was seen in his temple the ark of his testament: and there were lightnings, and voices, and thunderings, and an earthquake, and great hail. (Revelation 11:19, KJV)

### IN WHAT WAY WILL THE TEMPLE BE "OPENED IN HEAVEN"?

As mentioned previously, the innermost sanctuary of the Temple of Jerusalem—the Holy of Holies—symbolizes the eternal spiritual laws of God. In this verse, the temple of God being "opened in heaven" means that in the Dispensation of Bahá'u'lláh the spiritual laws of God will be universally apparent and fully realized throughout the world, bringing an era of enlightenment:

"And the temple of God was opened in heaven." This means that the divine Jerusalem has appeared and the Holy of Holies has become manifest. Among the people of true knowledge, the Holy of Holies refers to the essence of the religion of God and His true teachings, which have remained unchanged throughout all the prophetic Dispensations, as was explained previously, while Jerusalem encompasses the reality of the religion of God, which is the Holy of Holies, as well as all the laws, mutual relationships, rites, and material ordinances, which constitute the city. That is why it is called the heavenly Jerusalem. Briefly, in the course of the Dispensation of the Sun of Truth, the lights of God will shine forth with the utmost splendour, and thus the essence of the divine teachings will be realized in the world of being, the darkness of ignorance and folly will be dispelled, the world will become another world, spiritual illumination will encompass all, and hence the Holy of Holies will appear. ('Abdu'l-Bahá, *Some Answered Questions,* no. 11.42)

### WHAT IS "THE ARK OF HIS TESTAMENT"?

The "ark of His Testament" symbolizes Bahá'u'lláh's Will and Testament (Kitáb-i-'Ahd, the Book of the Covenant) in which He designates his son, 'Abdu'l-Bahá, as His successor and the Center of His Covenant:

"And there was seen in His temple the ark of His Testament." This means that the Book of His Covenant will appear in His Jerusalem, the Tablet of the Testament will be recorded, and the meaning of the Covenant and Testament will become evident. The call of God will resound throughout East and West, and the earth will be filled with the renown of the Cause of God. The violators of the Covenant will be humbled and abased, and the faithful will attain honour and glory, for they hold fast to the Book of the Covenant and are firm and unwavering in the path of the Testament. ('Abdu'l-Bahá, *Some Answered Questions,* no. 11.44)

### WHAT DOES THE ACCOMPANYING EARTHQUAKE, LIGHTNING, THUNDER, AND HAIL SIGNIFY?

The earthquake symbolizes doubts that will arise upon the passing of Bahá'u'lláh, the sound of thunder symbolizes how some will violate the Covenant of Bahá'u'lláh, and hail and lightning symbolize the torment that the violators of the Covenant will bring upon themselves:

"And there were lightnings, and voices, and thunderings, and an earthquake, and great hail," meaning that after the appearance of the Book of the Covenant there will be a great tempest, the lightning of divine anger and wrath will flash, the thunder of the violation of the Covenant will break, the tremor of doubt will shake the earth, the hail of torments will rain upon the violators of the Covenant, and those who claim to believe will be subjected to tests and trials. ('Abdu'l-Bahá, *Some Answered Questions*, no. 11.45)

Every Dispensation comes with chastisements, tests, and difficulties. That is why it is called a "woe."

This concludes selections from 'Abdu'l-Bahá's commentary on the eleventh chapter of the Book of Revelation. This one chapter addresses crisis and victory in the Dispensations of Muhammad, the Báb, and Bahá'u'lláh through the poetic language of prophecy. In the remainder of this section we will examine 'Abdu'l-Bahá's explanation of certain passages in Revelation chapters twelve, twenty-one, and twenty-two that lead up to "a new heaven and a new earth" (Revelation 21:1).

## CHAPTER 12: CLOTHED WITH THE SUN

How do we get to a new heaven and a new earth? It's a process and it's painful—like childbirth:

> And there appeared a great wonder in heaven; a woman clothed with the sun, and the moon under her feet, and upon her head a crown of twelve stars: And she being with child cried, travailing in birth, and pained to be delivered. (Revelation 12:1–2, KJV)

### WHO IS THE WOMAN AND WHAT DO THE SUN AND MOON SYMBOLIZE?

The woman symbolizes the religion of Muhammad standing clothed with Persia (the sun) and standing on the Ottoman Empire (the moon):

> This woman is that bride, the religion of God, that descended upon Muhammad. The sun with which she was clothed, and the moon which was under her feet, are the two governments which are under the shadow of that religion, the Persian and Ottoman, for the emblem of Persia is the sun and that of the Ottoman Empire is the crescent moon. Thus the sun and moon allude to two gov-

ernments under the shadow of the religion of God. ('Abdu'l-Bahá, *Some Answered Questions,* no. 13.4)

### WHAT DO THE
### TWELVE STARS SYMBOLIZE?

The twelve stars in the crown of Islam symbolize the twelve Imams who educated the people by promulgating the Law of Muhammad:

These twelve stars represent the twelve Imáms, who were the promoters of the religion of Muhammad and the educators of the nation, and who shone as stars in the heaven of guidance. ('Abdu'l-Bahá, *Some Answered Questions,* no. 13.4)

### WHAT IS THE SIGNIFICANCE
### OF THE CHILDBIRTH?

The childbirth indicates that the woman (the religion of Muhammad) travailed in pain before giving birth to the religion of the Báb. Every religion is, in a way, the child of the religion that precedes it. Another connection is that the Báb was actually of the hereditary lineage of Muhammad:

Then it is said: "And she being with child cried, travailing in birth, and pained to be delivered," meaning that this religion will suffer great difficulties and endure great toil and trouble until a perfect offspring is produced therefrom—that is, until the subsequent and promised Manifestation, Who is a perfect offspring, is reared in the bosom of this religion, which is even as its mother. By this offspring is meant the Báb, the Primal Point, Who was in truth born from the religion of Muhammad. ('Abdu'l-Bahá, *Some Answered Questions,* no. 13.5)

## A RED DRAGON

The vision continues with a seven-headed, ten-horned, red dragon positioned to devour the child when it is born:

And there appeared another wonder in heaven; and behold a great red dragon, having seven heads and ten horns, and seven crowns upon his heads. And his tail drew the third part of the stars of heaven, and did cast them to the earth: and the dragon stood before the woman which was ready to be delivered, for to devour her child as soon as it was born. (Revelation 12:3–4, KJV)

### WHAT DOES THE DRAGON SYMBOLIZE?

The dragon symbolizes the rulers of the Umayyad clan who suppressed the true religion of Muhammad. The seven crowned heads are the seven political areas over which the Umayyads ruled:

This dragon represents the Umayyads, who seized the reins of the religion of Muhammad; and the seven heads and seven crowns represent the seven dominions and kingdoms over which they came to rule: the Roman dominion in Syria; the Persian, the Arabian, and the Egyptian dominions; the dominion of Africa—that is, Tunisia, Morocco, and Algeria; the dominion of Andalusia, which is now Spain; and the dominion of the Turkish tribes of Transoxania. The Umayyads gained power over all these dominions. ('Abdu'l-Bahá, *Some Answered Questions,* no. 13.6)

### WHAT ABOUT THE "TEN HORNS"?

The ten horns signify the names, without repetition, of the Umayyad rulers who were hostile to the lineage of Muhammad:

The ten horns represent the names of the Umayyad rulers, for, barring repetition, they are ten sovereigns, or ten names of chiefs and rulers. The first is Abú Sufyán and the last is Marván. Some of their names have been repeated, including two Mu'áviyihs, three Yazíds, two Valíds, and two Marváns. If, however, these names are each counted only once, they number ten in total. These Umayyads— the first of whom was Abú Sufyán, the former chief of Mecca and founder of the dynasty, and the last of whom was Marván— destroyed a third of the holy and sanctified souls who descended from the pure lineage of Muhammad and who were even as the stars of heaven. ('Abdu'l-Bahá, *Some Answered Questions,* no. 13.6)

**WHY DID THE DRAGON WANT TO KILL THE CHILD?**

The Umayyads (the dragon) were afraid of the next Manifestation of God Who was prophesied to come from Muhammad's offspring. Therefore, they actually kept watch over His descendents with the intent to kill any males who were particularly well-regarded:

> The dragon's standing near her signifies that it was keeping watch to devour her child as soon as it had been delivered. This child was the promised Manifestation, Who is the offspring of the religion of Muhammad. The Umayyads were ever anxious to lay hold on the Promised One Who was to appear from the lineage of Muhammad, that they might destroy and annihilate Him, for they greatly feared His advent. And so wherever they found a descendant of Muhammad who was respected in the eyes of the people, they killed him. ('Abdu'l-Bahá *Some Answered Questions,* no. 13.7)

## HER CHILD

The woman gave birth to a "man child" who sat on the throne of God and ruled with a "rod of iron":

> And she brought forth a man child, who was to rule all nations with a rod of iron: and her child was caught up unto God, and to his throne. And the woman fled into the wilderness, where she hath a place prepared of God, that they should feed her there a thousand two hundred and threescore days. (Revelation 12:5–6, KJV)

**WHO IS THE "MAN CHILD"**
**AND WHAT DOES THE**
**ROD OF IRON SYMBOLIZE?**

The "man child" was the promised Manifestation of God of the lineage of Muhammad—the Báb. The iron rod is a symbol of strength and also an indication that He ruled with the compassion of the Good Shepherd:

This glorious son is the promised Manifestation, Who was born of the religion of God and reared in the bosom of the divine teachings. The iron rod is a symbol of might and power—it is not a sword—and means that He will shepherd all the nations of the earth by virtue of His divine might and power. And by this son is meant the Báb. ('Abdu'l-Bahá, *Some Answered Questions*, no. 13.8)

### WHAT IS THE "WILDERNESS"?

In these verses "wilderness" indicates the desert of Hijaz and the Arabian Peninsula:

"And the woman fled into the wilderness," that is, the religion of God betook itself to the desert, meaning the vast desert of Hijaz and the Arabian Peninsula. ('Abdu'l-Bahá, *Some Answered Questions*, no. 13.10)

### WHAT IS THE SIGNIFICANCE OF
### "A THOUSAND TWO HUNDRED
### AND THREESCORE DAYS"?

"A thousand two hundred and threescore days" (1,260 days), indicates, as we have seen, 1,260 years. And 1,260 years is the duration of the religion of Muhammad. After this time, the fruit or "man child" of Muhammad's Dispensation appeared: the religion of the Báb:

According to the terminology of the Bible, these 1,260 days mean 1,260 years, as was before explained. Thus for 1,260 years the religion of God was fostered in the vast desert of Arabia, until the Promised One appeared. After these 1,260 years that religion ceased to be in effect, for the fruit of that tree had been manifested and its result had been produced. ('Abdu'l-Bahá, *Some Answered Questions*, no. 13.12)

This brings us to the Revelation of the Báb, inaugurated on 23 May 1844—year 1260 of the Hejira of Muhammad. The Báb declared Himself to be the Promised One of Islam and heralded the imminent coming of the next Messenger of God, "Him Whom God shall make manifest." After a six-year ministry and intense persecution, the Báb was martyred—executed by the Persian government on July 9, 1850.

In 1853, Bahá'u'lláh, while imprisoned as a follower of the Báb, received the Revelation that He was the One promised by the Báb and ten years later He publicly proclaimed His station. Bahá'u'lláh's long and fruitful ministry was also characterized by persecution, imprisonment, and exile.

## CHAPTER 21: A NEW EARTH

We will now jump to the twenty-first chapter of Revelation, which celebrates the fruit of the aforementioned crises and victories. It is time to enter "a new heaven and a new earth":

And I saw a new heaven and a new earth: for the first heaven and the first earth were passed away; and there was no more sea. And I John saw the holy city, new Jerusalem, coming down from God out of heaven, prepared as a bride adorned for her husband. And I heard a great voice out of heaven saying, Behold, the tabernacle of God is with men, and he will dwell with them, and they shall be his people, and God himself shall be with them, and be their God. (Revelation 21:1–3, KJV)

### WHAT DO THE "FIRST HEAVEN AND EARTH" THAT "WERE PASSED AWAY" SYMBOLIZE?

The "first heaven and earth" that "were passed away" symbolize previous religious laws. That "there was no more sea" foreshadows the long-awaited culmination of the story—the Kingdom of God on earth where the laws and teachings of God will be universally realized:

Consider how unmistakably "the first heaven" and "the first earth" refer to the outward aspects of the former religion. For it is said that "the first heaven and earth were passed away; and there was no more sea." That is, the earth is the arena of the last judgment, and in this arena there will be no more sea, meaning that the law and teachings of God will have spread throughout the earth, all mankind will have embraced His Cause, and the earth will have been entirely peopled by the faithful. Thus there will be no more sea, for man dwells upon solid land and not the sea—that is, in that Dispensation the sphere of influence of that religion will encompass every land that man has trodden, and it will be established upon solid ground whereon the feet do not falter. ('Abdu'l-Bahá, *Some Answered Questions,* no. 13.2)

### WHAT IS THE "NEW JERUSALEM"?

As was noted previously, "Jerusalem" is a symbol for the Revelation of the laws and teachings of God. Therefore, the "new Jerusalem" is the latest Revelation:

Likewise, the religion of God is described as the Holy City or the New Jerusalem. Clearly, the New Jerusalem which descends from heaven is not a city of stone and lime, of brick and mortar, but is rather the religion of God which descends from heaven and is described as new. For it is obvious that the Jerusalem which is built of stone and mortar does not descend from heaven and is not renewed, but that what is renewed is the religion of God.

Furthermore, the religion of God is likened to an adorned bride who appears with the utmost grace, as it has been said in chapter 21 of the Revelation of John: "And I John saw the holy city, new Jerusalem, coming down from God out of heaven, prepared as a bride adorned for her husband." ('Abdu'l-Bahá, *Some Answered Questions,* no. 13.3–4)

### HAS THE NEW JERUSALEM DESCENDED FROM HEAVEN AS PROPHESIED IN THE BOOK OF REVELATION?

Bahá'u'lláh brought the new Jerusalem; that is, the new laws and teachings of God, for the current stage of our ever-advancing civilization. It is prophesied that through this Revelation, and after a tumultuous global maturing, mankind will see the long-promised era of peace. The following is an excerpt of a Tablet in which 'Abdu'l-Bahá, in the symbolic language of biblical Scripture, celebrates the Bahá'í Faith as the coming of the new Jerusalem:

Verily, verily, the new heaven and the new earth are come. The holy City, new Jerusalem, hath come down from on high in the form of a maid of heaven, veiled, beauteous, and unique, and prepared for reunion with her lovers on earth. The angelic company of the Celestial Concourse hath joined in a call that hath run throughout the universe, all loudly and mightily acclaiming: "This is the City of God and His abode, wherein shall dwell the pure and holy among His servants. He shall live with them, for they are His people and He is their Lord." ('Abdu'l-Bahá, *Selections from the Writings of 'Abdu'l-Bahá,* no. 3.1)

The new Jerusalem has descended from heaven, but not as a celestial kingdom, nor earthly city, nor even as a place. It has come in the form of a do-it-yourself kit with comprehensive instructions delivered by the Word of God for the purpose of building a new civilization.

## CHAPTER 22: ALPHA AND OMEGA

The visions recorded in the Book of Revelation begin with Christ stating His reality as "Alpha and Omega" (Revelation 1:8), and end with the same declaration:

I am Alpha and Omega, the beginning and the end, the first and the last. (Revelation 22:13, KJV)

### WHY DID CHRIST SAY THAT HE WAS "THE FIRST AND THE LAST"?

Christ's reality as "the first and the last" describes His eternal spiritual station as a Manifestation of God:

Their heavenly station encompasses all things, is aware of all mysteries, is informed of all signs, and rules supreme over all things. And this is equally true both before and after the intimation of Their mission. That is why Christ said: "I am Alpha and Omega, the first and the last"—that is, there has never been, nor shall there ever be, any change or alteration in Me. ('Abdu'l-Bahá, *Some Answered Questions,* no. 58.5)

### IS "THE FIRST AND THE LAST" TITLE SPECIFIC TO CHRIST?

As has already been noted, all of the titles of the Manifestations are, in the station of essential unity as the voice of God, shared:

And were they all [the Manifestations of God] to proclaim, "I am the Seal of the Prophets," they, verily, utter but the truth, beyond the faintest shadow of doubt. For they are all but one person, one soul, one spirit, one being, one revelation. They are all the manifestation of the "Beginning" and the "End," the "First" and the "Last," the "Seen" and the "Hidden"—all of which pertain to Him Who is the Innermost Spirit of Spirits and Eternal Essence of Essences. (Bahá'u'lláh, The Kitáb-i-Íqán, ¶196)

In the Bahá'í Writings, Bahá'u'lláh is identified as the return of "Alpha and Omega" for this age:

He [Bahá'u'lláh] is Alpha and Omega. He is the One that will give unto him that is athirst of the fountain of the water of life and bestow upon the sick the remedy of true salvation. He whom such grace aideth is verily he that receiveth the most glorious heritage from the Prophets of God and His holy ones. ('Abdu'l-Bahá, *Selections from the Writings of 'Abdu'l-Bahá,* no. 3.3)

And at the same time, every Manifestation of God is Alpha and Omega, the First and the Last, the Beginning and the End.

Inasmuch as these Birds of the celestial Throne are all sent down from the heaven of the Will of God, and as they all arise to proclaim His irresistible Faith, they, therefore, are regarded as one soul and the same person. For they all drink from the one Cup of the love of God, and all partake of the fruit of the same Tree of Oneness. (Bahá'u'lláh, The Kitáb-i-Íqán, ¶161)

# REFLECTIONS ON THE
# NEW TESTAMENT:
# SWADDLING CLOTHES

To conclude this introductory collection of New Testament topics in the Bahá'í Writings, I offer this brief reflection on a New Testament story that we have not yet examined—the Nativity as told in the Gospel of Luke. First, let's review the Scripture:

> And she gave birth to her firstborn son and wrapped him in bands of cloth, and laid him in a manger, because there was no place for them in the inn.
>
> In that region there were shepherds living in the fields, keeping watch over their flock by night. Then an angel of the LORD stood before them, and the glory of the LORD shone around them, and they were terrified. But the angel said to them, "Do not be afraid; for see—I am bringing you good news of great joy for all the people: to you is born this day in the city of David a Savior, who is the Messiah, the LORD. This will be a sign for you: you will find a child wrapped in bands of cloth and lying in a manger." And suddenly there was with the angel a multitude of the heavenly host, praising God and saying, "Glory to God in the highest heaven, and on earth peace among those whom he favors!"
>
> When the angels had left them and gone into heaven, the shepherds said to one another, "Let us go now to Bethlehem and see this thing that has taken place, which the LORD has made known to us." So they went with haste and found Mary and Joseph, and the child lying in the manger. (Luke 2:7–16)

I know of no commentary in the Bahá'í Writings on the Nativity scene. However, I do know that all Scripture is rich in spiritual meanings, and we are encouraged to ponder those meanings. So, as a personal and not authoritative interpretation, and for my love of this Scripture since my early childhood, this is what I envision now when I ponder the significance of the Nativity from a Bahá'í perspective:

*No room at the inn:* An "inn" is a public house—a popular place for travelers and merry-makers. That there was "no room in the inn" may symbolize the lack of acceptance of the Manifestation of God by the generality of the population. The appearance of the Word of God never gets the popular vote early in the Revelation.

*Swaddling clothes:* To "swaddle" means to restrain or bind. Babies are often swaddled (wrapped with a large cloth so that they look like burritos) to keep them secure and restrict their movements. It is notable that "swaddling clothes" are mentioned twice in Luke's story. It is likely that most babies were swaddled in that period, so, not being a distinctive infant wrap, why does the Scripture mention swaddling clothes at all? Perhaps the importance of the swaddling clothes is that they symbolize the restrictions that every Manifestation of God accepts when born in a human body. The swaddling may also symbolize that the mission of the Manifestation cannot be declared until the situation is mature. Even though born upon the earth, every Manifestation is "bound" or "swaddled" until His announcement is timely. In addition, the message of the Manifestation of God is delivered in words familiar to human sensory experience and so we have metaphysical truths necessarily "swaddled" in the language of the physical world.

*Laid in a manger:* Of all the imagery in the Nativity story, I think that the manger calls the loudest for symbolic interpretation. A manger is a feeding trough—a dinner table for animals. So I ask you, if you (or your wife) had just given birth in a stable, would you multiply the overwhelming hazards of the event by putting your delicate and precious newborn in the animals' feeding trough? Perhaps the placing of baby Jesus in the manger (literally on a plate) may be symbolic of the offering of the Manifestation of God as the "Bread of Life" (John 6:35)—the Word required for spiritual development. The image, contrasting the most pure spiritual station with the lowliest animal nature, certainly communicates the willingness to sacrifice that characterizes the life of every Manifestation of God.

***Shepherds keeping watch by night hear news of the Messiah and are afraid:*** Shepherds lead, feed, and protect flocks of sheep. Shepherds have long been symbolic of religious leaders. In Christian tradition, Jesus is identified as the Good Shepherd. Perhaps the shepherds in the Nativity scene symbolize those religious leaders with "ears to hear" who recognized the Reality of Christ early in the Revelation. That they were watching over their flocks (or congregations) by night describes the spiritual deprivation of that time—the Return of the Manifestation of God always happens in the darkness of spiritual winter. Luke indicates that the shepherds were afraid; this is for good reason. Change can be frightening. The new Revelation always challenges the status quo, and leaders of religion generally do not benefit socially or materially by challenging the status quo of the religious organizations in which they are invested.

***Domestic animals:*** Though not mentioned in the Scripture, farm animals often appear in Nativity scenes. These animals, such as horses, sheep, cows, and donkeys that normally feed from a manger, may be symbolic of the animal nature of the people of the world who need the Bread of Life to awaken and nurture their spiritual realities.

To me, the Nativity story symbolizes elements of every Dispensation: the darkness of a world ignorant of its own spiritual potential; the birth of a new Revelation; the lack of acceptance by the general population; the miracle of the all-powerful Word of God born into a human body; the civilization-changing flood of spiritual nutrition that flows from the Word of God; the courage of leaders who have eyes to see; and the miraculous stories of everyday people who transform themselves and their communities by attending to the new Revelation. This is truly the "good news" of the Gospel!

# APPENDIX A

# The Bahá'í Faith

The following is excerpted from *The Bahá'ís: A Profile of the Bahá'í Faith and its Worldwide Community*, a publication of the Bahá'í International Community.

Founded a century and a half ago, the Bahá'í Faith is today among the fastest growing of the world's religions. With more than five million followers, who reside in virtually every nation on earth, it is the second-most widespread faith, surpassing every religion but Christianity in its geographic reach. Bahá'ís reside in more than 100,000 localities around the world, an expansion that reflects their dedication to the ideal of world citizenship.

The Bahá'í Faith's global scope is mirrored in the composition of its membership. Representing a cross section of humanity, Bahá'ís come from virtually every nation, ethnic group, culture, profession, and social or economic class. More than 2,100 different ethnic and tribal groups are represented.

Since it also forms a single community, free of schism or factions, the Bahá'í Faith comprises what is very likely the most diverse and widespread organized body of people on earth.

The Faith's Founder was Bahá'u'lláh, a Persian nobleman from Tehran Who, in the mid-nineteenth century, left a life of princely comfort and security and, in the face of intense persecution and deprivation, brought to humanity a stirring new message of peace and unity.

Bahá'u'lláh claimed to be nothing less than a new and independent Messenger from God. His life, work, and influence parallel that of Abraham, Krishna, Moses, Zoroaster, Buddha, Christ, and Muhammad. Bahá'ís view Bahá'u'lláh as the most recent in this succession of divine Messengers.

The essential message of Bahá'u'lláh is that of unity. He taught that there is only one God, that there is only one human race, and that all the world's religions represent stages in the revelation of God's will and purpose for humanity. In this day, Bahá'u'lláh said, humanity has collectively come of age. As foretold in all of the world's Scriptures, the time has arrived for the uniting of all peoples into a peaceful and integrated global society. "The earth is but one country, and mankind its citizens," He wrote.

The youngest of the world's independent religions, the Faith founded by Bahá'u'lláh stands out from other religions in a number of ways. It has a unique system of global administration, with freely elected governing councils in nearly 10,000 localities.

It takes a distinctive approach to contemporary social problems. The Faith's Scriptures and the multifarious activities of its membership address virtually every important trend in the world today, from new thinking about cultural diversity and environmental conservation to the decentralization of decision making; from a renewed commitment to family life and moral values to the call for social and economic justice in a world that is rapidly becoming a global neighborhood.

The Faith's most distinctive accomplishment by far, however, is its unity. Unlike every other religion—not to mention most social and political movements—the Bahá'í community has successfully resisted the perennial impulse to divide into sects and subgroups. It has maintained its unity despite a history as turbulent as that of any religion of antiquity.

In the years since Bahá'u'lláh lived, the process of global unification for which He called has become well advanced. Through historical processes, the traditional barriers of race, class, creed, and nation have steadily broken down. The forces at work, Bahá'u'lláh predicted, will eventually give birth to a universal civilization. The principal challenge facing the peoples of the earth is to accept the fact of their oneness and assist in the creation of this new world.

For a global society to flourish, Bahá'u'lláh said, it must be based on certain fundamental principles. They include the elimination of all forms of prejudice; full equality between the sexes; recognition of the essential oneness of the world's great religions; the elimination of extremes of poverty and wealth; universal education; the harmony of science and religion; a sustainable balance between nature and technology; and the establishment of a world federal system, based on collective security and the oneness of humanity. Bahá'ís around the world express their commitment to these principles chiefly through individual and community transformation, including the large number of small-scale, grassroots-based social and economic development projects that Bahá'í communities have launched in recent years.

In building a unified network of local, national, and international governing councils, Bahá'u'lláh's followers have created a far-flung and diverse worldwide community—marked by a distinctive pattern of life and activity—which offers an encouraging model of cooperation, harmony, and social action. In a world so divided in its loyalties, this is in itself a singular achievement.

For more information about the Bahá'í Faith, visit www.bahai.org. In the United States, call 1-800-22-UNITE.

# APPENDIX B

# The Central Figures and Institutions of the Bahá'í Faith

The Central Figures of the Bahá'í Faith are the Báb, Bahá'u'lláh, and 'Abdu'l-Bahá. The supreme Institutions of the Bahá'í Faith are the Guardianship (Shoghi Effendi) and the Universal House of Justice.

## BAHÁ'U'LLÁH (1817–1892)

Bahá'u'lláh (meaning "the Glory of God") is the Prophet-Founder of the Bahá'í Faith. He was born Mírzá Husayn-'Alí on 12 November 1817 to a noble family in Mazindaran, Iran. At age twenty-seven He became a follower of the Báb and shortly afterwards became known by the name of Bahá (Glory). "Bahá'u'lláh suffered from the persecution waged against the Bábís at the time and was made to endure imprisonment and the bastinado" (Momen, p. 39). While imprisoned in the Síyáh-Chál (an underground prison in Tihrán) He received a revelation that He was the One promised by the Báb.

Under order of the Persian Empire Bahá'u'lláh was exiled from Iran, whereby He went to Baghdád, Iraq where He became recognized as a spiritual leader. Because of His spreading influence, authorities of the Ottoman Empire exiled Him from Baghdád to Constantinople. "Bahá'u'lláh departed for Constantinople and soon afterwards was banished to Adrianople where He publicly proclaimed His Mission, addressing His proclamation to the kings and rulers of the earth and calling on them to establish world peace, justice, and unity" (Momen, p. 40). Shortly afterwards He was condemned to perpetual imprisonment in the prison-city of 'Akká (in present-day Israel).

Despite hardships and isolation, Bahá'u'lláh continued His proclamation to world leaders. The revelation of foundational principles of the Bahá'í Faith and the teachings required to establish unity, equality, and justice in this age poured from His pen until His ascension on 29 May 1892. In His Will and Testament (The Book of the Covenant), Bahá'u'lláh named His eldest son, 'Abdu'l-Bahá, as His successor and the authorized interpreter of His Teachings. "Bahá'u'lláh's Writings are considered by Bahá'ís to be revelation from God, and some 15,000 of His Tablets have so far been collected" (Momen, p. 41).

## THE BÁB (1819–1850)

"The Báb" (meaning "the Gate") is the Herald of the Bahá'í Faith. He was born Siyyid 'Alí-Muhammad to a merchant family in Shiraz, Iran on 20 October 1819. On 23 May 1844 "the Báb proclaimed Himself to be the Promised One of Islam, the Qá'im, and said that the Mission of His Dispensation was to alert the people to the imminent advent of another Prophet, 'Him Whom God shall make manifest'" (Momen, p. 28). The Báb and His followers eventually broke ties with Islam.

The fanatical Shí'ih clergy attempted to stamp out the new religion, but the number of the Báb's followers grew. The Báb was imprisoned and subjected to the bastinado and His followers (Bábís) were subjected to brutal persecution. On July 9, 1850 the Báb was martyred by execution before a firing squad in Tabríz, Persia. "Bahá'ís revere the Báb as the Forerunner or Herald of Bahá'u'lláh, but also as a Manifestation of God in His own right, considering His Writings to be Holy Scripture. The beginning of the Bahá'í Era is dated from the day of His Declaration" (Momen, p. 30).

*Appendix B*

## ‘ABDU’L-BAHÁ (1844–1921)

‘Abdu’l-Bahá (meaning "Servant of the Glory"), the eldest son of Bahá’u’lláh, was born ‘Abbás Effendi on 23 May 1844, the very night that the Báb declared His mission. ‘Abdu’l-Bahá recognized His Father's station before Bahá’u’lláh's public Declaration. "He shared Bahá’u’lláh's banishment and exile and often served as His Father's deputy when dealing with officials and the public" (Momen, p. 2).

‘Abdu’l-Bahá assumed the role as the Head of the Bahá’í Faith (as ordained in Bahá’u’lláh's Will and Testament) following the passing of Bahá’u’lláh, and it was at this time that He chose the name ‘Abdu’l-Bahá, Servant of the Glory, for Himself. Bahá’u’lláh's appointment of ‘Abdu’l-Bahá as His successor and the Center of His Covenant ensured the unity of the Bahá’í community and the preservation of Bahá’u’lláh's teachings. Shoghi Effendi explains ‘Abdu’l-Bahá's unique station: "Though essentially human and holding a station radically and fundamentally different from that occupied by Bahá’u’lláh and His Forerunner, . . . ‘Abdu’l-Bahá was the perfect Exemplar of His Faith . . . endowed with superhuman knowledge, and to be regarded as the stainless mirror reflecting His light" (Shoghi Effendi, *God Passes By*, p. 381).

‘Abdu’l-Bahá, Whose Writings are considered Scripture by Bahá’ís, wrote many books and Tablets interpreting and explaining His Father's Teachings. He traveled extensively from 1911 to 1913 throughout Europe and North America proclaiming the principles of the Faith. A model of selfless service within the Bahá’í community, ‘Abdu’l-Bahá was also renowned for humanitarian activities in the greater community. He "was knighted in 1920 by the British government for His efforts for the relief of hunger in Palestine during World War I" (Momen, p. 3). In His Will and Testament, ‘Abdu’l-Bahá named His grandson, Shoghi Effendi, to succeed Him as Guardian of the Bahá’í Faith.

## SHOGHI EFFENDI (1897–1957)

Upon 'Abdu'l-Bahá's passing, His grandson, Shoghi Effendi—who had grown up under the guidance of 'Abdu'l-Bahá—assumed the position of Guardian of the Bahá'í Faith as ordained in 'Abdu'l-Bahá's Will and Testament, which proclaims that the Institution of the Guardianship is "under the care and protection of the Abhá Beauty, under the shelter and unerring guidance of His Holiness, the Exalted One . . ." (p. 11).

Shoghi Effendi's many achievements include the establishment of the Administrative Order of the Faith as conceived by Bahá'u'lláh, and the spread of the Faith to all parts of the world. His writings, many in the form of letters, continue to clarify the teachings of the Central Figures (Bahá'u'lláh, the Báb, and 'Abdu'l-Bahá) and guide the community. He translated many of the Bahá'í Writings from the language in which they were revealed (either Persian or Arabic) into a majestic style of English, and wrote extensively on the history of the Faith, its long-range vision, and the practical steps necessary to turn that vision into reality. Shoghi Effendi worked tirelessly, with 'Abdu'l-Bahá and after Abdu'l-Bahá's passing, to establish the conditions required for the election of the Universal House of Justice.

## THE UNIVERSAL HOUSE OF JUSTICE (1963–PRESENT)

The Universal House of Justice is the international governing body for the world Bahá'í community as ordained by Bahá'u'lláh in the Kitáb-i-Aqdas. In His Will and Testament, 'Abdu'l-Bahá states that the Universal House of Justice is "under the care and protection of the Abhá Beauty, under the shelter and unerring guidance of His Holiness, the Exalted One . . ." (p. 11). The House of Justice has the authority to legislate on all matters not specifically laid down in the Bahá'í Scriptures. The first Universal House of Justice was elected in 1963. The council chamber and offices of the Universal House of Justice are housed on the Arc of Mount Carmel in Haifa, Israel.

# BIBLIOGRAPHY

## Works of Bahá'u'lláh

*Epistle to the Son of the Wolf.* New ed. Translated by Shoghi Effendi. Wilmette, IL: Bahá'í Publishing Trust, 1988.

*Gems of Divine Mysteries.* Australia: Bahá'í Publications Australia, 2002.

*Gleanings from the Writings of Bahá'u'lláh.* 1st ps ed. Translated by Shoghi Effendi. Wilmette, IL: Bahá'í Publishing, 2005.

*The Hidden Words.* Translated by Shoghi Effendi. Wilmette, IL: Bahá'í Publishing, 2002.

*The Kitáb-i-Aqdas: The Most Holy Book.* 1st ps ed. Wilmette, IL: Bahá'í Publishing Trust, 1993.

*The Kitáb-i-Íqán: The Book of Certitude.* 1st pocket-size ed. Translated by Shoghi Effendi. Wilmette, IL: Bahá'í Publishing, 2003.

*Prayers and Meditations.* Translated by Shoghi Effendi. 1st pocket-size ed. Wilmette, IL: Bahá'í Publishing Trust, 2008.

*The Proclamation of Bahá'u'lláh to the Kings and Leaders of the World.* Haifa: Bahá'í World Centre, 1967.

*Seven Valleys and the Four Valleys.* New ed. Translated by Ali-Kuli Khan and Marzieh Gail. Wilmette, IL: Bahá'í Publishing Trust, 1991.

*The Summons to the Lord of Hosts, Tablets of Bahá'u'lláh.* Wilmette, IL: Bahá'í Publishing, 2006.

*The Tabernacle of Unity: Bahá'u'lláh's Responses to Mánikchí Sáhib and other Writings.* Haifa: Bahá'í World Center, 2006.

*Tablets of Bahá'u'lláh revealed after the Kitáb-i-Aqdas.* 1st pocket-size ed. Compiled by the Research Department of the Universal House of Justice. Translated by Habib Taherzadeh et al. Wilmette, IL: Bahá'í Publishing Trust, 1988.

## Works of the Báb

*Selections from the Writings of the Báb.* Compiled by the Research Department of the Universal House of Justice. Translated by Habib Taherzadeh et al. Wilmette, IL: Bahá'í Publishing Trust, 2006.

## Works of 'Abdu'l-Bahá

*'Abdu'l-Bahá in London: Addresses &Notes of Conversations.* London: Bahá'í Publishing Trust, 1987.

*Memorials of the Faithful.* New ed. Translated by Marzieh Gail. Wilmette, IL: Bahá'í Publishing Trust, 1996.

*Paris Talks: Addresses Given By 'Abdu'l-Bahá in Paris in 1911.* Wilmette, IL: Bahá'í Publishing, 2011.

*Promulgation of Universal Peace: Talks Delivered by 'Abdu'l-Bahá during His Visit to the United States and Canada in 1912.* Compiled by Howard MacNutt. Wilmette, IL: Bahá'í Publishing, 2012.

*The Secret of Divine Civilization.* Translated from the Persian by Marzieh Gail in consultation with Ali-Kuli Khan. 1st pocket-size ed. Wilmette, IL: Bahá'í Publishing, 2015.

*Selections from the Writings of 'Abdu'l-Bahá.* Compiled by the Research Department of the Universal House of Justice. Translated by a Committee at the Bahá'í World Center and by Marzieh Gail. Wilmette, IL: Bahá'í Publishing, 2010.

*Some Answered Questions.* Collected and translated from the Persian by Laura Clifford Barney. Newly revised by a committee at the Bahá'í World Center. Haifa: Bahá'í World Centre, 2014.

*Tablet to August Forel.* Oxford: George Ronald, 1978.

*Will and Testament of 'Abdu'l-Bahá.* Wilmette, IL: Bahá'í Publishing Trust, 2010.

## Works of Shoghi Effendi

*Arohanui: Letters from Shoghi Effendi to New Zealand.* Suva, Fiji: Bahá'í Publishing Trust, 1982.

*Citadel of Faith.* Wilmette, IL: Bahá'í Publishing Trust, 1965.

*The Dawn-Breakers: Nabíl's Narrative of the Early Days of the Bahá'í Revelation.* Translated by Shoghi Effendi. Wilmette, IL: Bahá'í Publishing Trust, 1990.

*God Passes By.* Wilmette, IL: Bahá'í Publishing Trust, 1974.

*High Endeavors: Messages to Alaska.* Anchorage: National Spiritual Assembly of the Bahá'ís of Alaska, 1976.

*The Light of Divine Guidance: Letters from the Guardian of the Bahá'í Faith to Individual Believers, Groups and Bahá'í Communities in Germany and Austria.* Hofheim-Langenhain: Bahá'í Verlag, 1985.

*Messages to America: Selected Letters and Cablegrams Addressed to the Bahá'ís of North America, 1932–1946.* Wilmette, IL: Bahá'í Publishing Trust, 1947.

*Messages to the Antipodes.* Victoria: Bahá'í Publishing Trust of Australia, 1965.

*Messages to the Bahá'í World 1950–1957.* Wilmette IL: Bahá'í Publishing Trust, 1971.

*The Promised Day is Come.* Rev. ed. Wilmette, IL: Bahá'í Publishing Trust, 1996.

*The Unfolding Destiny of the British Bahá'í Community: The Messages of the Guardian of the Bahá'í Faith to the Bahá'ís of the British Isles.* London: Bahá'í Publishing Trust, 1981.

*The World Order of Bahá'u'lláh.* Wilmette, IL: Bahá'í Publishing Trust, 1991.

### Works of the Universal House of Justice

*Messages from the Universal House of Justice, 1963–1986: The Third Epoch of the Formative Age.* Compiled by Geoffrey W. Marks. Wilmette, IL: Bahá'í Publishing Trust, 1996.

*The Promise of World Peace.* Wilmette, IL: Bahá'í Publishing Trust, 1985.

*Century of Light.* Written on behalf of and commissioned by the Universal House of Justice. Haifa: Bahá'í World Centre, 2001.

### Works of the Bahá'í International Community

*The Bahá'ís: A Profile of the Bahá'í Faith and its Worldwide Community.* London: Bahá'í Publishing Trust, 1994.

*The Prosperity of Humankind.* Haifa: Bahá'í World Center, 1995.

*Seizing the Opportunity: Redefining the Challenge of Climate Change.* New York: United Nations Office, 2008. (https://www.bic.org/statements/seizing-opportunity-redefining-challenge-climate-change)

*Turning Point for All Nations: A Statement of the Bahá'í International Community on the Occasion of the 50$^{th}$ Anniversary of the United Nations.* New York: United Nations Office, 1995.

Sustaining Societies—Towards a New 'We': The Bahá'í International Community's Statement to the United Nations Conference on Sustainable Development, June 2012. www.bic.org.

Rethinking Prosperity—Forging Alternatives to a Culture of Consumerism The Bahá'í International Community's Contribution to the 18th Session of the United Nations Commission on Sustainable Development, 3 May 2010, New York. www.big.org.

### Bahá'í Compilations

Bahá'u'lláh, 'Abdu'l-Bahá, Shoghi Effendi and the Universal House of Justice. *The Compilation of Compilations: Prepared by the Universal House of Justice*. 3 vols. Australia: Bahá'í Publications Australia, 1991.

———. *Lights of Guidance*. Compiled by Helen Hornby. New ed. New Delhi, India: Bahá'í Publishing Trust, 1994.

Bahá'u'lláh, the Báb, and 'Abdu'l-Bahá. *Bahá'í Prayers: A Selection of Prayers Revealed by Bahá'u'lláh, the Báb, and 'Abdu'l-Bahá*. New ed. Wilmette, IL: Bahá'í Publishing Trust, 2002.

Bahá'u'lláh, the Báb, 'Abdu'l-Bahá, Shoghi Effendi, and the Universal House of Justice. *Fire and Gold: Benefiting From Life's Tests*. Compiled by Brian Kurzius. Oxford: George Ronald, 1995.

### Other Works

Aitken, K. T. "Proverbs" in *The Oxford Bible Commentary*. Ed. John Barton and John Muddiman. Oxford: Oxford University Press, 2013, pp 405–22.

Alexander, Loveday. "Acts" in *The Oxford Bible Commentary*. Ed. John Barton and John Muddiman. Oxford: Oxford University Press, 2013, pp. 1028–61.

Allison, Dale C. "Matthew" in *The Oxford Bible Commentary*. Ed. John Barton and John Muddiman. Oxford: Oxford University Press, 2013, pp. 844–86.

Attridge, Harold W. "1 and 2 Kings" in *The Oxford Bible Commentary*. Ed. John Barton and John Muddiman. Oxford: Oxford University Press, 2013, pp. 1236–54.

Barclay, John. "1 Corinthians" in *The Oxford Bible Commentary*. Ed. John Barton and John Muddiman. Oxford: Oxford University Press, 2013, pp. 1108–33.

Barton, John. "Introduction to the Old Testament" in *The Oxford Bible Commentary*. Ed. John Barton and John Muddiman. Oxford: Oxford University Press, 2013, pp. 5–12.

Bauckham, Richard. "Revelation" in *The Oxford Bible Commentary*. Ed. John Barton and John Muddiman. Oxford: Oxford University Press, 2013, pp. 1287–1306.

Brenner, Athalya. "The Song of Solomon" in *The Oxford Bible Commentary*. Ed. John Barton and John Muddiman. Oxford: Oxford University Press, 2013, pp. 429–33.

Black, Matthew. *Peake's Commentary on the Bible*. London: Routledge, 2001, section 607.

Borg, Marcus J. and John Dominic Crossan. *The First Paul: Reclaiming the Radical Visionary Behind the Church's Conservative Icon*. NY: Harper One, 2009.

Borovicka, JoAnn. "The Ten Plagues of the Exodus in Light of the Bahá'í Writings" in *Lights of 'Irfán: Papers Presented at the 'Irfán Colloquia and Seminars, Book Sixteen*. Darmstadt, Germany: 'Asr-i-Jadíd Publisher, 2015, pp. 9–26.

Bruns, Gerald L. "Midrash and Allegory: The Beginnings of Scriptural Interpretation." in *The Literary Guide to the Bible*. Ed. Robert Alter and Frank Kermode. Cambridge: Harvard University Press, 1987.

Bultmann, Christoph. "Deuteronomy" in *The Oxford Bible Commentary*. Ed. John Barton and John Muddiman. Oxford: Oxford University Press, 2013, pp. 135–158.

Buss, Martin J. *Biblical Form Criticism in its Context*. Sheffield: Sheffield Academic Press, 1999.

Carter, Jimmy. *A Call to Action: Women, Religion, Violence, and Power*. New York: Simon & Schuster, 2014.

Chakrabarty, Bidyut. *Social and Political Thought of Mahatma Gandhi*. New York: Routledge, 2006.

Cline, Eric H. *1177 B.C.: The Year Civilization Collapsed*. Princeton: Princeton University Press, 2014.

———. *Jerusalem Besieged–From Ancient Canaan to Modern Israel*. Ann Arbor: University of Michigan Press, 2004.

Coggins, R. "Isaiah" in *The Oxford Bible Commentary*. Ed. John Barton and John Muddiman. Oxford: Oxford University Press, 2013, pp. 433–86.

*Comparative Study Bible, Revised Edition.* Grand Rapids: Zondervan, 1999.

Crenshaw, James L. "Job" in *The Oxford Bible Commentary.* Ed. John Barton and John Muddiman. Oxford: Oxford University Press, 2013, pp. 331–55.

Crossan, John Dominic. *The Historical Jesus: The Life of a Mediterranean Jewish Peasant.* San Francisco: Harper, 1992.

Davies, P. R. "Daniel" in *The Oxford Bible Commentary.* Ed. John Barton and John Muddiman. Oxford: Oxford University Press, 2013, pp. 563–71.

Day, John. "Hosea" in *The Oxford Bible Commentary.* Ed. John Barton and John Muddiman. Oxford: Oxford University Press, 2013, pp. 571–78.

Deger-Jalkotzy, S. "Decline, Destruction, Aftermath." *The Cambridge Companion to the Aegean Bronze Age.* Ed. C. W. Shelmerdine. Cambridge: Cambridge University Press, 2008, pp. 387–415.

Dietrich, Walter. "1 and 2 Kings" in *The Oxford Bible Commentary.* Ed. John Barton and John Muddiman. Oxford: Oxford University Press, 2013, pp. 232–66.

Dines, Jennifer M. "Amos" in *The Oxford Bible Commentary.* Ed. John Barton and John Muddiman. Oxford: Oxford University Press, 2013, pp. 581–90.

Drury, Clare. "The Pastoral Epistles" in *The Oxford Bible Commentary.* Ed. John Barton and John Muddiman. Oxford: Oxford University Press, 2013, pp. 1220–33.

Duff, Jeremy. "2 Peter" in *The Oxford Bible Commentary.* Ed. John Barton and John Muddiman. Oxford: Oxford University Press, 2013, pp. 1270–74.

Dunbar, Hooper C. *Forces of Our Time: The Dynamics of Light and Darkness.* Oxford: George Ronald, 2009.

Dunn, J. D. G. "Ephesians" in *The Oxford Bible Commentary.* Ed. John Barton and John Muddiman. Oxford: Oxford University Press, 2013, pp. 1165–79.

Durant, Will. *The Story of Civilization IV–The Age of Faith.* New York: Simon and Schuster, 1950.

Elliott, Neil. *Liberating Paul: The Justice of God and the Politics of the Apostle.* Maryknoll, NY: Orbis Books, 1994.

Emerson, Grace I. "Ruth" in *The Oxford Bible Commentary*. Ed. John Barton and John Muddiman. Oxford: Oxford University Press, 2013, pp. 192–95.

Esler, Philip F. "1 Thessalonians" in *The Oxford Bible Commentary*. Ed. John Barton and John Muddiman. Oxford: Oxford University Press, 2013, pp. 1199–1220.

Esslemont, Dr. J. E. *Bahá'u'lláh and the New Era: An Introduction to the Bahá'í Faith*. Wilmette, IL: Bahá'í Publishing, 2006.

Eve, Eric. "1 Peter" in *The Oxford Bible Commentary*. Ed. John Barton and John Muddiman. Oxford: Oxford University Press, 2013, pp. 1263–70.

Finkel, Irving. *The Ark Before Noah: Decoding the Story of the Flood*. London: Hodder and Stoughton, 2014.

Finkelstein, Israel and Neil Asher Silberman. *The Bible Unearthed: Archaeology's New Vision of Ancient Israel and the Origin of its Sacred Texts*. New York: The Free Press, 2001.

Franklin, Eric. "Luke" in *The Oxford Bible Commentary*. Ed. John Barton and John Muddiman. Oxford: Oxford University Press, 2013, pp. 922–59.

Foltz, Richard C. *Spirituality in the Land of the Noble: How Iran Shaped the World's Religions*. Oxford: Oneworld Publications, 2004.

Freedman, David Noel, ed. *The Anchor Bible Dictionary*. New Haven: Yale University Press, 2007.

Fretheim, Terence E. "Numbers" in *The Oxford Bible Commentary*. Ed. John Barton and John Muddiman. Oxford: Oxford University Press, 2013, pp. 110–34.

Friedman, Richard Elliott. *The Bible with Sources Revealed: A New View Into the Five Books of Moses*. New York: Harper Collins, 2005.

———. *Who Wrote the Bible?* New York: Harper Collins, 1997.

Gail, Marzieh. *Bahá'í Glossary*. Wilmette, IL: Bahá'í Publishing, 1957.

———. *Dawn Over Mount Hira*. Oxford: George Ronald, 1976.

Galambush, J. "Ezekiel" in *The Oxford Bible Commentary*. Ed. John Barton and John Muddiman. Oxford: Oxford University Press, 2013, pp. 533–62.

Goodall, Helen S. and Ella Goodall Cooper. *Daily Lessons Received at 'Akká: January 1908*. Wilmette, IL: Baha'i Publishing Trust, 1979.

Gowan, Donald E. "Habakkuk" in *The Oxford Bible Commentary*. Ed. John Barton and John Muddiman. Oxford: Oxford University Press, 2013, pp. 601–4.

Grabbe, Lester L. "Leviticus" in *The Oxford Bible Commentary*. Ed. John Barton and John Muddiman. Oxford: Oxford University Press, 2013, pp. 91–110.

Gulpáygání, Mírzá Abu'l-Fadl. *Miracles and Metaphors*. Los Angeles: Kalimat Press, 1981.

Gunkel, Hermann. *The Legends of Genesis: The Biblical Saga & History*. New York: Schocken Books, 1964.

Harris, Mark J. "How Did Moses Part the Red Sea? - Science as Salvation in the Exodus Tradition" in *Moses in Biblical and Extra Biblical Traditions*. Ed. Alex Graupner and Michael Wolten. Germany: Walter De Gruyter, 2007, pp. 5–31.

Harris, Stephen L. *Understanding the Bible*. Palo Alto: Mayfield, 1985.

Hays, J. Daniel. *The Message of the Prophets: A Survey of the Prophetic and Apocalyptic Books of the Old Testament*. Grand Rapids: Zondervan, 2010.

Heschel, Abraham J. *The Prophets*. New York: Harper Perennial, 1962.

Hill, Craig. "Romans" in *The Oxford Bible Commentary*. Ed. John Barton and John Muddiman. Oxford: Oxford University Press, 2013, pp. 1083–1108.

Horrell, David G. "The First Letter of Paul to the Thessalonians" in *The New Oxford Annotated Bible*. Oxford: Oxford University Press, 2010, pp. 2074–79.

*The Holy Bible*, King James Version. Nashville, Tennessee: Thomas Nelson, 1982.

Houston, Walter. "Exodus" in *The Oxford Bible Commentary*. Ed. John Barton and John Muddiman. Oxford: Oxford University Press, 2013, pp. 67–91.

Hyers, Conrad. *The Meaning of Creation: Genesis and Modern Science*. Atlanta: John Knox Press, 1984.

Jones, Gwilym H. "1 and 2 Samuel" in *The Oxford Bible Commentary*. Ed. John Barton and John Muddiman. Oxford: Oxford University Press, 2013, pp. 196–232.

Joyce, P. M. "Lamentations" in *The Oxford Bible Commentary.* Ed. John Barton and John Muddiman. Oxford: Oxford University Press, 2013, pp. 528–33.

Karlberg, Michael. *Beyond the Culture of Contest.* Oxford: George Ronald, 2004.

Kieffer, René. "John" in *The Oxford Bible Commentary.* Ed. John Barton and John Muddiman. Oxford: Oxford University Press, 2013, pp. 960–1000.

Lambden, Stephen. "An Episode in the Childhood of the Báb" in *Studies in Bábi and Bahá'í History, vol. 3,* ed Peter Smith. Los Angeles: Kalimat Press, 1986, pp. 1–32.

Larkin, Katrina J. A. "Zechariah" in *The Oxford Bible Commentary.* Ed. John Barton and John Muddiman. Oxford: Oxford University Press, 2013, pp. 610–15.

Leff, Rabbi Zev. *Shimoneh Esrei: The Depth and Beauty of Our Daily Tefillah.* Southfield, MI: Targum Press Inc., 2008.

Lieu, Judith. "1 John, 2 John, 3 John" in *The Oxford Bible Commentary.* Ed. John Barton and John Muddiman. Oxford: Oxford University Press, 2013, pp. 1274–83.

MacDonald, Margaret. "2 Corinthians" in *The Oxford Bible Commentary.* Ed. John Barton and John Muddiman. Oxford: Oxford University Press, 2013, pp. 1134–51.

Mason, Rex. "Obadiah" in *The Oxford Bible Commentary.* Ed. John Barton and John Muddiman. Oxford: Oxford University Press, 2013, pp. 590–93.

———."Zephaniah" in *The Oxford Bible Commentary.* Ed. John Barton and John Muddiman. Oxford: Oxford University Press, 2013, pp. 604–7.

Matthews, Gary L. *Afraid to Speak Against Moses: Was the Bearer of the Ten Commandments Guilty of Sin?* Knoxville: Stonehaven Press, 2002.

———.*The Challenge of Bahá'u'lláh.* Wilmette, IL. Bahá'í Publishing, 2005.

———.*He Cometh with Clouds: A Bahá'í View of Christ's Return.* Oxford: George Ronald, 2000.

————. *The Metropolis of Satan: Evil and the Devil in Bahá'í/Christian Dialogue*. Knoxville: Stonehaven Press, 1998.

Matthews, Victor H. and Don C. Benjamin. *Old Testament Parallels: Laws and Stories From the Ancient Near East*. Mahwah, New Jersey: Paulist Press, 2006.

Mathys, H. P. "1 and 2 Chronicles" in *The Oxford Bible Commentary*. Ed. John Barton and John Muddiman. Oxford: Oxford University Press, 2013, pp. 268–308.

McConville, Gordon. "Joshua" in *The Oxford Bible Commentary*. Ed. John Barton and John Muddiman. Oxford: Oxford University Press, 2013, pp. 158–76.

McLean, J. A. *Dimensions in Spirituality*. Oxford: George Ronald, 1994.

Merton, Thomas. *Praying the Psalms*. Collegeville, MN: Order of St. Benedict Inc., 1956.

Meyers, Carol. "Esther" in *The Oxford Bible Commentary*. Ed. John Barton and John Muddiman. Oxford: Oxford University Press, 2013, pp. 324–30.

————. *Exodus*. New York: Cambridge University Press, 2005.

Middleton, G. D. "Nothing Lasts Forever: Environmental Discourses on the Collapse of Past Societies." *Journal of Archaeological Research* 20.3 (2012), pp. 357–87. Print.

Miller, Kenneth R. *Finding Darwin's God*. New York: Harper Perennial, 2007.

Mills, Lawrence H. *Our Own Religion in Ancient Persia: Being Lectures Delivered in Oxford Presenting the Zend Avesta as Collated with the Pre-Christian Exilic Pharisaism, Advancing the Persian Question to the Foremost Position in Our Biblical Research*. Los Angeles: Reprint from the University of California Libraries, 1913.

Momen, Moojan. "The God of Bahá'u'lláh." *The Bahá'í Faith and the World's Religions: Papers Presented at the Irfan Colloquia*. Ed. Moojan Momen. George Ronald Baha'i Study Series. Oxford: George Ronald, 2003, pp. 1–38.

————. *Understanding Religion: A Thematic Approach*. Oxford: One World, 2009.

Momen, Wendi. *A Basic Bahá'í Dictionary*. Oxford: George Ronald, 1996.

Murphy-O'Connor. "Colossians" in *The Oxford Bible Commentary*. Ed. John Barton and John Muddiman. Oxford: Oxford University Press, 2013, pp. 1191–99.

Murray, Robert. "Philippians" in *The Oxford Bible Commentary*. Ed. John Barton and John Muddiman. Oxford: Oxford University Press, 2013, pp. 1179–90.

Nakhjavání, Bahíyyih. *Asking Questions: A Challenge to Fundamentalism*. Oxford: George Ronald, 1990.

Niditch, Susan. "Judges" in *The Oxford Bible Commentary*. Ed. John Barton and John Muddiman. Oxford: Oxford University Press, 2013, pp. 176–91.

Nigosian, S. A. *The Zoroastrian Faith: Tradition and Modern Research*. Montreal: McGill-Queen's University Press, 2003.

Nova, PBS. "Invisible Universe Revealed—25 years of Hubble" (2015).

O'Brien, Julia M. "Nahum" in *The Oxford Bible Commentary*. Ed. John Barton and John Muddiman. Oxford: Oxford University Press, 2013, pp. 599–601.

O'Connor, Kathleen M. "Jeremiah" in *The Oxford Bible Commentary*. Ed. John Barton and John Muddiman. Oxford: Oxford University Press, 2013, pp. 487–528.

Oswalt, John N. *The Bible Among the Myths: Unique Revelation or Just Ancient Literature?* Grand Rapids: Zondervan, 2009.

Petersen, D. L. "Haggai" in *The Oxford Bible Commentary*. Ed. John Barton and John Muddiman. Oxford: Oxford University Press, 2013, pp. 607–10.

Pinker, Steven, *The Better Angels of our Nature: Why Violence has Declined*. New York: Viking Penguin, 2011.

Pritchard, James B. (ed.). *Ancient Near Eastern Texts Relating to the Old Testament*. Princeton: Princeton University Press: 1969.

Rabbani, Rúhíyyih. *The Guardian of the Bahá'í Faith*. Oakham: Bahá'í Publishing Trust of the UK, 1988.

Redford, Donald B. *Egypt, Canaan, and Israel in Ancient Times*. Princeton: Princeton University Press, 1992.

Riesner, Rainer. "James" in *The Oxford Bible Commentary*. Ed. John Barton and John Muddiman. Oxford: Oxford University Press, 2013, pp. 1255–63.

Rodd, C. S. "Psalms" in *The Oxford Bible Commentary*. Ed. John Barton and John Muddiman. Oxford: Oxford University Press, 2013, pp. 355–405.

Rogerson, John. "Malachi" in *The Oxford Bible Commentary*. Ed. John Barton and John Muddiman. Oxford: Oxford University Press, 2013, pp. 615–17.

———. *The Oxford Illustrated History of the Bible*. Oxford: Oxford University Press, 2001.

Rowland, C. "Jude" in *The Oxford Bible Commentary*. Ed. John Barton and John Muddiman. Oxford: Oxford University Press, 2013, pp. 1284–87.

St Rain, Justice. *Why Me? A Spiritual Guide to Growing Through Tests*. Heltonville, IN: Special Ideas, 2013.

Sanders, E. P. *Paul, the Law, and the Jewish People*. Minneapolis: Fortress Press, 1983.

Schniedewind, William M. *How the Bible Became a Book: The Textualization of Ancient Israel*. New York: Cambridge University Press, 2004.

Sears, William. *Thief in the Night: The Case of the Missing Millenium*. Oxford: George Ronald, 1997.

Skehan, James W. *Modern Science and the Book of Genesis*. Washington: National Science Teachers Association, 1986.

Smith-Christopher, Daniel L. "Ezra–Nehemiah" in *The Oxford Bible Commentary*. Ed. John Barton and John Muddiman. Oxford: Oxford University Press, 2013, pp. 308–24.

Smith, Peter. *In Iran: Studies in Bábí and Bahá'í History*, Volume 3, Los Angeles: Kalimat Press, 1986.

Sours, Michael. *The Station and Claims of Bahá'u'lláh*. Wilmette, IL: Bahá'í Publishing Trust, 1997.

Southwell, Peter J. M. "Jonah" in *The Oxford Bible Commentary*. Ed. John Barton and John Muddiman. Oxford: Oxford University Press, 2013, pp. 593–95.

Stanton, G. N. "Galatians" in *The Oxford Bible Commentary*. Ed. John Barton and John Muddiman. Oxford: Oxford University Press, 2013, pp. 1152–65.

Stetzer, Frank. *Religion on the Healing Edge: What Bahá'ís Believe*. Wilmette, IL: Baha'i Publishing, 2007.

Stockman, Robert. "The Bahá'í Faith and Higher Biblical Criticism." *The Bahá'í Faith and the World's Religions: Papers Presented at the Irfan Colloquia.* Ed. Moojan Momen. George Ronald Baha'i Study Series. Oxford: George Ronald, 2003, pp. 107–14.

Taherzadeh, Adib. *The Revelation of Bahá'u'lláh: Adrianople 1863–68.* Oxford: George Ronald, 1977.

———. *The Revelation of Bahá'u'lláh: Mazra'ih & Bahjí 1877–1892.* Oxford: George Ronald, 1987.

*The New Oxford Annotated Bible: New Revised Standard Version With the Apocrypha.* Ed. Michael D. Coogan. Oxford: Oxford University Press, 2010.

*The Oxford English Dictionary, Volume 1 A–Basouki.* Oxford: Clarendon Press, 1989.

*The Oxford English Dictionary, Volume IX Look–Mouke.* Oxford: Clarendon Press, 1989.

*The Oxford English Dictionary, Volume XII Poise–Quelt.* Oxford: Clarendon Press, 1989.

The Ruhi Institute. *Reflections on the Life of the Spirit: Book 1* Riviera Beach: Palabra Publications, 1999.

Thompson, Juliet. *The Diary of Juliet Thompson.* Los Angeles: Kalimat Press, 1983.

Townsend, George. *The Heart of the Gospel.* London: George Ronald, 1960.

Toynbee, Arnold. *An Historians Approach to Religion.* New York: Oxford University Press, 1956.

Tuckett, C. M. "Mark" in *The Oxford Bible Commentary.* Ed. John Barton and John Muddiman. Oxford: Oxford University Press, 2013, pp. 886–922.

Vafai, Shahin. *The Path Toward Spirituality: Sacred Duties and Practices of the Bahá'í Life.* Riviera Beach: Palabra Publications, 1996.

Walton, John H. *Ancient Near Eastern Thought and the Old Testament: Introducing the Conceptual World of the Hebrew Bible.* Grand Rapids: Baker Academic, 2006.

Wansbrough, Henry. "The Four Gospels in Synopsis" in *The Oxford Bible Commentary.* Ed. John Barton and John Muddiman. Oxford: Oxford University Press, 2013, pp. 1001–27.

Wansink, Craig S. "Philemon" in *The Oxford Bible Commentary*. Ed. John Barton and John Muddiman. Oxford: Oxford University Press, 2013, pp. 1233–36.

Weeks, Stuart. "Ecclesiastes" in *The Oxford Bible Commentary*. Ed. John Barton and John Muddiman. Oxford: Oxford University Press, 2013, pp. 423–29.

Whybray, R. N. "Genesis" in *The Oxford Bible Commentary*. Ed. John Barton and John Muddiman. Oxford: Oxford University Press, 2013, pp. 38–66.

Williamson, H. G. M. "Micah" in *The Oxford Bible Commentary*. Ed. John Barton and John Muddiman. Oxford: Oxford University Press, 2013, pp. 595–99.

Worthington, Frances. *Abraham: One God, Three Wives, Five Religions*. Wilmette, IL: Bahá'í Publishing, 2011.

Zaehner, R. C. *The Dawn & Twilight of Zoroastrianism*. Whitefish, MT: Literary Licensing LLC, 2011.

**Internet Sources**

The Bahá'í Encyclopedia Project. "FAQ: Does the Bahá'í Encyclopedia Project have a policy of using gender-neutral language?" http://www.bahai-encyclopedia-project.org

Bahá'í Reference Library. http://reference.bahai.org

*The Resurrection of Christ Memorandum* 14 September 1987, Research Department of the Universal House of Justice. http://bahai-library.com/uhj/resurrection. bible.html

The Universal House of Justice. *Letter to the World's Religious Leaders*. 2002. http://www.bahai.org/library/authoritative-texts/the-universal-house-of-justice/messages/#

———.Ridván 150: Message to the Bahá'ís of the World. http://www.bahai.org/library/authoritative-texts/the-universal-house-of-justice/messages/

# Index

as Collective Center, 90–91
Covenants of, 65, 71–74, 299
cycles of, 42, 43, 96, 175–77, 178–79
distinction of, 198, 248
Divinity of, 41, 43, 90–91, 215, 216, 308
    as Divine Educators, 41, 44, 52, 61, 67, 87–88, 217
    as Divine Physicians, 70–71, 233
God's attributes embodied by, 17–18, 41–42, 196–98, 215–16,
        297–98, 306–9
grace from, 88, 241–42, 244, 265
Holy Spirit's power possessed by, 44, 268
human bodies of, 181, 212–13, 214–16
influence of, 51–52, 112
knowledge of, 17–18, 41, 204, 233–34, 293–94
laws of God brought by, 67–71, 95, 157–59, 162, 185, 311
mercy of, 154, 161, 257
names and titles of, 41–42, 180–82, 349
oneness with God, 219, 242, 248, 296, 349
opposition to, 60–63, 154–56, 240–44, 313–14, 352
pattern of, 50–51, 56
perfections of, 296–97, 306–8, 319–20
plural pronouns used for, 26
proofs of, 231, 261
protecting humanity from punishment, 65–66, 149
purpose of, 42–43, 44–45, 73, 298
realities of, 265–66
recognition of, 53, 159–61, 292
return of, 246–48, 248–51, 353
sacrifices of, 67, 117, 217–18, 242–44, 255, 299, 351, 352
sinless nature of, 65, 66
stations of, 39, 181–82, 204–5, 212–13, 248
    human, 160–61, 352
    spiritual, 40, 41–42, 86, 200, 214–15, 216, 274, 295–96
as three woes from Book of Revelation, 335
time in seclusion, 218
truth brought by, 43, 47, 155, 156, 231
unity among, 92, 180–83, 300–301

For more information about the Bahá'í Faith,
or to contact Bahá'ís near you,
visit http://www.bahai.us/
or call
1-800-22-UNITE

PUBLISHING

# BAHÁ'Í PUBLISHING AND THE BAHÁ'Í FAITH

Bahá'í Publishing produces books based on the teachings of the Bahá'í Faith. Founded over 160 years ago, the Bahá'í Faith has spread to some 235 nations and territories and is now accepted by more than five million people. The word "Bahá'í" means "follower of Bahá'u'lláh." Bahá'u'lláh, the founder of the Bahá'í Faith, asserted that He is the Messenger of God for all of humanity in this day. The cornerstone of His teachings is the establishment of the spiritual unity of humankind, which will be achieved by personal transformation and the application of clearly identified spiritual principles. Bahá'ís also believe that there is but one religion and that all the Messengers of God—among them Abraham, Zoroaster, Moses, Krishna, Buddha, Jesus, and Muḥammad—have progressively revealed its nature. Together, the world's great religions are expressions of a single, unfolding divine plan. Human beings, not God's Messengers, are the source of religious divisions, prejudices, and hatreds.

The Bahá'í Faith is not a sect or denomination of another religion, nor is it a cult or a social movement. Rather, it is a globally recognized independent world religion founded on new books of scripture revealed by Bahá'u'lláh.

Bahá'í Publishing is an imprint of the National Spiritual Assembly of the Bahá'ís of the United States.

## What Good Will Come

*Jana Hannigan*
*Illustrated by Henry Warren*
$14.00 US / $16.00 CAN
Hardcover
ISBN 978-1-61851-103-4

*A heartwarming story that will help children learn problem solving and discover the importance of relying on God during times of tests.*

Pasha Dev lives in Delhi, India with his beloved cat, Mustafa. The two enjoy a good life in Pasha's simple apartment, but one evening during a rainstorm Mustafa goes missing, and Pasha ends up sleeping next to the window he has left open in the hope that Mustafa will return. When Pasha wakes the following morning, he finds that he has come down with a cold and that Mustafa has not returned. Still, Pasha must travel to the Bahá'í House of Worship, where he will serve as the keeper of people's shoes—a responsibility he takes very seriously. During his day of service, Pasha worries about Mustafa and faces some challenges that leave him with some riddles to solve. Along the way, he learns to put his faith in prayer and God, and comes to realize that tests and challenges can lead to some exciting, life-changing opportunities.

**The First Gift**
*Judith A. Cobb*
*Illustrated by Wendy Cowper-Thomas*
$8.95 US / $10.95 CAN
Trade Paper
ISBN 978-0-87743-708-6

*A heartwarming story that will help young children begin to understand their spiritual reality.*

*The First Gift* tells the story of six-year-old Griffin, who attends Bahá'í children's class, where he learns that he has a soul that was given to him by God. But where is his soul? Intrigued, Griffin asks his brother Paul for more detail, but Paul is in a hurry and can only tell him briefly that his soul is God's first gift to him. Griffin checks everywhere he can think of—his pockets, the car he rides home in, his bedroom. When he doesn't find his soul, he worries that he doesn't have one after all. His mother, sensing something is wrong, begins to talk to him, learns of his fears, and comforts him with an explanation of his soul that is based on the Bahá'í teachings. After talking to his mother, Griffin feels better and understands more clearly how he received his soul as well as God's love.

**Fountain of Wisdom**
A COLLECTION OF WRITINGS FROM BAHÁ'U'LLÁH
*Bahá'u'lláh*
$24.00 US / $26.00 CAN
Hardcover
ISBN 978-1-61851-104-1

*A timeless collection of writings penned by the Prophet-Founder of the Bahá'í Faith with a universal message that all humanity is one race, destined to live in peace and harmony.*

*Fountain of Wisdom: A Collection of Writings from Bahá'u'lláh* is a collection of the writings of Bahá'u'lláh, the Prophet-Founder of the Bahá'í Faith, in which He explains some of the "precepts and principles that lie at the very core of His Faith." Revealed during the final years of His ministry, the sixteen tablets contained in this volume cover a wide range of topics and place emphasis on principles such as the oneness and wholeness of the human race, collective security, justice, trustworthiness, and moderation in all things.

# From Sin to Salvation
## The Ascent of the Soul
*John S. Hatcher*
$17.00 US / $19.00 CAN
Trade Paper
ISBN 978-1-61851-102-7

*An exploration of how sin has traditionally been defined by major religions, the view of the Bahá'í Faith toward sin, and how the soul can escape sin and advance spiritually.*

*From Sin to Salvation: The Ascent of the Soul* takes the reader on a quest to understand the concept of sin. The first part of the book is dedicated to defining moral reality and what words such as "sin," "evil," and "salvation" actually mean. Author John S. Hatcher delves deep into the concepts of evil, Hell, and Satan, as they are portrayed in religious and contemporary literature, and he introduces the Bahá'í concept of "the insistent self"—the ego. He then explores whether we can protect ourselves from sin and whether everyday behavior seen in the news—such as bullying, nonfeasance, and apathy—are sins. Hatcher then analyzes other concepts found in various world religions, such as atonement and penance, and explores whether, through practices commonly found in religion, such as the fear of God, it is possible to overcome the temptation of evil, to live free from guilt, and for the soul to ascend into a higher spiritual state.